INSTRUCTOR'S ANNOTATED

Grassroots

with Readings

THE WRITER'S WORKBOOK

SIXTH EDITION

Susan Fawcett

Alvin Sandberg

HOUGHTON MIFFLIN COMPANY   Boston   New York

Senior Sponsoring Editor: Mary Jo Southern
Senior Associate Editor: Ellen Darion
Senior Project Editor: Chere Bemelmans
Senior Production/Design Coordinator: Sarah Ambrose
Senior Manufacturing Coordinator: Priscilla Bailey
Senior Marketing Manager: Nancy Lyman
Senior Designer: Henry Rachlin
Editorial Assistants: Kate O'Sullivan and Joy Park

Cover Design: Judy Arisman
Cover Image: Robert C. Gordon Photographs, Old Lyme, Connecticut

Acknowledgments appear on page 459.

Printed in the U.S.A.

Library of Congress Catalog Card number: 97-72978

Student Edition, Otabind, ISBN: 0-395-88169-2
Student Edition, Spiral, ISBN: 0-395-88167-6
Instructor's Annotated Edition ISBN: 0-395-88165-X

1 2 3 4 5 6 7 8 9-WC-01 00 99 98 97

As part of Houghton Mifflin's ongoing
commitment to the environment, this text
has been printed on recycled paper.

Contents

UNIT 1 — Writing Forceful Paragraphs   2

UNIT 3   *Using Verbs Effectively*   94

© 1998 Houghton Mifflin Company

UNIT 9 Reading Selections and Quotation Bank   404

Preface

Grassroots with Readings combines in one book the exciting Sixth Edition of our widely used basic writing text *Grassroots* and nineteen high-interest reading selections. *Grassroots* grew out of our classroom experience at Bronx Community College of the City University of New York; it is designed for students who have not yet mastered the basic writing skills so necessary for success in college and in many careers. Through clear, paced lessons and a variety of engaging practices and writing assignments, *Grassroots* has helped more than 900,000 students write better.

In *Grassroots with Readings,* instructors who wish to incorporate reading in their basic writing classes may choose from a diverse group of readings chosen with an eye to thought-provoking subject matter, stylistic excellence, and ethnic and gender balance. Authors include Amy Tan, Malcolm X, Anna Quindlen, Julia Alvarez, Daniel Goleman, Maya Angelou, and Dave Barry. Each selection is accompanied by a headnote, vocabulary glosses, comprehension questions, and writing assignments.

In this new Sixth Edition, we have kept the carefully honed grammar and sentence-skills lessons that prompt so many instructors and students to tell us that *Grassroots* keeps fulfilling its promise: to help students become better writers. We have more effectively emphasized the connection between grammar and writing; added many inspiring examples of student writing; strengthened our coverage of the writing process; concluded every grammar chapter with a writing assignment, often collaborative; and, of course, updated and replaced practice material throughout the book.

Features of the Sixth Edition

■ **GRAMMAR IN A WRITING CONTEXT**

Two-Page Unit Openers. Each unit now begins with a list of topics to be covered and with a well-crafted paragraph by a professional writer such as Judith Ortiz Cofer, Pete Hamill, or Brent Staples. Through their stimulating ideas and style, these paragraphs kindle student interest while illustrating the grammar and sentence skills taught in each unit. Providing a motivating launch to instruction, each opener can also be used to prompt discussion or writing.

More Writing-Based Practices. Exercises now include more sentence combining and other tasks requiring critical thinking and sentence creation.

New High-Interest Practice Material. We have replaced numerous practice sets with engaging new paragraphs, essays, and continuous discourses for proofreading and editing. These exercises sustain interest as students apply the concepts they have learned to longer pieces of writing. Topics include singer Gloria Estefan, the Tuskegee Airmen, Brazil's Carnivale, young computer geniuses, Rollo May's four types of courage, and comic action hero Jackie Chan.

■ **MORE STUDENT WRITING**

Writers' Workshops. This versatile new feature at the end of every unit showcases a student paragraph or essay—carefully processed with discussion and peer-editing questions and followed by writing and revising assignments. Ideal for class work or individual study, these exciting workshops reinforce grammar and sentence skills in context, highlight the writing process, and inspire student writers by example.

More Student Models and Practice Material. Because students are inspired by the excellent writing of their peers, student as well as professional paragraphs are now used as models for teaching writing and revising techniques. In addition, more practices now use student paragraphs or essays.

■ **ENHANCED COVERAGE OF THE WRITING PROCESS**

New Chapter 1, "Exploring the Writing Process." This short chapter introduces subject, audience, and purpose, and also lists guidelines for submitting written work.

Expanded Writing and Revising Instruction in Unit 1. Topic sentence development, transitional expressions, and revision are now presented more fully. Sections on revising for support and peer editing have been added to Chapter 3, now called "Developing Effective Paragraphs." Exact and concise language has been moved to Chapter 4, "Improving Your Paragraphs."

New Chapter 5, "Moving from Paragraph to Essay." For instructors who wish to use it, this brief chapter shows students how to apply their paragraph skills to the short essay. A model student essay, "Tae Kwon Do," is included.

■ **COLLABORATIVE WRITING AND REVISING TASKS**

New End-of-Chapter Writing Activities. A writing assignment—often collaborative—now concludes every grammar chapter. These assignments ask students to apply the skills they have learned to tasks such as writing an unusual restaurant menu using past participles or writing a class lesson on courtesy for young children using coordinating conjunctions.

Peer Editing. Chapter 3 now includes instruction on peer editing, plus a helpful Peer Feedback Sheet that students can use as they respond to one another's work. The Writers' Workshops afford additional peer-editing opportunities.

■ **THREE NEW READING SELECTIONS**

We have replaced three readings with dynamic new selections about arranged marriage, the day a child learns to read, and emotional intelligence.

■ **EXTENSIVE ANCILLARY PACKAGE**

Available on adoption of the text, the following ancillaries provide the instructor with rich materials to expand his or her teaching options:

Instructor's Annotated Edition

Student Answer Key

Test Package

Computerized Diagnostic and Mastery Tests (Mac and DOS)

GRASP, a dynamic new assessment software program (Mac and Windows)

Test Bank Data Disk (Mac and Windows)

Writing Director's Resource Package

Houghton Mifflin Web Site

Organization of the Text

The range of materials and flexible format of *Grassroots* make this worktext adaptable to almost any teaching/learning situation: classroom, laboratory, or self-teaching. Each chapter is a self-contained lesson, so instructors may teach the chapters in any sequence that fits their course designs. *Grassroots with Readings* is versatile enough to support many different approaches to basic writing instruction.

Acknowledgments

We wish to thank those people whose thoughtful comments and suggestions helped us develop the Sixth Edition.

John Bell, New York City Technical College

Marilyn Black, Middlesex Community College

Chandler Clifton, Edmonds Community College

Mark Connelly, Milwaukee Area Technical College

Judy D. Covington, Trident Technical College

Marsha Cummins, Bronx Community College

Jane Gamber, Hutchinson Community College

Jennifer L. Hurd, Harding University

Jill A. Lahnstein, Cape Fear Community College

Mary Ann Merz, Oklahoma City Community College

Raymond E. Mort, Oakland Community College

Marcus H. Patton, Sacramento City College

Dee Pruitt, Florence-Darlington Technical College

Betsy Ray, Indiana Business College

Martha Rogers, Aiken Technical College

Mike Rovasio, California State University

Ann Marie Shackelford, Bacone College

Linda Whisnant, Guilford Technical Community College

David L. White, Walters State Community College

Gary Zacharias, Palomar College

For her invaluable contribution to this latest edition, we owe a special debt of gratitude to our talented Developmental Editor, Melody Davies. During the demanding revision process, we appreciated more than ever Melody's tireless commitment to excellence, her great ideas, her generous heart, and her enviable calm under pressure. That Melody shares our love of *Grassroots* and its mission is a gift.

For her rare vision and enthusiastic support over the years, we thank our Senior Sponsoring Editor and friend, Mary Jo Southern. She has championed us and our books, generously sharing her national perspective and keen understanding of the needs of developmental students. Thanks also to our friends and former colleagues in the English Department at Bronx Community College; to Neil Grill, Carol Zavin, and Registrar Harvey Erdsnecker; and to Susan Yaeger of Monroe College for kindly helping us identify and track down exceptional student authors.

Susan Fawcett thanks her husband, Richard Donovan, for loving her through bright times and grieving times, for making her laugh every day, and for his example of lifelong dedication to students—his own and, through the Urban Partnership Program, students all over the country who make up in hard work what they may lack in privilege. For their example of creativity, enthusiasm, and endurance, Susan thanks her parents, Harriet and Millard Fawcett.

Alvin Sandberg thanks Marilyn Weissman for her excellent editorial assistance. Much credit also goes to Beth and Miriam for their love and support.

Most of all, the two of us thank our students, who inspired us to write this book.

S. F.
A. S.

Suggestions to the Writing Instructor

Although most teachers of English agree that students learn to write by writing, effective course designs are probably as numerous and varied as good instructors. In the paragraphs that follow, we offer a few suggestions based on our own experience with teaching basic writing.

Student Attitude and Motivation

A student's attitude toward writing can affect both motivation and performance. He or she must feel comfortable enough to write freely and to learn, instead of trying to hide errors by writing as little as possible. Since basic writing students may bring to your classroom negative attitudes about English class and about their own abilities, you may need to fight the "I can't write" attitude by helping students see that their reluctance is the cause of many writing problems rather than the result of them. Remember, too, that your own expectations will have an enormous impact on your students. Studies document what many teachers have long suspected: that the instructor's attitude and expectations are key factors in student learning.

Creating a Writers' Community

Beware your own sense of grammatical urgency ("But I have so many errors to correct and only one short term to work miracles!"). The first weeks of any basic writing course can make or break student attitude and, thus, affect student progress. The two of us have come up with a method of starting off the term that we use in our separate classrooms. For the first one to two weeks, the students write nearly every day, as they will all term. These writings might be short, get-acquainted exercises like having each student write for five minutes on his or her name—how it was chosen, whether the student likes it, and so forth. Samples of student writing (perhaps anonymous at the outset) are either read aloud by volunteers or reproduced for the class and then discussed. Here's the catch: *no grammar is marked for the full one to two weeks.* Instead, we talk about the content of the papers or about what strikes us as "powerful writing." Further, the classroom rule is this: *we talk only about what is good in each paper.* If we don't like anything about a particular paper, we don't say anything. The result? Students open up, write regularly, learn that they can write something "good" and show it to a group without derision, and find that their own reactions to other people's writing have value. Meanwhile, the instructor has a chance to survey the grammatical needs of the class and to plan the term accordingly.

The second or third week, when discussion enlarges to include criticism and we begin marking errors in the papers, we continue to emphasize what the student is doing right, not just what is wrong. For every error cited, we cite something positive as well—the sense of humor, the vivid example, the honesty of the writing. As the term progresses, groups or pairs of students can read, critique, and revise work, thus honing their skills. Such collaborative activities create a writers' community in the classroom and enhance learning.

Writing Assignments

Beginning the term with frequent short compositions done in class will avoid the problem of students getting stuck at home and giving up altogether or seeking outside help. Further, the communal experience of writing and reading papers in class will create a subtle but important dynamic as the term progresses. We use dyads, groups, and full class discussions to hone writing and revising skills. Once the class begins to enjoy its work and to sense its own strength, at-home compositions will prove that there is no magic in the classroom that is responsible for success. Students will begin to see that the skills are *within them,* not in Room 303, their text, or their teacher.

Theme topics should be snappy enough to hold the attention of the class but difficult enough to provide a challenge, point to a new perspective, or foster a new skill. Developmental students generally write more easily about things they know best—their neighborhoods, families, themselves. It is often helpful to begin with these familiar sources of material and to build toward more sophisticated issues, questions, and modes of expression. Even if some topics do not produce the desired results, assigning many themes will ease the pain of a few poor choices on your part and a few poor showings on the students'.

We trust that the assignments in the chapters and at the end of each unit in *Grassroots* will provide you and your students with a number of interesting and accessible writing tasks, some of them collaborative. We have tried to present a wide range of topics, from interviewing a classmate to discussing whether family shopping excursions were a wonderful or terrible experience to writing a letter of compliment or complaint.

In any case, varying the kinds of writing assignments you give is usually a good idea. Letters, for example, can force students to focus on audience and purpose. For this reason, we have included some letters in the end-of-unit writing assignments. Journals can provide regular writing practice, a sense of the power of personal expression, and a source of ideas for classroom papers. You may wish to base some writing assignments on the grammar lesson just covered, so students can immediately apply what they have learned. For example, if you have just taught verb agreement, have the class visit the student lounge or the gymnasium and describe in the present tense what is happening there.

The many high-interest paragraphs and essays for proofreading in *Grassroots* also can serve as stimuli for class discussion and writing. For example, portraits of such people as Nelson Mandela, Simón Bolívar, athlete Jim Thorpe, action hero Jackie Chan, Gloria Estefan, Sitting Bull, Spike Lee, or celebrities recovering from addiction can shed light on achievers and the obstacles they overcome. Topics like underwater missions of the Navy SEALs, the history of the Olympics, training killer whales at Sea World, improving study habits, the effects of alcohol on pregnancy, and the creation of the most-used rock guitar in the world are likely to elicit lively student responses. Additional short readings you bring in can both model and inspire good writing.

Using Collaborative Assignments Effectively

Although this edition of *Grassroots* contains more collaborative writing and revising assignments, we offer this caution: Collaborative work at this level must be carefully set up and supervised to be effective. For example, putting students in groups and asking them to edit one another's papers won't accomplish much if they don't know what to look for. Our "writers' community" approach just described is one way to teach writing and editing principles to the whole class first and to establish "quality control." The Writers' Workshop that concludes each unit also provides closely guided discussion of student work, as well as practical opportunities for peer editing. The new end-of-chapter writing assignments include many that are collaborative, letting students interact while they apply the grammar skills learned to their writing. For peer editors, Chapter 3 includes a list of useful questions students can answer as they respond to a classmate's paper.

Evaluation

The challenge of many basic writing courses is balance: of grammar work with writing assignments, of student motivation with high standards. In addition to marking papers, you may wish to rely on other ways of letting students know where they stand. Frequent conferences, for example, provide a good way of keeping them informed of their progress. Some instructors write lengthy comments, both positive and negative, on every batch of papers. Peer evaluation is an excellent tool, provided you guide students through the process first and supply guidelines as they read and respond to one another's work. A simple peer evaluation sheet might include such questions as these: *What is most effective about this paper? What is the main idea? What one change would most improve this paper?* To prepare students for the realities of writing final examinations or assessments, consider administering "mock finals" several times toward the end of the term. Evaluate these (or have a colleague do so) just as if they were the finals themselves; then return them to the students, who will be highly motivated to correct any writing problems that are still keeping them from passing the course.

Lightening the Paper Load

As basic writing teachers, we all fight the paper load, but, in fact, we do not have to do all the correcting, reading, and grading ourselves. Not only can students help, but doing so will improve their writing and revising skills. First, a Student Answer Key is available to all instructors using *Grassroots;* just reproduce and distribute the answers for those practices or chapters that you want your students to correct. Remember too that the short, frequent writings appropriate to basic writing classes may be read quickly and need not always be graded. Peer evaluation of first drafts not only lightens your load but helps students internalize and apply the principles of revision. Peer evaluations must be prepared for—with full group discussions of student work early in the term—if, later, students are to respond thoughtfully to each other's papers. We have students swap first drafts in dyads or small groups, answering in writing a series of simple questions listed on a "peer evaluation form." Finally, journal writing based on periodic assignments provides excellent writing practice and need not be read word for word; however, students should know that their journals will be collected at the end of the term. Ask them to tell you which sections they would like you to read, and read just those.

Notes on Using GRASSROOTS

Organization of Grassroots

The units in *Grassroots* reflect the major problem clusters encountered in composition classrooms: "Writing Forceful Paragraphs," "Writing Complete Sentences," "Using Verbs Effectively," "Joining Ideas Together," and so on. The order of units and chapters in *Grassroots* represents one possible way to organize a developmental English course—teaching paragraph writing first and building from there. Another instructor might see the sentence as central and will start the term with Chapter 6, "Subjects and Verbs." Someone else might begin with lessons in verb agreement. Obviously, your preferences and the needs of your students will determine the best shape of your course.

    Grassroots is extremely versatile. Each unit is a sequence of self-contained chapters, so the book may be adapted to almost any course design. A careful look through the book will suggest possibilities. In addition, each unit begins and ends with writing-based features that place grammar study firmly in the context of the writing process. A two-page unit opener introduces material to be covered, using an interesting, well-written professional paragraph. These openers can provide a dynamic launch to instruction or, through their ideas and style, prompt discussion or writing. At the end of each unit are varied review practices, usually dealing with essays and other whole pieces of writing; four high-interest writing assignments; and a Writers' Workshop. The eight Writers' Workshops showcase inspiring student paragraphs or essays, each processed carefully with questions and followed by writing ideas. The Workshops make excellent full-class or collaborative activities, teaching the arts of peer editing and revision and inspiring students by example.

    Whatever concepts you wish to stress, whatever the order of presentation, it is probably a good idea to assign some important chapters to the whole class and to go over the exercises in class together. This procedure familiarizes students with the text at the outset. Furthermore, students enjoy this activity because it affords them a chance to share not only "answers" but also creations—sentences and paragraphs.

    Finally, *Grassroots* lends itself to tutorials and self-teaching. Individuals and small groups with special problems can complete appropriate chapters on their own.

Organization of Each Chapter

Each chapter is a self-contained lesson, short enough so that flagging concentration will not interfere with learning. Each stresses the development of writing skills rather than mere error correction. Points that frequently confuse students receive the most exact attention. We assume that the student brings very little prior knowledge to each task; we present, step by logical step, the vocabulary and concepts necessary to the skill being taught, keeping explanations simple but accurate. For example, after the student learns to spot subjects in Chapter 6, he or she then practices distinguishing between singular and plural subjects, an ability vital to the rest of the lesson and one that cannot be presupposed. Similarly, the treatment of subject-verb agreement in Chapter 8 includes an exercise on transforming noun subjects into pronouns; only after completing this exercise does the student tackle sentences in which pronoun subjects appear.

In general, the exercises in each chapter move from the very elementary to the more demanding, repeating basic skills and building upon them. Because the exercises are varied in form and difficulty and often explore engaging or humorous topics, students will not be bored or be able simply to fill in right answers without really learning anything. Many exercises—often paragraph or essay length—require students to spot and correct particular errors, thus honing their proofreading and revising skills.

Each chapter in the book ends with Chapter Highlights; these summarize important points covered in the chapter and can be used by students as a brief review. Beginning with Unit 2, each chapter ends with two additional elements: a Chapter Review and a Writing Assignment. The Chapter Review is composed of paragraph- or essay-length practices that provide an opportunity for students to revise and proofread in context. Often a collaborative effort, the Writing Assignment is a structured writing task that helps students think through the issues of audience and purpose.

Unit 1: Writing Forceful Paragraphs

Unit 1 consists of five chapters: "Exploring the Writing Process," "Prewriting to Generate Ideas," "Developing Effective Paragraphs," "Improving Your Paragraphs," which presents more advanced material like illustration and coherence, and "Moving from Paragraph to Essay," a brief optional chapter that prepares students for later courses.

Chapter 1 introduces the writing process itself, as well as subject, audience, and purpose. It contains a list of guidelines for submission of written college work, which the instructor can amend as desired. Chapter 2 presents four prewriting techniques, each illustrated with student examples: freewriting, brainstorming, clustering, and keeping a journal. We believe that journals work best if you periodically assign topics and let students know you will be collecting the journals at some point. Encourage your students to try all four prewriting techniques and discover what works best for them.

Chapter 3 guides the student through the process of writing simple paragraphs. We realize that the actual writing process may be messier than this chapter makes it appear, but the steps presented provide beginning writers with a reassuring way of writing basic paragraphs. Part A defines the paragraph and introduces the idea of the topic sentence. Part B shows the student how to turn a broad topic into a specific topic sentence, a step that many students have trouble with because they believe that a broad topic is easier to write about. You should stress that the topic sentence controls the paragraph, that limiting the topic will help students write more easily later. Students who have trouble writing the topic sentence should be encouraged to try brainstorming first to help focus the topic and then to compose the topic sentence.

Parts C, D, and E detail the generation and arrangement of ideas within the paragraph. Students usually enjoy Part C, "Generating Ideas for the Body," which covers brainstorming. Those who have completed Chapter 2, "Prewriting to Generate Ideas," will see how freewriting, brainstorming, and clustering can be rich sources of details and examples that will later make the paragraph effective and interesting. In teaching this material, consider writing a sample topic sentence on the board and having the class brainstorm or freewrite ideas to develop it, select the best ideas, and then arrange them in some logical order.

Parts F and G guide students through the revision process, stressing revision for clear topic sentences, good support, basic transitions, and unity. Model first and revised drafts are given, showing revision techniques. A section on peer revision is included, with a specific and useful list of questions for students to answer if you ask them to respond to one another's written work. The more guidance peer editors are given, the more helpful the result. Attention is paid as well to proofreading, especially for omitted words.

Chapter 4 covers somewhat more difficult material: using examples, types of order, revising for exact and concise language, and turning assignments into paragraphs. If your students' level of preparedness is quite low, this full chapter may not be appropriate. Part A explains just what examples are and how they can be used to develop a paragraph. Many students have trouble understanding the relationship between a general statement and a specific example, but putting example topic sentences on the board—and having students suggest and evaluate examples that support them—is an excellent way to address this problem.

Part B explains time order, space order, and order of importance. Your students, like ours, will probably be inspired by the model paragraphs of space order and importance, both written by students. You may wish to go over the three kinds of order in class and then to assign an at-home paragraph, allowing each student to choose one kind of order. Later, have successful paragraphs read to the class.

Part D, "Turning Assignments into Paragraphs," helps students see the practical application of the writing instruction they receive in English class to other course work. Here they learn how to turn an exam question into a topic sentence and to plan their answer. Even if you do not assign the rest of Chapter 4, you may wish to assign Part D. Consider giving a "mock exam," using this material as the basis of a lesson: students love this kind of academic "basic training."

For instructors who wish to use it, Chapter 5, "Moving from Paragraph to Essay," briefly applies paragraph-writing skills to essay writing. It includes an actual student essay called "Tae Kwon Do" that will probably provoke interest and discussion. Instructors who teach short essays in this course will find that the four Writers' Workshops showcasing student essays and the many essay-based practices throughout the text work well with Chapter 5 to enrich basic essay instruction.

Unit 2: Writing Complete Sentences

This unit concerns itself with the basics of the complete sentence. Chapter 6, "Subjects and Verbs," provides students with practice in spotting and using these two essential parts of a thought, thereby preparing them for the next chapter on fragments and for Chapter 8, "Present Tense," where the ability to recognize subjects and verbs is crucial. Part C, "Spotting Prepositional Phrases, " helps students find the real subject and not be confused by prepositional phrases that intervene between subject and verb. Since students often assume that a verb is necessarily a single word, Part F of Chapter 6 focuses on verbs of more than one word: this section can also be helpful in a discussion of compound tenses.

Chapter 7, "Avoiding Sentence Fragments," covers the three sentence fragment errors most common to developmental writing—the incomplete past participle, the incomplete progressive, and the subordinate clause written as an entire sentence. These problems are also covered in Chapters 10, 11, and 14. In Chapter 7, once students have corrected fragments by writing sentences with complete subjects and verbs, they proofread paragraphs for sentence fragments since fragments are most likely in longer pieces of writing. Some instructors may wish to teach Chapter 26, "Parallelism," in conjunction with Unit 2: the principle of parallelism is fairly easy for students to master and helps them to develop a sense of balance and style in sentence writing.

Unit 3: Using Verbs Effectively

A large portion of this text is devoted to verbs because they present the most difficulties for the developmental writing student. Many grammar handbooks cover only sophisticated problems in agreement, but Chapter 8, "Present Tense," concentrates on the third person singular ending, that elusive *-s* or *-es* that is so conspicuously absent from the themes of developmental writers. *To be, to have,* and *to do* are singled out for special attention: these verbs appear incorrectly so often on such a large number of papers that they deserve separate treatment. More subtle problems in agreement are explained in Part G.

Chapter 9, "Past Tense," stresses the student's ability to recognize the past tense and to form it by adding *-ed* or *-d* to regular verbs. Except for *to be,* which requires special work, students generally have less trouble with irregular verbs than with regular verbs in the past tense. This phenomenon may be due to the fact that the *-ed* or *-d* ending is often virtually absent from students' spoken vocabulary, but irregular verbs are easier to remember and more apt to be taught in the lower grades. In any case, it would be wise to reinforce the section on regular verbs with extra sentences or short themes written exclusively in the past tense. Beware: Students usually "catch on" to the *-ed* or *-d* quickly but then tend to return after a short time to their old habits. Periodic reviews and constant correction of themes can counteract this tendency.

Chapter 10, "The Past Participle in Action," is central to a multitude of problems for the developmental writer and should be covered carefully and, whenever possible, in class. This chapter introduces the student to new tenses and time relationships; it shows the function of the past participle in the passive voice; and finally, it explains the use of the past participle form as an adjective. The greatest difficulty students face in understanding these areas is their assumption that the *-ed* or *-d* ending always signifies past tense.

Students also have trouble understanding the subtle differences between the perfect tenses and the other tenses. We have attempted to clarify these differences in the charts and examples provided in Parts D and E; however, our experience has been that a teacher's explanation is required in addition to the charts and examples. You may wish to skip the sections on present perfect tense and past perfect tense altogether and go straight to work on the passive voice and past participles as adjectives.

Chapter 11, "Progressive Tenses," explains the difference between the progressive tense and the simple present or past. This chapter will be of special value to nonnative writers of English who often overuse the progressive tenses. Part D reminds students to make progressive verb forms complete with the use of *to be* as a helper; this section may be combined with Chapter 7, "Avoiding Sentence Fragments."

Chapter 12, "Fixed-Form Helping Verbs and Verb Problems," begins with a discussion of the fixed form of the modal helping verbs and the simple form that their main verbs must take. This emphasis is necessary because students learning about verb endings sometimes develop a penchant for affixing *-es, -s, -ed,* or *-d* to the modals or to their main verbs.

Can, could, will, and *would* are singled out for special treatment; many students confuse the present and past tenses of these verbs and do not understand their conditional forms. Parts C and D, which deal with these problems, might be covered directly after Chapter 9, "Past Tense," while the difference between past and present is fresh in students' minds.

Part E, "Writing Infinitives," covers a common student error—putting endings on infinitives. This problem occurs when developmental writers attempt to make all verbs show tense or time. Part F, "Revising Double Negatives," could be assigned selectively to those students who use double negatives, although at times enough students require the explanation to warrant covering this part with the entire class.

Unit 4: Joining Ideas Together

This unit teaches the student six ways to combine simple ideas and create more complicated and interesting sentences. It builds upon the concept of the sentence expounded in Unit 2; the instructor may wish to combine material from this unit with the work on sentence fragments in Chapter 7, "Avoiding Sentence Fragments." Each chapter presents one method of joining ideas and highlights the correct punctuation necessary for that construction. A number of practices in this unit provide extra work in sentence combining. Please note the useful chart on page 230 and on the inside cover; this chart provides a handy reference for students once they have learned these methods.

Chapters 13 to 15, "Coordination," "Subordination," and "Avoiding Run-ons and Comma Splices," will probably be the best-thumbed chapters in this unit. Chapter 13, "Coordination," presents a compact explanation of the seven common coordinating conjunctions. Since many students do not really understand the precise meanings of these words, the chapter contains exercises that require the student to choose the conjunction that correctly expresses the relationship between paired ideas.

Chapter 14, "Subordination," is also reduced to essentials and gives the student a basic list of subordinating conjunctions. Special attention is paid to the order of main idea and subordinate idea and to punctuation, when to use a comma and when not to. This chapter may be used with Chapter 7, "Avoiding Sentence Fragments," for work on one kind of sentence fragment problem.

Chapter 15, "Avoiding Run-ons and Comma Splices," defines these two errors and encourages students to use either coordination or subordination—discussed in the previous two chapters—to correct them. Here, as elsewhere in the book, we stress skill building rather than error correction. The Chapter Review provides students with paragraphs to proofread and revise so that they will be better able to transfer these skills to their own writing.

Chapter 16, "Semicolons," is followed by a related chapter on adverbial conjunctions. Many instructors of developmental English choose not to teach these two areas at all. However, those who do will find these lessons simplified and clear, teaching basic patterns, not all possible uses. In this spirit, Chapter 17, "Conjunctive Adverbs," introduces only eight common conjunctive adverbs.

The student is given two other options for joining ideas together—Chapter 18, "Relative Pronouns," and Chapter 19, "-ING Modifiers." These two chapters, like Chapter 14, may be used with Chapter 7 to address the problem of sentence fragments.

Unit 5: Choosing the Right Noun, Pronoun, Adjective, Adverb, or Preposition

This unit zeroes in on five parts of speech. You may wish to assign these chapters individually to students or to entire classes needing work in certain areas, say, plural endings or possessive pronouns. Relevant sections of Unit 5 may also be assigned to students working on verb agreement. Chapter 20, "Nouns," and Part F, "Demonstrative Adjectives," in Chapter 22, "Adjectives and Adverbs," provide the extensive practice in singular and plural formations that some students need. Singulars and plurals are introduced in Chapter 6, "Subjects and Verbs."

Chapter 21, "Pronouns," deals exhaustively with pronouns, a source of much bafflement, and clears up most of the confusion that students experience. Part A introduces the concept of the antecedent. Parts B through D explain the basics of pronoun-antecedent agreement: indefinite pronouns, collective nouns, and so forth. Part E deals with vague and redundant pronouns. Parts F, G, and H discuss case: often, however, choosing the correct case can be taught by ear without a great deal of drill in case forms and usage. Finally, Part I, "Using Pronouns with -SELF and -SELVES," can be covered at almost any time during the term since it is largely concerned with spelling.

Chapter 22, "Adjectives and Adverbs," differentiates between these two forms. Practices here stress the formation of comparatives and superlatives, with special attention paid to *good* and *well*. Also included is work on the demonstratives *this/that* and *these/those*.

Chapter 23, "Prepositions," explains the difference between *on* and *in* and *like* and *as/as if*. The chapter also contains a chart of common phrases containing prepositions, which can present problems for nonnative speakers of English. Students requiring work with this part of speech can be assigned the chapter on an individual basis.

Unit 6: *Revising for Consistency and Parallelism*

The chapters in this unit can be taught together or used separately as follow-ups to earlier chapters. Chapter 24, "Consistent Tense," might be effectively taught after Chapters 8 and 9, on present and past tense verbs, because students often shift from present to past tense and from past to present. Similarly, Chapter 25, "Consistent Person," might be taught after Chapter 21, "Pronouns"; students often use singular, plural, and indefinite pronouns in a single paragraph without being aware of their lack of consistency. The paragraph practices at the end of each chapter provide exercises in proofreading and revising for consistency.

Chapter 26, "Parallelism," can be taught as early in the term as you feel your students can benefit from such a lesson. In fact, beginning writers are apt to understand parallelism rather easily. They perceive the balance, shape, and form in their sentences and are often able to eliminate problems like inconsistent tenses, incomplete verb forms, and poor transitions by applying the principles of parallelism.

Unit 7: *Mastering Mechanics*

This unit explains not only those marks of punctuation that frequently trouble students, but also the rules of capitalization. Basic rules governing capitalization are briefly listed in Chapter 27; students proofread for and correct capitalization errors in practice sentences and in a practice essay.

The comma is a mark of punctuation that often bewilders students. Chapter 28 explains eight basic uses of the comma, each rule reinforced by a practice. Note that the correct use of the comma with coordinating and subordinating conjunctions, covered in Chapters 13 and 14, is reinforced in this chapter.

Chapter 29 explains the two basic uses of the apostrophe—contractions and possessives. Since students who misunderstand the apostrophe often add one when they form the plural of nouns, you may wish to refer them to Part A of Chapter 20, "Nouns." Additional work on commonly confused pairs of words—*it's* and *its*, *you're* and *your*—is found in Chapter 32, "Look-alikes/Sound-alikes."

Chapter 30 teaches the difference between direct and indirect quotations and how to punctuate them.

Unit 8: *Improving Your Spelling*

Chapter 31, "Spelling," provides students with clear explanations of some basic spelling rules and their exceptions, each reinforced with lots of practice. It is best to teach this entire chapter slowly since the rules take time to digest and since spelling drills can quickly become tedious.

Part A might be discussed early in the term so that students can begin to keep spelling lists and to devise tricks for remembering difficult words. This part can be assigned individually or to a class as needed. Part B is often a necessary preface to further work in spelling because many students are not really sure what vowels and consonants are. Since Parts C and D deal with the doubling of consonants, they might logically be discussed after Chapter 9, "Past Tense," and Chapter 11, "Progressive Tenses." The rules discussed in Parts F and G can likewise be related to lessons on present tense verbs, past tense verbs, and noun plurals.

Chapter 32, "Look-alikes/Sound-alikes," treats groups of words that writing students tend to confuse, like *to, too,* and *two,* or *where, were,* and *we're.* A simple explanation of each word in the group is given, followed by practice—an approach we have found to be effective in clearing up these errors. Assign these sections to individuals or to the class as the need arises.

Appendix

The Appendix defines the eight parts of speech and provides examples of their use. It can serve as a review or as an introduction to the principles of grammar.

Unit 9: Reading Selections and Quotation Bank

The nineteen reading selections in *Grassroots with Readings* were chosen for their high-interest subjects, readability, and variety. The introduction, "Effective Reading: Strategies for the Writer," explains to the student some basic techniques of effective reading—underlining main ideas, preparing questions, and so on—and provides a sample annotated reading. Difficult words within the readings are glossed on the bottom of the pages. Each reading is followed by questions to stimulate class discussion or journal assignments and by three writing assignments.

The Quotation Bank contains more than seventy brief quotations. An admixture of the profound and the whimsical, these quotations may be used in a variety of ways. They can provide topics for discussion and written assignments. Students may wish to agree or disagree with a quotation, using their own experience to support their stand, or simply to read through the quotation bank, seeking inspiration or ideas. One of these quotations might start or augment a composition. You might tell your students about such volumes as *Bartlett's Familiar Quotations,* available in libraries and bookstores.

Notes on the Readings

Malcolm X, "A Homemade Education"

This essay stimulates keen interest and discussion—especially now that Spike Lee's film has increased public awareness of Malcolm X. The essay begins with an honest assessment of Malcolm X's stumbling attempts to write letters to his spiritual mentor and the contrast between his speaking and writing abilities. Most students will identify with Malcolm X's struggle to read and write effectively, although Malcolm X is set apart by his impressive determination in copying the dictionary. Ask your students how many would go to this length to improve their skills. What motivated Malcolm X? Did his incarceration make learning easier? Is the author exaggerating when he claims that reading freed him, even though he was in prison?

The essay provides an excellent lead-in to early class discussions about learning to write and the motivation, means, and ongoing hard work this requires. Ask students what motivates them to learn—and to keep on when frustration occurs. Consider connecting this essay with a lesson in dictionary use. Writing Assignment 3 asks students to copy several dictionary entries and then write about the experience—or discuss it in groups. This piece works nicely with Leo Buscaglia's "Papa, the Teacher" or Martorano and Kildahl's "Say Yes to Yourself."

Maya Angelou, "Mrs. Flowers"

This selection from Angelou's autobiographical *I Know Why the Caged Bird Sings* describes the young Angelou's life-changing relationship with a neighbor who saw her specialness and invited her into the world of spoken poetry. (Earlier in the book, Angelou has described being raped by her mother's live-in friend Mr. Freeman, his mysterious murder after the trial, and her own self-imposed silence.) Angelou's style is rich and evocative; consider combining this essay with a lesson on specific language or description.

This essay provides an opportunity to discuss the kinds of friendships or activities that help us through tough, even traumatic, times. Students might enjoy sharing such transformative relationships—either as the recipients or the givers of "gifts." Some of your students may have trouble speaking up, perhaps because of the way they speak or their accent. Ask students if they think it is important to be able to speak up, in class and elsewhere, or where they feel most and least comfortable speaking up. Consider pairing this essay with Malcolm X's "A Homemade Education," in which Malcolm X is skilled at speaking but not writing, Amy Tan's "Four Directions," in which a girl loses confidence when her mother withdraws support, or Courtland Milloy's "The Gift."

David Goddy, "The First Read"

This essay begins with Goddy's nostalgic memories of parenthood—specifically, teaching his daughter, Sonya, to read. As it turns out, however, Sonya claims that she learned to read pretty much by herself. This is probably the first of many

© 1998 Houghton Mifflin Company

transitions his daughter will experience as she develops a sense of self; he hints at the inevitability of being left behind in his last line as he turns the pages "a little bit too slowly."

Use the three conflicting stories of how Sonya learned to read to spark a discussion of different perceptions of reality. Students, for instance, might wish to share incidents from their own family life in which no one could agree on who started an argument or who gave in first. Parents may wish to recall how they taught a skill: what problems they encountered and what rewards they garnered. Discuss what kinds of skills parents should teach—and perhaps what kind they should leave to the schools.

This essay can be paired with "A Homemade Education," in which Malcolm X describes how he taught himself, or with Sherwood Anderson's "Discovery of a Father." Here Anderson gains a new perspective on his father's influence on his life and skills.

Leo Buscaglia, "Papa, the Teacher"

What can parents do to inspire children with a respect for learning? Buscaglia gives one answer, using his father as an example. The author says his father had "natural wisdom" and believed that the greatest sin is to go to bed as ignorant as we were on waking. In great detail, using quotations, he describes their dinner ritual. What do your students think of this ritual? Did it put needless pressure on the children? Does it sound too good to be true? And if a child has no such parent to promote excellence, can he or she overcome this lack? How? This piece leads naturally to discussing or writing about specific ways that parents encourage children to learn—or discourage them from learning. It might lead to writing about a family "ritual," either positive or negative, that students have experienced. An interesting group on teaching and learning can include Malcolm X's "A Homemade Education" and David Goddy's "The First Read." In "Four Directions," Amy Tan creates a more complex, fictional portrait of a parent who first supported and then sabotaged her daughter's talent.

Francine Klagsbrun, "Forever"

This article explores the unrealistic expectations that many of us have about our partners; it also suggests fruitful ways of going beyond them. Using one couple as an example, Klagsbrun draws on dialogue, anecdotes, and quotations from an expert in the field to make her points accessible and concrete. Ask students if some of Klagsbrun's examples of unrealistic expectations sound familiar: "I'll change him/her after we marry," for example, or "If she loved me, she'd know how I feel." Depending on the type of communication the class has established, students may be willing to share past and present expectations about spouses or partners, the results of holding unrealistic expectations, the attempts (or unwillingness) to give up these expectations, and the benefits of a more realistic relationship. If students are not able to talk about themselves, they may be willing to talk about other people's experiences.

Discuss with the class whether Klagsbrun's point of view is ultimately positive or negative. Some students may need help in understanding Klagsbrun's final point about the process of marriage, the paradox that the greatest happiness may involve growth, change, acceptance, frustration, and "incompleteness." This selection may be used in conjunction with others about relationships and idealized expectations, for example, Sherwood Anderson's "Discovery of a Father," Amy Tan's "Four Directions," or Courtland Milloy's "The Gift." It also works well with Martorano and Kildahl's self-help piece, "Say Yes to Yourself."

Shoba Narayan, "In This Arranged Marriage, Love Came Later"

This firsthand account of an arranged marriage is sure to provoke intense discussion. Here Ms. Narayan, an American-educated Indian journalist, explains her decision to let her family choose her husband and describes her subsequent journey within the marriage from open-mindedness to active dislike to love. At first, most American students are appalled by the idea of not marrying for love. Ask them whether there are different kinds of love or whether love alone can meet the day-to-day requirements of marriage. The author mentions such factors as horoscopes that Indian families consider as they match mates. Would these provide at least as solid a partnership as romantic love? Some of your students may share firsthand knowledge of arranged marriages from their birth countries. Do they agree with the author that arranged marriages work only in the context of stable traditional societies and close family relationships? You will need to explain such references as those to Giacometti, Munch, and Kandinsky, by which Ms. Narayan contrasts her artistic temperament with her husband's more practical nature. This article works well with "Forever"—in which author Francine Klagsbrun claims that romantic love, an illusion, cannot last—or with Courtland Milloy's "The Gift"—about a young man who is moved to donate a kidney to his friend after her boyfriend and family refuse.

Anna Quindlen, "Homeless"

Here, through carefully chosen details and particulars, Quindlen movingly brings to life the much-discussed problem of homelessness. She begins with the example of Ann, a woman who treasures pictures of a house. "Concentrate on details" is the advice Quindlen gives about social problems; it could as well apply to writing. She replaces the word "homeless" with "a woman without a bureau, a man with no mirror—no drawer that holds the spoons, no window to look out upon the world." In fact, this essay provides a wonderful model of how to make an abstract problem come alive for the reader. By concentrating on details as they write, your students may wish to bring such a problem to life or describe the typical day of a homeless person in their neighborhood or document what they love about their own homes. This essay can be taught to good effect with Chapter 4, Part A, "More Work on Support: Examples," or Part C, "More Work on Revising: Exact and Concise Language."

Joseph T. Martorano and John P. Kildahl, "Say Yes to Yourself"

Students usually enjoy discussing this essay and applying to their own lives its provocative main idea: "When people think differently, they feel and act differently." The authors describe five steps for changing our thoughts, each supported with examples, anecdotes, or quotations. Point out to your students the Quotation Bank in *Grassroots with Readings*—a good source of quotations to use in their writing—and introduce them to the collections of quotations available in libraries and bookstores. Ask students to share recurrent negative thoughts they would like to change or to contribute stories about a time when they were able to change their thoughts. An excellent writing assignment is number 3, in which students are asked to isolate a negative thought, apply the authors' strategies for a day or two, and then write about the experience. In paragraph 24, the authors urge us to "remember our best selves"; if you teach this essay early in the term, ask students in groups or the full class to tell others about some quality or action for which they've been complimented or to share "their best selves." This piece provides an interesting conceptual lens through which to preview personal narratives of success and failure; for example, Sherwood Anderson's "Discovery of a Father," Maya

Angelou's "Mrs. Flowers," Amy Tan's "Four Directions," or Shoba Narayan's "In This Arranged Marriage, Love Came Later."

Julia Alvarez, "Yolanda"

This brief fictional narrative, from *How the Garcia Girls Lost Their Accents*, evokes one child's immigrant experience. Through precise descriptions, like that of the nuns in the opening paragraph, and well-chosen particulars, Alvarez captures not only the confusion and humor of learning a new language, but the tenseness of an era. The author emphasizes words—*Yo-lan-da*—and effectively mixes the innocuous terms of everyday American life with the vocabulary of annihilation—*laundromat, corn flakes, snow, bomb shelter, fallout.* If appropriate, ask your ESL students to share their learning stories. What did they find most amazing, wondrous, or upsetting in the new country? What important words did they confuse? Sister Zoe was an attentive and a sympathetic teacher. How typical do students think she is? Alvarez's final image unifies the piece; as snow falls, we hear Sister Zoe's moving simile: "Each flake was different . . . like a person, irreplaceable and beautiful." This narrative may be clustered with others on teaching and learning: Ana Veciana-Suarez's "For a Parent, There's No Language Dilemma," David Goddy's "The First Read," and Daniel Goleman's "Emotional Intelligence."

Courtland Milloy, "The Gift"

Most students are inspired and provoked by this newspaper account of Jermaine Washington's gift to a friend of a kidney. His act is all the more amazing because his relationship with Michelle Stevens is platonic, and her own brothers and fiancé have refused to help her. The author, through quotations and scenes like the one in the barbershop (paragraph 1), underlines the bafflement that others felt at Washington's act. Ask students what they would have done in his place. Why do they think he did it? What did he give up, and what did he get in return? Was it worth it? And how do your students feel about Washington? Would they like to have him as a friend? An interesting writing assignment is to have students recount someone's act of extreme generosity or bravery, trying as well to capture the reaction of others. This essay is fascinating taught in conjunction with Francine Klagsbrun's "Forever" about the limits of romantic love. Have students in groups answer the question raised in paragraph 20. Does romance "mess up a good thing" between two people?

Langston Hughes, "Salvation"

This narrative captures in lucent, accurate prose the author's youthful disillusionment with the church—a painful conflict between the expectations of others and his inner experience. Hughes opens with these powerful, attention-gripping sentences: "I was saved from sin when I was going on thirteen. But not really saved. It happened like this." He sets the scene through exact details (paragraphs 3 and 4, for example), quoting the minister and his aunt. The young man himself is waiting to "see Jesus," and when he doesn't, he ceases to believe. Ask your class whether this means that Jesus doesn't exist. What is this story about? Religion? Peer pressure? Coming of age? Consider having your students use Hughes' opening as a model for their own narrative that begins "_____ when I was going on _____. It happened like this." But first, help them analyze Hughes' rich details, his effective conclusion. This essay and Amy Tan's "Four Directions" give a realistic glimpse into the painful and perhaps unavoidable transformations that occur during adolescence.

Daniel Goleman, "Emotional Intelligence"

This article, based on the author's much discussed best-selling book, raises important questions about the nature of intelligence and its relationship to success. Your students may find the concepts and vocabulary in this piece challenging, but we believe the ideas explored here are worth the effort. The material lends itself nicely to both collaborative class activities and to exercises in critical thinking. Goleman names five qualities that constitute emotional intelligence. Discuss these one by one in class. An enjoyable exercise that encourages critical thinking is to have students cite, for each trait, two examples: one, a situation in which someone showed "emotional genius" and another in which someone showed "emotional ignorance."

A fertile area for class discussion and writing is the handling of anger. The author cautions against "ventilating." Of course, uncontrolled anger and violence loom large in American society, and many school programs are attempting to teach young people to be more emotionally intelligent through "conflict resolution" and other skills. Can these skills be taught in school if they are not taught in the home? Have groups of students think of constructive ways to handle anger or create a lesson on the subject for fifth grade boys and girls. Make sure your students grasp the point of the marshmallow study Goleman refers to: the article makes a connection between the ability to resist a marshmallow in childhood and the impulse control that predicts success in school and work. Of course, having students assess their own emotional intelligence can be instructive.

Consider having students apply the concepts learned here to people and situations in other reading selections. For example, in "Papa, the Teacher," does the author's father draw on emotional intelligence as he teaches his children to love learning? What are his skills? In "The Gift," is the young man who donates his kidney emotionally intelligent or just crazy (as some of his neighbors think)? Does emotional intelligence include changes of heart and perception like the son's discovery of his father in Sherwood Anderson's story?

Dave Barry, "Sports Nuts"

In this humorous essay, Dave Barry explores the obsession many men have with sports. By directing his irony and wit not only toward men in general but toward himself, Barry makes the piece doubly appealing. The selection is a gold mine for a discussion of the use of language. You might start at the beginning, asking students what kind of language Barry is exploiting with the words "Today, in our continuing series on How Guys Think . . ." Or you might want to draw students' attention to Barry's ironic use of specific words—for example, the use of the word *legendary* in paragraph 3 (where he describes his "legendary athletic career"). Barry's parting shot is also directed at himself. Have students make the connection between Philadelphia Phillies Barry (paragraph 10) and "Pittsburgh Penguin Johnson" (paragraph 3). Ask students what Barry is telling us about himself by ending the essay in this way.

Students might also discuss whether this essay has changed the way they look at sports. Do they now have a somewhat different perspective on the subject? This reading can be paired with any essay that provides readers with a different perspective on any subject, like Narayan's "In This Arranged Marriage, Love Came Later," Quindlen's "Homeless," Klagsbrun's "Forever," or Abbey's "Desert Kin." Students might consider how each author goes about showing us his or her point of view.

Edward Abbey, "Desert Kin"

In this excerpt from *Desert Solitaire: A Season in the Wilderness*, Abbey examines his complex relationships with the creatures who share his habitat. He tells us that he prefers not to kill animals (paragraph 4). Students may want to discuss their views on this subject. How do they feel about hunting deer, using monkeys for medical research, spraying ants? Under what circumstances do they feel that it is either necessary or justifiable to kill an animal? Do they agree that Abbey needed to kill the rattlesnake (paragraph 8)? How do they feel about Abbey's conclusion in this piece—that all living things are kindred? How connected do they feel to the natural world?

Abbey is a master of description and detail. Draw students' attention to the vivid writing in this piece, for example, to passages like "On guard, head aloft—that evil slit-eyed weaving head shaped like the ace of spades—tail whirring, the rattler slithers sideways, retreating slowly before me until he reaches the shelter of a sandstone slab. He backs under it" (paragraph 6). This selection might be discussed in conjunction with Chapter 4, Part C, "More Work on Revising: Exact and Concise Language." It might be compared with other pieces in which the authors manifest strong personal convictions, for example, with Quindlen's "Homeless," and Veciana-Suarez's "For a Parent, There's No Language Dilemma."

Barbara Garson, "Perfume"

Reporting on her observations and interviews in a perfume factory, Garson describes in detail the repetitive, mind- and body-numbing tasks that the workers perform hour after hour, day after day. Ask your students if they have ever worked at jobs like those that Garson describes. What were the effects of such jobs on them and on their co-workers? Discuss the strategies that the women use to maintain their identity as human beings, including the strong bonds they form as they unite against stultifying tasks and against management. Which do your students think is more important: interesting work or good wages?

Because Garson's descriptions of processes are so clear and concise (for example, the progress of the assembly line for Herbescence in paragraph 3), this selection might be used fruitfully in conjunction with Chapter 4, Part B, "More Work on Arranging Ideas: Coherence." It could also be grouped with other selections that deal with overcoming adverse conditions, like Angelou's "Mrs. Flowers," Milloy's "The Gift," Klagsbrun's "Forever," and Malcolm X's "A Homemade Education." An interesting cluster that focuses on gifts, gift giving, and gift givers might include this piece, Milloy's "The Gift," and Narayan's "In This Arranged Marriage, Love Came Later."

Sherwood Anderson, "Discovery of a Father"

In this excerpt from his *Memoirs*, Sherwood Anderson recalls a childhood plagued by shame and embarrassment over his father's "ridiculous" and alcoholic behavior. Anderson also recalls the dramatic experience that not only helped him understand and accept his father but made him aware of his father's legacy to him, the gift of storytelling. Your class may enjoy discussing the personalities of their own parents or guardians. Some students may never have tried to look objectively at their parents' strengths and weaknesses. Some may describe their disillusionment; others may describe realistic—or unexamined—acceptance. You might also want to lead students to discuss the effects of their parents' (or teachers' or others') nurturance—or neglect—on the development of their skills and talents.

Students could try to describe Anderson's style as a storyteller (direct, simple, colloquial, "natural"). Students might also enjoy finding words and phrases that show when and where the piece was written. (You might want to briefly describe Anderson's masterpiece, *Winesburg, Ohio*.) "Discovery of a Father" makes a very interesting pair with Amy Tan's "Four Directions." How does the parent's attitude—and the child's attitude toward the parent—affect the child? affect the child's skill? affect the child in relationship to his or her peers? Julia Alvarez's "Yolanda" could add another perspective to the discussion.

Amy Tan, "Four Directions"

In this excerpt from *The Joy Luck Club*, Tan describes a young girl who loses confidence in herself—and consequently loses her skill as a chess player—because of her mother's withdrawal of support. Discuss with your class what has actually happened to this child. What stages does she go through before she finally gives up? What strategies does she use to try to get her mother back on her side? Why does the mother make such a complete about-face? Has she helped her daughter in the long run—or has she damaged her?

This excerpt begins with the words "I was ten years old" and ends with the words "I was fourteen." Ask why Tan brackets the section with this information about age. Students might enjoy discussing changes that took place in their own personalities between the ages of ten and fourteen. Did any of them lose their childhood confidence? Why? Are the pressures greater on girls or boys? Were any of them disillusioned by others?

This narrative might be clustered with other selections about parents and children, including Anderson's "Discovery of a Father" and Buscaglia's "Papa, the Teacher." For an interesting comparison and contrast with another young teenager who loses faith, "Four Directions" may be discussed along with Langston Hughes' "Salvation."

Ana Veciana-Suarez, "For a Parent, There's No Language Dilemma"

Having not insisted that her youngest son learn to speak Spanish, Veciana-Suarez voices her deep regret and her "urgent" attempt to make up for lost time. Her reasons are cultural, economic, and emotional. Interestingly enough, she does not address the issue of bilingual education in the schools. After students have discussed and evaluated Veciana-Suarez's reasons for wanting her boys to speak Spanish as well as English, you might want to ask how this goal can best be accomplished. Veciana-Suarez works with her son at home. Are your students in favor of this approach? Do they believe in formal bilingual education? What are the arguments for teaching children their native language in the schools? What are the arguments against it? Are there solutions other than parents teaching their children at home and bilingual education in the schools?

Ask students to discuss the first sentence of this newspaper article. How does this lead get our attention and also let us know what the piece will be about? Veciana-Suarez discusses a serious subject and has a definite point of view, but she peppers her argument with humor (paragraph 2, for example). This piece might also be discussed with other selections that take a particular stand: for example, "Emotional Intelligence" and "In This Arranged Marriage, Love Came Later." Points of comparison might include the seriousness of the theme and the techniques and arguments used (personal anecdote, testimony by others, humor, irony, and so forth).

Grassroots

Writing Forceful Paragraphs

The goal of *Grassroots* is to make you a better writer, and Unit 1 is key to your success. In this unit, you will

✔ Learn the importance of subject, audience, and purpose

✔ Learn the parts of a good paragraph

✔ Practice the paragraph-writing process

✔ Learn how to revise and improve your paragraphs

✔ Apply these skills to exam questions and short essays

Here, writer Maya Angelou remembers the preparations for graduation night. If possible, read her paragraph aloud.

The weeks until graduation were filled with heady activities. A group of small children were to be presented in a play about buttercups and daisies and bunny rabbits. They could be heard throughout the building practicing their hops and their little songs that sounded like silver bells. The older girls (non-graduates, of course) were assigned the task of making refreshments for the night's festivities. A tangy scent of ginger, cinnamon, nutmeg and chocolate wafted around the home economics building as the budding cooks made samples for themselves and their teachers.

Maya Angelou, *I Know Why the Caged Bird Sings*

■ Ms. Angelou's words bring to life some preparations for the big event. Are any details especially vivid? Which ones?

■ Words have power: they can make us remember, see, feel, or think in a certain way.

Unit 1 will introduce you to the power of writing well.

■ Preparations for some important event

■ A school day—joyful or terrible—that you won't forget

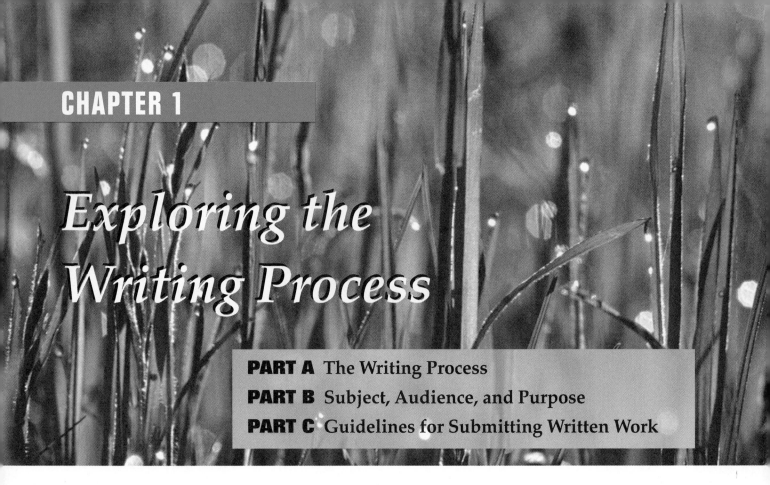

CHAPTER 1

Exploring the Writing Process

PART A The Writing Process
PART B Subject, Audience, and Purpose
PART C Guidelines for Submitting Written Work

Good writing is the end result of a *writing process,* a series of steps the writer has taken. This chapter will give you an overview of that process—explored in more depth throughout Unit 1—as well as some tips on how to approach your writing assignments.

PART A   The Writing Process

Experienced writers go through a *process* consisting of steps like these:

1 Prewriting
- Thinking about possible subjects
- Freely jotting ideas on paper or computer
- Narrowing the subject and writing it as one sentence
- Deciding which ideas to include
- Arranging ideas in a plan or outline

2 Writing
- Writing a first draft

3 Rewriting
- Rethinking, rearranging, and revising as necessary
- Writing one or more new drafts
- Proofreading for grammar and spelling errors

Writing is a personal and sometimes messy process. Writers don't all perform these steps in the same order, and they may have to go through some steps more than once. However, most writers *prewrite, write, rewrite*—and *proofread.* The rest of this unit and much of the book will show you how.

Choose a paper that you wrote recently for an English class or for some other class, and think about the *process* you followed in writing it. With a group of three or four classmates, or in your notebook, answer these questions:

1. Did I do any planning or prewriting—or did I just start writing the paper?

2. How much time did I spend improving and revising my paper?

3. Was I able to spot and correct my own grammar and spelling errors?

4. In the past, have any instructors or others made useful comments about my writing?

5. What one change in my writing process would most improve my writing? (Taking more time for prewriting? Spending more time revising? Improving my grammar or spelling skills?)

PART B   Subject, Audience, and Purpose

As you begin a writing assignment, give some thought to your *subject, audience,* and *purpose.*

When your instructor assigns a broad subject, try to focus on one aspect that interests you. For example, suppose the subject is *music,* and you play the conga drums. You might focus on why you play them rather than some other instrument, or on what drumming means to you. If the subject is *a change you have made,* you might focus on how you recently improved your study habits.

Whenever possible, choose subjects you know and care about: observing your neighborhood come to life in the morning, riding a dirt bike, helping a child resist peer pressure, maintaining a recent weight loss, achieving a dream. Ask yourself:

■ What special experience or knowledge do I have?

■ What angers, saddens, or inspires me?

■ What do I love to do?

■ What news story got to me recently?

■ What community problem do I have ideas about solving?

Your answers to such questions will suggest promising writing ideas.

How you approach your subject will depend on your *audience,* your readers. Are you writing for classmates, a professor, people who know about your subject, or people who do not? For instance, if you are writing about weight training and your readers have never been inside a gym, you will approach your subject in a simple and basic way, perhaps stressing the benefits of weightlifting. An audience of bodybuilders, however, already knows these things; for them, you would write in more depth, perhaps focusing on how to develop one muscle group.

Finally, keeping your *purpose* in mind helps you know what to write. Do you want to explain something to your readers, persuade them that a certain point of view is correct, entertain them, or just tell a good story? If your purpose is to persuade parents to support having school uniforms, you can explain that uniforms lower clothing costs and may reduce student crime. But if your purpose is to convince students that uniforms are a good idea, you might approach the subject differently, emphasizing how stylish the uniforms look or how students from other schools feel that uniforms improve their school atmosphere.

PRACTICE 1

List five subjects you might like to write about. For ideas, reread the questions on page 5.

1. _____

2. _____

3. _____

4. _____

5. _____

PRACTICE 2

With a group of three or four classmates, or on your own, jot down ideas for the following two writing tasks. Notice how your points and details differ, depending on your audience and purpose. (If you are not employed, write about a job with which you are familiar.)

1. For a new coworker, you plan to write a description of a typical day on your job. Your purpose is to help train this person, who will perform the same duties you do. Your boss will need to approve what you write.

2. For one of your closest friends, you plan to write a description of a typical day on your job. Your purpose is to make your friend laugh because he or she has been feeling down recently.

PART C   Guidelines for Submitting Written Work

Learn your instructor's requirements for submitting written work, as these may vary from class to class. Here are some general guidelines. Write in any special instructions.

1. Choose sturdy white 8½-by-11-inch paper (not onionskin), lined if you write by hand, plain if you use a computer or type.

2. Clearly write your name, the date, and any other required information, using the format requested by your instructor.

3. If you write by hand, do so neatly in black or dark blue ink.

4. Write on only one side of the paper.

5. Double-space if you write on computer or type. Some instructors also want handwriting double-spaced.

6. Leave margins of at least one inch on all sides.

7. Number each page of your assignment, starting with page 2. Place the numbers at the top of each page, either centered or in the top right corner.

Other guidelines: _____

_____

_____

 Chapter Highlights

Tips for succeeding in this course:

■ Remember that writing is a process: prewriting, writing, and rewriting.

■ Before you write, always be clear about your subject, audience, and purpose.

■ Follow your instructor's guidelines for submitting written work.

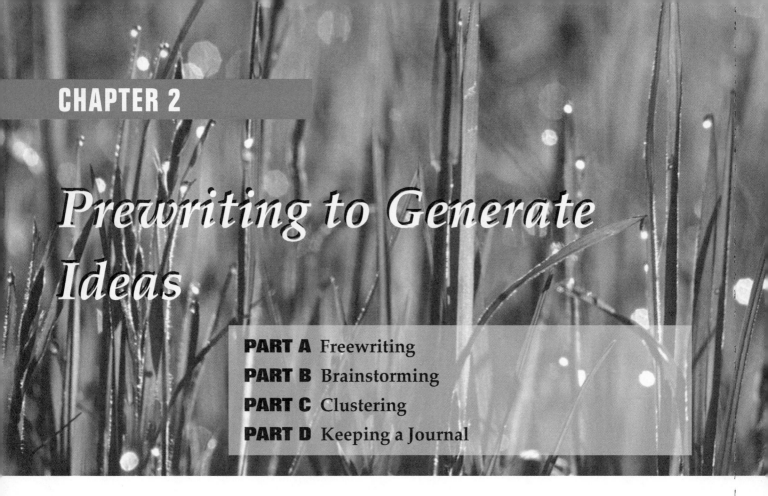

CHAPTER 2

Prewriting to Generate Ideas

PART A Freewriting
PART B Brainstorming
PART C Clustering
PART D Keeping a Journal

One of the authors of this book used to teach ice skating. On the first day of class, the students practiced falling. Once they knew how to fall without fear, they were free to learn to skate.

Writing is much like ice skating: The more you practice, the better you get. If you are free to make mistakes, you'll want to practice, and you'll look forward to new writing challenges.

The problem is that many people avoid writing. Faced with an English composition or a report at work, they put it off and then scribble something at the last minute. Or they sit staring at that blank page—writing a sentence, crossing it out, unable to get started. In this chapter, you will learn four useful prewriting techniques that will help you jump-start your writing process and put ideas on paper: freewriting, brainstorming, clustering, and keeping a journal.

PART A   Freewriting

Freewriting is a method many writers use to warm up and get ideas on paper. Here are the guidelines: For five or ten full minutes, write without stopping about anything that comes into your head. Don't worry about grammar or about writing complete sentences; just set a timer and go. If you get stuck, repeat or rhyme the last word you wrote, but keep writing nonstop until the timer sounds.

Afterward, read what you have written, and underline any parts you like. Here is one student's first freewriting, with her underlinings:

> Freewrite free without stopping hopping popping pills and Mark in trouble <u>the more he messes up, the harder I work,</u> explain that. Go to school, work nights, study late, no privacy, no sleep, no fun fun fun. This is fast all right and I'm getting lost cost coasting on my pen I never wrote before without bending my brain for hours first this doesn't feel like writing it feels like flying or a fast car at night; no—like something quick and quiet except for the sound of all these pens maybe 30 pens on paper <u>what a weird noise scratch scratch hiss hiss</u> and sleeves, left handed sleeves <u>dragging in the ink</u> sink pink skies and blue sounds. <u>Fast ink is a blue sound, the sea is a blue sound.</u>

■ This example has the vital energy of many freewritings.

■ Why do you think the student underlined what she did?

■ Would you have underlined any other words or phrases? Why?

_____

_____

Freewriting is a wonderful way to let ideas pour onto paper without getting stuck by worrying too soon about correctness or "good writing." Sometimes freewriting produces nonsense, but often it provides interesting ideas for further thinking and writing.

PRACTICE 1

1. Set a timer for ten minutes, or have someone time you. Freewrite without stopping for the full ten minutes. Repeat or rhyme words if you get stuck, but keep writing! Don't let your pen or pencil leave the page.

2. When you finish, write down one or two words that describe how you feel

   while freewriting. _____

3. Now read your freewriting. Underline any words or lines you like—anything that strikes you as powerful, moving, funny, or important. If nothing strikes you, that's okay.

PRACTICE 2

Try two more freewritings at home, each one ten minutes long. Do them at different times of the day when you have a few quiet moments. If possible, use a timer: set it for ten minutes, and then write fast until it rings. Later, read your freewritings, and underline any striking lines or ideas.

Focused Freewriting

In *focused freewriting,* just try to focus your thoughts on one subject as you freewrite. The subject can be one assigned by your instructor, one you choose, or one you have discovered in unfocused freewriting.

Here is one student's focused freewriting on the topic *someone who strongly influenced you.*

> Queen, queen of the feathery sofa where we are not allowed to sit, so clean, the gleaming Tiffany lamp, the elegance, the smoke that chokes me. Puff puff, red nails, puffing away at her eternal cigarette she calls herself the master of the house and threatens me without a word. I sit on a bridge chair afraid to look her way. Her seersucker robe is exactly like mine her hair is like mine and her eyes are as blue but she weighs 10 pounds less she fits into jeans I threw away and loves it loves. We are so alike, Amy, she says popping grapes into her mouth and drinking wine. Laurel leaves of success should have been on her head but instead I have found them on mine.
>
> Amy Adler, student

■ This student later used her freewriting as the basis for an excellent paragraph.

■ Underline any words or lines that you find especially striking or powerful. Be prepared to discuss your choices.

■ Can you guess the relationship between the writer and the woman she describes?

PRACTICE 1

Read over your earlier freewritings, and notice your underlinings. Do you find any words or ideas that you would like to write more about? List two or three of them here:

_____

_____

_____

_____

_____

PRACTICE 2

Now choose one word or idea from your freewriting or from the following list. Focus your thoughts on it, and do a ten-minute focused freewriting. Try to stick to the topic, but don't worry too much about it. Just keep writing! When you finish, read and underline as usual.

1. winning
2. trees
3. the biggest lie
4. a dream

5. someone who influenced you
6. your experiences with writing
7. the smell of _____
8. blue

PART B   Brainstorming

Brainstorming means freely jotting ideas about a topic. As in freewriting, the purpose of brainstorming is to get as many ideas as possible onto paper, so you will have something to work with later. Just write down everything that comes to mind about a topic—words and phrases, ideas, details, examples, little stories. Once you have brainstormed, read over your list, underlining any ideas you might want to develop further.

Here is one student's brainstorming list on *an interesting job:*

> midtown messenger
>
> frustrating but free
>
> I know the city backwards and forwards
>
> good bike needed
>
> fast, ever-changing, dangerous
>
> drivers hate messengers—we dart in and out of traffic
>
> old clothes don't get respect
>
> I wear the best Descent racing gear, a Giro helmet
>
> people respect you more
>
> I got tipped $100 for carrying a crystal vase from the showroom to Wall Street in 15 minutes
>
> other times I get stiffed
>
> lessons I've learned—controlling my temper
>
> having dignity
>
> staying calm no matter what—insane drivers, deadlines, rudeness
>
> weirdly, I like my job

As he brainstormed, this writer produced many interesting facts and details about his job as a bicycle messenger, all in just a few minutes. He might want to underline the ideas that most interest him—perhaps the time he was tipped $100—and then brainstorm again for more details.

Choose one of the following topics that interests you, and write it at the top of your paper. Then brainstorm! Write anything that comes into your head about the topic. Let your ideas flow.

1. a singer or musician
2. the future
3. an intriguing job
4. a story in the news

5. the best/worst class I've had
6. making a difference
7. a place to which I never want to return
8. a community problem

After you fill a page with your list, read it over, underlining the most interesting ideas. Draw arrows to connect related ideas. Do you find one idea that might be the subject of a paper?

PART C   Clustering

Some writers find *clustering* or *mapping* an effective way to get ideas on paper. To begin clustering, write one idea or topic—usually one word—in the center of your paper. Then let your mind make associations, and write these ideas down, branching out from the center, like this:

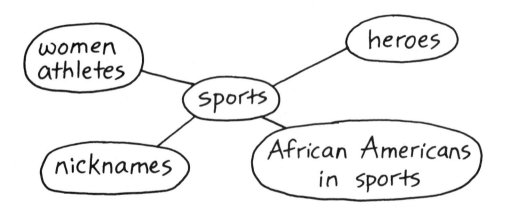

When one idea suggests other ideas, details, or examples, jot these around it in a cluster. When you finish, pick the cluster that most interests you, and write further. You might want to freewrite for more ideas.

PRACTICE 1

Read over the clustering map on page 13. If you were giving advice to the writer, which cluster or branch do you think would make the most interesting paper? Why?

PRACTICE 2

Choose one of these topics or another topic that interests you. Write it in the center of a piece of paper and then try clustering. Keep writing down associations until you have filled the page.

1. movies
2. a villain
3. a lesson
4. sports
5. my hometown
6. self-esteem
7. the good student
8. Mr. or Ms. Right

PART D   Keeping a Journal

Keeping a journal is an excellent way to practice your writing skills and to discover ideas for future writing. Most of all, your journal is a place to record your private thoughts and important experiences. Set aside a section of your notebook, or get yourself a special book with 8½-by-11-inch lined paper. Every night, or several times a week, write for at least ten minutes in your journal.

What you write about will be limited only by your imagination. Here are some ideas:

■ Write in detail about things that matter to you—family relationships, falling in (or out) of love, an experience at school or work, something important you just learned, something you did well.

■ List your personal goals, and brainstorm possible steps toward achieving them.

■ Write about problems you are having, and "think on paper" about ways to solve them.

■ Comment on classroom instruction or assignments, and evaluate your learning progress. What needs work? What questions do you need to ask? Write out a study plan for yourself and refer to it regularly.

■ Write down your responses to your reading—class assignments, newspaper items, magazine articles that impress or anger you.

■ Read through the quotations at the end of this book until you find one that strikes you. Then copy it into your journal, think about it, and write. For example, Agnes Repplier says, "It is not easy to find happiness in ourselves, and it is not possible to find it elsewhere." Do you agree with her?

■ Be alert to interesting writing topics all around you. If possible, carry a notebook during the day for "fast sketches." Jot down moving or funny moments, people, or things that catch your attention—a homeless person in your neighborhood, a scene at the day-care center where you leave your child, a man trying to persuade an officer not to give him a parking ticket.

You will soon find that writing ideas will occur to you all day long. Before they slip away, capture them in words.

PRACTICE 1

Write in your journal for at least ten minutes three times a week.

At the end of each week, read what you have written. Underline striking passages, and put a check beside interesting topics and ideas that you would like to write more about.

As you complete the exercises in this book and work on the writing assignments, try all four techniques—freewriting, brainstorming, clustering, and keeping a journal—and see which ones work best for you.

PRACTICE 2

From your journal, choose one or two passages that you might want to rewrite and allow others to read. Put a check beside each of those passages so you can find them easily later. Underline the parts you like best. Can you already see ways you might rewrite and improve the writing?

Chapter Highlights

To get started and to discover your ideas, try these techniques.

■ **Freewriting:** writing for five or ten minutes about anything that comes into your head

■ **Focused freewriting:** freewriting for five or ten minutes about one topic

■ **Brainstorming:** freely jotting many ideas about a topic

■ **Clustering:** making word associations on paper

■ **Keeping a journal:** writing regularly about things that interest and move you

Developing Effective Paragraphs

The *paragraph* is the basic unit of writing. This chapter will guide you through the process of writing paragraphs.

PART A Defining the Paragraph and the Topic Sentence

A *paragraph* is a group of related sentences that develops one main idea. Although a paragraph has no definite length, it is often four to twelve sentences long. A paragraph usually occurs with other paragraphs in a longer piece of writing—an essay, a letter, or an article, for example.

A paragraph looks like this on the page:

- Clearly *indent* the first word of every paragraph about one-half inch or five spaces on the keyboard.

- Extend every line of a paragraph to the right-hand margin.

- However, if the last word of the paragraph comes before the end of the line, leave the rest of the line blank.

Topic Sentence and Body

Most paragraphs contain one main idea to which all the sentences relate. The *topic sentence* states this main idea. The *body* supports this main idea with specific details, facts, and examples.

> When I was growing up, my older brother Joe was the greatest person in my world. If anyone teased me about my braces or buckteeth, he fiercely defended me. When one boy insisted on calling me "Fang," Joe threatened to knock his teeth out. It worked—no more teasing. My brother always chose me to play on his baseball teams though I was a terrible hitter. Even after he got his driver's license, he didn't abandon me. Instead, every Sunday, the two of us went for a drive. We might stop for cheeseburgers, go to a computer showroom, drive past some girl's house, or just laugh and talk. It was one of childhood's mysteries that such a wonderful brother loved me.
>
> Jeremiah Woolrich, student

- The first sentence of this paragraph is the *topic sentence.* It states in a general way the main idea of the paragraph: that *Joe was the greatest person in my world.* Although the topic sentence can appear anywhere in the paragraph, it is often the first sentence.

- The rest of the paragraph, the *body,* fully explains this statement with details about braces and buckteeth, baseball teams, Sunday drives, cheeseburgers, and so forth.

- Note that the final sentence provides a brief conclusion so that the paragraph *feels* finished.

Each group of sentences below can be arranged and written as a paragraph. Circle the letter of the sentence that would be the best topic sentence. REMEMBER: The topic sentence states the main idea of the entire paragraph and includes all the other ideas.

EXAMPLE: a. Speed-walking three times a week is part of my routine.

(b.) Staying healthy and fit is important to me.

c. Every night, I get at least seven hours of sleep.

d. I eat as many fresh fruits and vegetables as possible.

(Sentence b is more general than the other sentences; it would be the best topic sentence.)

1. a.   My father looks handsome in his old-fashioned top hat and tails.

   b.   My mother is seated before him wearing a lacy gown.

   (c.)   I will always treasure this wedding picture of my parents.

   d.   In the background is the old arched gate of my grandparents' garden.

2. a.   In 1988, three students at a Philadelphia high school for the arts were singing in the men's room.

   b.   Singing dates in Philadelphia clubs led to their first recording contract.

   c.   A fourth student came by, added a bass note, and was asked to join the group, then called Unique Attraction.

   (d.)   The group Boyz II Men rose quickly from lunch-hour vocalizing to international fame.

   e.   Their first album, *Coolie High Harmony,* earned platinum.

   f.   Today the Boyz' silky mix of doo-wop and gospel is loved all over the world.

3. a.   Physical courage allows soldiers or athletes to endure bodily pain or danger.

   b.   Those with social courage dare to expose their deep feelings in order to build close relationships.

   c.   Those rare people who stand up for their beliefs despite public pressure possess moral courage.

   d.   Inventors and artists show creative courage when they break out of old ways of seeing and doing things.

   (e.)   Psychologist Rollo May believed that four different types of courage exist.

4. (a.) Many old toys and household objects are now collectors' items.

   b. A Barbie or Madame Alexander doll from the 1950s can bring more than $1,000.

   c. Old baseball cards are worth money to collectors.

   d. Fiesta china, made in the 1930s, has become popular again.

5. a. Horses are available for day trips.

   b. There are many scenic hiking trails.

   c. The Sierra Nevada mountains are a challenge to rock climbers.

   (d.) Yosemite National Park offers a variety of activities to the visitor.

   e. Those who like to fish can cast for trout in Yosemite's lakes and rivers.

PART B   Narrowing the Topic and Writing the Topic Sentence

The rest of this chapter will guide you through the *process* of writing paragraphs of your own. Here are the steps we will discuss:

1. Narrowing the topic and writing the topic sentence

2. Generating ideas for the body

3. Selecting and dropping ideas

4. Grouping ideas in a plan

5. Writing and revising the paragraph

6. Writing the final draft

Narrowing the Topic

Often your first step as a writer will be *narrowing* a broad topic—one assigned by your instructor, one you have thought of yourself, or one suggested by a particular writing task, like a letter. That is, you must cut the topic down to size and choose one aspect that interests you.

Assume, for example, that you are asked to write a paragraph describing a person you know. The trick is to choose someone you would *like* to write about, someone who interests you and would probably also interest your audience of readers.

At this point, many writers find it helpful to think on paper by *brainstorming, freewriting,* or *clustering.** As you jot down or freely write ideas, ask yourself questions. Whom do I love, hate, or admire? Who is the funniest or most unusual person I know? Is there a family member or friend about whom others might like to read?

Suppose you choose to write about your friend Beverly. Beverly is too broad a topic for one paragraph. Therefore, you should limit your topic further, choosing just one of her qualities or acts. What is unusual about her? What might interest others? Perhaps what stands out in your mind is that Beverly is a determined person who doesn't let difficulties defeat her. You have now *narrowed* your broad topic to just *Beverly's determination.*

---

*Brainstorming is discussed further in Part C. Also see Chapter 2 for more information about prewriting.

Writing the Topic Sentence

The *topic sentence* states your narrowed topic clearly in sentence form. It makes one point that the rest of your paragraph will support and explain. A topic sentence can be very simple *(Beverly is a determined person)* or, better yet, it can state your attitude or point of view about the topic *(Beverly inspires admiration because she is so determined)*. A good topic sentence should be limited and complete.

Your topic sentence should be *limited*. It should make a point that is neither too broad nor too narrow to be supported in a paragraph. As a rule, the more specific and well-defined the topic sentence, the better the paragraph. Which of these topic sentences do you think will produce the best paragraphs?

(1)　My recent trip to Colorado was really bad.

(2)　My recent trip to Colorado was disappointing because the weather ruined my camping plans.

■　Topic sentence (1) is so broad that the paragraph could include almost anything.

■　Topic sentence (2), on the other hand, is *limited* enough to provide the main idea for a good paragraph: how terrible weather ruined the writer's camping plans.

(3)　The Each-One-Reach-One tutoring program encourages academic excellence at Chester Elementary School.

(4)　Tutoring programs can be found all over the country.

■　Topic sentence (3) is limited enough to provide the main idea for a good paragraph. Reading this topic sentence, what do you expect the paragraph to include?

It might explain ways in which the program encourages academic excellence

at Chester.

■　Topic sentence (4) lacks a limited point. Reading this sentence, a reader cannot guess what the paragraph will be about.

In addition, the topic sentence must be a *complete sentence;* it must contain a subject and a verb and express a complete thought.* Do not confuse a topic with a topic sentence. For example, *the heroism of Christopher Reeve* cannot be a topic sentence because it is not a complete sentence. Here is one possible topic sentence: *Christopher Reeve's work with other spinal-cord injury patients makes him a true hero.*

For now, it is best to place your topic sentence at the beginning of the paragraph. After you have mastered this pattern, you can try variations. Placed first, the topic sentence clearly establishes your paragraph's focus and helps grab the reader's attention. Wherever the topic sentence appears, all other sentences must relate to it and support it with specific details, facts, examples, arguments, and

---

*For more work on writing complete sentences, see Chapters 6 and 7.

explanations. If necessary, you can revise the topic sentence later to make it more accurately match the paragraph you have written.

Do not begin a topic sentence with *This paragraph will be about . . .* or *I am going to write about. . . .* These extra words contribute nothing. Instead, make your point directly. Make every word in the topic sentence count.

PRACTICE 1

Put a check beside each topic sentence that is limited enough to write a good paragraph about. If you think a topic sentence is too broad, limit the topic according to your own interests; then write a new, specific topic sentence.

EXAMPLES: ✔ Owning a computer has improved my writing in three ways.

Rewrite: _____

I am going to write about my family.

Rewrite: My mother finds gardening a creative and financially rewarding hobby.

1. ✔ Working in the complaint department taught me tolerance.

   Rewrite: _____

   _____

2. Children are really something.

   Rewrite: The play behavior of two-year-olds is different from that of

   five-year-olds.

3. A subject I want to write about is date rape.

   Rewrite: Discussions led by a counselor can help college students define

   date rape for themselves.

4. This paragraph will discuss music.

   Rewrite: Celine Dion's husband has supported her career in three ways.

   _____

5. Some things about college have been great.

   Rewrite: Being able to set my own study schedule in college has been great.

   _____

6. ✔ It is hard to change many of the attitudes about food that we learn as children.

   Rewrite: _____

   _____

7. ✔ Lana's tendency to spend too much time on the phone is a problem in the office.

Rewrite: _____

_____

8. Single parents have a hard time.

Rewrite: _Single parents often have little time for themselves._

_____

9. ✔ Welfare recipients should be able to use their welfare checks to pay their college tuition.

Rewrite: _____

_____

10. ✔ Living in a one-room apartment forces a person to be organized.

Rewrite: _____

_____

PRACTICE 2

From the following list of broad topics, choose three that interest you. Then narrow each one to a subject that could be developed in one paragraph. Finally, write both a limited topic and a complete topic sentence for each one.

a celebrity you'd love to meet   aging

your first impressions of college   hair or clothing styles

overcoming fears   the value of humor

marriage or relationships   a dream job

1. Topic: _Aging_

   Limited topic: _Mr. Nosco—active despite advancing age_

   Topic sentence: _At seventy-eight, Mr. Nosco still lectures on astronomy and watches the stars from his roof._

2. Topic: _Marriage_

   Limited topic: _Staying married_

   Topic sentence: _Staying married requires communication and understanding._

   _____

3. Topic: _Overcoming Fears_

   Limited topic: _Overcoming fear of speaking before large groups_

   Topic sentence: _I practice in front of a mirror to overcome my fear of speaking before large groups._

PART C   Generating Ideas for the Body

Rich supporting detail is one key to effective writing. A good way to generate ideas for the body of a paragraph is by *brainstorming*, freely jotting down ideas. This important step may take just a few minutes, but it gets your ideas on paper and may pull ideas out of you that you didn't even know you had!

Freely jot down anything that might relate to your topic—details, examples, little stories. Don't worry at this point if some ideas don't seem to belong. For now, just keep jotting.

Here is a possible brainstorming list for the topic sentence *Beverly inspires admiration because she is so determined.*

1. saved enough money for college

2. worked days, went to school nights

3. has beautiful brown eyes

4. nervous about learning to drive but didn't give up

5. failed road test twice—passed eventually

6. her favorite color—wine red

7. received degree in accounting

8. she is really admirable

9. with lots of will power, quit smoking

10. used to be a heavy smoker

11. married to Virgil

12. I like Virgil too

13. now a good driver

14. never got a ticket

15. hasn't touched another cigarette

As you saw in Part B, some writers also brainstorm or use other prewriting techniques *before* they write the topic sentence. Do what works best for you.

PRACTICE 1

Here are three topic sentences. For each one, brainstorm, freewrite, or cluster for several specific details that you might use to develop an interesting paragraph.

1. The van was painted from bumper to bumper with nature scenes.

_____

_____

_____

2. Bailey gave a wonderful party.

_____

_____

_____

3. The best course I ever took was _____.

_____

_____

_____

Now choose the topic from Part B, Practice 2, that most interests you. Write that topic and your topic sentence here.

Topic:_____

Topic sentence: _____

Next, brainstorm. On a sheet of notebook paper, write anything that comes to you about your topic sentence. Just let your ideas pour onto paper! Try to fill the page.

Many writers adjust the topic sentence after they have finished drafting the paragraph. In a group of three or four classmates, study the body of each of the following paragraphs. Then, working together, write the most exact and interesting topic sentence you can.

a. _Celia Johnson's collection of Wild West objects is taking over her living room._

_____

    The chairs in Celia's living room are printed with pony heads and stand on legs that resemble hooves. The bases of her four table lamps are statues of cowboys or cowgirls, each topped with a matching shade. On three walls, floor-to-ceiling shelves sag under the weight of Roy Rogers and Hopalong Cassidy lunch boxes from the 1940s and hundreds of salt-and-pepper shakers in the form of cowboy boots or cacti. The most amazing object in Celia's collection is a huge motorized bucking bronco that guests in her house can ride on.

b. _Winter mornings in Minnesota were bitterly cold but beautiful._

_____

    Frigid air would hit us in the eyes when we stepped out the door to catch the school bus. Even though our faces were wrapped in scarves and our heads covered with wool caps, the cold snatched our breath away. A thin layer of snow crunched loudly under our boots as we ran gasping out to the road. I knew that the famous Minnesota wind chill was pulling temperatures well below zero, but I tried not to think about that. Instead, I liked to see how everything in the yard was frozen motionless, even the blades of grass that shone like little glass knives.

(Ari Henson, student)

PART D   # Selecting and Dropping Ideas

This may be the easiest step in paragraph writing because all you have to do is to select those ideas that best support your topic sentence and drop those that do not. Also drop ideas that just repeat the topic sentence but add nothing new to the paragraph.

Here is the brainstorming list for the topic sentence *Beverly inspires admiration because she is so determined.* Which ideas would you drop? Why?

1. saved enough money for college

2. worked days, went to school nights

3. has beautiful brown eyes

4. nervous about learning to drive but didn't give up

5. failed road test twice—passed eventually

6. her favorite color—wine red

7. received degree in accounting

8. she is really admirable

9. with lots of will power, quit smoking

10. used to be a heavy smoker

11. married to Virgil

12. I like Virgil too

13. now a good driver

14. never got a ticket

15. hasn't touched another cigarette

You probably dropped ideas 3, 6, 11, and 12 because they do not relate to the topic. You also should have dropped idea 8 because it merely repeats the topic sentence.

PRACTICE

Now read through your own brainstorming list in Part C, Practice 2. Select the ideas that best support your topic sentence, and cross out those that do not. In addition, drop ideas that merely repeat the topic sentence. You should be able to give good reasons for keeping or dropping each idea in the list.

PART E   Arranging Ideas in a Plan or Outline

Now choose an *order* in which to arrange your ideas. First, group together ideas that have something in common, that are related or alike in some way. Then decide which ideas should come first, which second, and so on. Many writers do this by numbering the ideas on their list.

Here are the ideas for a paragraph about Beverly arranged in one possible way.

> worked days, went to school nights
> saved enough money for college
> received degree in accounting

> nervous about learning to drive but didn't give up
> failed road test twice—passed eventually
> now a good driver
> never got a ticket

> used to be a heavy smoker
> with lots of will power, quit smoking
> hasn't touched another cigarette

■ How are the ideas in each group related?   *The first group of ideas deals with*

school, the second with driving, and the third with smoking.

■ Does it make sense to discuss college first, driving second, and smoking last?

Why? *This may be the order of importance to the writer.*

Keep in mind that there is more than one way to arrange ideas. As you group your own brainstorming list, think of what you want to say; then arrange ideas accordingly.*

PRACTICE

On a separate sheet of paper, group the ideas from your brainstorming list into a plan. First, group together related ideas. Then decide which ideas will come first, which second, and so on.

---

*For more work on choosing an order, see Chapter 4, Part B.

PART F — Writing and Revising the Paragraph

Writing the First Draft

By now, you should have a clear plan or outline from which to write the first draft of your paragraph. The *first draft* should contain all the ideas you have decided to use, in the order in which you have chosen to present them. Writing on every other line will leave room for later corrections.

Explain your ideas fully, including details that will interest or amuse the reader. If you are unsure about something, put a check in the margin and come back to it later, but avoid getting stuck on any one word, sentence, or idea. If possible, set the paper aside for several hours or several days; this will help you read it later with a fresh eye.

PRACTICE

On a separate sheet of paper, write a first draft of the paragraph you have been working on.

Revising

Whether you are a beginning writer or a professional, you must *revise*—that is, rewrite what you have written in order to improve it. You might cross out and rewrite words or entire sentences. You might add, drop, or rearrange details.

As you revise, keep the reader in mind. Ask yourself these questions:

■ Is my topic sentence clear?

■ Can the reader easily follow my ideas?

■ Is the order of ideas logical?

■ Will this paragraph keep the reader interested?

In addition, revise your paragraph for *support* and for *unity*.

Revising for Support

Make sure your paragraph contains excellent *support*—that is, specific details, facts, and examples that fully explain your topic sentence.

Avoid simply repeating the same idea in different words, especially the idea in the topic sentence. Repeated ideas are just padding, a sign that you need to brainstorm or freewrite again for new ideas. Which of the following two paragraphs contains the best and most interesting support?

> A.   Every Saturday morning, Fourteenth Street is alive with activity. From one end of the street to the other, people are out doing everything imaginable. Vendors sell many different items on the street, and storekeepers will do just about anything to get customers into their stores. They will use signs, and they will use music. There is a tremendous amount of activity on Fourteenth Street, and just watching it is enjoyable.

> B.   Every Saturday morning, Fourteenth Street is alive with activity. Vendors line the sidewalks, selling everything from cassette tapes to wigs. Trying to lure customers inside, the shops blast pop music into the street or hang brightly colored banners announcing "Grand Opening Sale" or "Everything Must Go." Shoppers jam the sidewalks, both serious bargain hunters and families just out for a stroll, munching chilidogs as they survey the merchandise. Here and there, a panhandler hustles for handouts, taking advantage of the Saturday crowd.

- The body of *paragraph A* contains vague and general statements, so the reader gets no clear picture of the activity on Fourteenth Street.

- The body of *paragraph B*, however, includes many specific *details* that clearly explain the topic sentence: *vendors selling everything from cassette tapes to wigs, shops blasting pop music, brightly colored banners.*

- What other details in paragraph B help you see just how Fourteenth Street is alive with activity?

  serious bargain hunters

  strolling families

  chili dogs

  a panhandler

PRACTICE

Check these paragraphs for strong, specific support. Mark places that need more details or explanation, and cross out any weak or repeated words. Then revise and rewrite each paragraph *as if you had written it,* inventing and adding support when you need to.

Paragraph A: Aunt Alethia was one of the most important people in my life. She had a strong influence on me. No matter how busy she was, she always had time for me. She paid attention to small things about me that no one else seemed to notice. When I was successful, she praised me. When I was feeling down, she gave me pep talks. She was truly wise and shared her wisdom with me. My aunt was a great person who had a major influence on my life.

Paragraph B: Just getting to school safely can be a challenge for many young people. Young as he is, my son has been robbed once and bullied on several occasions. The robbery was very frightening, for it involved a weapon. What was taken was a small thing, but it meant a lot to my son. It angers me that just getting to school is so dangerous. Something needs to be done.

Revising for Unity

While writing, you may sometimes drift away from your topic and include information that does not belong in the paragraph. It is important, therefore, to revise your paragraph for *unity*; that is, drop any ideas or sentences that do not relate to the topic sentence.

This paragraph lacks unity:

> (1) Franklin Mars, a Minnesota candy maker, created many popular candy snacks. (2) Milky Way, his first bar, was an instant hit. (3) Snickers, which he introduced in 1930, also sold very well. (4) Milton Hershey developed the very first candy bar in 1894. (5) M&Ms were a later Mars creation, supposedly designed so that soldiers could enjoy a sugar boost without getting sticky trigger fingers.

■ What is the topic sentence in this paragraph? _____*sentence (1)*_____

■ Which sentence does *not* relate to the topic sentence? _____*sentence (4)*_____

■ Sentence (4) has nothing to do with the main idea, that *Franklin Mars created many popular candy snacks.* Therefore, sentence (4) should be dropped.

PRACTICE

Check the following paragraphs for unity. If a paragraph is unified, write *U* in the blank. If not, write the number of the sentence that does not belong in the paragraph.

1. __*3*__ (1) Personalized license plates have become very popular since they were introduced in the 1970s. (2) These "vanity plates" allow car owners to express their sense of humor, marital status, pet peeves, or ethnic pride. (3) Of course, every car must display a plate on the rear bumper or in the back window. (4) California was one of the first states to allow vanity plates, and its drivers created such messages as NUTS 2U and 55IZ2LO. (5) Now in some states, as many as one in seven autos has a personalized plate. (6) A recent *Car and Driver* poll picked the nation's best vanity plates, including NT GUILTY (on an Arkansas sports car), NOBODY (on a Rolls Royce in California), and NO WIFE (on a mid-sized sedan in Illinois).

2. __*U*__ (1) Families who nourish their children with words as well as food at dinner time produce better readers later on. (2) Researchers at Harvard University studied the dinner conversations of sixty-eight families. (3) What they found is that parents who use a few new words in conversation with their three- and four-year-olds each night quickly build the children's vocabularies and their later reading skills. (4) The researchers point out that children can learn from eight to twenty-eight new words a day, so they need to be "fed" new words. (5) Excellent "big words" for preschoolers include *parachute, emerald, instrument,* and *education,* the researchers say.

3. __*5*__ (1) Swimming is excellent exercise. (2) Swimming vigorously for just twelve minutes provides aerobic benefits to the heart. (3) Unlike jogging and many other aerobic sports, however, swimming does not jolt the bones and muscles with sudden pressure. (4) Furthermore, the motions of swimming, such as reaching out in the crawl, stretch the muscles in a healthy, natural way. (5) Some swimmers wear goggles to keep chlorine or salt out of their eyes, while others do not.

Peer Feedback for Revising

You may wish to show your first draft or read it aloud to a respected friend or classmate. You will be asking this person to give an honest reader response, not to rewrite your work. To elicit useful responses, ask specific questions of your own or use this peer feedback sheet.

PEER FEEDBACK SHEET

To _____   From _____   Date _____

1. What I like about this piece of writing is _____
   _____

2. Your main point seems to be _____
   _____

3. These particular words or lines struck me as powerful:

   Words or lines: I like them because:

   _____   _____

   _____   _____

   _____   _____

4. But some things aren't clear to me. These lines or parts could be improved (meaning not clear, supporting points missing, order seems mixed up, writing not lively):

   Lines or parts: Need improving because

   _____   _____

   _____   _____

   _____   _____

   _____   _____

5. The one change you could make that would make the biggest

   improvement in this piece of writing is _____
   _____

PRACTICE 1

Now read the first draft of your paragraph with a critical eye. Revise and rewrite it, checking especially for a clear topic sentence, strong support, and unity.

Exchange *revised* paragraphs with a classmate. Ask specific questions or use the Peer Feedback Sheet.

When you *give* feedback, try to be as honest and specific as possible; saying a paper is "good," "nice," or "bad" doesn't really help the writer. When you *receive* feedback, think over your classmate's responses; do they ring true?

Now revise a second time, with the aim of writing a fine paragraph.

PART G   Writing the Final Draft

When you are satisfied with your revisions, recopy your paper. Be sure to include all your corrections, and write neatly and legibly—a carelessly scribbled paper seems to say that you don't care about your work.

The first draft of the paragraph about Beverly, with the writer's changes, and the revised, final draft follow. Compare them.

First Draft with Revisions

(1) Beverly inspires admiration because she is so determined. (2) Although she

doing what? add details

could not afford to attend college right after high school, she worked to save

How long?! Better support needed—show her hard work!

money. (3) It took a long time, but she got her degree. (4) She is now a good

driver. (5) At first, she was very nervous about getting behind the wheel and even

The third time,

failed the road test twice, but she didn't quit. (6) She passed eventually.

Drop Virgil—he doesn't belong

(7) Her husband, Virgil, loves to drive; he races cars on the weekend. (8) Anyway,

Beverly has never gotten a ticket. (9) A year ago, Beverly quit smoking. (10) For

how long??   too general—add details here

awhile, she had a rough time, but she hasn't touched a cigarette. (11) Now she

better conclusion needed

says that the urge to smoke has faded away. (12) She doesn't let difficulties

defeat her.

Guide the reader better from point to point! Choppy—

Final Draft

(1) Beverly inspires admiration because she is so determined. (2) Although she could not afford to attend college right after high school, she worked as a cashier to save money for tuition. (3) It took her five years working days and going to school nights, but she recently received a B.S. in accounting. (4) Thanks to this same determination, Beverly is now a good driver. (5) At first, she was very nervous about getting behind the wheel and even failed the road test twice, but she didn't give up. (6) The third time, she passed, and she has never gotten a ticket. (7) A year ago, Beverly quit smoking. (8) For a month or more, she chewed her nails and endless packs of gum, but she hasn't touched a cigarette. (9) Now she says that the urge to smoke has faded away. (10) When Beverly sets a goal for herself, she doesn't let difficulties defeat her.

■ This paragraph provides good support for the topic sentence. The writer has made sentences (2) and (3) more specific by adding *as a cashier; for tuition; five years working days and going to school nights;* and *recently received a B.S. in accounting.*

■ What other revisions did the writer make? How do these revisions improve

the paragraph? *The writer made sentence (6) more exact and combined it*

with sentence (8), dropped the sentence about Virgil, added details to sentence

(10), and expanded sentence (12) to relate it to the topic sentence. The paragraph

is now more unified and specific.

■ *Transitional expressions* are words and phrases that guide the reader smoothly from point to point. In sentence (5) of the final draft, *At first* is a transitional expression showing time. What other transitional expressions of time are

used? *The third time, a year ago, for a month or more, now*

■ What phrase provides a transition from sentence (3) to (4)?

Thanks to this same determination

■ Note that the last sentence now provides a brief *conclusion*, so that the paragraph *feels* finished.

Proofreading

Finally, carefully *proofread* your paper for grammatical and spelling errors, consulting your dictionary and this book as necessary. Errors in your writing will lower your grades in almost all college courses and will seriously limit your job opportunities. Units 2 through 8 of this text will help you improve your grammar, punctuation, and spelling skills.

Some students find it useful to point to each word and say it softly. This also helps them catch errors, as well as any words they may have left out as they wrote, especially little words like *and, at, of,* and *on.*

In which of these sentences have words been omitted?

(1) Despite its faulty landing gear, the 747 managed land safely.

(2) Plans for the new gym were on display the library.

(3) Mr. Sampson winked at his reflection in the bathroom mirror.

■ Sentences (1) and (2) are missing words.

■ Sentence (1) requires *to* before *land.*

■ What word is omitted in sentence (2)? *in*

■ Where should this word be placed? *after display*

Proofread these sentences for omitted words. Add the necessary words above the lines. Some sentences may already be correct.

EXAMPLE: People were not always able ^to^ tell time accurately.

1. People used to guess the time ^of^ day by watching the sun move across the sky.

2. Sunrise and sunset were easy ^to^ recognize.

3. Recognizing noon ^was^ easy, too.

4. However, telling time by the position of ^the^ sun was very difficult at other times.

5. People noticed that shadows lengthened during the day.

6. They found it easier to tell time by looking at the shadows than by looking ^at^ the sun.

7. People stuck poles into the ground to ^tell^ time by the length of the shadows.

8. These ^were^ the first shadow clocks, or sundials.

9. In 300 B.C., ^a^ Chaldean astronomer invented a more accurate, bowl-shaped sundial.

10. Today, most sundials ^are^ decorative, but they can still be used to tell time.

Proofread the final draft of your paragraph, checking for grammar or spelling errors and omitted words.

Writing and Revising Paragraphs

The assignments that follow will give you practice in writing and revising basic paragraphs. In each assignment, aim for (1) a clear topic sentence and (2) a body that fully supports and explains the topic sentence. As you write, refer to the checklist in the Chapter Highlights.

Paragraph 1: Describe a public place. Reread paragraph B on page 28. Then choose a place in your neighborhood that is "alive with activity"—a park, street, restaurant, or club. In your topic sentence, name the place and say when it is most active. For example, "Every Saturday night, the Planet Hollywood Cafe is alive with activity." Begin by freewriting or by jotting down as many details about the scene as possible. Then describe the scene, choosing lively and interesting details that will help the reader to see the place as clearly as you do. Arrange your observations in a logical order. Revise for support.

Paragraph 2: Choose your time of day. Many people have a favorite time of day—the freshness of early morning, 5 p.m. when work ends, late at night when the children are asleep. In your topic sentence, name your favorite time of day. Then develop the paragraph by explaining why you look forward to this time and exactly how you spend it. Remember to conclude the paragraph; don't just stop.

Paragraph 3: Describe a person. Choose someone you strongly do (or do not) admire. In your topic sentence, focus on just *one* of the person's qualities. For example, "I admire Jamal's courage (athletic ability, unusual sense of humor, and so on)." Then discuss two or three incidents or actions that clearly show this quality. Freewrite, brainstorm, or cluster for details and examples. Revise for unity; make sure that every sentence supports your topic sentence. Check your final draft for omitted words.

Paragraph 4: Create a holiday. Holidays honor important people, events, or ideas. If you could create a new holiday for your town or state, or for the country, what would that holiday be? In your topic sentence, name the holiday and tell exactly whom or what it honors. Then explain why this holiday is important, and discuss how it should be celebrated. Take a humorous approach if you wish. For instance, you might invent a national holiday in honor of the first time you got an A in English composition. As you revise, make sure you have arranged your ideas in a logical order. Proofread carefully.

✔ Chapter Highlights

Checklist for Writing an Effective Paragraph

☐ 1. Narrow the topic: Cut the topic down to one aspect that interests you and will probably interest your readers.

☐ 2. Write the topic sentence. (You may wish to brainstorm or freewrite first.)

☐ 3. Brainstorm, freewrite, or cluster ideas for the body: Write down anything and everything that might relate to your topic.

☐ 4. Select and drop ideas: Select those ideas that relate to your topic and drop those that do not.

☐ 5. Group together ideas that have something in common; then arrange the ideas in a plan.

☐ 6. Write your first draft.

☐ 7. Read what you have written, making any necessary corrections and additions. Revise for support and unity.

☐ 8. Write the final draft of your paragraph neatly and legibly, making sure to indent the first word.

☐ 9. Proofread for grammar, punctuation, spelling, and omitted words. Make neat corrections in ink.

In Chapter 3, you practiced the steps of the paragraph-writing process. This chapter builds on that work. It explains several skills that can greatly improve your writing: using examples; achieving coherence; choosing exact, concise language; and turning assignments into paragraphs.

PART A   More Work on Support: Examples

One effective way to make your writing specific is by using *examples*. Someone might write, "Divers in Monterey Bay can observe many beautiful fish. For instance, tiger-striped treefish are common." The first sentence makes a general statement about the beautiful fish in Monterey Bay. The second sentence gives a specific example of such fish: *tiger-striped treefish.*

Use one, two, or three well-chosen examples to develop a paragraph.

> Many of the computer industry's best innovators were young when they first achieved success. For example, David Filo and Jerry Yang were graduate students at Stanford when they realized that their hobby of listing the best pages on the World Wide Web might become a business. They created Yahoo!, a Web index now used by more than 500,000 people every day. Another youthful example is Marc Anderssen, who helped start the software company Netscape and designed one of the most popular computer programs ever, the Navigator. At age twenty-four, Mr. Anderssen suddenly had $58 million in the bank. A third young computer genius is Masayoshi Son. As a Berkeley undergraduate, he started importing the Space Invaders video game from his native Japan and made a small fortune. After graduation, at twenty-four, Mr. Son returned to Japan, started the Softbank company, and built a worldwide computer empire.

■ The writer begins this paragraph with a topic sentence about the youth of many computer innovators.

■ What three examples does the writer provide as support?

Example 1: _____ *David Filo and Jerry Yang* _____

Example 2: _____ *Marc Anderssen* _____

Example 3: _____ *Masayoshi Son* _____

■ Note that the topic sentence and the examples make a rough plan for the paragraph.

The simplest way to tell a reader that an example will follow is to say so, using a transitional expression: *For example, David Filo. . . .*

Transitional Expressions to Introduce Examples	
for example	for instance
to illustrate	another example

PRACTICE 1

Each example in a paragraph must clearly relate to and explain the topic sentence. Each of the following topic sentences is followed by several examples. Circle the letter of any example that does not clearly illustrate the topic sentence. Be prepared to explain your choices.

EXAMPLE: Some animals and insects camouflage themselves in interesting ways.

a. Snowshoe rabbits turn from brown to white in winter, thus blending into the snow.

b. The cheetah's spotted coat makes it hard to see in the dry African bush.

(c.) The bull alligator smashes its tail against the water and roars during mating season.

d. The walking stick is brown and irregular, much like the twigs among which this insect hides.

1. Mrs. Makarem is well loved in this community for her generous heart.

   a. Her door is always open to neighborhood children, who stop by for lemonade or advice.

   b. When the Padilla family had a fire, Mrs. Makarem collected clothes and blankets for them.

   c. "Hello, dear," she says with a smile to everyone she passes on the street.

   (d.) Born in Caracas, Venezuela, she has lived on Bay Road for thirty-two years.

2. A number of unusual, specialized scholarships are offered by colleges across the United States.

   a. North Carolina State University offers up to $7,000 to undergraduates with the last name Gatlin or Gatling.

   (b.) The University of Vienna in Austria has funds for "noncommunist creative writers ages 22 to 35."

   c. Left-handed, financially needy students can get special scholarships at Juniata College in Pennsylvania.

   d. Wisconsin's Ripon College offers $1,500 to students with a 3.0 average who once were Badger Girls or Badger Boys.

3. English borrows words from many other languages.

   a. The Spanish *la reata* gives us *lariat,* "a rope."

   b. The expression *gung ho* comes from the Chinese *keng ho,* which literally means "more fire."

   (c.) *Diss* is a term meaning "disrespect."

   d. *Kimono* is the Japanese word for "thing for wearing."

4. Cinnamon had many unusual uses in the ancient world.

   a. In Biblical times, cinnamon was burned as incense during religious ceremonies.

   b. Wealthy Romans perfumed their bath water with cinnamon.

   (c.) Cinnamon sticks tied with ribbon make an unusual gift.

   d. Egyptians used cinnamon to embalm the dead.

5. In recent years, scientists have learned that human genes play a role in causing many diseases.

   (a.) Once thought to be an illness of the past, T.B.—tuberculosis—is common again.

   b. New research shows that women with a certain pair of genes have an increased chance of getting breast cancer.

   c. The discovery that cystic fibrosis has a genetic cause is suggesting new treatments.

   d. Sickle cell anemia has long been known to have a genetic cause.

The secret of good illustration lies in well-chosen and well-written examples. Think of one example that illustrates each of the following general statements. Write out the example in sentence form—one to three sentences—as clearly and exactly as possible.

1. Many films today employ amazing special effects.

   Example: *In* Independence Day, *for instance, a huge spaceship hovers over* _____

   major cities. _____

2. Roberta has had several disappointing blind dates.

   Example: *One young man brought a comic book and read it at the restaurant.* _____

   _____

3. Dan is always buying strange gadgets.

   Example: *Tuesday, he bought a combination lint-remover-beard brush, and* _____

   Thursday, he couldn't resist an automatic sauce-stirring device. _____

4. Grace owns an impressive collection of old records.

   Example: *She has seven Elvis Presley hits recorded on 45s.* _____

   _____

5. Children often say surprising things.

   Example: *My five-year-old niece Rachel once told me that God wears a* _____

   blue nightshirt. _____

Write a paragraph developed by examples. Make sure your topic sentence can be supported by examples. Prewrite and pick the best one to three examples to explain your topic sentence. Here are some ideas:

disastrous wedding stories	ads that appeal to _____
great places to study on campus	offensive talk show topics

PART B   More Work on Arranging Ideas: Coherence

Every paragraph should have *coherence*. A paragraph *coheres*—holds together—when its ideas are arranged in a clear and logical order.

Sometimes the order of ideas will flow logically from your topic. However, three basic ways to organize ideas are *time order, space order,* and *order of importance.*

Time Order

Time order means arranging ideas chronologically, from present to past or from past to present. Careful use of time order helps to avoid such confusing writing as *Oops, I forgot to mention before that. . . .*

Most instructions, histories, processes, and stories follow the logical order of time.

> The life of Grandma Moses proves that a person is never too old to develop her talents. As a child, Anna Robertson Moses loved to draw; she often made pictures with berry juice when paint was scarce. When Anna eventually married and had a large family, she found little time to paint. Years later, with her children grown, she began to knit pictures with yarn, but her fingers ached, and she returned to her first love, painting. She was seventy years old! An art dealer saw her pictures in a local drugstore and bought them. Grandma Moses, as she was called, soon became famous, with her paintings of simple country life exhibited throughout the world. She continued to paint until her death at age 101.

■ The paragraph moves in time from Grandma Moses's childhood to her fame as an elderly artist.

■ Note how these transitional expressions—*as a child, when Anna . . . married,* and *years later*—show time and connect the events in the paragraph.

Transitional Expressions to Show Time

first, second, third

then, next, finally

before, during, after

soon, the following month, the next year

Arrange each set of sentences in time order, numbering them 1, 2, 3, and so on. Be prepared to explain your choices.

1. In eighty years, the T-shirt rose from simple underwear to fashion statement.

   __2__ During World War II, women factory workers started wearing T-shirts on the job.

   __3__ Hippies in the 1960s tie-dyed their T-shirts and wore them printed with messages.

   __4__ Now, five billion T-shirts are sold worldwide each year.

   __1__ The first American T-shirts were cotton underwear, worn home by soldiers returning from France after World War I.

2. Scientists who study the body's daily rhythms can suggest the ideal time of day for different activities.

   __1__ Taking vitamins with breakfast will help the body absorb them.

   __4__ Allergy medication should be taken just before bedtime to combat early-morning hay fever—usually the worst of the day.

   __3__ The best time to work out is 3 P.M. to 5 P.M., when strength, flexibility, and body temperature are greatest.

   __2__ Ideal naptime is 1 P.M. to 3 P.M., when body temperature falls, making sleep easier.

3. The short life of Sadako Sasaki has inspired millions to value peace.

   __1__ Sadako was just two years old in 1945 when the atom bomb destroyed her city, Hiroshima.

   __3__ From her sickbed, Sadako set out to make 1,000 paper cranes, birds that, in Japan, symbolize long life and hope.

   __4__ Although she died before making 1,000, classmates finished her project and published a book of her letters.

   __2__ At age eleven, already a talented runner, she was crushed to learn that she had leukemia, caused by radiation from the bomb.

   __5__ Now, every year, the Folded Crane Club places 1,000 cranes at the foot of a statue of Sadako, honoring her wish that all children might enjoy peace and a long life.

Have you ever been through something that lasted only a few moments but was unforgettable—for example, a sports victory, an accident, or a kiss? Write a paragraph telling about such an event. As you prewrite, pick the highlights of the experience and arrange them in time order. As you write, try to capture the drama of what happened. Use transitional expressions of time to make the story flow smoothly.

Space Order

Space order means describing a person, a place, or a thing from top to bottom, from left to right, from foreground to background, and so on.

Space order is most often used in descriptions because it moves from detail to detail, like a camera's eye.

> When the city presses in on me, I return in my mind to my hometown in St. Mary, Jamaica. I am alone, high in the mango tree on our property on the hilltop. The wind is blowing hard as usual, making a scared noise as it passes through the lush vegetation. I look down at the coconut growth with its green flooring of banana plants. Beyond that is a wide valley and then the round hills. Further out lies the sea, and I count the ships as they pass to and from the harbor while I relax on my special branch and eat mangoes.
>
> Daniel Dawes, student

■ The writer describes this scene from his vantage point high in a tree. His description follows space order, moving from the plants below him, further out to the valley and the hills, and then even further, to the sea.

■ Notice how *transitional expressions* indicating space—*beyond that*, *then*, and *further out*—help the reader to follow and "see" the details.

> **Transitional Expressions to Show Space Order**
>
> to the left, in the center, to the right
>
> behind, beside, in front of
>
> next, beyond that, further out

PRACTICE 1

Arrange each set of details according to space order, numbering them 1, 2, 3, and so on. Be prepared to explain your choices.

1. The last woman to board the bus had to stand until the last stop.

    _1_ stylish brown high-heeled shoes

    _2_ heavy leather purse dangling from left hand

    _4_ grinding teeth

    _5_ hat slipping over eyes

    _3_ tensed shoulders

2. After the party, the living room was a complete mess.

    _2_ greasy pizza boxes on the coffee table

    _1_ empty soda cans on the floor

    _4_ deflated balloons on the ceiling light

    _3_ pictures hanging at odd angles on the wall

3. We took in the sights of Rue Sherbrook West in Montreal.

   __3__ grand towers of the Ritz Carlton hotel

   __1__ lunch-hour crowds on the sidewalks

   __2__ pigeons sitting on top of the streetlights

   __4__ an airplane passing in the blue sky

PRACTICE 2   WRITING ASSIGNMENT

Select an object that interests you. It can be something natural—like a plant or a wasps' nest, or something made by human hands—like a police shield or a cellular phone. Study the object closely; then describe it in a detailed paragraph. Arrange the details in space order, from top to bottom, left to right, and so forth. As you revise, make sure your sentences flow clearly and smoothly.

Order of Importance

Order of importance means starting your paragraph with the most important idea (or the largest, most expensive, most surprising).

> State legislators should provide more money to community colleges. Most important, more teachers are needed. Faculty size has not kept pace with the great increase in community college students. Therefore, classes keep getting larger, and students get less personal attention. In addition, colleges need better learning facilities. Many community colleges occupy old buildings. Classrooms are often small and in poor condition. These schools often lack the well-equipped science labs and computer centers needed to prepare students for the twenty-first century. Finally, community colleges also need more parking lots. Currently, students spend so much time looking for parking spaces that they are frequently late to class.

■ The three reasons in this paragraph are discussed from the most important reason to the least important.

■ Note that the words *most important, in addition,* and *also* help the reader move from one reason to another.

Sometimes you may wish to begin with the least important idea and build toward a climax at the end of the paragraph. Paragraphs arranged in this way can have dramatic power.

> Although my fourteen-year-old daughter learned a great deal from living with a Pennsylvania Amish family last summer, adjusting to their strict lifestyle was difficult for her. Kay admitted that the fresh food served on the farm was great, but she missed her diet colas. More difficult was the fact that she had to wear long dresses—no more jeans and baby tees. Still worse in her view were the hours. A suburban girl and self-confessed night person, my daughter had to get up at 5 A.M. to milk cows! By far the most difficult adjustment concerned boys. If an Amish woman is not married, she cannot spend time with males, and this rule now applied to Kay. Yes, she suffered and complained, but by summer's end, she was a different girl—more open-minded and proud of the fact that all these deprivations put her more in touch with herself.
>
> Lucy Auletta, student

■ The adjustment difficulties this writer's daughter had are arranged from least to most important. How many difficulties are discussed? _____*four*_____

■ Note how the words *more difficult, still worse,* and *by far the most difficult adjustment* help the reader move from one idea to the next.

Transitional Expressions to Show Importance

first, next, finally

more, most

less, least

PRACTICE 1

Arrange the ideas that develop each topic sentence in order of importance, numbering them 1, 2, and 3. Begin with the most important idea (largest, most expensive, and so on). Or reverse the order if you think that a paragraph would be more effective if it began with the least important idea. Be prepared to explain your choices. Then, on a separate sheet of paper, write the ideas in a paragraph.

1. For three reasons, joining a serious study group is an excellent idea.

   __2__ A study group will expose you to new points of view and effective study habits.

   __3__ Joining a study group is a good way to make new friends.

   __1__ Statistics show that students who regularly attend a study group get better grades and are less likely to drop out of college.

2. Steven Spielberg has directed many of the world's most successful movies.

   _2_   *Jurassic Park,* which he directed in 1993, earned nearly $360 million at the box office.

   _1_   Spielberg's 1975 thriller, *Jaws,* the most-watched movie of its time, grossed $260 million.

   _3_   *E.T.* is still the most popular film ever made, generating $400 million in ticket sales.

3. At 2 A.M., arriving on the scene of a rollover with injuries, the fire rescue team had to act quickly.

   _2_   One team member lit flares and placed them on the road to warn other drivers to slow down.

   _3_   On the ambulance radio, a team member called for "sanders" to drop sand on local roads, which were becoming slippery in the falling snow.

   _1_   A lone woman, conscious with head injuries, was carefully moved from the driver's seat into the ambulance.

   _4_   Someone held the woman's dog, who was shivering but seemed unhurt.

PRACTICE 2   WRITING ASSIGNMENT

Your college is offering free classes in photography, money management, or fitness for senior citizens in the area. Choose just one of these classes, and write a paragraph encouraging local seniors to sign up. Discuss the three most important reasons why this class would benefit them, and arrange these reasons in order of importance—least to most or most to least, whichever you think would make a better paragraph. Don't forget to use transitional expressions. If you wish, use humor to win over your audience.

PART C   More Work on Revising:
Exact and Concise Language

Good writers do not settle for the first words that spill onto their paper or computer screen. Instead, they *revise* what they have written, replacing vague words with exact language and repetitious words with concise language.

Exact Language

As a rule, the more specific, detailed, and exact the language is, the better the writing. Which sentence in each of the following pairs contains the more vivid and exact language?

> (1) The office was noisy.
> (2) In the office, phones jangled, faxes whined, and copy machines hummed.
> (3) What my tutor said made me feel good.
> (4) When my tutor whispered, "Fine job," I felt like singing.

■ Sentence (2) is more exact than sentence (1) because *phones jangled, faxes whined, and copy machines hummed* provides more vivid information than the general word *noisy.*

■ What exact words does sentence (4) use to replace the general words *said* and *made me feel good?* _whispered, "Fine job," I felt like singing._

You do not need a large vocabulary to write exactly and well, but you do need to work at finding the right words to fit each sentence.

PRACTICE

These sentences contain vague language. Revise each one, using vivid and exact language wherever possible.

EXAMPLE: A man went through the crowd.

Revise: _A man in a blue leather jacket pushed through the crowd._

1. An automobile went down the street.

Revise: _A late-model Infiniti roared down Maple Street._

_____

2. This apartment has problems.

Revise: _This apartment has peeling paint and leaky water pipes._

_____

3. When Allison comes home, her pet greets her.

   Revise: _When Allison walks in the door, her cat meows and rubs up against her leg._

4. The moon made everything look pretty.

   Revise: _The moon cast a soft glow on the treetops._

5. The expression on his face made me feel comfortable.

   Revise: _His reassuring eyes and warm smile made me feel comfortable._

6. My work is interesting.

   Revise: _Teaching high school science challenges me._

7. There was a big storm here last week.

   Revise: _A freak electrical storm swept through Cleveland last week._

8. Hobbies can be nice.

   Revise: _I have learned much about history by collecting stamps._

9. The emergency room has a lot of people in it.

   Revise: _Crying children, people with broken bones, and busy nurses fill the emergency room._

10. Your paper is okay.

    Revise: _Your paper is very clearly organized, but the language is vague and lacks exactness._

Concise Language

Concise writing never uses five or six words when two or three will do. It avoids repetitious and unnecessary words that add nothing to the meaning of a sentence. As you revise your writing, cross out unnecessary words and phrases.

Which sentence in each of the following pairs is more concise?

> (1) Because of the fact that Larissa owns an antiques shop, she is always poking around in dusty attics.
>
> (2) Because Larissa owns an antiques shop, she is always poking around in dusty attics.
>
> (3) Mr. Tibbs entered a large, dark blue room at the end of the hallway.
>
> (4) Mr. Tibbs entered a room that was large in size and dark blue in color at the end of the hallway.

■ Sentences (2) and (3) are concise; sentences (1) and (4) are wordy.

■ In sentence (1), *because of the fact that* is a wordy way of saying *because*.

■ In sentence (4), *in size* and *in color* just repeat which ideas?

large and dark blue

Of course, conciseness does not mean writing short, choppy sentences. It does mean dropping unnecessary words and phrases.

PRACTICE 1

The following sentences are wordy. Make them more concise by deleting unnecessary words. Write each revised sentence on the lines provided.

EXAMPLE: We celebrate Halloween on October 31 in the autumn.

Revise: *We celebrate Halloween on October 31.*

1. For a great many thousands of years, people have celebrated the holiday of Halloween.

Revise: *For thousands of years, people have celebrated Halloween.*

2. The Celts of ancient Britain in their opinion believed that Samhain, the god of death, held a meeting on October 31.

Revise: *The Celts of ancient Britain believed that Samhain, the god of death, held a meeting on October 31.*

3. He gathered together at a gathering the evil and bad souls that had died during the year.

Revise: *He gathered the evil souls that had died during the year.*

4. The reason why the Celts lit candles was because they hoped the candlelight would scare away these evil spirits.

Revise: *The Celts lit candles because they hoped the candlelight would scare away these evil spirits.*

5. Children also dressed in costumes that were ugly in looks to scare away these spirits.

   Revise: *Children also dressed in ugly costumes to scare away these spirits.*

6. By coincidence, the Romans also held an autumn festival in the fall of the year on October 31.

   Revise: *By coincidence, the Romans also held a festival on October 31.*

7. Their autumn festival honored Pomona, a goddess who was the goddess of fruits and vegetables.

   Revise: *Their autumn festival honored Pomona, the goddess of fruits and vegetables.*

8. Our Halloween seems to combine together in one both the Celt and Roman festivals.

   Revise: *Our Halloween seems to combine the Celt and Roman festivals.*

9. Children dress up in frightening costumes that scare people, put candles into pumpkins, and eat fruits and other treats.

   Revise: *Children dress up in frightening costumes, put candles into pumpkins, and eat fruits and other treats.*

PRACTICE 2   REVIEW

Following are statements from real accident reports collected by an insurance company. As you will see, these writers need help with more than their fenders!

In a group of four or five classmates, read each statement and try to understand what each writer *meant* to say. Then revise each statement so that it says, exactly and concisely, what the writer intended.

1. "The guy was all over the place. I had to swerve a number of times before I hit him."

2. "The telephone pole was approaching fast. I was attempting to swerve out of its path when it struck my front end."

3. "Coming home, I drove into the wrong house and collided with a tree I don't have."

4. "I was on my way to the doctor's with rear-end trouble when my universal joint gave way, causing me to have an accident."

5. "I was driving my car out of the driveway in the usual manner when it was struck by the other car in the same place it had been struck several times before."

PRACTICE 3   REVIEW

Choose a paragraph or paper you have written recently. Read it with a fresh eye, checking for exact and concise language. Then rewrite it, eliminating all vague or wordy language.

PART D   Turning Assignments into Paragraphs

In Chapter 3, Part B, you learned how to narrow down a broad topic and write a specific topic sentence. Sometimes, however, your assignment may take the form of a specific question, and your job may be to answer the question in one paragraph.

     For example, this question asks you to take a stand on—for or against—a particular issue.

Are professional athletes overpaid?

You can often turn this kind of question into a topic sentence:

(1) Professional athletes are overpaid.

(2) Professional athletes are not overpaid.

(3) Professional athletes are sometimes overpaid.

■ These three topic sentences take different points of view.

■ The words *are, are not,* and *sometimes* make each writer's opinion clear.

     Sometimes you will be asked to agree or disagree with a statement:

(4) Salary is the most important factor in job satisfaction. Agree or disagree.

■ This is really a question in disguise: *Is salary the most important factor in job satisfaction?*

     In the topic sentence, make your opinion clear, and repeat key words.

(5) Salary is the most important factor in job satisfaction.

(6) Salary is not the most important factor in job satisfaction.

(7) Salary is only one among several important factors in job satisfaction.

■ The words *is, is not,* and *is only one among several* make each writer's opinion clear.

■ Note how the topic sentences repeat the key words from the statement— *salary, important factor, job satisfaction.*

     Once you have written the topic sentence, follow the steps described in Chapter 2—brainstorming or clustering, selecting, grouping—and then write your paragraph. Be sure that all ideas in the paragraph support the opinion you have stated in the topic sentence.

PRACTICE 1

Here are four exam questions. Write one topic sentence to answer each of them. REMEMBER: Make your opinion clear in the topic sentence, and repeat key words from the question.

1. Should computer education be required in every public high school?

   Topic sentence: *Computer education should be required in every public*

   high school.

2. Do you pay more attention to what you eat now than you did a few years ago?

   Topic sentence: *I am more concerned now about eating balanced meals than I*

   was a few years ago.

3. Is there too much bad news on television news programs?

   Topic sentence: *There is too much bad news on television news programs.*

4. How has your neighborhood changed in the last ten years?

   Topic sentence: *My neighborhood has become more crowded in the last ten*

   years.

PRACTICE 2

Imagine that your instructor has just written the exam questions from Practice 1 on the board. Choose the question that most interests you, and write a paragraph answering that question. Prewrite, select, and arrange ideas before you compose your paragraph. Then read your work, making neat corrections in ink.

PRACTICE 3

Here are four statements. Agree or disagree, and write a topic sentence for each.

1. Parents should forbid a child to see friends they disapprove of. Agree or disagree.

   Topic sentence: *Parents who forbid their children to see "undesirable" friends are*

   asking for trouble.

2. All higher education should be free. Agree or disagree.

   Topic sentence: *All high school graduates should be able to continue their higher*

   education free of charge.

3. Silence is golden. Agree or disagree.

Topic sentence: *It is usually better to speak out on important issues than to remain silent.*

4. Marriage seems to be back in style. Agree or disagree.

Topic sentence: *Marriage, once an unpopular, old-fashioned institution, seems to be back in style.*

PRACTICE 4

Choose the statement that most interests you in Practice 3. Then write a paragraph in which you agree or disagree.

Chapter Highlights

To improve your writing, try these techniques:

- Use well-chosen examples to develop a paragraph.

- Organize your ideas by time order.

- Organize your ideas by space order.

- Organize your ideas by order of importance, either from the most important to the least or from the least important to the most.

- Use language that is exact and concise.

- Turn assignment questions into topic sentences.

CHAPTER 5

Moving from Paragraph to Essay

PART A Defining the Essay and the Thesis Statement

PART B The Process of Writing an Essay

So far, you have written single paragraphs, but to succeed in college and at work, you will need to handle longer writing assignments as well. This chapter will help you apply your paragraph-writing skills to planning and writing short essays.

PART A   Defining the Essay and the Thesis Statement

An *essay* is a group of paragraphs about one subject. In many ways, an essay is like a paragraph in longer, fuller form. Both have an introduction, a body, and a conclusion. Both explain one main idea with details, facts, and examples.

However, an essay is not just a padded paragraph. An essay is longer because it contains more ideas.

The paragraphs in an essay are part of a larger whole, so each one has a special purpose.

■ The *introductory paragraph* opens the essay and tries to catch the reader's interest. It usually contains a *thesis statement*, one sentence that states the main idea of the entire essay.

■ The *body* of an essay contains one, two, three, or more paragraphs, each one making a different point about the main idea.

■ The *conclusion* brings the essay to a close. It might be a sentence or a paragraph long.

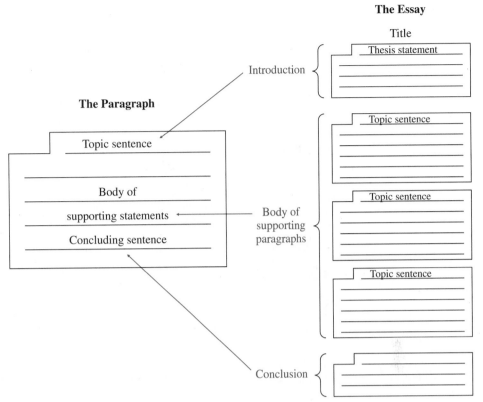

The Essay

Title

Thesis statement

Introduction

The Paragraph

Topic sentence

Body of

supporting statements

Concluding sentence

Body of
supporting
paragraphs

Topic sentence

Topic sentence

Topic sentence

Conclusion

Here is a student essay:

Tae Kwon Do

Wineth Williams

(1) Tae kwon do is a Korean martial art. It is a way of fighting and self-defense based on an understanding of both body and mind. As a college student, I discovered tae kwon do. Even though I was physically fit and planned to become a police officer, I thought that women needed special skills to protect themselves. Tae kwon do teaches these skills and much more. The person who practices tae kwon do gains discipline, maturity, and a changed self-concept.

(2) First, the discipline of tae kwon do helps the student to outfight and outsmart her opponent. For a while, I didn't appreciate the discipline. We had to move in certain ways, and we had to yell. Yelling made me laugh. Our teacher told us to shout with great force, "Keeah!" Yelling keeps the mind from focusing on being tired and helps the fighter call out the life force, or "chi," from inside her. Once we started sparring, I also had to get past not wanting to hurt anyone. Later I understood that if I punched or kicked my opponent, it meant that he or she should have been blocking and was not using good skills.

(3) Second, with practice, tae kwon do increases maturity. I have a hot temper. Before tae kwon do, I would walk dark streets and take chances, almost daring trouble. I reacted to every look or challenge. Practicing this martial art, I started to see the world more realistically. I developed more respect for the true danger in the streets. I spoke and behaved in ways to avoid trouble. My reactions became less emotional and more rational.

(4) Finally, after a year or so, tae kwon do can change the student's self-concept. This happened to me. On one hand, I became confident that I had the skills to take care of business if necessary. On the other hand, the better I got, the more I acted like a pussycat instead of a lion. That may sound strange, but inside myself, I knew that I had nothing to prove to anybody.

(5) As I discovered firsthand, the practice of tae kwon do can bring personal benefits that go far beyond self-defense.

- The last sentence in the introduction is the *thesis statement*. The thesis statement must be general enough to include the topic sentence of every paragraph in the body.

- Underline the topic sentences of paragraphs (2), (3), and (4). Note that the thesis statement and the topic sentences make a rough plan of the entire essay.

- *Transitional expressions* are words and phrases that guide the reader from point to point and from paragraph to paragraph. What transition does this student use between paragraphs (1) and (2)? Between (2) and (3)? Between (3) and (4)?

  First, Second, Finally

- The last paragraph provides a brief *conclusion.**

PRACTICE 1

To help you understand the structure of an essay, complete this plan for "Tae Kwon Do." Under each topic sentence, jot down the writer's two or three main supporting points, as if you were making a plan for the essay. (In fact, the writer probably made such a plan before she wrote her first draft.)

Paragraph 1. INTRODUCTION

> **Thesis statement:** The person who practices tae kwon do gains discipline, maturity, and a changed self-concept.

Paragraph 2. Topic Sentence: First, the discipline of tae kwon do helps the student to outfight and outsmart her opponent.

Point 1 ___*didn't appreciate discipline*___

Point 2 ___*yelling made me laugh*___

Point 3 ___*didn't want to hurt people*___

---

*To read essays by other students, see the Writers' Workshops in Units 3, 6, 7, and 8.

© 1998 Houghton Mifflin Company

Paragraph 3. Topic Sentence: Second, with practice, tae kwon do increases maturity.

Point 1 _____ *before—reacted to challenges* _____

Point 2 _____ *after—saw danger realistically* _____

Paragraph 4. Topic Sentence: Finally, after a year or so, tae kwon do can change the student's self-concept.

Point 1 _____ *I am more confident* _____

Point 2 _____ *pussycat, not lion* _____

Point 3 _____ *nothing to prove* _____

Paragraph 5.   CONCLUSION

PRACTICE 2

Discuss with several classmates or write your answers to these questions.

1. Did Ms. Williams' introduction (paragraph 1) catch and hold your interest? Would this essay be just as good or better if it had no introduction but started right in with the thesis statement? Why or why not?

2. In paragraph (4), the writer says she now can "take care of business." Is this language appropriate for a college essay? Will readers know what this means?

3. Is the conclusion effective, or is it too short?

4. Ms. Williams' audience was her English class. Her purpose (though not directly stated in the essay) was to let people know some of the benefits that come from practicing tae kwon do. Did she achieve her purpose?

5. What did you like best about the essay? What, if anything, would you change?

PART B   The Process of Writing an Essay

Whether you are writing a paragraph or an essay, the writing process is the same. Of course, writing an essay will probably take longer. In this section, you will practice these steps of the essay-writing process:

■ Narrowing the subject and writing the thesis statement

■ Generating ideas for the body

■ Selecting and arranging ideas in a plan

■ Writing and revising your essay

Narrowing the Subject and Writing the Thesis Statement

While an essay subject should be broader than a paragraph topic, a good essay subject also must be narrow enough to write about in detail. For example, the topic *jobs* is broad enough to fill a book. But the far narrower topic *driving a bulldozer at the town dump* could make a good essay. Remember to select or narrow your subject in light of your intended audience and purpose. Who are your readers, and what do you want your essay to achieve?

Writing the *thesis statement* forces you to narrow the topic further: *driving a bulldozer for the Department of Highways was the best job I ever had*. That could be an intriguing thesis statement, but the writer could focus it even more: *For three reasons, driving a bulldozer for the Department of Highways was the best job I ever had*. The writer might discuss one reason in each of three paragraphs.

Here are two more examples of the narrowing process:

(1) Subject:	music
Narrowed subject:	Babyface Edmunds, songwriter to the stars
Thesis statement:	Hit maker Babyface Edmunds studies a singer's personality and style before he writes a song.
(2) Subject:	pets
Narrowed subject:	Pains and pleasures of owning a parrot
Thesis statement:	Owning a parrot will enrich your life with noise, occasional chaos, and lots of laughs.

■ On the basis of each thesis statement, what do you expect the essays to

discuss? *Writer 1 will show how Babyface tailors his songs to the singer. Writer 2*

will discuss the noise, chaos, and laughs of parrot ownership.

Although the thesis statement must include all the ideas in the body, it should also be clear and specific. Which of these thesis statements is specific enough to write a good essay about?

(1) Three foolproof techniques will help you avoid disastrous first dates.
(2) NBA basketball is the most exciting sport in the world.
(3) Dr. Villarosa is a competent and caring physician.

■ Thesis statements (1) and (3) are both specific. From (1), a reader might expect to learn about the "three foolproof techniques," each one perhaps explained in a paragraph.

■ On the basis of thesis statement (3), what supporting points might the essay

discuss? *1. Dr. Villarosa's competence and*

2. his or her caring ways

■ Thesis statement (2), however, is too broad for an essay—or even a book. It gives the reader (and writer) no direction.

© 1998 Houghton Mifflin Company

PRACTICE

Choose one of these topics to write your own essay about. Then narrow the topic, and write a clear and specific thesis statement.

> The benefits of a sport or practice
>
> The most fascinating/boring/important job I ever had
>
> Qualities of an excellent husband/wife/partner

Narrowed subject: _____

_____

Thesis statement: _____

_____

Generating Ideas for the Body

Writers generate support for an essay just as they do for a paragraph—by prewriting to get as many interesting ideas as possible. Once you know your main point and have written a thesis statement, use your favorite prewriting method— freewriting, for example. If you feel stuck, change to brainstorming or clustering. Just keep writing.

PRACTICE

Now, generate as many good ideas as possible to support your thesis statement. Fill at least one or two pages with ideas. As you work, try to imagine how many paragraphs your essay will contain and what each will include.

Selecting and Arranging Ideas in a Plan

Next, underline or mark the most interesting ideas that support your thesis statement. Cross out the rest.

Make a rough plan or outline that includes an introductory paragraph, two or three paragraphs for the body, and a brief conclusion. Choose a logical order in which to present your ideas. Which idea will come first, second, third?

For example, the bulldozer operator might explain why that job was "the best" with three reasons, arranged in this order: 1. *On the job, I learned to operate heavy equipment.* 2. *Working alone at the controls gave me time to think.* 3. *One bonus was occasionally finding interesting items beside the road.* This arrangement moves logically from physical skills to mental benefits to a surprising bonus.

PRACTICE

Read over your prewriting pages, selecting your best ideas and a logical order in which to present them. Make an outline or plan that includes an introduction and a thesis statement; two or three supporting paragraphs, each with a clear topic sentence; and a brief conclusion.

Writing and Revising Your Essay

Drafting

Now write your first draft. Try to express your ideas clearly and fully. If a section seems weak or badly written, put a check in the margin and go on; you can come back to that section later, prewriting again if necessary for fresh ideas. Set aside your draft for an hour or a day.

Revising and Proofreading

Revising may be the most important step in the writing process. Reread your essay as if you were reading someone else's work, marking it up as you answer questions like these:

- Are my main idea and my thesis statement clear?

- Have I supported my thesis in a rich and convincing way?

- Does each paragraph in the body clearly explain the main idea?

- Does my essay *cohere* (have logical order, good transitions)?

- Are there any parts that don't belong or don't make sense?

- What one change would most improve my essay?*

    You also might wish to ask a respected friend to read or listen to your essay, giving peer feedback before you revise.**

PRACTICE 1

Now read your first draft to see how you can improve it. Trust your instincts about what is alive and interesting and what is dull. Take your time. As you revise, try to make this the best paper you have ever written.

Finally, write a new draft of your essay, using the format preferred by your instructor. Proofread carefully, correcting any grammar or spelling errors.

PRACTICE 2

Exchange essays with a classmate. Write a one-paragraph evaluation of each other's work, saying as specifically as possible what you like about the essay and what might be improved. If you wish, use the Peer Feedback Sheet (see page 30).

* See Chapter 3, Part F, for more revising ideas.
** See Chapter 3, Part F, for a sample Peer Feedback Sheet.

Possible Topics for Essays

1. The Best/Worst Class I Ever Had
2. Three Things That _____ Taught Me
3. Two Surefire Ways to Relax
4. The Bill I Most Hated to Pay
5. How to Solve a Community Problem
6. A Major Decision
7. Tips for the New Driver (College Student, NBA Draft Pick, Dieter, and so forth)
8. A Valuable/Worthless Television Show
9. Why _____ Is a Great Entertainer
10. A Good Friend
11. Can Anger Be Used Constructively?
12. What Success Meant in My High School (Family, Country)
13. How I Fell in Love with Books (German Shepherds, Rock Climbing, Video Games, and so forth)
14. Why Babies Have Babies
15. What Childhood Taught Me About Boys/Girls in Society

 Chapter Highlights

Checklist for Writing an Effective Essay

■ Narrow the topic in light of your audience and purpose. Be sure you can discuss this topic fully in a short essay.

■ Write a clear thesis statement. If you have trouble, freewrite or brainstorm first; then narrow the topic and write the thesis statement.

■ Freewrite, brainstorm, or cluster to generate facts, details, and examples to support your thesis statement.

■ Plan or outline your essay, choosing from two to three main ideas to support the thesis statement.

■ Write a topic sentence that expresses each main idea.

■ Decide on a logical order in which to present the paragraphs.

■ Plan the body of each paragraph, using all you have learned about support and paragraph development.

■ Write the first draft of your essay.

■ Revise as necessary, checking your essay for support, unity, and coherence.

■ Proofread carefully for grammar, punctuation, and spelling.

UNIT 1   WRITING ASSIGNMENTS

As you complete each writing assignment, remember to perform these steps:

- ■ Write a clear, complete topic (or thesis) sentence.

- ■ Use freewriting, brainstorming, or clustering to generate ideas.

- ■ Arrange your best ideas in a plan.

- ■ Revise for support, unity, coherence, and exact language.

- ■ Proofread for grammar, punctuation, and spelling errors.

Writing Assignment 1: *Discuss a goal.* Complete this topic sentence: "An important goal in my life is to _____." You might wish to finish school, master the Internet, visit Hawaii, or stop smoking, for example. Begin by jotting all your reasons for having this goal. Then choose the three most important reasons, and arrange them in order of importance—either from least to most important, or the reverse. Explain each reason, making clear to the reader why you feel as strongly as you do.

Writing Assignment 2: *Interview a classmate about an achievement.* Write about a time when your classmate achieved something important, like winning a sales prize at work, losing thirty pounds, or helping a friend through a bad time. To gather interesting facts and details, ask your classmate questions like these, and take notes: *Is there one accomplishment of which you are very proud? Why was this achievement so important? Did it change the way you feel about yourself?* Keep asking questions until you feel you can give your reader a vivid sense of your classmate's triumph.

In your first sentence, state the person's achievement—for instance, *Getting her first A in English was a turning point in Jessica's life.* Then explain specifically why the achievement was so meaningful.

Writing Assignment 3: *Describe an annoying trait.* Choose someone you like or love, and describe his or her most annoying habit or trait. In your topic sentence, name the trait. For instance, you might say, "My husband's most annoying trait is carelessness." Then give one to three examples explaining the topic sentence. Make your examples as specific as possible; be sure they support the topic sentence.

Writing Assignment 4: *Develop a paragraph with examples.* Below are topic sentences for possible paragraphs. Pick the topic sentence that most interests you, and write a paragraph using one to three examples to explain the topic sentence. Or choose a quotation from the Quotation Bank, and explain it with one or more examples.

a. A sense of humor can make difficult times easier to bear.

b. Mistakes can be great teachers.

c. Television commercials often insult my intelligence.

UNIT 1 REVIEW

Choosing a Topic Sentence

Each group of sentences could be unscrambled and written as a paragraph. Circle the letter of the sentence that would be the best topic sentence.

1. a. Rooftops and towers made eye-catching shapes against the winter sky.

   b. Far below, the faint sounds of slush and traffic were soothing.

   c. From the apartment-house roof, the urban scene was oddly relaxing.

   d. Stoplights changing color up and down the avenues created a rhythmic pattern invisible from the street.

2. a. Julio Iglesias, the Spanish singer, has settled in Miami.

   b. Famous Mexican actress and singer Lucía Méndez has moved there, as has Venezuelan soap star José Luis Rodríguez.

   c. The largest Spanish-language TV networks now have headquarters in Miami.

   d. In recent years, Miami has become the Hollywood of Latin America.

Selecting Ideas

Below is a topic sentence and a brainstormed list of possible ideas for a paragraph. Check "Keep" for ideas that best support the topic sentence and "Drop" for ideas that do not.

Topic sentence: Probably the greatest female athlete of all time was Texan Babe Didrikson.

Keep	Drop	
✔		1. during the 1940s, she won every women's golf title at least once
✔		2. in 1932, won eight out of ten track and field events in the Amateur Athletic Union's national championships
	✔	3. married George Zaharias in 1939
	✔	4. in photos, intelligent, dark-haired woman
✔		5. after 1932 Olympics, she became a professional athlete, excelling in basketball, baseball, swimming, diving, and billiards!
	✔	6. Babe was the daughter of Norwegian immigrants
	✔	7. a woman of many talents in our time is Oprah Winfrey
	✔	8. Oprah overcame many obstacles on her way to the top
✔		9. at 1932 Olympics, Didrikson broke world records in the javelin throw and 80-meter hurdles.
✔		10. also broke world high-jump record, but Olympic judges disqualified her for using what they called the "Texas roll"

Examining a Paragraph

Read this paragraph and answer the questions.

(1) Students at some American colleges are learning a lot from trash by study-ing "garbology." (2) Wearing rubber gloves, they might sift through the local dump, counting and collecting treasures that they examine back at the laboratory. (3) First, they learn to look closely and to interpret what they see, thus reading the stories that trash tells. (4) More important, they learn the truth about what Americans buy, what they eat, and how they live. (5) Students at the University of Arizona, for instance, were surprised to find that low-income families in certain areas buy more educational toys for their children than nearby middle-income families. (6) Most important, students say that garbology courses can motivate them to be better citizens of planet Earth. (7) One young woman, for example, after seeing from hard evidence in her town's landfill how many people really recycled their glass, cans, and newspapers and how many cheated, organized an annual recycling awareness day.

1. Write the number of the topic sentence in the paragraph._____*1*_____

2. What kind of order does this writer use?_____*order of importance*_____

3. Students learn three things in garbology courses. (a) Write the numbers of the sentences stating these. (b) Which two ideas are supported by examples?

   (a)___*3, 4, 6*___   (b)___*4 and 6*___

UNIT 1 WRITERS' WORKSHOP

Describe an Interesting Person

Good writers are masters of careful observation and exact language. In your group or class, read this student's description of her classmate, aloud if possible. Underline any words or details that strike you as well written or powerful.

> In this paragraph, I will describe my classmate Benny. His most riveting feature is the contrast between his close-cropped black hair and his light skin. Two slight scars on his left cheek add to instead of detract from his appearance. His eyelashes are not prominent, but dark brown eyes gaze at you from under a canopy of thick black eyebrows. His nose is short and straight, befitting his oval face. The cheekbones *are* high but not prominent, and the well-kept mustache gives a promise of luxuriant growth if given free rein. Benny's mouth *is* small and full, and though the braces are off-putting, that shy smile will someday break a lot of hearts. All these factors put together with a mischievous gleam in his eyes draw the picture *of* an intelligent, personable young man.
>
> Carmen Crawford, student

1. How effective is Ms. Crawford's description of Benny?

   <u>N</u> Good topic sentence?   <u>Y</u> Rich supporting details?

   <u>Y</u> Logical organization?   <u>Y</u> Effective conclusion?

2. Underline the words, details, and sentences you like best. Put a check beside anything that needs improvement.

3. Now discuss your underlinings with your group or class. Try to explain why a particular word or sentence is effective. For instance, in the second sentence, the interesting word *riveting* introduces a contrast between Benny's "close-cropped black hair" (we can almost see it) and his light skin.

4. The best descriptions feel as if they were observed from real life, not memory. Do you think Ms. Crawford was *with* Benny when she wrote about him. Why?

5. Is the topic sentence as good as the rest of the paragraph? If not, how might you change it? *No, topic sentence should be rewritten.*

6. Last, proofread for grammar, spelling, and omitted words. Do you see any error patterns (the same type of error made two or more times) that this student should watch out for? *Yes, omitted words*

Writing and Revising Ideas

1. Describe a classmate.

2. Describe an interesting person from your neighborhood or job.

For help writing your paragraph, see Chapter 3 and Chapter 4, Parts B and C. As you revise your first draft, pay special attention to writing a clear, catchy topic sentence supported by well-observed (even riveting) details.

Writing Complete Sentences

The sentence is the basic unit of all writing, so good writers must know how to write clear and correct sentences. In this unit, you will

✔ Learn to spot subjects and verbs

✔ Practice writing complete sentences

✔ Learn to avoid or correct any sentence fragments

Notice the way this writer uses strong, simple sentences to capture a moment with her grandfather, her *abuelo*. If possible, read the paragraph aloud.

My grandfather has misplaced his words again. He is trying to find my name in the kaleidoscope of images that his mind has become. His face brightens like a child's who has just remembered his lesson. He points to me and says my mother's name. I smile back and kiss him on the cheek. It doesn't matter what names he remembers anymore. Every day he is more confused, his memory slipping back a little further in time. Today he has no grandchildren yet. Tomorrow he will be a young man courting my grandmother again, quoting bits of poetry to her. In months to come, he will begin calling her Mama.

Judith Ortiz Cofer, "The Witch's Husband"

- How does the writer feel about her grandfather? What sentences tell you this?
- Why do you think the writer arranges the last three sentences in the order that she does?

- A visit with a loved (or feared) relative
- Your relationship with someone who has a disability

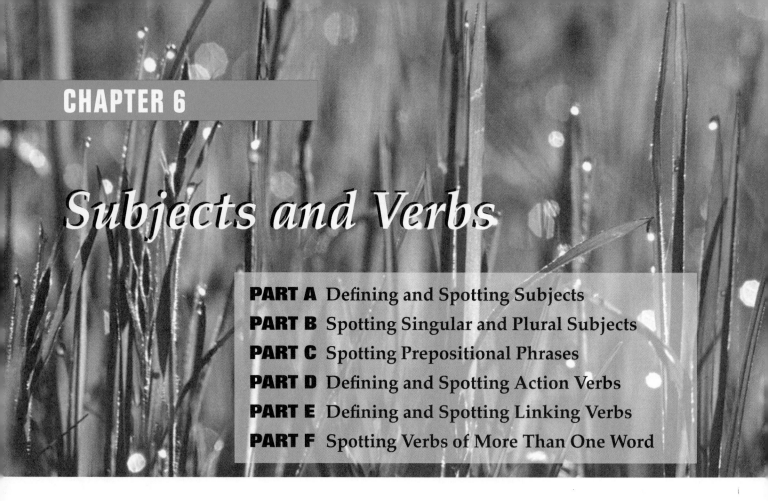

CHAPTER 6

Subjects and Verbs

PART A — Defining and Spotting Subjects

The sentence is the basic unit of all writing. To write well, you need to know how to write correct and effective sentences. A *sentence* is a group of words that expresses a complete thought about something or someone. It contains a subject and a verb.

> (1) _____ jumped over the black Buick, scaled the building, and finally reached the roof.
>
> (2) _____ needs a new coat of paint.

These sentences might be interesting, but they are incomplete.

■ In sentence (1), *who* jumped, scaled, and reached? Bruce Willis, Mariah Carey, the English teacher?

■ Depending on *who* performed the action—jumping, scaling, or reaching—the sentence can be exciting, surprising, or strange.

■ What is missing is the *who* word—the *subject*.

■ In sentence (2), *what* needs a new coat of paint? The house, the car, the old rocking chair?

■ What is missing is the *what* word—the *subject*.

For a sentence to be complete, it must contain a *who* or *what* word—a *subject*. The subject tells you *who* or *what* does something or exists in a certain way.

The subject is often a *noun*, a word that names a person, place, or thing (such as *Mariah Carey, English teacher,* or *house*). However, a *pronoun* (*I, you, he, she, it, we,* or *they*) also can be the subject.*

PRACTICE 1

In each of these sentences, the subject (the *who* or *what* word) is missing. Fill in your own subject to make the sentence complete.

EXAMPLE: A(n) _____ *fox* _____ dashed across the road.

1. The _____ *hockey puck* _____ skidded across the ice.

2. The _____ *student* _____ was eager to begin the semester.

3. Because of the crowd, _____ *the spy* _____ slipped out unnoticed.

4. For years, _____ *comic books* _____ piled up in the back of the closet.

5. The slinky black _____ *cape* _____ looked wonderful on Sheila.

6. _____ *Papers* _____ and _____ *pencils* _____ were scattered all over the doctor's desk.

7. The _____ *singer* _____ believed that his _____ *voice* _____ would return someday.

8. The _____ *farmhouse* _____ was in bad shape. The _____ *ceiling* _____ was falling in, and the _____ *downstairs windows* _____ were all broken.

As you may have noticed, the subject can be a noun only, but it can also include *words that describe the noun* (such as *the, slinky,* or *black*).

The noun or pronoun alone is called the *simple subject;* the noun or pronoun plus the words that describe it are called the *complete subject.*

(3) Three yellow roses grew near the path.
(4) A large box was delivered this morning.

■ The simple subject of sentence (3) is the noun *roses*.

■ The complete subject is *three yellow roses*.

■ What is the simple subject of (4)? _____ *box* _____

■ What is the complete subject of (4)? _____ *a large box* _____

PRACTICE 2

Circle the complete subjects in these sentences. REMEMBER: The complete subject includes the *who* or *what* word (the noun or pronoun) and any words that describe it.

EXAMPLE: (The typist) became a millionaire.

(1) (Bette Nesmith) was a good secretary. (2) However, (employers) constantly complained about her messy typing. (3) One day, (the young office worker) had an inspired idea. (4) (She) covered her typing errors with dots of white paint. (5) Soon

_____
*For more on pronoun subjects, see Chapter 21, Part F.

© 1998 Houghton Mifflin Company

other secretaries wanted to try her method. (6) Bette's kitchen became a small factory. (7) A local chemistry teacher helped her improve the formula. (8) Her son bottled the new product in the garage. (9) Quickly, orders began pouring in. (10) By 1980, six hundred people worked for the company, Liquid Paper.

<table>
<tr><td>**PRACTICE 3**</td></tr>
</table>

In these sentences, the subject has been omitted. You must decide where it belongs and fill in a subject (a *who* or *what* word) that makes sense. (You may have to fill in more than one subject in a sentence.)

EXAMPLE: Raced down the street.

My friend raced down the street.

1. Trained day and night for the big event.

   The gymnasts trained day and night for the big event.

2. Always talks about his childhood after he sees his sister.

   Grandpa always talks about his childhood after he sees his sister.

3. Landed in the corn field.

   A small plane landed in the corn field.

4. After the show, applauded and screamed for fifteen minutes.

   After the show, the crowd applauded and screamed for fifteen minutes.

5. Got out of the large gray van.

   Mr. Sandhurst got out of the large gray van.

PART B   Spotting Singular and Plural Subjects

Besides being able to spot subjects in sentences, you need to know whether a subject is singular or plural.

(1) The man jogged around the park.

■ The subject of this sentence is *the man.*

■ Because *the man* is one person, the subject is *singular*.

Singular means only one of something.

(2) The man and his friend jogged around the park.

■ The subject of sentence (2) is *the man and his friend.*

■ Because *the man and his friend* refers to more than one person, the subject is *plural*.

Plural means more than one of something.

PRACTICE 1

Here is a list of possible subjects of sentences. If the subject is singular, put a check in the Singular column; if the subject is plural, put a check in the Plural column.

Possible Subjects	Singular (one)	Plural (more than one)
EXAMPLES: an elephant	✔	
children		✔
1. our cousins		✔
2. a saxophone and a trumpet		✔
3. Horace	✔	
4. their trophy	✔	
5. women		✔
6. a rock star and her band		✔
7. his three pickup trucks		✔
8. pecan pie	✔	

PRACTICE 2

Circle the complete subjects in these sentences. Then, in the space at the right, write *S* if the subject is singular or *P* if the subject is plural.

EXAMPLE: (Spike Lee) inspired a new generation of African-American filmmakers.　　　　*S*

1. (Lee's first hit) was *She's Gotta Have It* in 1986.　　　*S*

2. (Many African-American moviemakers) have had success since then.　　　*P*

3. (These young artists) write, direct, and even act in their own movies.　　　*P*

4. Often (their goal) is to combine exciting entertainment with a social message.　　　*S*

5. (John Singleton) wrote and directed the acclaimed *Boyz N the Hood* at age twenty-three.　　　*S*

6. (*Poetic Justice* and *Higher Learning*) followed soon after.　　　*P*

7. (Reading) turned another young man into a filmmaker.　　　*S*

8. At nineteen, (Matty Rich) made *Straight Out of Brooklyn*, after studying more than 250 film books!　　　*S*

9. (The talented Hudlin brothers) produced *House Party*, *Boomerang*, and *Bebe's Kids*.　　　*P*

10. (Reginald Hudlin) later directed *The Great White Hype*, a popular satire on the world of boxing.　　　*S*

PART C Spotting Prepositional Phrases

One group of words that may confuse you as you look for subjects is the prepositional phrase. A *prepositional phrase* contains a *preposition* (a word like *at, from, in,* or *of*) and its *object* (a *noun* or *pronoun*). Here are some prepositional phrases:*

Prepositional Phrase	=	Preposition	+	Object
at work		at		work
behind her		behind		her
of the students		of		the students
on the blue table		on		the blue table

The object of a preposition *cannot* be the subject of a sentence. Therefore, crossing out prepositional phrases can help you find the real subject.

(1) On summer evenings, girls in white dresses stroll under the trees.
(2) ~~On summer evenings,~~ girls ~~in white dresses~~ stroll ~~under the trees~~.
(3) ~~From dawn to dusk,~~ we hiked.
(4) The president ~~of the college~~ will speak tonight.

■ In sentence (1), you may have trouble spotting the subject. However, once the prepositional phrases are crossed out in (2), the subject, *girls,* is easy to see.

■ Cross out the prepositional phrase in sentence (3). What is the subject of the sentence? _____ we _____

■ Cross out the prepositional phrase in sentence (4). What is the subject of the sentence? _____ the president _____

Here are some common prepositions you should know:

Common Prepositions		
about	beside	off
above	between	on
across	by	over
after	during	through(out)
against	except	to
along	for	toward
among	from	under
around	in	until
at	into	up
before	like	with
behind	of	without

*For more work on prepositions, see Chapter 23.

PRACTICE

Cross out the prepositional phrase or phrases in each sentence. Then circle the subject of the sentence.

EXAMPLE: (Millions) of people walk on the Appalachian Trail each year.

1. (That famous trail) stretches from Springer Mountain in Georgia to Mount Katahdin in Maine.
2. (One quarter) of the trail goes through Virginia.
3. (The majority) of walkers hike for one day.
4. Of the four million trail users, (two hundred people) will hike the entire trail every year.
5. For most hikers, (the trip) through fourteen states takes four or five months.
6. In the spring, (many hardy souls) begin their 2,158 mile-long journey.
7. (These lovers) of the wilderness must reach Mount Katahdin before winter.
8. On the trail, (men and women) battle heat, humidity, bugs, blisters, muscle sprains, and food and water shortages.
9. After beautiful green scenery, (the path) becomes rocky and mountainous.
10. (Hikers) in the White Mountains of New Hampshire struggle against high winds.
11. (A pebble) from Georgia is sometimes added to the pile of stones at the top of Mount Katahdin.
12. At the bottom of the mountain, (the conquerors) of the Appalachian Trail add their names to the list of successful hikers.

PART D   Defining and Spotting Action Verbs

(1) The pears _____ on the trees.

(2) Robert _____ his customer's hand and _____ her dog on the head.

These sentences tell you what or who the subject is—*the pears* and *Robert*—but not what each subject does.

■ In sentence (1), what do the pears do? Do they *grow, ripen, rot, stink,* or *glow*?

■ All these *action verbs* fit into the blank space in sentence (1), but the meaning of the sentence changes depending on which action verb you use.

■ In sentence (2), what actions does Robert perform? Does he *shake, ignore, kiss, pat,* or *scratch*?

■ Depending on which verb you use, the meaning of the sentence changes.

■ Some sentences, like sentence (2), contain two or more action verbs.

For a sentence to be complete, it must have a *verb*. An *action verb* tells what action the subject is performing.

PRACTICE 1

Fill in each blank with an action verb.

1. Michael Jordan _____*sailed*_____ through the air for a slam dunk.

2. An artist _____*sketched*_____ the scene at the waterfront.

3. When Francine _____*screamed*_____, the waiter _____*jumped*_____.

4. A fierce wind _____*raged*_____ and _____*howled*_____.

5. The audience _____*clapped*_____ while the conductor _____*bowed*_____.

6. This new kitchen gadget _____*chops*_____ and _____*slices*_____ any vegetable you can think of.

7. When the dentist _____*broke*_____ his drill, Earl _____*cheered*_____.

8. David Bowie _____*leaped*_____ and _____*strutted*_____ across the stage.

PRACTICE 2

Circle the action verbs in these sentences. Some sentences contain more than one action verb.

An Unusual Businessman

(1) On the night of December 11, 1995, fire (raged) through Malden Mills, a Massachusetts fabric company. (2) Several people (suffered) severe burns. (3) Workers (feared) unemployment. (4) However, mill owner Aaron Feuerstein (turned) the tragedy around for his 1,400 employees.

(5) The textile manufacturer already (had) a reputation for generosity, persistence, and high-quality products. (6) Now, after the tragic fire, Feuerstein (gave) his unemployed workers a Christmas bonus and their full salaries for three months. (7) He (restarted) operations and (rebuilt) the company within the incredibly short time of one month.

(8) Feuerstein's actions (amazed) many people. (9) These days, a company president often (pockets) the insurance money after a fire and (closes) the business. (10) Instead, Feuerstein (paid) $15 million to nonworking employees and (kept) his company in the same high-cost location. (11) Nine months after the fire, Malden Mills even (introduced) a new line of upholstery fabrics.

PART E   Defining and Spotting Linking Verbs

The verbs you have been examining so far show action, but a second kind of verb simply links the subject to words that describe or rename it.

> (1) Aunt Claudia sometimes seems a little strange.

■ The subject in this sentence is *Aunt Claudia,* but there is no action verb.

■ Instead, *seems* links the subject, *Aunt Claudia,* with the descriptive words *a little strange.*

Aunt Claudia	seems	a little strange.
↓	↓	↓
subject	linking verb	descriptive words

> (2) They are reporters for the newspaper.

■ The subject is *they.* The word *reporters* renames the subject.

■ What verb links the subject, *they,* with the word *reporters*? _____*are*_____

For a sentence to be complete, it must contain a *verb.* **A** *linking verb* **links the subject with words that describe or rename that subject.**

The box below lists linking verbs you should know.

Common Linking Verbs	
be (am, is, are, was, were)	look
act	seem
appear	smell
become	sound
feel	taste
get	

■ The most common linking verbs are the forms of *to be,* but verbs of the senses, such as *feel, look,* and *smell,* also may be used as linking verbs.

© 1998 Houghton Mifflin Company

PRACTICE 1

The subjects and descriptive words in these sentences are boxed. Circle the linking verbs.

1. Jerry sounds sleepy today.

2. Ronda always was the best debater on the team.

3. His brother often appeared relaxed and happy.

4. By evening, Harvey felt confident about the exam.

5. Mr. Forbes became a long-distance runner.

PRACTICE 2

Circle the linking verbs in these sentences. Then underline the subject and the descriptive word or words in each sentence.

1. The sweet potato pie tastes delicious.

2. You often seem worried.

3. During the summer, she looks calm.

4. Under heavy snow, the new dome roof appeared sturdy.

5. Raphael is a gifted animal trainer.

6. Lately, I feel very competent at work.

7. Luz became a medical technician.

8. Yvonne acted surprised at her baby shower.

PART F   Spotting Verbs of More Than One Word

All the verbs you have dealt with so far have been single words—*look, walked, saw, are, were,* and so on. However, many verbs consist of more than one word.

> (1) Sarah is walking to work.

- The subject is *Sarah*. What is *Sarah* doing?
- Sarah is walking.
- *Walking* is the *main verb. Is* is the *helping verb*; without *is*, *walking* is not a complete verb.

> (2) Should I have written sooner?

- The subject is *I*.
- *Should have written* is the *complete verb*.

■ *Written* is the *main verb. Should* and *have* are the *helping verbs; without should have, written* is not a complete verb.

> (3) Do you eat fish?

■ What is the subject? _____ *you* _____

■ What is the main verb? _____ *eat* _____

■ What is the helping verb? _____ *do* _____

The *complete verb* **in a sentence consists of all the helping verbs and the main verb.**

PRACTICE 1

The blanks following each sentence tell you how many words make up the complete verb. Fill in the blanks with the complete verb; then circle the main verb.

EXAMPLE: Ordinary people have been fighting crime in many creative ways.

_____ *have* _____   _____ *been* _____   _____ (*fighting*) _____

1. They are turning their fear of crime into preventive action.

_____ *are* _____   _____ (*turning*) _____

2. Do you know about community policing programs?

_____ *do* _____   _____ (*know*) _____

3. These programs have increased all over the country, from Florida to Oregon.

_____ *have* _____   _____ (*increased*) _____

4. Many volunteers have been walking the streets in civilian crime patrols.

_____ *have* _____   _____ *been* _____   _____ (*walking*) _____

5. Suspicious activities are reported to the police.

_____ *are* _____   _____ (*reported*) _____

6. Walkie-talkies, car patrols, and volunteer security guides can be very helpful in civilian crime prevention programs.

_____ *can* _____   _____ (*be*) _____

7. Neighborhood groups in Brooklyn, New York, have found those measures particularly effective in their campaign against burglaries.

_____ *have* _____   _____ (*found*) _____

8. Residents of some communities have been photographing drug dealers and exchanges. _____ *have* _____   _____ *been* _____   _____ (*photographing*) _____

9. On the basis of these photographs, police have made drug raids.

_____ *have* _____   _____ (*made*) _____

10. Private citizens are arranging recreation, tutoring, and leadership programs

   for restless teenagers. _____are_____ _____(arranging)_____

11. They have also created antiviolence training for students in public schools.

   _____have_____ _____(created)_____

12. In Los Angeles, California, people have been campaigning against violence
   through billboards and television ads.

   _____have_____ _____been_____ _____(campaigning)_____

13. Are these measures working?

   _____are_____ _____(working)_____

14. Because of community action, crime has decreased in both large cities

   and small towns. _____has_____ _____(decreased)_____

15. Perhaps someday all neighborhoods will be safer.

   _____will_____ _____(be)_____

PRACTICE 2

Box the subjects, circle the main verbs, and underline any helping verbs in these sentences.

EXAMPLE: Most [people] have (wondered) about the beginning of the universe.

1. [Scientists] have (developed) one theory.
2. According to this theory, [the universe] (began) with a huge explosion.
3. [The explosion] has been (named) the Big Bang.
4. First, [all matter] must have been (packed) into a tiny speck under enormous pressure.
5. Then, about 15 billion years ago, [that speck] (burst) with amazing force.
6. [Everything] in the universe has (come) from the original explosion.
7. In fact, [the universe] still is (expanding) from the Big Bang.
8. [All the planets and stars] are (moving) away from each other at an even speed.
9. Will [the universe] (expand) forever?
10. [Scientists] may be (debating) that question for a long time.

PRACTICE: WRITING ASSIGNMENT

Whether you have just graduated from high school or have worked for several years, the first year of college can be difficult. Imagine that you are writing to an incoming student who needs advice and encouragement. Pick one serious problem you had as a first-year student, and explain how you coped with it. State the problem clearly. Use examples from your own experience or the experience of others to make your advice more vivid.

Chapter Highlights

- **A sentence contains a subject and a verb, and expresses a complete thought:**

  $\quad\quad\quad$ *S* $\quad\quad$ *V*
  Jennifer bakes often.
  $\quad\quad\quad\quad\quad\quad$ *S* $\quad\quad\quad$ *V*
  The two students have tutored at the writing lab.

- **An action verb tells what the subject is doing:**

  Toni Morrison *writes* novels.

- **A linking verb links the subject with words that describe or rename it:**

  Her novels *are* bestsellers.

- **Don't mistake the object in a prepositional phrase for a subject:**

  $\quad\quad$ *S* $\quad\quad\quad\quad$ *PP*
  The red car [in the showroom] is a Corvette.
  $\quad\quad\quad$ *PP* $\quad\quad\quad\quad\quad\quad$ *S*
  [In my dream,] *a sailor and his parrot* were singing.

Chapter Review

Circle the subjects, crossing out any confusing prepositional phrases. Then underline the complete verbs. If you have difficulty with this review, consider rereading the lesson.

Nobel Peace Prize Winners

(1) In 1901, a committee presented the first yearly Nobel Peace Prize. (2) That important prize honors individuals for outstanding work toward world peace. (3) Mother Teresa and Nelson Mandela are among the well-known winners of the award. (4) Those champions of peace have devoted their lives to the welfare of others. (5) However, less famous figures also have been honored for their work toward a more peaceful world.

(6) Dr. Joseph Rotblat received the Nobel Peace Prize in 1995 for his opposition to nuclear weapons. (7) During World War II, Rotblat and other distinguished scientists had worked for the secret U.S. Manhattan Project. (8) In 1944, however, he resigned from that atomic bomb project because of moral concerns. (9) Since the cold war of the 1950s and 1960s, the talented physicist has campaigned against the development, manufacture, and use of atomic weapons.

(10) In 1996, two peace workers shared the prize. (11) Bishop Carlos Belo and José Ramos-Horta have struggled for years against the military occupation of East Timor, a small country in Asia. (12) The fearless bishop protests within the country. (13) In exile for more than twenty years, Ramos-Horta speaks in other countries on behalf of his people. (14) The 1996 Nobel Peace Prize brought the tragedy of their land to the attention of nations all over the world.

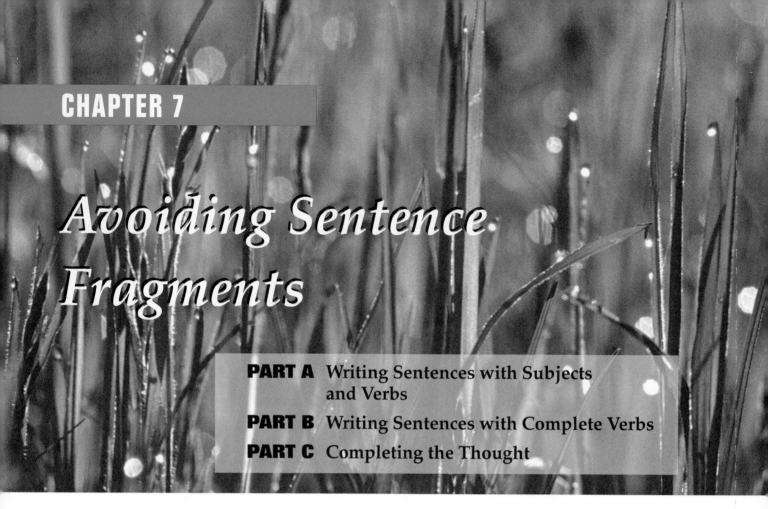

CHAPTER 7

Avoiding Sentence Fragments

PART A	Writing Sentences with Subjects and Verbs
PART B	Writing Sentences with Complete Verbs
PART C	Completing the Thought

PART A   Writing Sentences with Subjects and Verbs

Which of these groups of words is a sentence? Be prepared to explain your answers.

(1) People will bet on almost anything.

(2) For example, every winter the Nenana River in Alaska.

(3) Make bets on the date of the breakup of the ice.

(4) Must guess the exact day and time of day.

(5) Last year, the lucky guess won $300,000.

■ In (2), you probably wanted to know what the Nenana River *does*. The idea is not complete because there is no *verb*.

■ In (3) and (4), you probably wanted to know *who* makes bets on the date of the breakup of the ice and *who* must guess the exact day and time of day. The ideas are not complete. What is missing? _____*the subjects*_____

■ But in sentences (1) and (5), you knew *who did what*. These ideas are complete. Why? ____*They have a subject and a verb, and express a complete thought.*____

_____

78

Below is the same group of words written as complete sentences:

(1) People will bet on almost anything.
(2) For example, every winter the Nenana River in Alaska freezes.
(3) The townspeople make bets on the date of the breakup of the ice.
(4) Someone must guess the exact day and time of day.
(5) Last year, the lucky guess won $300,000.

Every *sentence* **must have both a subject and a verb and must express a complete thought.**

A *fragment* **lacks either a subject or a complete verb—or does not express a complete thought.**

PRACTICE

All of the following are *fragments*; they lack a subject, a verb, or both. Add a subject, a verb, or both in order to make the fragments into sentences.

EXAMPLE: Raising onions in the backyard.

Rewrite:_____ *Charles was raising onions in the backyard.*_____

1. Laughed loudly at the antics of the clown.

   Rewrite: _____ *The audience laughed loudly at the antics of the clown.*_____

2. Melts easily.

   Rewrite: _____ *On a hot day in Alabama, butter melts easily.*_____

3. The two-year-old in the red overalls.

   Rewrite: _____ *Her child is the two-year-old in the red overalls.*_____

4. One of the fans.

   Rewrite: _____ *One of the fans caught a fly ball.*_____

5. Manages a Software City store.

   Rewrite: _____ *My next-door neighbor manages a Software City store.*_____

6. The tip of her nose.

   Rewrite: _____ *The tip of her nose was red from the cold.*_____

7. A VCR with remote control.

   Rewrite: _____ *Many American homes have a VCR with remote control.*_____

8. Makes me nervous.

   Rewrite: _____ *Parking my car on the street overnight makes me nervous.*___

9. Tuition and fees.

   Rewrite: _Tuition and fees rose again last spring._

10. A person who likes to take risks.

    Rewrite: _Eli is a person who likes to take risks._

PART B   Writing Sentences with Complete Verbs

Do not be fooled by incomplete verbs.

> (1) She leaving for the city.
> (2) The students gone to the cafeteria for dessert.

■ *Leaving* seems to be the verb in (1).

■ *Gone* seems to be the verb in (2).

But . . .

■ An *-ing* word like *leaving* is not by itself a verb.

■ A word like *gone* is not by itself a verb.

> (1) She $\left.{is \atop was}\right\}$ leaving for the city.
>
> (2) The students $\left.{have \atop had}\right\}$ gone to the cafeteria for dessert.

■ To be a verb, an *-ing* word (called a *present participle*) must be combined with some form of the verb *to be*.*

Helping Verb	Main Verb
am	
is	
are	
was	
were	jogging
has been	
have been	
had been	

___

*For a detailed explanation of present participles, see Chapter 11.

■ To be a *verb*, a word like *gone* (called a *past participle*) must be combined with some form of *to have* or *to be*.*

Helping Verb	Main Verb
am	
is	
are	
was	
were	
has	forgotten
have	
had	
has been	
have been	
had been	

PRACTICE 1

All of the following are fragments; they have only a partial or an incomplete verb. Complete each verb in order to make these fragments into sentences.

EXAMPLE: The children grown taller this year.

Rewrite: *The children have grown taller this year.*

1. The Australian winning the tennis match.

   Rewrite: *The Australian is winning the tennis match.*

2. My friends gone to a dude ranch.

   Rewrite: *My friends have gone to a dude ranch.*

3. Steve's letter published in the *Miami Herald*.

   Rewrite: *Steve's letter was published in the* Miami Herald.

4. My physics professor always forgetting the assignment.

   Rewrite: *My physics professor is always forgetting the assignment.*

5. These shirts made in Korea.

   Rewrite: *These shirts were made in Korea.*

*For a detailed explanation of past participles, see Chapter 10.

6. For two years, Joan working at a computer.

   Rewrite: *For two years, Joan has been working at a computer.*

7. You ever been to San Francisco?

   Rewrite: *Have you ever been to San Francisco?*

8. Yesterday, Ed's wet gloves taken from the radiator.

   Rewrite: *Yesterday, Ed's wet gloves were taken from the radiator.*

PRACTICE 2

All of the following are fragments; they lack a subject, and they contain only a partial verb. Make these fragments into sentences by adding a subject and by completing the verb.

EXAMPLE: Written by Ray Bradbury.

Rewrite: *This science fiction thriller was written by Ray Bradbury.*

1. Forgotten the codeword.

   Rewrite: *The spy has forgotten the codeword.*

2. Now running the copy center.

   Rewrite: *Students are now running the copy center.*

3. Making sculpture from old car parts.

   Rewrite: *Jim is making sculpture from old car parts.*

4. Been working at the state capitol building.

   Rewrite: *My aunt has been working at the state capitol building.*

5. Talking about the good old days.

   Rewrite: *My brother was talking about the good old days.*

6. Driven that tractor for years.

   Rewrite: *Phil Hamilton has driven that tractor for years.*

7. Broken the computer through carelessness.

   Rewrite: *The secretary had broken the computer through carelessness.*

8. Been to a wrestling match.

   Rewrite: *None of my friends had been to a wrestling match.*

PRACTICE 3

Fragments are most likely to occur in paragraphs or longer pieces of writing. Proofread the paragraph below for fragments; check for missing subjects or incomplete verbs. Circle the number of any fragments; then write your corrections above the lines.

(1) *was*
Lois Weber the first female American film director. (2) She was born

Florence Lois Weber in Allegheny, Pennsylvania, in 1881. (3) By the age of sixteen,
was   *was*
she touring the United States as a concert pianist. (4) At twenty, she working as a

singer and an actress. (5) After she married, she and her stage-manager husband

would accept only jobs together. (6) That decision brought them to the motion

picture industry. (7) Weber acted, directed, wrote, designed sets, and even
                              She became
operated the camera. (8) Became a successful, respected director. (9) Some of her
were
films censored because they dealt with difficult social problems and moral issues.
Weber died
(10) Died at fifty-eight. (11) She had made hundreds of films. (12) Incredibly

enough, she had written or adapted all but seven of them.

PART C Completing the Thought

Can these ideas stand by themselves?

> (1) Because oranges are rich in vitamin C.
> (2) Although Sam is sleepy.

- These ideas have a subject and a verb (find them), but they cannot stand alone because you expect something else to follow.

- Because oranges are rich in vitamin C, then *what?* Should you *eat them, sell them,* or *make marmalade?*

- Although Sam is sleepy, *what will he do?* Will he *work on the computer, walk the dog,* or *go to the gym?*

> (1) Because oranges are rich in vitamin C, *I eat one every day.*
> (2) Although Sam is sleepy, *he will work late tonight.*

- These sentences are now complete.

- Words like *because* and *although* make an idea incomplete unless another idea is added to complete the thought.*

———————
*For more work on this type of sentence, see Chapter 14.

Make these fragments into sentences by adding some idea that completes the thought.

EXAMPLE: Because I miss my family, _I am going home for the weekend._

1. As May stepped off the elevator, _she bumped into her old boyfriend._

2. Whenever I vote, _I feel like a good citizen._

3. While Kimi studied chemistry, _Maurie did his math homework._

4. Because you believe in yourself, _you will succeed._

5. Although spiders scare most people, _I find them fascinating._

6. Unless the surgery is absolutely necessary, _I do not want to have it._

7. If Ronald sings "True Colors" one more time, _I will scream!_

8. Although these air conditioners are expensive to run, _we have to keep them on all night._

Can these ideas stand by themselves?

(3) Graciela, who has a one-year-old daughter.
(4) A course that I will always remember.

■ In each of these examples, you expect something else to follow. Graciela, who has a one-year-old daughter, *is doing what?* Does she *attend PTA meetings, knit sweaters,* or *fly planes?*

■ A course that I will always remember *is what?* The thought must be completed.

(3) Graciela, who has a one-year-old daughter, *attends Gordon College.*
(4) A course that I will always remember *is documentary filmmaking.*

■ These sentences are now complete.*

Make these fragments into sentences by completing the thought.

EXAMPLE: Kent, who is a good friend of mine, _rarely writes to me._

1. The horoscopes that appear in the daily papers _make me laugh._

2. Couples who never argue _seem unreal._

*For more work on this type of sentence, see Chapter 18, Part A.

3. Robert, who is a superb pole-vaulter, _will compete in the Olympics._

4. Radio programs that ask listeners to call in are _often very funny._

5. A person who has overcome great loss _often can help others._

6. Potholes, which can cause accidents, _are often the result of changing weather conditions._

7. Doctors who spend a lot of time with their patients _gain their patients' trust and respect._

8. The video that we watched last night _was rented from Video Watch._

9. A person who becomes upset easily _should never go into sales._

10. A country that I have always wanted to visit _is Kenya._

To each fragment, add a subject, a verb, or whatever is required to complete the thought.

1. Visiting the Vietnam Memorial.

    Rewrite: _Are they visiting the Vietnam Memorial?_

2. That digital clock blinking for hours.

    Rewrite: _That digital clock has been blinking for hours._

3. People who can't say no to their children.

    Rewrite: _People who can't say no to their children will probably regret it._

4. Wanted to become a chiropractor.

    Rewrite: _Jerome wanted to become a chiropractor._

5. Over the roof and into the garden.

    Rewrite: _The squirrel scampered over the roof and into the garden._

6. Dave went to camp as a counselor, but back now.

    Rewrite: _Dave went to camp as a counselor, but he is back now._

7. Chess, which is a difficult game to play.

    Rewrite: _Six-year-old Eric loves chess, which is a difficult game to play._

8. Whenever Dolly starts to yodel.

    Rewrite: _Whenever Dolly starts to yodel, her dog starts to howl._

PRACTICE 4

Proofread the paragraph for fragments. Circle the numbers of any fragments, and then write your corrections above the lines.

program that

(1) The Special Olympics is an international program. (2) That is held for mentally impaired children and adults. (3) Special Olympics athletes train and

sports, which

compete in regular sports. (4) Which include floor hockey, skiing, soccer, swimming, speed skating, and tennis. (5) The Special Olympics winter and summer international games are held every other year. (6) Although 140 countries

games, Special

participate in the world games. (7) Special Olympics are also held yearly at local and state levels. (8) Altogether, more than a million athletes participate.

(9) Whereas Special Olympics competitors may not swim as fast or jump as high

stars, they

as Olympics stars. (10) They are very eager to do their best. (11) Their courage

everyone, and

and accomplishments inspire everyone. (12) And change these athletes' lives forever.

PRACTICE: WRITING ASSIGNMENT

Working in small groups, choose one of the sentences below that could begin a short story.

1. As soon as Sean replaced the receiver, he knew he had to take action.

2. Suddenly, the bright blue sky turned dark.

3. No matter where she looked, Elena could not find her diary.

Next, each person in the group should write his or her own short story, starting with that sentence. First decide what type of story yours will be—science fiction, romance, action, comedy, murder mystery, and so on; perhaps each person will choose a different type. It may help you to imagine the story later becoming a TV show. As you write, be careful to avoid fragments, making sure each thought has a subject and a complete verb, and expresses a complete thought.

Then exchange papers, checking each other's work for fragments. If time permits, read the papers aloud to the group. Which story gets the best reaction?

✔ Chapter Highlights

A sentence fragment is an error because it lacks

■ **a subject:** Was buying a gold ring. *(incorrect)*
Diamond Jim was buying a gold ring. *(correct)*

■ **a verb:** The basketball game Friday at noon. *(incorrect)*
The basketball game *was played* Friday at noon. *(correct)*

■ **or a complete thought:** While Teresa was swimming. *(incorrect)*
While Teresa was swimming, she lost a contact lens. *(correct)*

The woman who bought your car. *(incorrect)*
The woman who bought your car is walking down the highway. *(correct)*

Chapter Review

Proofread each paragraph below for fragments. Circle the numbers of any fragments; then correct the fragments in any way that makes sense, making them into separate ideas or adding them to other sentences. Write your corrections above the lines.

A. (1) Steel drums wonderful and unusual musical instruments. *[are]* (2) Steel bands use them to perform calypso, jazz, and popular music. (3) And even classical symphonies. *[music, and]* (4) Steel drums were invented in Trinidad. (5) Where they were made from the ends of discarded oil drums. *[Trinidad, where]* (6) That had been left by the British navy. *[drums that]* (7) Although the first steel drums produced only rhythm. (8) Now they can be tuned to play up to five octaves. *[rhythm, now]* (9) Steel orchestras produce music. (10) That surrounds and delights listeners without the use of amplifiers. *[music that]* (11) The worldwide popularity of steel drums has been increasing steadily. (12) The Trinidad All Steel Percussion Orchestra was a smash hit. (13) When it first performed in England a number of years ago. *[hit when]* (14) In the 1990s, the Northern Illinois University Steel Band thrilled audiences from the United States to Taiwan.

B. (1) In 1986, people in the Ganges Delta of India began wearing masks to protect themselves from Bengal tigers. (2) *were* These deadly tigers protected in the region. (3) *They were killing* Killing up to sixty people a year. (4) Someone noticed. (5) *noticed that* That the big cat attacked only from behind. (6) Workers put face masks on the back of their heads. (7) The inexpensive rubber masks showed a pale-faced human with a thin mustache. (8) *were* The results excellent. (9) The confused animals thought the masks were real faces and did not attack.

C. (1) Chocolate is made from dried beans of the cacao tree. (2) When the beans arrive at the chocolate mill. (3) *mill, they* They are first cleaned. (4) *cleaned and* And then roasted. (5) Roasting loosens the husks. (6) *husks, which* Which machines blow away, leaving the inner kernels, or nibs. (7) Heavy stone mills grind the nibs. (8) *nibs until* Until they turn into a thick paste called chocolate liquor. (9) This hardens into bitter chocolate, from which candy and baked goods are made.

D. (1) Braille, which is a system of reading and writing now used by blind people all over the world. (2) *world, was* Was invented by a fifteen-year-old French boy. (3) In 1824, when Louis Braille entered a school for the blind in Paris. (4) *Paris, he* He found that the library had only fourteen books for the blind. (5) These books used a system that Louis and the other blind students found hard to use. (6) Most of them just gave up. (7) Louis Braille devoted himself to finding a better way. (8) *Working* With the French army method called night-writing. (9) *night-writing, he* He came up with a new system in 1829. (10) Although his classmates liked and used Braille. (11) *Braille, it was* It not widely accepted in England and the United States for another hundred years.

UNIT 2   WRITING ASSIGNMENTS

As you complete each writing assignment, remember to perform these steps:

■ Write a clear, complete topic sentence.

■ Use freewriting, brainstorming, or clustering to generate ideas.

■ Arrange your best ideas in a plan.

■ Revise for support, unity, coherence, and exact language.

■ Proofread for grammar, punctuation, and spelling errors.

Writing Assignment 1: *Write a love letter.* From the Quotation Bank, choose a quotation on *love,* and include it in a letter to someone who is or was dear to you—perhaps a spouse or a "significant other." You may even want to write to someone you would like to meet but are too shy to approach. Use the quotation as an opener, explaining how the words apply to your feelings, or use it to show why you think this person and you should part—a "Dear John" letter. Proofread your letter for fragments.

Writing Assignment 2: *Describe your place in the family.* Your psychology professor has asked you to write a brief description of your place in the family—as an only child, the youngest child, the middle child, or the oldest child. Did your place provide you with special privileges or lay special responsibilities on you? For instance, youngest children often are babied; oldest children may be expected to act like parents. Did your place in the family have an effect on you as an adult? In your topic sentence, state what role your place in the family played in your development: "Being the _____ child in my family has made me _____." Proofread for fragments.

Writing Assignment 3: *Explain your feelings about a prized possession.* If your home caught fire and you could save just one thing you owned, what would it be? (Assume no one was harmed.) A reporter saw you run out of your house with your prized possession. She asks you why it means so much to you. If your explanation is interesting enough, it will be quoted in her newspaper story. Proofread for any fragments.

Writing Assignment 4: *Ask for a raise.* Compose a memo to a boss, real or imagined, persuading him or her to decide to raise your pay. In your first sentence, state that you are asking for an increase. Be specific: Note how the quality of your work, your extra hours, or any special projects you have been involved in have made the business run more smoothly or become more profitable. Do not sound vain, but do praise yourself honestly. Proofread for fragments.

UNIT 2   REVIEW

Proofreading and Revising

Proofread the following essay to eliminate all sentence fragments. Circle the numbers of any fragments; then correct them in any way you choose—by connecting them to a sentence before or after, by completing any incomplete verbs, and so on. Make your corrections above the lines.

The Greatest Athlete of All

(1) James Francis Thorpe was probably the most talented American athlete of all time. (2) Born in Oklahoma in 1888. *1888, the* (3) The future sports great was named Bright Path by his parents, who were both half Native American. (4) Thorpe first achieved national recognition in 1911. (5) When he played halfback for the *1911 when* Carlisle Indian School in Pennsylvania. (6) He led his team to an upset victory against the undefeated Harvard team. (7) In the Carlisle-Army game. *game, Thorpe* (8) Thorpe scored twenty-two of twenty-seven winning points. (9) Running ninety-seven *points, running* yards at amazing speed for one of his touchdowns. (10) In that year, and again in 1912, he was named to the All-American football team.

(11) In track as well, 1912 was a banner year for Thorpe. (12) He won the pentathlon and decathlon in the Olympics in Sweden. (13) An incredible *Sweden, an* achievement never matched before or since. (14) In the pentathlon, Thorpe took four out of a possible five first places—in the 200-meter dash, the 1,500-meter run, the broad jump, and the discus throw. (15) He placed third in the javelin throw. (16) Although he had never picked up a javelin until two months before *throw although* the meet. (17) At six feet tall, weighing 180 pounds. (18) Thorpe was at the peak *pounds, Thorpe* of his powers.

(19) Then tragedy struck. (20) In 1913, Thorpe admitted that he had earned $15 a week as a semiprofessional pitcher. (21) During the summer before his *victories, Thorpe* Olympic victories. (22) Thorpe had violated his amateur status. (23) The Amateur Athletic Association took away his gold medals and wiped his name from the Olympic records.

down, he

(24) Although he was down. (25) He was not out. (26) Thorpe played

Braves

baseball for the New York Giants, Cincinnati Reds, and Boston Braves.

between

(27) Between 1913 and 1919. (28) Then he began one of the longest professional

1929, he

football careers ever. (29) When he retired in 1929. (30) He was forty-one.

(31) Thorpe died in 1953. (32) In that same year, sportswriters from all over

athlete of

the country voted him the greatest American athlete. (33) Of the first half of the

twentieth century. (34) Thirty years later, Thorpe's name was cleared. (35) His

gold medals were returned to his family, and his Olympic victories were officially

accepted again.

Discuss an Event That Influenced You

Readers of a final draft can easily forget that they are reading the *end result* of someone else's writing process. The following paragraph is one student's response to the assignment "Write about an event in history that influenced you."

In your class or group, read it aloud if possible. As you read, underline any words or lines that strike you as especially powerful.

> Though the Vietnam War ended almost before I was born, it
> *father, a*
> changed my life. My earliest memory is of my father. A grizzled
>
> Vietnam warrior who came back spat upon, with one less brother. He
>
> wore a big smile playing ball with my brother and me, but even then I
>
> felt the grin was a coverup. When the postwar reports were on, his face
>
> became despondent. What haunted his heart and mind, I could not
>
> know, but I tried in my childish way to reason with him. A simple "It'll
>
> be all right, Dad" would bring a bleak smirk to his face. When he was
>
> happy, I was happy. When he was down, I was down. Soon the fatherly
>
> horseplay stopped, and once-full bottles of liquor were empty. He was
> *body, yet*   *gone, either*
> there in body. Yet not there. Finally, he was physically gone. Either
>
> working a sixty-hour week or out in the streets after a furious fight
>
> with my mother. Once they divorced, she moved us to another state. I
>
> never came to grips with the turmoil inside my father. I see him as an
>
> intricate puzzle, missing one piece. That piece is his humanity, tangled
>
> up in history and blown up by a C-19.
>
> *Brian Pereira, student*

1. How effective is Mr. Pereira's paragraph?

   __Y__ Good topic sentence?   __Y__ Rich supporting details?

   __Y__ Logical organization?   __Y__ Effective conclusion?

2. Discuss your underlinings with the group or class. Did others underline the same parts? Explain why you feel particular words or details are effective. For instance, the strong words *bleak smirk* say so much about the father's hopeless mood and the distance between him and his young son.

3. The topic sentence says that the writer's life changed, yet the body of the paragraph speaks mostly about his troubled father. Does the body of the paragraph explain the topic sentence?

4. What order, if any, does this writer follow? *Time order*

5. If you do not know what a "C-19" is in the last sentence, does that make the conclusion less effective for you?

6. Would you suggest any changes or revisions?

7. Proofread for grammar and spelling. Do you notice any error patterns (two or more errors of the same type) that this student should watch out for? *Yes, sentence fragments.*

> This fine paragraph was the end result of a difficult writing process. Mr. Pereira writes:
>
> > The floor in my room looked like a writer's battleground of crumpled papers. Before this topic was assigned, I had not the slightest idea that this influence even existed, much less knew what it was. I thought hard, started a sentence or two, and threw a smashed paper down in disgust, over and over again. After hours, I realized it—the event in history that influenced me was Vietnam, even though I was too young to remember it! That became my topic sentence.

Writing and Revising Ideas

1. Discuss an event that influenced you.

2. Choose your best recent paper and describe your own writing process—what you did well and not so well.

For help with writing your paragraph, see Chapter 3 and Chapter 4, Part B (see "Time Order"). Give yourself plenty of time to revise. Stick with it, trying to write the best possible paper. Pay special attention to fully supporting your topic with interesting facts and details.

Using Verbs Effectively

Every sentence contains at least one verb. Because verbs often are action words, they add interest and punch to any piece of writing. In this unit, you will

✔ Learn to use present, past, and other verb tenses correctly

✔ Learn when to add -s or -ed

✔ Recognize and use past participle forms

✔ Recognize -ing verbs, infinitives, and other special forms

Notice how vividly this writer describes the scene before her. Her verbs are shown in italics.

A huge glittering tower *sparkles* across the Florida marshlands. Floodlights *reach* into the heavens all around it, rolling out carpets of light. Helicopters and jets *blink* around the launch pad like insects drawn to flame. Oz never *filled* the sky with such diamond-studded improbability. Inside the cascading lights, a giant trellis *holds* a slender rocket to its heart, on each side a tall thermos bottle filled with solid fuel the color and feel of a hard eraser, and on its back a sharp-nosed space shuttle, clinging like the young of some exotic mammal. A full moon *bulges* low in the sky, its face turned toward the launch pad, its mouth open.

Diane Ackerman, "Watching a Night Launch of the Space Shuttle"

■ Well-chosen verbs help bring this description to life. Which verbs most effectively help you see and experience the scene?

■ In the last sentence, the author describes the moon as if it were watching the launch—with "its mouth open." Why do you think she does this?

Writing Ideas

■ The takeoff of a rocket, plane, speedboat, or other vehicle

■ A historical event that you feel is important

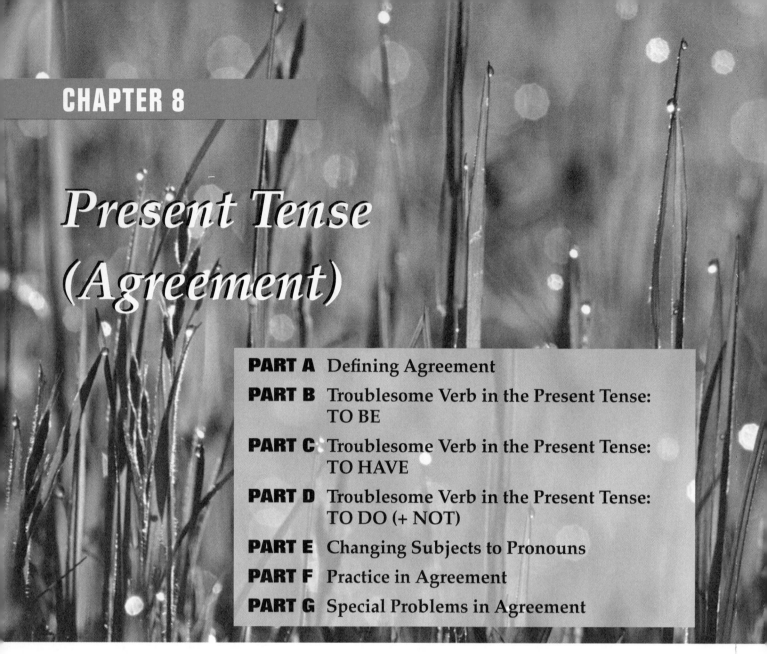

CHAPTER 8

Present Tense (Agreement)

PART A   Defining Agreement

A subject and a present tense verb *agree* if you use the correct form of the verb with each subject. The chart on the following page shows which form of the verb to use for each kind of pronoun subject (we discuss other kinds of subjects later).

Verbs in the Present Tense
(example verb: to write)

Singular		Plural	
If the subject is	the verb is	If the subject is	the verb is
↓	↓	↓	↓
1st person: I	write	1st person: we	write
2nd person: you	write	2nd person: you	write
3rd person: he she it }	writes	3rd person: they	write

PRACTICE 1

Fill in the correct present tense form of the verb.

1. You *ask* questions.
2. They *decide.*
3. I *travel.*
4. They *wear* glasses.
5. We *hope* so.
6. I *laugh* often.
7. We *study* daily.
8. He *interests* me.

1. He _____asks_____ questions.
2. She _____decides_____.
3. He _____travels_____.
4. She _____wears_____ glasses.
5. He _____hopes_____ so.
6. She _____laughs_____ often.
7. He _____studies_____ daily.
8. It _____interests_____ me.

Add -*s* or -*es* to a verb in the present tense only when the subject is *third person singular (he, she, it).*

Third Person Singular

If the subject is	the verb in the present tense must take an -*s* or -*es*.
he	wins
she	promises
it	wishes

PRACTICE 2

Write the correct form of the verb in the space to the right of the pronoun subject.

EXAMPLE: **to see**

I _____see_____

they _____see_____

she _____sees_____

	to fall		**to ask**		**to go**
he	falls	I	ask	he	goes
they	fall	she	asks	you	go
it	falls	he	asks	we	go

	to rest		**to hold**		**to purchase**
I	rest	it	holds	she	purchases
they	rest	we	hold	he	purchases
she	rests	you	hold	I	purchase

PRACTICE 3

First, underline the subject or subjects in each sentence below. Then circle the correct verb form. REMEMBER: If the subject of the sentence is *he, she,* or *it* (third person singular), the verb must end in *-s* or *-es* to agree with the subject.

1. In Dr. Deborah Tannen's book *You Just Don't Understand,* she (write, (writes)) about how men and women communicate.

2. They often ((differ), differs) in predictable ways, Tannen reports.

3. In the book, she (describe, (describes)) the following argument between a husband and wife.

4. For the third time in twenty minutes, they ((drive), drives) through the same neighborhood.

5. She (press, (presses)) him to stop and ask for directions.

6. He (insist, (insists)) on finding the way himself.

7. In the twilight, they ((struggle), struggles) to read street signs.

8. To the woman, it (make, (makes)) no sense not to get help.

9. She (remind, (reminds)) him that they are already late.

10. He (keep, keeps) driving.

11. According to Dr. Tannen, they (represent, represents) common male-female differences.

12. Like many other men, he (feel, feels) strong when finding his own way, but weak asking for help.

13. Like many women in this situation, she (fail, fails) to understand his need for independence.

14. She just (get, gets) angry or (criticize, criticizes) him.

15. Stereotypes or truth? You (decide, decides) for yourself whether or not you (agree, agrees) with Dr. Tannen's analysis.

PART B   Troublesome Verb in the Present Tense: TO BE

A few present tense verbs are formed in special ways. The most common of these verbs is *to be*.

Reference Chart: TO BE *(present tense)*			
Singular		**Plural**	
If the subject is	the verb is	If the subject is	the verb is
↓	↓	↓	↓
1st person: I	am	1st person: we	are
2nd person: you	are	2nd person: you	are
3rd person: he she it	is	3rd person: they	are

The chart also can be read like this:

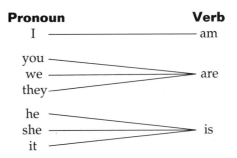

Pronoun	**Verb**
I	am
you we they	are
he she it	is

Use the charts to fill in the present tense form of *to be* that agrees with the subject.

1. She _____*is*_____ a member of the Olympic softball team.

2. We _____*are*_____ both jewelers, but he _____*is*_____ more skilled than I.

3. We _____*are*_____ sorry about your accident; you _____*are*_____ certainly unlucky with rollerblades.

4. They _____*are*_____ salmon fishermen.

5. He _____*is*_____ a musician in the firefighters' band.

6. I _____*am*_____ a weekend seamstress.

7. Because she _____*is*_____ a native of Morocco, she _____*is*_____ able to speak both Arabic and French.

8. I _____*am*_____ too nervous to sleep because we _____*are*_____ having an accounting exam tomorrow.

9. So you _____*are*_____ the one we have heard so much about!

10. It _____*is*_____ quite cool today, but she _____*is*_____ sunbathing.

11. Of course we _____*are*_____ excited about the rodeo.

12. Try this seafood soup; it _____*is*_____ delicious.

13. They _____*are*_____ interpreters at the United Nations.

14. I _____*am*_____ sure that she _____*is*_____ a marine biologist.

15. If it _____*is*_____ sunny tomorrow, we _____*are*_____ going hot air ballooning.

PART C   Troublesome Verb in the Present Tense: TO HAVE

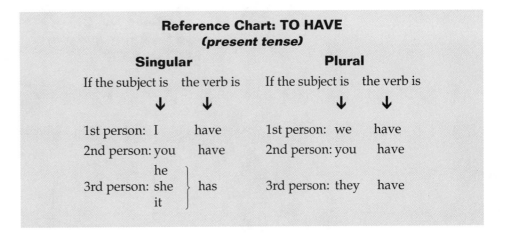

The chart also can be read like this:

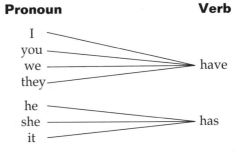

PRACTICE

Fill in the present tense form of *to have* that agrees with the subject. Use the charts.

1. He _____*has*_____ a cabin on Lake Superior.

2. You _____*have*_____ a wonderful sense of style.

3. We _____*have*_____ to protect our rivers, lakes, and oceans.

4. It _____*has*_____ to be spring because the cherry trees _____*have*_____ pink blossoms.

5. She _____*has*_____ the questions, and he _____*has*_____ the answers.

6. You _____*have*_____ a suspicious look on your face, and I _____*have*_____ to know why.

7. They _____*have*_____ doubts about the plan, but we _____*have*_____ none.

8. You _____*have*_____ one ruby earring, and she _____*has*_____ the other.

9. It _____*has*_____ to be repaired, and I _____*have*_____ just the person to do it for you.

10. If you _____*have*_____ $50, they _____*have*_____ an offer you can't refuse.

PART D   Troublesome Verb in the Present Tense: TO DO (+ NOT)

Reference Chart: TO DO
(present tense)

Singular		Plural	
If the subject is	the verb is	If the subject is	the verb is
↓	↓	↓	↓
1st person: I	do	1st person: we	do
2nd person: you	do	2nd person: you	do
3rd person: he she it }	does	3rd person: they	do

The chart also can be read like this:

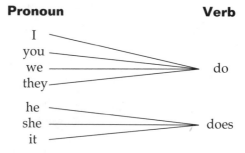

Pronoun	Verb
I you we they	do
he she it	does

PRACTICE

Use the charts to fill in the correct present tense form of *to do*.

1. She always _____*does*_____ well in math courses.

2. I always _____*do*_____ badly under pressure.

3. It _____*does*_____ matter if you forget to vote.

4. They most certainly _____*do*_____ sell muscle shirts.

5. You _____*do*_____ what I say, or you will be sorry.

6. If you _____*do*_____ the dishes, I'll _____*do*_____ the laundry.

7. He _____*does*_____ seem sorry about forgetting your dog's birthday.

8. You really _____*do*_____ irritate me.

9. _____*Do*_____ they dance the mambo?

10. _____*Does*_____ she like being a salesperson?

To Do + Not

Once you know how to use *do* and *does*, you are ready for *don't* and *doesn't*.

do + not = don't

does + not = doesn't

In the Positive columns, fill in the correct form of *to do* (*do* or *does*) to agree with the pronoun. In the Negative columns, fill in the correct form of *to do* with the negative *not* (*don't* or *doesn't*).

Pronoun	Positive	Negative
1. he	*does*	*doesn't*
2. we	*do*	*don't*
3. I	*do*	*don't*
4. they	*do*	*don't*
5. she	*does*	*doesn't*
6. they	*do*	*don't*
7. it	*does*	*doesn't*
8. you	*do*	*don't*

Fill in either *doesn't* or *don't* in each blank.

1. If they ____*don't*____ turn down that music, I'm going to scream.

2. It just ____*doesn't*____ make sense.

3. You ____*don't*____ have to reply in writing.

4. He ____*doesn't*____ always lock his door at night.

5. We ____*don't*____ want to miss *60 Minutes*.

6. If you ____*don't*____ stop calling collect, I ____*don't*____ want to talk to you.

7. He ___doesn't___ know the whole truth, and they ___don't___ want to know.

8. They ___don't___ realize how lucky they are.

9. Although you ___don't___ like biking five miles a day to work, it ___doesn't___ do your health any harm.

10. When I ___don't___ try, I ___don't___ succeed.

PRACTICE 3   REVIEW

As you read this paragraph, fill in the correct present tense form of *be, have,* or *do* in each sentence. Make sure all your verbs agree with their subjects.

(1) He ___has___ the expertise of a James Bond or an Indiana Jones, but he ___is___ the real thing, not a movie hero performing fantasy stunts. (2) Right now, he ___is___ calm, even though he ___is___ ready to leap from the open door of a Navy aircraft. (3) On his back he ___has___ an oversized parachute capable of supporting both him and the extra hundred pounds of special equipment packed in his combat vest. (4) When he ___does___ hit the water, he ___is___ ready to face the real challenge: finding and defusing a bomb sixty feet under rough, murky seas. (5) He ___has___ a mission and a very tight time frame, and he ___does___ not want to let the enemy know he ___is___ there. (6) Swimming underwater in special scuba gear, he ___does___ not release any air bubbles to mark the water's surface. (7) Working in semidarkness, performing dangerous technical tasks, he quickly ___does___ the job. (8) However, unlike media heroes, he ___does___ n't work alone. (9) He ___is___ a member of a highly trained team of Navy SEALs. (10) Among the most respected special forces in the world, they ___are___ commando divers ready for hazardous duty on sea, air, and land.

PART E   Changing Subjects to Pronouns

So far, you have worked on pronouns as subjects (*I, you, he, she, it, we, they*) and on how to make verbs agree with them. Often, however, the subject of a sentence is not a pronoun but a noun—like *dog, banjo, Ms. Callas, José and Robert, swimming* (as in *Swimming keeps me fit*).

To be sure that your verb agrees with your subject, *mentally* change the subject into a pronoun, and then select the correct form of the verb.

If the subject is	**it can be changed to the pronoun**
1. the speaker himself or herself ──────────→	I
2. masculine and singular ──────────→ (*Bill, one man*)	he
3. feminine and singular ──────────→ (*Sondra, a woman*)	she
4. neither masculine nor feminine and singular (a thing or an action) ──────→ (*this pen, love, running*)	it
5. a group that includes the speaker (I) ──────→ (*the family and I*)	we
6. a group of persons or things not including the speaker ──────────→ (*Jake and Wanda, several pens*)	they
7. the person or persons spoken to ───────→	you

PRACTICE 1

Change the subjects into pronouns. REMEMBER: If you add *I* to a group of people, the correct pronoun for the whole group is *we*; if you add *you* to a group, the correct pronoun for the whole group is *you*.

	Possible Subject	**Pronoun**
EXAMPLE:	Frank	*he*
1.	a huge moose	*it*
2.	a calculator and a checkbook	*they*
3.	my buddies and I	*we*
4.	you and the other nurses	*you*
5.	the silk blouse	*it*
6.	his daughter	*she*
7.	their tent	*it*
8.	deep sea fishing	*it*

Change each subject into a pronoun. Then circle the present tense verb that agrees with that subject. (Use the reference chart if you need to.)

EXAMPLES: Harry = _____*he*_____   Harry (whistle, (whistles)).

Sam and I = _____*we*_____   Sam and I ((walk,) walks).

1. Camilla = _____*she*_____
2. Their concert = _____*it*_____
3. Tod and you = _____*you*_____
4. The men and I = _____*we*_____
5. This blender = _____*it*_____
6. This church = _____*it*_____
7. Our printer = _____*it*_____
8. Scuba diving = _____*it*_____
9. The house and garden = _____*they*_____
10. Aunt Lil and I = _____*we*_____

1. Camilla (own, (owns)) a horse farm.
2. Their concert ((is,) are) sold out.
3. Tod and you ((look,) looks) alike.
4. The men and I ((repair,) repairs) potholes.
5. This blender (grate, (grates)) cheese.
6. This church ((is,) are) very old.
7. Our printer (jam, (jams)) too often.
8. Scuba diving ((is,) are) her one passion.
9. The house and garden (is, (are)) well cared for.
10. Aunt Lil and I ((give,) gives) Swedish massages.

PART F   Practice in Agreement

Circle the correct verb in each sentence, making sure it agrees with its subject.

Not Exactly Rocky Road

(1) Ben Cohen and Jerry Greenfield (is, (are)) famous. (2) Yet most people ((do,) does) not even know their last names. (3) Their friendly, unkempt faces (stares,

(stare) at us every time we (tear, tears) the top from a pint of their sherbet or frozen yogurt. (4) These two men (run, runs) their ice cream business in a rather unusual way. (5) Of course their company (has, have) to make a profit. (6) However, Ben and Jerry also (believe, believes) in having fun and in giving back to the community.

(7) One important goal (is, are) to make their factory in Vermont an enjoyable place to work. (8) Ben (call, calls) himself the firm's Minister of Joy. (9) He (lead, leads) a Joy Gang consisting of six employees. (10) Ben and this unusual group (roam, roams) the factory, acting goofy and making the daily grind more fun. (11) Urged on by the Joy Gang, employees (celebrate, celebrates) such little-known holidays as National Clash-Dressing Day. (12) On Clash Day, the company (award, awards) prizes like glow-in-the-dark rubber lobsters to the worker wearing the ugliest outfit. (13) The Joy Gang also (sponsor, sponsors) monthly events like delicious Italian dinners served to workers on the night shift.

(14) On a more serious note, the company (give, gives) each worker fifty hours off a year to volunteer in community programs. (15) For this time, the worker (receive, receives) full pay. (16) A loan fund (offer, offers) money to help employees start socially responsible businesses. (17) Other benefits (include, includes) profit sharing, maternity and paternity leave, free massages, and three pints of ice cream a day.

(18) Ben and Jerry (admit, admits) they are not great managers. (19) After several strong years, profits (is, are) down. (20) A new, more traditional manager now (run, runs) the business. (21) However, the two founders still (own, owns) 42 percent of voting stock. (22) As leaders of the company's Philanthropic Department, Ben and Jerry still (love, loves) their jobs. (23) Every day, they (roar, roars) in to work on their Harley-Davidsons.

PRACTICE 2   REVIEW

In each blank, write the *present tense* form of one of the verbs from this list. Your sentences can be funny; just make sure that each verb agrees with each subject.

talk	punch	tickle	drink
kiss	arrive	sing	dance

(1) Many famous people _____*arrive*_____ at the party. (2) Tiger Woods _____*tickles*_____ a baby. (3) Madonna and I

_____*dance*_____ near the punchbowl, not far from the Vice President, who

_____ *drinks* _____ with a small poodle. (4) Several rock stars

_____ *kiss* _____ in one corner of the room. (5) Then Sly Stallone

_____ *talks* _____ , and everybody goes home.

PRACTICE 3   REVIEW

The sentences that follow have singular subjects and verbs. To gain skill in verb agreement, rewrite each sentence, changing the subject from *singular* to *plural*. Then make sure the verb agrees with the new subject. Keep all verbs in the present tense.

EXAMPLE: The train stops at Cold Spring.

Rewrite: _____ *The trains stop at Cold Spring.* _____

1. The movie ticket costs too much.

   Rewrite: _____ *The movie tickets cost too much.* _____

2. The pipeline carries oil from Alaska.

   Rewrite: _____ *The pipelines carry oil from Alaska.* _____

3. A white horse grazes by the fence.

   Rewrite: _____ *White horses graze by the fence.* _____

4. My brother owns a variety store.

   Rewrite: _____ *My brothers own a variety store.* _____

5. The family needs good health insurance.

   Rewrite: _____ *The families need good health insurance.* _____

6. The backup singer wears green contact lenses.

   Rewrite: _____ *The backup singers wear green contact lenses.* _____

7. My daughter wants striped tights.

   Rewrite: _____ *My daughters want striped tights.* _____

8. A wave laps softly against the dock.

   Rewrite: _____ *Waves lap softly against the dock.* _____

PRACTICE 4   REVIEW

The sentences that follow have plural subjects and verbs. Rewrite each sentence, changing the subject from *plural* to *singular*. Then make sure the verb agrees with the new subject. Keep all verbs in the present tense.

1. My neighbors vacation in Bermuda.

    Rewrite: _____ *My neighbor vacations in Bermuda.* _____

2. The engines roar loudly.

    Rewrite: _____ *The engine roars loudly.* _____

3. The students invest in the stock market.

    Rewrite: _____ *The student invests in the stock market.* _____

4. The inmates watch *America's Most Wanted*.

    Rewrite: _____ *The inmate watches* America's Most Wanted. _____

5. Overhead, seagulls ride on the wind.

    Rewrite: _____ *Overhead, a seagull rides on the wind.* _____

6. Good card players know when to bluff.

    Rewrite: _____ *A good card player knows when to bluff.* _____

7. On Saturday, the pharmacists stay late.

    Rewrite: _____ *On Saturday, the pharmacist stays late.* _____

8. The jewels from Bangkok are on display.

    Rewrite: _____ *The jewel from Bangkok is on display.* _____

PRACTICE 5   REVIEW

Rewrite this paragraph in the present tense by changing the verbs.

(1) Ralph loved to shop. (2) Night after night, he dreamed of spending a month at the West Edmonton Mall in Edmonton, Canada. (3) He needed that much time in one of the largest shopping malls in the world. (4) Its 800 shops fascinated him. (5) In his dream, Ralph eyed merchandise, tried on clothing, and bargained with salespeople. (6) He dashed around the mall's 110 acres while he thought about other purchases he wanted to make. (7) When he finished shopping, he and a friend went to a different theater every night and ate in a different restaurant. (8) They did all this without ever leaving the mall. (9) Only one thing was wrong with Ralph's dream. (10) Every morning, Ralph woke up totally exhausted.

_____ *(1) Ralph loves to shop. (2) Night after night, he dreams of spending a* _____

_____ *month at the West Edmonton Mall in Edmonton, Canada. (3) He needs that* _____ *much time in one of the largest shopping malls in the world. (4) Its 800 shops*

fascinate him. (5) In his dream, Ralph eyes merchandise, tries on clothing,

and bargains with salespeople. (6) He dashes around the mall's 110 acres

while he thinks about purchases he wants to make. (7) When he finishes

shopping, he and a friend go to a different theater every night and eat in a

different restaurant. (8) They do all this without ever leaving the mall. (9)

Only one thing is wrong with Ralph's dream. (10) Every morning, Ralph

wakes up totally exhausted.

PART G Special Problems in Agreement

So far, you have learned that if the subject of a sentence is third person singular (*he, she, it*) or a word that can be changed into *he, she,* or *it,* the verb takes *-s* or *-es* in the present tense.

In special cases, however, you will need to know more before you can make your verb agree with your subject.

Focusing on the Subject

---

(1) A box of chocolates sits on the table.

- ◼ *What* sits on the table?
- ◼ Don't be confused by the prepositional phrase before the verb—*of chocolates.*
- ◼ Just one *box* sits on the table.
- ◼ *A box* is the subject. *A box* takes the third person singular verb—*sits.*

A box (of chocolates) sits on the table.
    ↓   ↓
 subject   verb
(singular)   *(singular)*

---

(2) The children in the park play for hours.

- ◼ *Who* play for hours?
- ◼ Don't be confused by the prepositional phrase before the verb—*in the park.*
- ◼ *The children* play for hours.
- ◼ *The children* is the subject. *The children* takes the third person plural verb—*play.*

The children (in the park) play for hours.
    ↓   ↓
 subject   verb
(plural)   *(plural)*

(3) The purpose of the exercises is to improve your spelling.

■ *What* is to improve your spelling?

■ Don't be confused by the prepositional phrase before the verb—*of the exercises.*

■ *The purpose* is to improve your spelling.

■ *The purpose* is the subject. *The purpose* takes the third person singular verb—*is.*

The purpose (of the exercises) is to improve your spelling.
   ↓   ↓
subject   verb
(singular)   *(singular)*

As you can see from these examples, sometimes what seems to be the subject is really not the subject. Prepositional phrases (groups of words beginning with *of, in, at,* and so on) *cannot* contain the subject of a sentence. One way to find the subject of a sentence that contains a prepositional phrase is to ask yourself *what makes sense as the subject.*

My friends from the old neighborhood often $\begin{matrix} \text{visits} \\ \text{visit} \end{matrix}$ me.

■ Which makes sense as the subject of the sentence: *my friends* or *the old neighborhood?*

(a) My friends . . . visit me.   (b) The old neighborhood . . . visits me.

■ Obviously, sentence (a) makes sense; it clearly expresses the intention of the writer.

PRACTICE

Now try these sentences. Cross out any confusing prepositional phrases, and circle the correct verb.

1. The houses ~~in that neighborhood~~ ((cost) costs) too much.

2. The traffic lights ~~along Clark Street~~ ((blink) blinks) to a salsa beat.

3. The price ~~of the repairs~~ (seem, (seems)) high.

4. His lack ~~of knowledge~~ (amaze, (amazes)) me.

5. The coffee stains ~~on his résumé~~ ((show) shows) his carelessness.

6. The secret ~~of her success~~ ((is) are) persistence.

7. The cause ~~of many illnesses~~ ((is) are) poor diet.

8. The polar bears ~~in the zoo~~ ((miss) misses) the Arctic.

9. One American ~~in ten~~ (drink, (drinks)) too much.

10. The laboratories ~~on the fifth floor~~ (has, (have)) new equipment.

Spotting Special Singular Subjects

> *Either* of the students
> *Neither* of the students
> *Each* of the students   }   seems happy.
> *One* of the students
> *Every one* of the students

- ■ *Either, neither, each, one,* and *every one* are the real subjects of these sentences.

- ■ *Either, neither, each, one,* and *every one* are special singular subjects. They always take a singular verb.

- ■ REMEMBER: The subject is never part of a prepositional phrase, so *the students* cannot be the subject.

PRACTICE 1

Circle the correct verb.

1. One of our satellites (is, are) lost in space.
2. Each of my brothers (wear, wears) cinnamon after-shave lotion.
3. Each of us (carry, carries) a snakebite kit.
4. Neither of those excuses (sound, sounds) believable.
5. One of the mirrors (have, has) a thick gold frame.
6. Either of the watches (cost, costs) about $30.
7. Neither of those cities (is, are) the capital of Brazil.
8. One of the butlers (commit, commits) the crime, but which one?
9. One of the desserts in front of you (do, does) not contain sugar.
10. Each of the taxi drivers (speed, speeds).

PRACTICE 2

On separate paper, write five sentences using the special singular subjects. Make sure your sentences are in the present tense.

Using THERE to Begin a Sentence

> (1) *There* is a squirrel in the yard.
> (2) *There* are two squirrels in the yard.

- ■ Although sentences sometimes begin with *there*, *there* cannot be the subject of a sentence.

- ■ Usually, the subject *follows* the verb in sentences that begin with *there*.

To find the real subject (so you will know how to make the verb agree), mentally drop the *there* and rearrange the sentence to put the subject at the beginning.

(1) There is a squirrel in the yard.
becomes

A squirrel   *is* in the yard.
↓   ↓
subject   verb
(singular)   *(singular)*

(2) There are two squirrels in the yard.
becomes
Two squirrels   *are* in the yard.
↓   ↓
subject   verb
(plural)   *(plural)*

BE CAREFUL: Good writers avoid using *there* to begin a sentence. Whenever possible, they write more directly: *Two squirrels are in the yard.*

PRACTICE 1

In each sentence, mentally drop the *there* and rearrange the sentence to put the subject at the beginning. Then circle the verb that agrees with the subject of the sentence. *Answers to Practice 2 are above the lines.*

A day-care center is on campus.
1. There (**is**, are) a day-care center on campus.
A beluga whale swims in the city aquarium.
2. There (**is**, are) a beluga whale in the city aquarium.
Two beluga whales are in the city aquarium.
3. There (is, **are**) two beluga whales in the city aquarium.
One good reason to quit this job is my supervisor.
4. There (**is**, are) one good reason to quit this job—my supervisor.
Six customers are waiting ahead of you.
5. There (is, **are**) six customers ahead of you.
A water fountain is in the lounge.
6. There (**is**, are) a water fountain in the lounge.
A house and a barn stand in the wheat field.
7. There (is, **are**) a house and a barn in the wheat field.
Only two shopping days are left before my birthday.
8. There (is, **are**) only two shopping days left before my birthday.
Thousands of plant species grow in the rain forest.
9. There (is, **are**) thousands of plant species in the rain forest.
A single blue egg is in the nest over the kitchen door.
10. There (**is**, are) a single blue egg in the nest over the kitchen door.

PRACTICE 2

On a separate sheet of paper, rewrite each sentence in Practice 1 so that it does not begin with *there is* or *there are*. Sentences (1) and (2) are done for you. *Answers to Practice 2 are above the lines in Practice 1.*

EXAMPLES: 1. A day-care center is on campus.

2. A beluga whale swims in the city aquarium.

Choosing the Correct Verb in Questions

> (1) Where is Bob?
> (2) Where are Bob and Lee?
> (3) Why are they singing?
> (4) Have you painted the hall yet?

■ In questions, the subject usually *follows* the verb.

■ In sentence (1), the subject is *Bob*. *Bob* takes the third person singular verb *is*.

■ In sentence (2), the subject is *Bob and Lee*. *Bob and Lee* takes the third person plural verb *are*.

■ What is the subject in sentence (3)? ___*they*___ What verb does it take? *third person plural verb* are + singing

■ What is the subject in sentence (4)? ___*you*___ What verb does it take? *second person plural verb* have + painted

If you can't find the subject, mentally turn the question around:

> (1) Bob is . . .
> (2) Bob and Lee are . . .

PRACTICE 1

Circle the correct verb.

1. Where (**is**, are) my leather bomber jacket?

2. (Have, **Has**) our waiter gone to lunch?

3. Why (is, **are**) so many children taking drugs?

4. Who (is, **are**) those people on the fire escape?

5. Which (**is**, are) your day off?

6. How (do, **does**) she like studying dentistry?

7. (**Have**, Has) you considered taking a cruise to Alaska?

8. Where (is, **are**) Don's power tools?

9. (Have, **Has**) the groundhog raided the zucchini patch today?

10. Well, what (**do**, does) you know about that?

PRACTICE 2

On separate paper, write five questions of your own. Make sure that your questions are in the present tense and that the verbs agree with the subjects.

Using WHO, WHICH, and THAT as Relative Pronouns

When you use a relative pronoun—*who, which,* or *that*—to introduce a dependent idea, make sure you choose the correct verb.*

> (1) I know a woman *who* plays expert chess.

■ Sentence (1) uses the singular verb *plays* because *who* relates or refers to *a woman* (singular).

> (2) Suede coats, *which* stain easily, should not be worn in the rain.

■ Sentence (2) uses the plural verb *stain* because *which* relates to the subject *suede coats* (plural).

> (3) Computers *that* talk make me nervous.

■ Sentence (3) uses the plural verb *talk* because *that* relates to what word?

    computers

PRACTICE 1

Write the word that the *who, which,* or *that* relates or refers to in the blank at the right; then circle the correct form of the verb.

EXAMPLE: I like people who (is, (are)) creative.
       people

1. My office has a robot that (fetch, (fetches)) the mail.
       robot

2. Always choose lemons that ((have,) has) smooth skins.
       lemons

3. My husband, who (take, (takes)) marvelous photographs, won the Nikon Prize.
       husband

4. He likes women who (is, (are)) very ambitious.
       women

5. The old house, which (sit, (sits)) on a cliff above the sea, is called Balston Heights.
       house

---

*For work on relative pronouns, see Chapter 18.

6. People who (love, loves) to read usually
   write well. _____people_____

7. I like a person who (think, thinks) for
   himself or herself. _____person_____

8. The only airline that (fly, flies) to
   Charlottesville is booked solid. _____airline_____

9. People who (live, lives) in glass houses
   should invest in blinds. _____people_____

10. Most students want jobs that (challenge,
    challenges) them. _____jobs_____

PRACTICE 2   REVIEW

Proofread the following paragraph for a variety of verb agreement errors. First underline all present tense verbs. Then correct any errors above the lines.

                                                         admire

(1) Many people who love exciting theater and talented actors admires Anna Deveare Smith. (2) She is well known for her thought-provoking one-woman
explore
shows. (3) Many of these dramas explores social conflicts in America and use just one actor. (4) Often, Smith herself brilliantly plays the roles of many different
examines
characters. (5) For example, one play, *Twilight: Los Angeles, 1992,* examine the Los Angeles riots and the beatings of Rodney King and Reginald Denny. (6) Ama-
brings
zingly, Smith, who is African-American, bring to life all the people involved: white people, black people, Korean shopkeepers, angry rioters, and frightened citizens. (7) Through Smith, theatergoers understand a moment in history from
does
many points of view. (8) How do she achieve this? (9) Once a shy and withdrawn child, Anna Deveare Smith now works to open her mind and heart to the experiences of others. (10) She believes that both successful acting and successful
require
democracy requires us to grow in tolerance. (11) Besides writing plays, this talented woman appears occasionally in Hollywood films and teaches drama at Stanford University in Palo Alto, California.

PRACTICE: WRITING ASSIGNMENT

In a group of three or four classmates, choose an area of the building or campus that contains some interesting action—the hallway, the cafeteria, or a playing field. Go there now and observe what you see, recording details and using verbs in the present tense. Choose as many good action verbs as you can. Keep observing and writing for ten minutes. Then head back to the classroom and write a first draft of a paragraph.

Next, exchange papers within your group. The reader should underline every verb, checking for verb agreement, and tell the writer what he or she liked about the writing and what could be improved.

 Chapter Highlights

■ **A subject and a present tense verb must agree:**

The light flickers. *(singular subject, singular verb)*

The lights flicker. *(plural subject, plural verb)*

■ **Only third person singular subjects** *(he, she, it)* **take verbs ending in** *-s* **or** *-es.*

■ **Three troublesome present tense verbs are** *to be,* **to have, and** *to do.*

■ **When a prepositional phrase comes between a subject and a verb, the verb must agree with the subject.**

The *chairs* on the porch *are* painted white.

■ **The subjects** *either, neither, each, one,* **and** *every one* **are always singular.**

Neither of the mechanics *repairs* transmissions.

■ **In a sentence beginning with** *there is* **or** *there are,* **the subject follows the verb.**

There are three *oysters* on your plate.

■ **In questions, the subject usually follows the verb.**

Where are *Kimi and Fred?*

■ **Relative pronouns** *(who, which,* **and** *that)* **refer to the word with which the verb must agree.**

A *woman who* has children must manage time skillfully.

Chapter Review

Proofread this essay carefully for verb agreement. First, underline all present tense verbs. Then correct any verb agreement errors in the space above the error.

The Killer Whales of Sea World

(1) Sea World maintains large parks in San Diego, California; Aurora, Ohio;

stars

and Orlando, Florida. (2) The show at each park star a killer whale, which is also

called an orca. (3) Audiences gasp when one of these fierce animals leaps twenty

plants

feet into the air and plant a gentle kiss on someone's cheek. (4) At first, this

amazing trick seems hard to understand.

deserve

(5) Killer whales certainly deserves their name. (6) Other whales weigh

are

more, and killer whales rarely grow longer than thirty feet, but they is the surest

killers in the sea. (7) Only the great white shark challenges them. (8) The orca

lives in every ocean of the world. (9) It is a successful predator because it out-

has

smarts and outraces all its prey. (10) It also have powerful teeth designed for

thinks

tearing flesh. (11) Though it usually eats fish, a hungry killer whale think nothing

of feasting on a sea lion or even an elephant seal, which weighs as much as two

tons. (12) Even giant hundred-ton blue whales are known to fall prey to the

powerful orca.

live   *hunt*

(13) However, killer whales are also very sociable. (14) They lives and hunts

in groups, or pods, of up to twenty-five animals. (15) They enjoy close family

nurse

relationships. (16) Children nurses for almost two years, and older males protect

youngsters and females. (17) Like other whales, killer whales help one another

is

when there are trouble.

understand

(18) Animal trainers at Sea World understands that the desire for companion-

is

ship in killer whales are almost as great as the need for food. (19) When regular

feeding satisfies the hunting instinct, the social urge becomes very important. (20)

teach

Using food and kindness as rewards, trainers teaches killer whales to perform

tricks that combine great physical skill and gentleness.

object
(21) Some people <u>objects</u> to keeping these magnificent creatures in captivity.

suffer
(22) They <u>say</u> that orcas who live away from their families <u>suffers</u>. (23) Whether

continue
Sea World and other parks <u>continues</u> to display killer whales or <u>find</u> new ways to

attract visitors, only time will tell.

CHAPTER 9

Past Tense

PART A Regular Verbs in the Past Tense
PART B Irregular Verbs in the Past Tense
PART C Troublesome Verb in the Past Tense: TO BE
PART D Review

PART A   Regular Verbs in the Past Tense

Verbs in the past tense express actions that occurred in the past. The italicized words in the following sentences are verbs in the past tense.

> (1) They *noticed* a dent in the fender.
> (2) She *played* the guitar very well.
> (3) For years I *studied* yoga.

■ What ending do all these verbs take?____-d or -ed____

■ In general, then, what ending do you add to put a verb in the past tense?____-d or -ed____

■ Verbs that add *-d* or *-ed* to form the past tense are called *regular verbs*.

PRACTICE 1

Some of the verbs in these sentences are in the present tense; others are in the past tense. Circle the verb in each sentence. Write *present* in the column at the right if the verb is in the present tense; write *past* if the verb is in the past tense.

1. Ricardo (stroked) his beard.   *past*

2. Light (travels) 186,000 miles in a second.   *present*

3. They (play) jazz on weekends.   *present*

4. Magellan (sailed) around the world.   _past_

5. The lake (looks) calm as glass.   _present_

6. All morning, Jennifer (studied) French.   _past_

7. Mount St. Helens (erupted) in 1980.   _past_

8. That chemical plant (pollutes) our water.   _present_

9. A robin (nested) in the mailbox.   _past_

10. He (owns) two exercise bikes.   _present_

PRACTICE 2

Read the following paragraph, written in the present tense. The verbs are shown in italics. Then, on the blank lines, rewrite the entire paragraph in the past tense, changing every verb to the correct past tense form.*

(1) Again this year, Carnival *transforms* Rio de Janiero, Brazil, into one of the most fantastic four-day parties on the planet. (2) On the Friday before Ash Wednesday, thousands of visitors *pour* into the city. (3) They *watch* all-night parades and *admire* the glittering costumes. (4) They *cheer, sweat,* and *dance* the samba. (5) Of course, preparation *starts* long before. (6) For months, members of the samba schools (neighborhood dance clubs) *plan* their floats, *practice* samba steps, and *stay* up nights making their costumes. (7) Using bright fabrics, sequins, feathers, and chains, both men and women *create* spectacular outfits. (8) Each samba school *constructs* a float that *features* a smoke-breathing dragon or a spouting waterfall. (9) During Carnival, judges *rate* the schools on costumes, dancing, and floats and then *award* prizes. (10) Together, Brazilians and their visitors *share* great music, drink, food, fun, and the chance to go a little bit crazy.

(1) Again this year, Carnival transformed Rio de Janiero, Brazil, into one of the most fantastic four-day parties on the planet. (2) On the Friday before Ash Wednesday, thousands of visitors poured into the city. (3) They watched all-night parades and admired the glittering costumes. (4) They cheered, sweated, and danced the samba. (5) Of course, preparation started long before. (6) For months, members of the samba schools (neighborhood dance clubs) planned their floats, practiced samba steps, and stayed up nights making their costumes. (7) Using bright fabrics, sequins, feathers, and chains, both men and women created spectacular outfits. (8) Each samba school constructed a float that featured a smoke-breathing dragon or a spouting waterfall. (9) During Carnival, judges rated the schools on costumes, dancing, and floats and then awarded prizes. (10) Together, Brazilians and their visitors shared great music, drink, food, fun, and the chance to go a little bit crazy.

---

*If you have questions about spelling, see Chapter 32.

As you can see from this exercise, many verbs form the past tense by adding either *-d* or *-ed*.

Furthermore, in the past tense, agreement is not a problem, except for the verb *to be*. This is because verbs in the past tense have only one form, no matter what the subject is.

PRACTICE 3

The verbs have been omitted from this paragraph. Choose verbs from the list below, and write the past tense form of each verb in the blank spaces. Do not use a verb twice.

approach	wink	shriek	stay
rustle	cry	leap	cook
move	burn	chase	help
camp	arrive	climb	laugh

(1) Last December, Tom and I _____camped_____ overnight in Everglades National Park. (2) We _____arrived_____ at sunset and _____cooked_____ eggs and beans over a campfire. (3) Suddenly, the dry grass near us _____rustled_____, and a very large alligator _____approached_____. (4) We _____shrieked_____ and _____leaped_____ into the van, where we _____stayed_____ all night.

PRACTICE 4

Fill in the past tense of each verb.

1. In 1923, Luis Angel Firpo _____challenged_____ (challenge) Jack Dempsey.

2. Firpo _____wanted_____ (want) to be the new heavyweight champion of the world.

3. The two boxers _____battled_____ (battle) in the fiercest title bout ever.

4. Excitement _____filled_____ (fill) the air as 85,000 fans _____crowded_____ (crowd) into New York City's Polo Grounds.

5. Scalpers _____charged_____ (charge) as much as $150 for a ticket.

6. From the opening bell, the fighters _____slugged_____ (slug) it out.

7. Dempsey _____knocked_____ (knock) Firpo down seven times and _____closed_____ (close) in to end the fight.

8. To everyone's surprise, Firpo _____unloaded_____ (unload) a powerful right-hand punch to Dempsey's jaw.

9. The champion _____sailed_____ (sail) through the ropes and out of the ring.

10. Only his legs _____remained_____ (remain) in view as they

    _____twisted_____ (twist) in the air.

11. The dazed Dempsey _____staggered_____ (stagger) back into the ring and

    barely _____managed_____ (manage) to finish the round.

12. Dempsey _____opened_____ (open) the second round by quickly floor-
    ing Firpo twice.

13. Then the champ _____flattened_____ (flatten) Firpo with a left to the jaw.

14. Bleeding, Firpo _____tried_____ (try) hard to get up, but

    he _____stiffened_____ (stiffen) and _____passed_____ (pass) out.

15. The whole match _____lasted_____ (last) just three minutes and fifty-
    seven seconds.

PART B   Irregular Verbs in the Past Tense

Instead of adding *-d* or *-ed*, some verbs form the past tense in other ways.

> (1) He *threw* a knuckle ball.
> (2) She *gave* him a dollar.
> (3) He *rode* from his farm into the town.

■ The italicized words in these sentences are also verbs in the past tense.

■ Do these verbs form the past tense by adding *-d* or *-ed*? _____no_____

■ *Threw, gave,* and *rode* are the past tense of verbs that do not add *-d* or *-ed* to
form the past tense.

■ Verbs that do not add *-d* or *-ed* to form the past tense are called *irregular verbs*.

A chart listing common irregular verbs follows.

Reference Chart: Irregular Verbs

Simple Form	Past	Simple Form	Past
be	was, were	come	came
become	became	cut	cut
begin	began	dive	dove (dived)
blow	blew	do	did
break	broke	draw	drew
bring	brought	drink	drank
build	built	drive	drove
buy	bought	eat	ate
catch	caught	fall	fell
choose	chose	feed	fed

Reference Chart: Irregular Verbs *(continued)*

Simple Form	Past	Simple Form	Past
feel	felt	rise	rose
fight	fought	run	ran
find	found	say	said
fly	flew	see	saw
forget	forgot	seek	sought
forgive	forgave	sell	sold
freeze	froze	send	sent
get	got	set	set
give	gave	shake	shook
go	went	shine	shone (shined)
grow	grew	sing	sang
have	had	sit	sat
hear	heard	sleep	slept
hide	hid	speak	spoke
hold	held	spend	spent
hurt	hurt	spring	sprang
keep	kept	stand	stood
know	knew	steal	stole
lay	laid	strike	struck
lead	led	swim	swam
leave	left	take	took
let	let	teach	taught
lie	lay	tear	tore
lose	lost	tell	told
make	made	think	thought
mean	meant	throw	threw
meet	met	understand	understood
pay	paid	wake	woke
put	put	wear	wore
quit	quit	win	won
read	read	wind	wound
ride	rode	write	wrote
ring	rang		

Learn the unfamiliar past tense forms by grouping together verbs that change from present tense to past tense in the same way. For example, some irregular verbs change *ow* in the present to *ew* in the past:

bl<u>ow</u>	bl<u>ew</u>	kn<u>ow</u>	kn<u>ew</u>
gr<u>ow</u>	gr<u>ew</u>	thr<u>ow</u>	thr<u>ew</u>

Another group changes from *i* in the present to *a* in the past:

beg<u>i</u>n	beg<u>a</u>n	s<u>i</u>ng	s<u>a</u>ng
dr<u>i</u>nk	dr<u>a</u>nk	spr<u>i</u>ng	spr<u>a</u>ng
r<u>i</u>ng	r<u>a</u>ng	sw<u>i</u>m	sw<u>a</u>m

As you write, refer to the chart. If you are unsure of the past tense form of a verb that is not in the chart, check a dictionary. For example, if you look up the verb *go* in the dictionary, you will find an entry like this:

go \ went \ gone \ going

The first word listed is used to form the *present* tense of the verb (I *go*, he *goes*, and so on). The second word is the *past* tense (I *went*, he *went*, and so on). The third word is the *past participle (gone)*, and the last word is the *present participle (going)*.

Some dictionaries list different forms only for irregular verbs. If no past tense is listed, you know that the verb is regular and that its past tense ends in *-d* or *-ed*.

PRACTICE 1

Use the chart to fill in the correct form of the verb in the past tense.

1. Beryl Markham _____*grew*_____ (grow) up in Kenya, East Africa.

2. As a child, this adventurer _____*went*_____ (go) hunting with African tribesmen.

3. Once, while a lion attacked her, she _____*lay*_____ (lie) still, thus saving her own life.

4. At age seventeen, she _____*sought*_____ (seek) a license to train horses, becoming the first woman trainer in Kenya.

5. Her friend Tom Black _____*taught*_____ (teach) her how to fly a small plane, the *D. H. Gipsy Moth.*

6. By her late twenties, she _____*was*_____ (be) a licensed pilot.

7. As Africa's first female bush pilot, Markham regularly

   _____*flew*_____ (fly) across East Africa, carrying supplies, mail, and passengers.

8. In 1936, she _____*made*_____ (make) a solo flight across the Atlantic Ocean.

9. Despite poor flying conditions, fatigue, and low fuel, she

   _____*kept*_____ (keep) her plane in the air for more than twenty hours.

10. Markham _____*set*_____ (set) a record as the first woman to fly alone nonstop from England to Nova Scotia.

11. In 1942, she _____*wrote*_____ (write) *West with the Night,* a book about her thrilling life.

12. Reprinted in 1983, this book _____*became*_____ (become) a great success.

Use the chart to fill in the correct past tense form of each verb.

(1) The story of the famous Hope diamond _____*began*_____ (begin) in India in 1701. (2) Jean Baptiste Tavernier, a French jeweler and traveler, _____*bought*_____ (buy) a huge blue diamond and _____*brought*_____ (bring) it home with him. (3) The jewel _____*became*_____ (become) known as the Blue Tavernier and eventually _____*wound*_____ (wind) up in the French royal collection. (4) During the French Revolution, someone _____*stole*_____ (steal) it. (5) Most people quickly _____*forgot*_____ (forget) about the stone. (6) However, forty years later, part of the diamond _____*did*_____ (do) show up in England. (7) H. T. Hope, a banker, _____*paid*_____ (pay) a great sum for it. (8) He _____*left*_____ (leave) it to his son, who soon _____*spent*_____ (spend) his fortune and _____*sold*_____ (sell) the diamond to the sultan of Turkey. (9) Finally, the Hope diamond _____*came*_____ (come) into the possession of Mrs. Edward B. McLean. (10) Soon after buying the jewel, she _____*lost*_____ (lose) a child in an accident, _____*saw*_____ (see) her family break up, and _____*went*_____ (go) bankrupt. (11) In the end, Mrs. McLean _____*took*_____ (take) her own life. (12) In 1958, the last private owner of the "unlucky" stone _____*sent*_____ (send) it to one of the Smithsonian museums in Washington, D.C., where it still can be seen.

Look over the list of irregular verbs on pages 123 and 124. Pick out the ten verbs that give you the most trouble, and list them here.

Simple	Past	Simple	Past
_____	_____	_____	_____
_____	_____	_____	_____
_____	_____	_____	_____
_____	_____	_____	_____
_____	_____	_____	_____

Now, on a separate sheet of paper, write one paragraph using *all ten* verbs. Your paragraph may be humorous; just make sure your verbs are correct.

PART C   Troublesome Verb in the Past Tense: TO BE

Reference Chart: TO BE
(past tense)

	Singular		Plural
1st person:	I was ———————→		we were
2nd person:	you were ———————→		you were
3rd person:	he she it } was ———————→		they were

■ Note that the first and third person singular forms are the same—*was.*

PRACTICE

In each sentence, circle the correct past tense of the verb *to be*—either *was* or *were.*

1. Our instructor (**was**, were) a pilot and skydiver.

2. You always (was, **were**) a good friend.

3. Georgia O'Keeffe (**was**, were) a great twentieth-century American painter.

4. Why (was, **were**) they wearing red ribbons?

5. Alanis Morisette (**was**, were) a Grammy Award winner in 1996.

6. You (was, **were**) right, and I (**was**, were) wrong.

7. The president and the first lady (was, **were**) both here.

8. I (**was**, were) seven when my sister (**was**, were) born.

9. Carmen (**was**, were) a Republican, but her cousins (was, **were**) Democrats.

10. Some people say that Greg Louganis (**was**, were) the world's greatest diver.

11. The bride and groom (was, **were**) present, but where (**was**, were) the minister?

12. (Was, **Were**) you happy working in sales?

13. Either they (was, **were**) late, or she (**was**, were) early.

14. Who (**was**, were) the woman we saw you with last night?

15. At this time last year, Sarni and I (was, **were**) in Egypt.

To Be + Not

Be careful of verb agreement if you use the past tense of *to be* with *not* as a contraction.

was + not = wasn't

were + not = weren't

In each sentence, fill in the blank(s) with either *wasn't* or *weren't*.

1. The printer cartridges _____*weren't*_____ on sale.

2. That papaya _____*wasn't*_____ cheap.

3. He _____*wasn't*_____ happy about the opening of the nuclear power plant.

4. _____*Weren't*_____ you here for the midterm?

5. She _____*wasn't*_____ bored, was she?

6. This fireplace _____*wasn't*_____ built properly.

7. The last time I saw Bonnie, she and Charles _____*weren't*_____ dating.

8. The parents _____*weren't*_____ willing to tolerate drug dealers near the school.

9. That _____*wasn't*_____ the point!

10. My car keys _____*weren't*_____ in my pocket.

11. Three of the paintings _____*weren't*_____ in the show.

12. That history quiz _____*wasn't*_____ so bad.

13. He and I liked each other, but we _____*weren't*_____ able to agree about anything.

14. That remark _____*wasn't*_____ very funny.

15. Many young couples _____*weren't*_____ able to afford homes.

PART D   Review

PRACTICE 1   REVIEW

Rewrite this paragraph, changing the verbs to the past tense.*

(1) Above the office where I work is a karate studio. (2) Every day as I go through my files, make out invoices, and write letters, I hear loud shrieks and crashes from the studio above me. (3) All day long, the walls tremble, the ceiling shakes, and little pieces of plaster fall like snow onto my desk. (4) Sometimes, the noise does not bother me; at other times, I wear earplugs. (5) If I am in a very bad mood, I stand on my desk and pound out reggae rhythms on the ceiling with my shoe. (6) However, I do appreciate one thing. (7) The job teaches me to concentrate, no matter what.

(1) Above the office where I worked was a karate studio. (2) Every day as I went through my files, made out invoices, and wrote letters, I heard loud shrieks and crashes from the studio above me. (3) All day long, the walls trembled, the ceiling shook, and little pieces of plaster fell like snow onto my desk. (4) Sometimes, the noise did not bother me; at other times, I wore earplugs. (5) If I was in a very bad mood, I stood on my desk and pounded out reggae rhythms on the ceiling with my shoe. (6) However, I did appreciate one thing. (7) The job taught me to concentrate, no matter what.

PRACTICE 2   REVIEW

Read the following paragraph for meaning. Then fill in a different past tense in every blank.

(1) In 1861, a French naturalist _____*hiked*_____ through a dense jungle of Cambodia in Southeast Asia. (2) He _____*came*_____ to a clearing and _____*looked*_____ across the treetops. (3) He _____*gasped*_____ in amazement. (4) Five enormous towers _____*loomed*_____ above him. (5) With a pounding heart, he _____*ran*_____ to the most gorgeous temple imaginable. (6) He _____*climbed*_____ 250 feet to the top of the highest

*See also Chapter 24, "Consistent Tense," for more practice.

tower. (7) A huge abandoned city _____ *stretched* _____ for miles all around him. (8) Carvings of gods and goddesses _____ *decorated* _____ the palaces and monuments. (9) Unlike the ruins of Greece and Rome, every stone in these buildings _____ *was* _____ in place. (10) Local people _____ *called* _____ this marvelous lost city Angkor. (11) Five hundred years before, it had been the largest city in Asia. (12) Then for unknown reasons, its entire population _____ *disappeared* _____ .

PRACTICE: WRITING ASSIGNMENT

With three or four classmates, invent a group fairy tale. Take five minutes to decide on a subject for your story. On a clean sheet of paper, the first student should write the first sentence—in the past tense, of course. Use vivid action verbs. Each student should write a sentence in turn, until the fairy tale is finished.

Have a group member read your story aloud. As you listen, make sure the verbs are correct. Should any verbs be replaced with livelier ones?

✔ Chapter Highlights

- **Regular verbs add -*d* or -*ed* in the past tense:**

  We *decided*.
  The frog *jumped*.
  He *outfoxed* the fox.

- **Irregular verbs in the past tense change in irregular ways:**

  We *took* a marketing course.
  Owen *ran* fast.
  Jan *brought* dessert.

- ***To be* is the only verb that takes more than one form in the past tense:**

I was	we were
you were	you were
he she it } was	they were

Chapter Review

Fill in the past tense form of each verb in parentheses. Some verbs are regular; others are irregular.

Scientist and Hero

(1) Marie Curie _____*led*_____ (lead) a heroic life. (2) Honored as one of the most brilliant scientists of the twentieth century, she also _____*triumphed*_____ (triumph) over great hardship and loss.

(3) Born in Poland in 1867, Marie Curie _____*began*_____ (begin) life as the daughter of a poor chemistry professor. (4) While a young woman, she _____*postponed*_____ (postpone) her own studies and _____*financed*_____ (finance) her older sister's medical education with the money she _____*earned*_____ (earn) as a governess. (5) Then Marie's turn _____*came*_____ (come). (6) She _____*moved*_____ (move) to Paris in 1891 and _____*became*_____ (become) the first woman to enroll in the Sorbonne, the greatest university in France. (7) For three years, she _____*studied*_____ (study) hard and _____*lived*_____ (live) in poverty. (8) Her work _____*paid*_____ (pay) off. (9) The young scholar _____*graduated*_____ (graduate) first in her class with a degree in physical science. (10) One year later, she _____*completed*_____ (complete) another degree, in mathematics.

(11) The eleven years from 1895 to 1906 _____*were*_____ (be) the happiest of her life. (12) She _____*married*_____ (marry) Pierre Curie, a well-known scientist. (13) The devoted couple _____*raised*_____ (raise) two daughters and _____*worked*_____ (work) together every day on their research in radiation. (14) In 1898, Madame Curie _____*found*_____ (find) two new radioactive elements. (15) One _____*was*_____ (be) radium. (16) The other she _____*called*_____ (call) polonium, after her native land. (17) In 1903, the Curies _____*shared*_____ (share) the Nobel Prize in physics. (18) When the French Legion of Honor _____*offered*_____ (offer) Pierre membership, he _____*refused*_____ (refuse) it because his wife _____*was*_____ (be) left out.

(19) A truck _____struck_____ (strike) and _____killed_____ (kill) Pierre in 1906. (20) This bitter blow _____drove_____ (drive) Madame Curie further into her work. (21) She _____stepped_____ (step) into Pierre's professorship to become the first woman teacher at the Sorbonne. (22) Then, in 1911, she _____achieved_____ (achieve) a second Nobel Prize, this one in chemistry.

(23) During World War I, the world-famous doctor _____risked_____ (risk) her life driving an ambulance and treating soldiers at the battlefront. (24) Later, she _____established_____ (establish) research centers in Paris and Warsaw, _____lectured_____ (lecture) in many countries, and _____continued_____ (continue) her studies. (25) Madame Curie _____died_____ (die) in 1934 of cancer, caused by years of exposure to radioactivity.

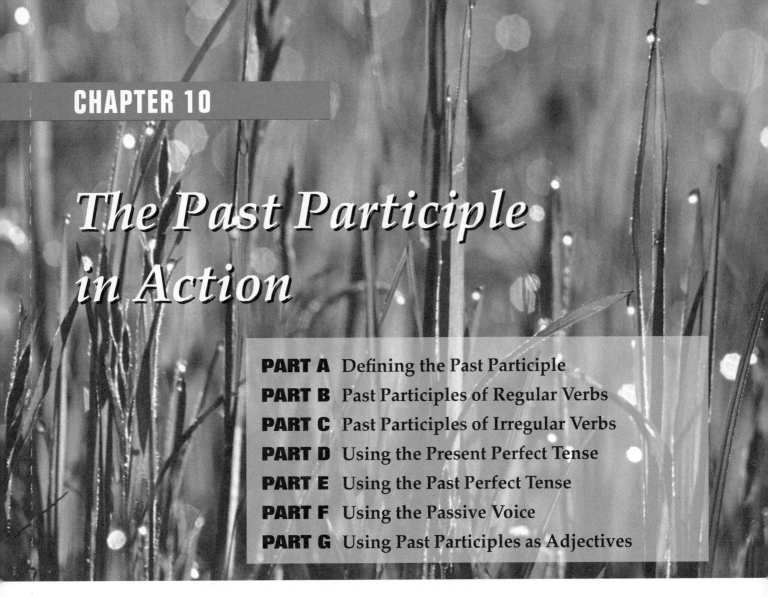

CHAPTER 10

The Past Participle in Action

PART A   Defining the Past Participle

Every verb has one form that can be combined with helping verbs like *has* and *have* to make verbs of more than one word. This form is called the *past participle*.

(1) She has solved the problem.
(2) I have solved the problem.
(3) He had solved the problem already.

■ Each of these sentences contains a two-part verb. Circle the first part, or *helping verb*, in each sentence, and write each helping verb in the blanks that follow:

(1) _____has_____

(2) _____have_____

(3) _____had_____

■ Underline the second part, or *main verb,* in each sentence. This word, a form of the verb *to solve,* is the same in all three. Write it here: _____*solved*_____

■ *Solved* is the past participle of *to solve.*

The past participle never changes, no matter what the subject is, no matter what the helping verb is.

PART B   Past Participles of Regular Verbs

Fill in the past participle in each series below:

Present Tense	Past Tense	Helping Verb + Past Participle
(1) Beth dances.	(1) Beth danced.	(1) Beth has *danced* .
(2) They decide.	(2) They decided.	(2) They have *decided* .
(3) He jumps.	(3) He jumped.	(3) He has *jumped* .

■ Are the verbs *to dance, to decide,* and *to jump* regular or irregular?

_____*regular*_____ How do you know? _*The past tense ends in -d or -ed.*_

■ What ending does each verb take in the past tense? _____*-d or -ed*_____

■ Remember that any verb that forms its past tense by adding *-d* or *-ed* is a *regular* verb. What past participle ending does each verb take?

_____*-d or -ed*_____

The past participle forms of regular verbs look exactly like the past tense forms. Both end in *-d* or *-ed.*

PRACTICE 1

The first sentence in each of these pairs contains a one-word verb in the past tense. Fill in the past participle of the same verb in the blank in the second sentence.

EXAMPLE: She designed jewelry all her life.

She has _____*designed*_____ jewelry all her life.

1. Several students worked in the maternity ward.

   Several students have _____*worked*_____ in the maternity ward.

2. The pot of soup boiled over.

   The pot of soup has _____*boiled*_____ over.

3. The mirror cracked.

   The mirror has _____cracked_____.

4. We congratulated Jorgé.

   We have _____congratulated_____ Jorgé.

5. Nelson always studied in the bathtub.

   Nelson has always _____studied_____ in the bathtub.

6. Many climbers scaled this mountain.

   Many climbers have _____scaled_____ this mountain.

7. The landlord asked for a rent increase.

   The landlord has _____asked_____ for a rent increase.

8. Sylvia tackled the man who took her purse.

   Sylvia has _____tackled_____ the man who took her purse.

9. The satellite circled Jupiter.

   The satellite has _____circled_____ Jupiter.

10. They signed petitions to save the seals.

    They have _____signed_____ petitions to save the seals.

PRACTICE 2

Write the missing two-part verb in each of the following sentences. Use the helping verb *has* or *have* and the past participle of the verb written in parentheses.

EXAMPLE: ___Have___ you ever _____wished_____ (to wish) for a new name?

1. Some of us ___have___ _____wanted_____ (to want) new names at one time or another.

2. Many famous people ___have___ _____fulfilled_____ (to fulfill) that desire.

3. Some ___have___ _____used_____ (to use) only their first names.

4. Madonna Louise Ciccone ___has___ _____dropped_____ (to drop) everything but Madonna.

5. Cherilyn LaPiere ___has___ _____shortened_____ (to shorten) her name to Cher.

6. Prince Roger Nelson ___has___ _____remained_____ (to remain) simply Prince, or recently, The Artist Formerly Known as Prince.

7. Other celebrities _____have_____ _____retained_____ (to retain) their first names and taken new last names.

8. Winona Horowitz _____has_____ _____converted_____ (to convert) her last name to Ryder.

9. Steveland Judkinds _____has_____ _____turned_____ (to turn) into Stevie Wonder.

10. Still others _____have_____ _____replaced_____ (to replace) their names altogether.

11. For many years, Caryn Johnson _____has_____ _____called_____ (to call) herself Whoopi Goldberg.

12. Carlos Irwin Estevez _____has_____ _____transformed_____ (to transform) himself into Charlie Sheen.

13. Annie Mae Bullock _____has_____ _____renamed_____ (to rename) herself Tina Turner.

14. Gordon Matthew Sumner _____has_____ _____changed_____ (to change) into Sting.

15. What new name would you _____have_____ _____picked_____ (to pick) for yourself?

PART C   Past Participles of Irregular Verbs

Present Tense	Past Tense	Helping Verb + Past Participle
(1) He sees.	(1) He saw.	(1) He has seen.
(2) I take vitamins.	(2) I took vitamins.	(2) I have taken vitamins.
(3) We sing.	(3) We sang.	(3) We have sung.

■ Are the verbs *to see, to take,* and *to sing* regular or irregular? _____irregular_____

■ Like all irregular verbs, *to see, to take,* and *to sing* do not add *-d* or *-ed* to show past tense.

■ Most irregular verbs in the past tense are also irregular in the past participle—like *seen, taken,* and *sung.*

■ Remember that past participles must be used with helping verbs.*

    Because irregular verbs change their spelling in irregular ways, there are no easy rules to explain these changes. Here is a list of some common irregular verbs.

———

*For work on incomplete verbs, see Chapter 7, Part B.

Reference Chart: Irregular Verbs

Simple Form	Past	Past Participle
be	was, were	been
become	became	become
begin	began	begun
blow	blew	blown
break	broke	broken
bring	brought	brought
build	built	built
buy	bought	bought
catch	caught	caught
choose	chose	chosen
come	came	come
cut	cut	cut
dive	dove (dived)	dived
do	did	done
draw	drew	drawn
drink	drank	drunk
drive	drove	driven
eat	ate	eaten
fall	fell	fallen
feed	fed	fed
feel	felt	felt
fight	fought	fought
find	found	found
fly	flew	flown
forget	forgot	forgotten
forgive	forgave	forgiven
freeze	froze	frozen
get	got	gotten (got)
give	gave	given
go	went	gone
grow	grew	grown
have	had	had
hear	heard	heard
hide	hid	hidden
hold	held	held

Reference Chart: Irregular Verbs (*continued*)

Simple Form	Past	Past Participle
hurt	hurt	hurt
keep	kept	kept
know	knew	known
lay	laid	laid
lead	led	led
leave	left	left
let	let	let
lie	lay	lain
lose	lost	lost
make	made	made
mean	meant	meant
meet	met	met
pay	paid	paid
put	put	put
quit	quit	quit
read	read	read
ride	rode	ridden
ring	rang	rung
rise	rose	risen
run	ran	run
say	said	said
see	saw	seen
seek	sought	sought
sell	sold	sold
send	sent	sent
set	set	set
shake	shook	shaken
shine	shone (shined)	shone (shined)
sing	sang	sung
sit	sat	sat
sleep	slept	slept
speak	spoke	spoken
spend	spent	spent
spring	sprang	sprung

Reference Chart: Irregular Verbs (*continued*)

Simple Form	Past	Past Participle
stand	stood	stood
steal	stole	stolen
strike	struck	struck
swim	swam	swum
take	took	taken
teach	taught	taught
tear	tore	torn
tell	told	told
think	thought	thought
throw	threw	thrown
understand	understood	understood
wake	woke (waked)	woken (waked)
wear	wore	worn
win	won	won
wind	wound	wound
write	wrote	written

You already know many of these past participle forms. One way to learn the unfamiliar ones is to group together verbs that change from the past tense to the present participle in the same way. For example, some irregular verbs change from *ow* in the present to *ew* in the past to *own* in the past participle.

bl<u>ow</u>	bl<u>ew</u>	bl<u>own</u>
gr<u>ow</u>	gr<u>ew</u>	gr<u>own</u>
kn<u>ow</u>	kn<u>ew</u>	kn<u>own</u>
thr<u>ow</u>	thr<u>ew</u>	thr<u>own</u>

Another group changes from *i* in the present to *a* in the past to *u* in the past participle:

beg<u>i</u>n	beg<u>a</u>n	beg<u>u</u>n
dr<u>i</u>nk	dr<u>a</u>nk	dr<u>u</u>nk
r<u>i</u>ng	r<u>a</u>ng	r<u>u</u>ng
s<u>i</u>ng	s<u>a</u>ng	s<u>u</u>ng
spr<u>i</u>ng	spr<u>a</u>ng	spr<u>u</u>ng
sw<u>i</u>m	sw<u>a</u>m	sw<u>u</u>m

As you write, refer to the chart. If you are unsure of the past participle form of a verb that is not on the chart, check a dictionary. For example, if you look up the verb *see* in the dictionary, you will find an entry like this:

see \ saw \ seen \ seeing

The first word listed is the present tense form of the verb (*I see, she sees,* and so on). The second word listed is the past tense form (*I saw, she saw,* and so on). The third word is the past participle form (*I have seen, she has seen,* and so on), and the last word is the present participle form.

Some dictionaries list different forms only for irregular verbs. If no past tense or past participle form is listed, you know that the verb is regular and that its past participle ends in *-d* or *-ed.*

PRACTICE 1

The first sentence in each pair contains an irregular verb in the past tense. Fill in *has* or *have* plus the past participle of the same verb to complete the second sentence.

EXAMPLE: I ate too much.

I ___have___ ___eaten___ too much.

1. The river rose over its banks.

   The river ___has___ ___risen___ over its banks.

2. She earned eighteen credits this term.

   She ___has___ ___earned___ eighteen credits this term.

3. For years, we sang in a gospel group.

   For years, we ___have___ ___sung___ in a gospel group.

4. Crime rates fell recently.

   Crime rates ___have___ ___fallen___ recently.

5. Ralph gave me a red satin bowling jacket.

   Ralph ___has___ ___given___ me a red satin bowling jacket.

6. They thought carefully about the problem.

   They ___have___ ___thought___ carefully about the problem.

7. I kept all your love letters.

   I ___have___ ___kept___ all your love letters.

8. The Joneses forgot to confirm the reservation.

   The Joneses ___have___ ___forgotten___ to confirm the reservation.

9. San Diego grew quickly.

   San Diego ___has___ ___grown___ quickly.

10. The children knew about these caves.

    The children ___have___ ___known___ about these caves.

PRACTICE 2

Now you will be given only the first sentence with its one-word verb in the past tense. Rewrite the entire sentence, changing the verb to a two-word verb: *has* or *have* plus the past participle of the main verb.

EXAMPLE: He took his credit cards with him.

He has taken his credit cards with him.

1. They brought their Great Dane to the party.

   They have brought their Great Dane to the party.

2. T. J. drove a city bus for two years.

   T. J. has driven a city bus for two years.

3. She paid cash for a cellular phone.

   She has paid cash for a cellular phone.

4. I saw a white fox near the barn.

   I have seen a white fox near the barn.

5. A tornado tore through the shopping center.

   A tornado has torn through the shopping center.

6. Margo became more self-confident.

   Margo has become more self-confident.

7. Councilman Gomez ran a fair campaign.

   Councilman Gomez has run a fair campaign.

8. The old barn stood there for years.

   The old barn has stood there for years.

9. Spring came to New England.

   Spring has come to New England.

10. Our conversations were helpful.

    Our conversations have been helpful.

For each verb in the chart that follows, fill in the present tense (third person singular form), the past tense, and the past participle. BE CAREFUL: Some of the verbs are regular, and some are irregular.

Simple	Present Tense (he, she, it)	Past Tense	Past Participle
know	knows	knew	known
catch	catches	caught	caught
stop	stops	stopped	stopped
break	breaks	broke	broken
reach	reaches	reached	reached
bring	brings	brought	brought
fly	flies	flew	flown
fall	falls	fell	fallen
feel	feels	felt	felt
take	takes	took	taken
go	goes	went	gone
see	sees	saw	seen
do	does	did	done
buy	buys	bought	bought
make	makes	made	made
answer	answers	answered	answered
hold	holds	held	held
say	says	said	said

Complete each sentence by filling in the helping verb *has* or *have* and the past participle of the verb in parentheses. Some verbs are regular, and some are irregular.

EXAMPLES: Millions ___*have*___ ___*heard*___ (hear) her sing.

She ___*has*___ ___*used*___ (use) words and music to connect

with others.

Gloria Estefan

(1) Singer Gloria Estefan ___*has*___ ___*inspired*___ (inspire)

millions of fans. (2) Since she joined the Miami Sound Machine in 1975, her

albums ___*have*___ ___*sold*___ (sell) millions of copies, and rousing

songs like "Rhythm of the Night" ___*have*___ ___*taken*___ (take) their

place in the memory banks of a generation. (3) For more than twenty years,

Gloria and her husband, Emilio Estefan, ___*have*___ ___*been*___ (be)

marriage partners as well as business partners.

(4) Yet Gloria ___*has*___ ___*endured*___ (endure) many hardships.

(5) Born in Cuba in 1957, she ___*has*___ ___*seen*___ (see) her father

imprisoned for political activities, and she ___*has*___ ___*known*___

(know) poverty. (6) After fleeing with her family to Miami, she often stayed home

to care for her sister and her dying father while her mother worked. (7) Ever since

those early years, however, Gloria ___*has*___ ___*found*___ (find)

strength in music—in singing and playing her guitar.

(8) Her talent ___*has*___ ___*turned*___ (turn) misfortune into real

fortune. (9) She and Emilio ___*have*___ ___*become*___ (become) rich in

friends as well as in material things. (10) But this is not a fairy tale: A 1990 bus tour

accident broke Gloria's back, and she ___*has*___ ___*suffered*___ (suffer)

through pain, 400 stitches, and two metal rods near her spine. (11) Her song

"Coming Out of the Dark" captures the spiritual power she ___*has*___

___*relied*___ (rely) on all her life.

(12) Recently, Gloria Estefan ___*has*___ ___*raised*___ (raise)

money for hurricane victims and ___*has*___ ___*volunteered*___ (volunteer) her time to publicize the dangers of jet skis (after a young man died racing a jet

ski into her boat). (13) She ___*has*___ ___*won*___ (win) two

Grammies, one for best Tropical Latin album, and she ___*has*___

___*written*___ (write) a song for the Olympics, "Reach."

PRACTICE 5   REVIEW

Now check your work in the preceding exercises, or have it checked. Do you see
any patterns in your errors? Do you tend to miss regular or irregular verbs? To help
yourself learn, copy all four forms of each verb that you missed into a chart like this
in your notebook, and use it to study.

Personal Review Chart

Simple	Present Tense (he, she, it)	Past Tense	Past Participle
go	*goes*	*went*	*gone*

PART D   Using the Present Perfect Tense

The *present perfect tense* is composed of the present tense of *to have (has* or *have)* plus
the past participle.

Present Perfect Tense

Singular	Plural
I *have* spoken	we *have* spoken
you *have* spoken	you *have* spoken
he she } *has* spoken it	they *have* spoken

Let us see how this tense is used.

(1) They *sang* together last Saturday.

(2) They *have sung* together for three years now.

■ In sentence (1), the past tense verb *sang* tells us that they sang together on one occasion, Saturday, but are no longer singing together. The action began and ended in the past.

■ In sentence (2), the present perfect verb *have sung* tells us something entirely different: that they have sung together in the past and *are still singing together now*.

(3) Janet *sat* on the beach for three hours.

(4) Valerie *has* just *sat* on the beach for three hours.

■ Which woman is probably still sunburned? _____*Valerie*_____

■ In sentence (3), Janet's action began and ended at some time in the past. Perhaps it was ten years ago that she sat on the beach.

■ In (4), the present perfect verb *has sat* implies that, although the action occurred in the past, it *has just happened*, and Valerie had better put some lotion on her sunburn *now*.

■ Notice how the word *just* emphasizes that the action occurred very recently.

Use the *present perfect tense* to show either (1) that an action began in the past and has continued until now or (2) that an action has just happened.

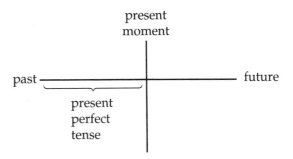

In writing about an action that began in the past and is still continuing, you will often use time words like *for* and *since.*

(5) We have watched the fireworks *for* three hours.

(6) John has sung in the choir *since* 1980.

In writing about an action that has just happened, you will often use words like *just, recently, already,* and *yet.*

(7) I have *just* finished the novel.

(8) They have *already* gone to the party.

PRACTICE 1

Paying close attention to meaning, circle the verb that best completes each sentence.

EXAMPLES: In recent years, many unusual museums (appeared, (have appeared).) For example, the International Museum of Cartoon Art first ((opened,) has opened) in 1974 in Greenwich, Connecticut.

1. The idea for the museum ((came,) has come) from cartoonist Mort Walker, the creator of "Beetle Bailey."

2. In the beginning, his museum ((had,) has had) only a small collection of original cartoons.

3. However, since 1974, the collection (grew, (has grown)) to include valuable first drawings of Mickey Mouse, Batman, Flash Gordon, Road Runner, Dumbo, Popeye, Garfield, and many others.

4. In 1995, the museum ((moved,) has moved) to a beautiful new building in Boca Raton, Florida.

5. For the past several years, visitors (laughed, (have laughed)) at classic comic books, cartoon movies, and the interactive Laugh Center.

6. Another interesting museum, the Bata Shoe Museum in Toronto, Canada, ((gained,) has gained) worldwide attention in 1995.

7. For years now, the Bata (held, (has held)) the world's largest collection of shoes.

8. In 1995, the museum ((moved,) has moved) its huge shoe collection into a new building shaped like a shoebox!

9. On a recent day, Elvis Presley's blue and white loafers, John Lennon's Beatle boot, and Queen Victoria's ivory satin flats ((seemed,) have seemed) to be the favorite items on view.

10. However, several history students never ((got,) have gotten) past the Bata's world-famous exhibit of Native American footwear.

PRACTICE 2

Fill in either the *past* tense or the *present perfect* tense form of each verb in parentheses.

(1) Lisa Rogers ____has worked____ (to work) as a nutritionist in the public schools since 1996. (2) That was the year her son first ____complained____ (to complain) about the poor quality of food in the school cafeteria. (3) Lisa ____applied____ (to apply) for a job as a nutritional adviser and ____got____ (to get) it. (4) Since then, she ____has taught____ (to teach) nutrition courses for staff members. (5) Lisa's hard work ____has paid____ (to pay) off. (6) Last year, her school system ____won____ (to win) an award for its excellent food.

PART E
Using the Past Perfect Tense

The *past perfect tense* is composed of the past tense of *to have (had)* plus the past participle.

Past Perfect Tense

Singular	**Plural**
I *had* spoken	we *had* spoken
you *had* spoken	you *had* spoken
he she } *had* spoken it	they *had* spoken

Let us see how this tense is used.

> (1) Because Bob *had broken* his leg, he *wore* a cast for six months.

■ The actions in both parts of this sentence occurred entirely in the past, but one occurred before the other.

■ At some time in the past, Bob *wore* (past tense) a cast on the leg that he *had broken* (past perfect tense) at some time before that.

When you are writing in the past tense, use the past perfect tense to show that something happened at an even earlier time.

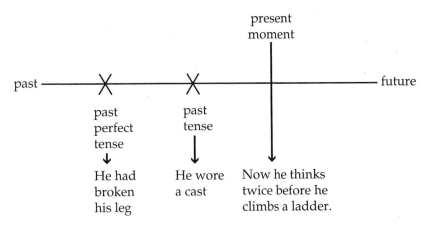

As a general rule, the present perfect tense is used in relation to the present tense, and the past perfect tense is used in relation to the past tense. Read the following pairs of sentences, and note the time relation.

> (2) Sid *says* (present) he *has found* (present perfect) a good job.
> (3) Sid *said* (past) he *had found* (past perfect) a good job.
>
> (4) Grace *tells* (present) us she *has won* (present perfect) first prize.
> (5) Grace *told* (past) us she *had won* (past perfect) first prize.

PRACTICE

Choose either the present perfect or the past perfect tense of the verb in parentheses to complete each sentence. Match present perfect tense with present tense and past perfect tense with past tense.

1. The newspaper reports that the dictator ___*has*___ ___*left*___ (to leave) the country.

2. The newspaper reported that the dictator ___*had*___ ___*left*___ (to leave) the country.

3. I plan to buy a red convertible; I ___*have*___ ___*wanted*___ (to want) a convertible for three years now.

4. Last year, I bought a red convertible; I ___*had*___ ___*wanted*___ (to want) a convertible for three years before that.

5. Jerry ___*had*___ ___*forgotten*___ (to forget) to pay his electric bill; he was unable to watch the news.

6. Jerry ___*has*___ ___*forgotten*___ (to forget) to pay his electric bill; he is unable to watch the news.

7. I am worried about my cat; she ___*has*___ ___*drunk*___ (to drink) bubble bath.

8. I was worried about my cat; she ___*had*___ ___*drunk*___ (to drink) bubble bath.

9. Sam told us he ___*had*___ ___*decided*___ (to decide) to major in English literature.

10. Sam tells us he ___*has*___ ___*decided*___ (to decide) to major in English literature.

PART F   Using the Passive Voice

So far in this chapter, you have combined the past participle with forms of *to have*. But the past participle also can be used with forms of *to be (am, is, are, was, were)*.

> (1) That jam was made by Aunt Clara.

■ The subject of the sentence is *that jam*. The verb has two parts: the helping verb *was* and the past participle *made*.

■ Note that the subject, *that jam*, does not act but is acted on by the verb. *By Aunt Clara* tells us who performed the action.

That jam *was made* by Aunt Clara.

When the subject is acted on or receives the action, it is passive, and the verb *(to be + past participle)* **is in the** *passive voice.*

Singular/plural
Somewhere

e voice with the active voice in these pairs of sentences:

ee gifts are given by the bank.

.he bank gives free gifts.

ice: We were robbed by a street gang.

voice: *A street gang robbed us.*

sentence (2), the subject, *free gifts,* is passive; it receives the action. In sen-
ence (3), *the bank* is active; it performs the action.

Note the difference between the passive verb *are given* and the active verb
gives.

■ However, the tense of both sentences is the same. The passive verb *are given* is
in the present tense, and so is the active verb *gives.*

■ Rewrite sentence (4) in the active voice. Be sure to keep the same verb tense in
the new sentence!

**Write in the passive voice only when you want to emphasize the receiver of the
action rather than the doer. Usually, however, write in the active voice because
sentences in the active voice are livelier and more direct.**

PRACTICE 1

Underline the verb in each sentence. In the blank at the right, write *A* if the verb is
written in the active voice and *P* if the verb is in the passive voice.

EXAMPLE: Nelson Mandela is respected worldwide as a leader.   *P*

1. Nelson Mandela was born in South Africa on July 18, 1918, a member
    of the Xhosa tribe.   *P*

2. Under the apartheid government, only whites enjoyed basic rights,
    not the black majority.   *A*

3. As a young lawyer, Mandela defended many black clients.   *A*

4. They were charged with such crimes as "not owning land" or "living
    in the wrong area."   *P*

5. Several times, Mandela was arrested for working with the African
    National Congress, a civil rights group.   *P*

6. In 1961, he sadly gave up his lifelong belief in nonviolence.   *A*

7. Training guerrilla fighters, he was imprisoned again, this time with a
    life sentence.   *P*

8. Thirty years in jail did not break Mandela.   *A*

9. Offered freedom to give up his beliefs, he said no.   *A*

10. Finally released in 1990, this man became a symbol of hope for a new
    South Africa.   *A*

11. In 1994, black and white South Africans <u>lined</u> up to vote in the first free elections. *A*

12. Gray-haired, iron-willed Nelson Mandela <u>was elected</u> president of his beloved country. *P*

PRACTICE 2

In each sentence, underline both parts of the passive verb, and circle the subject. Then draw an arrow from the verb to the word or words it acts on.

EXAMPLE: (I) <u>was approached</u> by a lost tourist.

1. (The skaters) <u>were applauded</u> vigorously by the crowd.

2. (The corn) <u>is picked</u> fresh every morning.

3. (These flowered bowls) <u>were imported</u> from Mexico.

4. (Milos, my cat,) <u>was ignored</u> by the mouse.

5. (Truer words) <u>were</u> never <u>spoken</u>.

6. (An antique train set) <u>was sold</u> at the auction.

7. (The computer) <u>was understood</u> by only one person.

8. (Customers) <u>are lured</u> into the store by loud music and bright signs.

9. (Dutch) <u>is spoken</u> on Curaçao.

10. (Our quarrel) <u>was</u> quickly <u>forgotten</u>.

PRACTICE 3

Rewrite each sentence, changing the verb into the passive voice. Make all necessary verb and subject changes. Be sure to keep each sentence in the original tense.

EXAMPLE: Smith broke the world record.

The world record was broken by Smith.

1. Thick makeup hides her beauty.

Her beauty is hidden by thick makeup.

2. Elton John first sang the song.

The song was first sung by Elton John.

3. The FDA took that drug off the market.

   That drug was taken off the market by the FDA.

4. My grandmother wore this wedding dress.

   This wedding dress was worn by my grandmother.

5. Your comments encouraged me.

   I was encouraged by your comments.

PRACTICE 4

Rewrite each sentence, changing the verb from the passive to the active voice. Make all necessary verb and subject changes. Be sure to keep each sentence in the original tense.

EXAMPLE: Corn was popped by Native Americans more than five hundred

years ago. *Native Americans popped corn more than five hundred years ago.*

1. In fact, popcorn was made by Native American women in many different

   ways. *In fact, Native American women made popcorn in many different ways.*

   _____

2. Bags of popcorn were brought to the first Thanksgiving by the Wampanoag

   guests. *The Wampanoag guests brought bags of popcorn to the first Thanksgiving.*

   _____

3. In 1907, the first electric corn popper was manufactured by an American

   company. *In 1907, an American company manufactured the first electric corn*

   popper.

4. By 1947, the snack was sold in movie houses all over the country.

   By 1947, movie houses all over the country sold the snack.

5. Now over one billion dollars' worth of popcorn is munched by Americans

   each year. *Now Americans munch over one billion dollars' worth of popcorn each*

   year.

PART G   Using Past Participles as Adjectives

Sometimes the past participle is not a verb at all, but an *adjective,* a word that describes a noun or pronoun.*

> (1) Jay is *married.*
> (2) The *broken* window looks terrible.
> (3) Two *tired* students slept in the hall.

- ■ In sentence (1), *married* is the past participle of the verb *to marry,* but here it is not a verb. Instead, it describes the subject, *Jay.*

- ■ *Is* links the subject, *Jay,* with the descriptive word, *married.*

- ■ In sentence (2), *broken* is the past participle form of *to break,* but it is used as an adjective to describe the noun *window.*

- ■ In sentence (3), what past participle is an adjective? _____ *tired* _____

- ■ Which word does it describe? _____ *students* _____

Past participles like *married, broken,* and *tired* are often used as adjectives.

Some form of the verb *to be* usually links descriptive past participles with the subjects they describe, but here are a few other common linking verbs that you learned in Chapter 6, Part E.

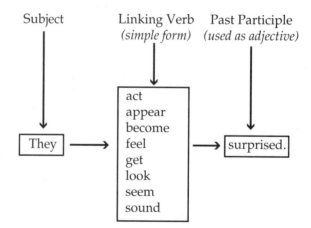

PRACTICE 1

Underline the linking verb in each sentence. Then circle the descriptive past participle or participles that complete the sentences.

EXAMPLES: The window <u>was</u> (polish, polished).

Harry <u>seems</u> very (worry, worried) these days.

1. This product <u>is</u> (guarantee, guaranteed) not to explode.
2. Nellie <u>seems</u> (qualify, qualified) for the job.

---

*For more work on adjectives, see Chapter 22.

3. My employer appears (prejudice, prejudiced).

4. After we read the chapter, we were still (confuse, confused).

5. The science laboratory is (air-condition, air-conditioned).

6. David feels (trap, trapped) in a low-paying job.

7. Did you know that one out of two American couples gets (divorce, divorced)?

8. We were (thrill, thrilled) to see Niagara Falls.

9. During the holidays, Paul feels (depress, depressed).

10. She is (interest, interested) in women's history.

11. You look so (dignify, dignified) in that tuxedo.

12. The garnet ring she wore was (borrow, borrowed).

13. I can't help you; my hands are (tie, tied).

14. Are the potatoes (fry, fried) (bake, baked) or (boil, boiled)?

15. After the trip, we felt (rest, rested) (pamper, pampered) and (relax, relaxed).

PRACTICE 2

Below is a list of verbs. Use the past participles of the verbs as adjectives, to describe each noun in the exercise. Then use your adjective-noun combination in a sentence. Use a different past participle for each noun.

bore	freeze	park	train
delight	hide	pollute	wear
dry	lose	tire	worry
embarrass	mask	toast	wrinkle

EXAMPLE: the _____dried_____ fruit

We served the dried fruit for dessert.

1. a(n) _____masked_____ bandit

   A masked bandit held up the stagecoach.

2. a(n) _____wrinkled_____ sheet

   The laundry basket held only a wrinkled sheet.

3. the _____polluted_____ river

   No one could swim in the polluted river.

4. a(n) _____worried_____ man

   A worried man searched the bus for his wallet.

5. the _____*hidden*_____ emeralds

   Indiana Jones could not find the hidden emeralds.

6. these _____*frozen*_____ muffins

   Please defrost these frozen muffins.

7. that _____*tired*_____ bear

   I remember when that old, tired bear was a cub.

8. a(n) _____*trained*_____ nurse

   A trained nurse must give the blood transfusion.

9. several _____*parked*_____ cars

   Several parked cars lined the narrow street.

10. a(n) _____*bored*_____ woman

    A bored woman balanced her checkbook throughout the meeting.

PRACTICE 3

Proofread the following ad copy for past participle errors. First, underline all the past participles. Then make any corrections above the line.

        pleased
(1) We are <u>please</u> to introduce three automobiles this year, each one <u>created</u> by our
experienced
<u>experience</u> team of engineers. (2) Our racy new sport model, the Hormone, is
                              equipped
<u>guaranteed</u> to provide adventure on the road. (3) It comes <u>equip</u> with a powerful
               steel-belted
fuel-<u>injected</u> engine, steel-<u>belt</u> tires, and orange flames <u>painted</u> across the hood.

(4) Growing families will prefer the Sesame ST. (5) Blue and modest on the out-
                made
side, the Sesame ST's interior is <u>make</u> for parents and children. (6) Its plastic

upholstery is <u>printed</u> with yellow Big Bird designs. (7) Pop-out soda and ham-
        preinstalled   *programmed*
burger holders come <u>preinstall</u>, and the sound system is <u>program</u> for soft rock

only, so your kids can't tune in to grunge, hard rock, or rap stations. (8) For the
                       equipped
budget-<u>minded</u> car shopper, we offer the Chintz. (9) It comes <u>equip</u> with a two-
                          named
cylinder engine, steering wheel, and seats. (10) Recently the Chintz was <u>name</u> "the

car that gives you less for less" on "The Tonight Show with Jay Leno."

PRACTICE 4

Combine each pair of short sentences. First, find and underline the past participle. Then rewrite the two short sentences as one smooth sentence, using the past participle as an adjective.

EXAMPLE: The book is lost. It is worth $1,000.

The lost book is worth $1,000.

1. The car was rented. Desi drove it into a fence.

   Desi drove the rented car into a fence.

2. This rug has been dry-cleaned. It looks new.

   This dry-cleaned rug looks new.

3. Your wallet was stolen. It is at the police station.

   Your stolen wallet is at the police station.

4. The envelope was sealed. Harriet opened it.

   Harriet opened the sealed envelope.

5. The player was injured. The coach took him out of the game.

   The coach took the injured player out of the game.

6. Your report is typed. It looks very neat.

   Your typed report looks very neat.

7. This bowl is broken. Can you fix it?

   Can you fix this broken bowl?

8. The weather forecast was revised. It calls for sunshine.

   The revised weather forecast calls for sunshine.

9. These gold chains are overpriced. Do not buy them.

   Do not buy these overpriced gold chains.

10. The box was locked. Divers brought it to the surface.

    Divers brought the locked box to the surface.

PRACTICE 5

The sentences in the left column are in the present tense; those in the right column are in the past tense. If the sentence is shown in the present tense on the left, write the sentence in the past tense on the right, and vice versa. REMEMBER: Only the *linking verb,* never the past participle, changes to show tense.

Present Tense	**Past Tense**
EXAMPLES: Smoking is forbidden.	Smoking was forbidden.
Lunches are served.	Lunches were served.
1. Your piano is tuned.	1. Your piano was tuned.
2. The store looks closed.	2. The store looked closed.
3. My feelings are hurt.	3. My feelings were hurt.
4. The seats are filled.	4. The seats were filled.
5. She is relaxed.	5. She was relaxed.
6. You seem qualified for the job.	6. You seemed qualified for the job.
7. He is supposed to meet us.*	7. He was supposed to meet us.
8. She is used to city life.*	8. She was used to city life.
9. It is written in longhand.	9. It was written in longhand.
10. You are expected to win.	10. You were expected to win.

PRACTICE: WRITING ASSIGNMENT

In a group of four or five classmates, write a wacky restaurant menu, using all the past participles as adjectives that you can think of: *steamed* fern roots, *fried* cherries, *caramel-coated* hamburgers, and so forth. Brainstorm. Get creative. Then arrange your menu in an order that makes sense (if that is the correct term for such a menu!).

---

* For more work on *supposed* and *used,* see Chapter 32, "Look-alikes/Sound-alikes."

✔ Chapter Highlights

■ Past participles of regular verbs add *-d* or *-ed*, just like their past tense forms:

Present	Past	Past Participle
decide	decided	decided
jump	jumped	jumped

■ Past participles of irregular verbs change in irregular ways:

Present	Past	Past Participle
bring	brought	brought
see	saw	seen
take	took	taken

■ Past participles can combine with *to have:*

He *has edited* many articles for us. *(present perfect tense)*

He *had edited* many articles for us. *(past perfect tense)*

■ Past participles can combine with *to be:*

The report *was edited* by Mary. *(passive voice)*

■ Past participles can be used as adjectives:

The *edited* report arrived today. *(adjective)*

Chapter Review

Proofread this student's essay for past participle errors. Then correct each error above the line.

Three Ways to Learn Smarter

(1) Once in a while, a rare person is born with a photographic memory, allowing him or her to memorize lots of information with almost no effort.
            struggled
(2) However, most of us have struggle on our own to find the best ways to learn.
                                                                            marked
(3) We have stayed up all night studying. (4) We have mark up our textbooks,
                                       skilled
highlighting and underlining like skill tattoo artists. (5) Maybe, in frustration, we

have even questioned our own intelligence. (6) Although everyone has his or her
                                                    made
own learning style, three techniques have make me and others better learners.

(7) The first technique is simple—sit at the front of the class! (8) A student
      chosen   *involved*
who has choose to sit up front is more likely to stay alert and involve than

students at the back and sides. (9) By sitting away from windows or talkative friends, many students discover that they take a greater interest in the classroom subject and take better notes. (10) An extra benefit of sitting up front is that teach-

impressed

ers are often <u>impress</u> by students with whom they make eye contact, students whose behavior says, "I care about this class."

(11) Second, make a smart friend. (12) During the first week of class, exchange phone numbers with another front-row student. (13) You are looking for an intelligent, responsible classmate who seems committed to learning—not

agreed

for a pizza buddy or a date. (14) Students who have <u>agree</u> in advance to help each

discussed

other can call if they miss a class. (15) What was <u>discuss</u> that day? (16) Was home-

assigned

work <u>assign</u> or a test announced? (17) Two students who "click" might want to become study partners, meeting regularly to review material and prepare for tests.

sat

(18) Third, ask questions. (19) The student who has <u>sit</u> up front, made a

paid

study friend, and <u>pay</u> close attention in class should not be worried about asking the professor questions. (20) Learning a subject is like building a tower. (21) Each

built

new level of understanding must be <u>build</u> solidly on the level below. (22) If an important point or term is unclear, ask for help, in or after class.

increased

(23) Students who use these techniques will be rewarded with <u>increase</u>

pulled

understanding and better grades. (24) And they haven't even <u>pull</u> out their pastel highlighters.

Maurice Jabbar, student

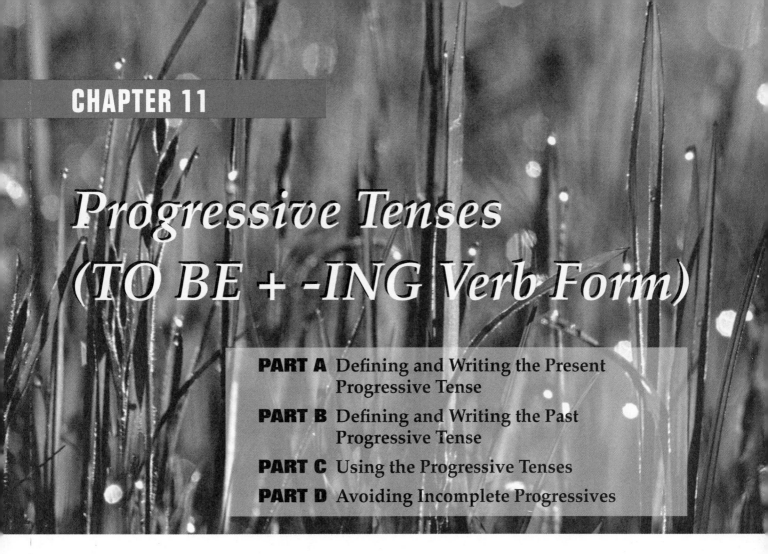

CHAPTER 11

Progressive Tenses (TO BE + -ING Verb Form)

PART A Defining and Writing the Present Progressive Tense

Verbs in the *present progressive tense* have two parts: the present tense form of *to be* (*am, is, are*) plus the *-ing* (or present participle) form of the main verb.

Present Progressive Tense	
(example verb: to play)	
Singular	**Plural**
I am playing	we are playing
you are playing	you are playing
he ⎫	
she ⎬ is playing	they are playing
it ⎭	

Compare the present tense with the present progressive tense below.

> (1) Larry works at the bookstore.
>
> (2) Larry is working at the bookstore.

■ Sentence (1) is in the present tense. Which word tells you this?

_____works_____

■ Sentence (2) is also in the present tense. Which word tells you this?

_____is_____

■ Note that the main verb in sentence (2), *working,* has no tense. Only the helping verb *is* shows tense.

PRACTICE 1

Change each one-word present tense verb in the left-hand column to a two-part present progressive verb in the right-hand column. Do this by filling in the missing helping verb (*am, is,* or *are*).

Present Tense	**Present Progressive Tense**
EXAMPLES: I fly.	I ____am____ flying.
He wears my sweater.	He ____is____ wearing my sweater.
1. Elsa and I set goals together.	1. Elsa and I ____are____ setting goals together.
2. You write rapidly.	2. You ____are____ writing rapidly.
3. He plans the wedding.	3. He ____is____ planning the wedding.
4. Our work begins to pay off.	4. Our work ____is____ beginning to pay off.
5. We pose for the photographer.	5. We ____are____ posing for the photographer.
6. Maryann smiles.	6. Maryann ____is____ smiling.
7. Sal does his Elvis impression.	7. Sal ____is____ doing his Elvis impression.
8. I speak Portuguese to Manuel.	8. I ____am____ speaking Portuguese to Manuel.
9. Frank gets lazy.	9. Frank ____is____ getting lazy.
10. You probably wonder why.	10. You ____are____ probably wondering why.

REMEMBER: Every verb in the present progressive tense must have two parts: a helping verb (*am, is,* or *are*) and a main verb ending in *-ing*. The helping verb must agree with the subject.

PRACTICE 2

Below are sentences in the regular present tense. Rewrite each one in the present progressive tense by changing the verb to *am, is,* or *are* plus the *-ing* form of the main verb.

EXAMPLE: We play cards.

We are playing cards.

1. The telephone rings.

   The telephone is ringing.

2. Dexter wrestles with his math homework.

   Dexter is wrestling with his math homework.

3. James and Judy work in the emergency room.

   James and Judy are working in the emergency room.

4. I keep a journal of thoughts and observations.

   I am keeping a journal of thoughts and observations.

5. We build a house.

   We are building a house.

PART B — Defining and Writing the Past Progressive Tense

Verbs in the *past progressive tense* have two parts: the past tense form of *to be* (*was* or *were*) plus the *-ing* form of the main verb.

Past Progressive Tense
(example verb: to play)

Singular	Plural
I was playing	we were playing
you were playing	you were playing
he she it } was playing	they were playing

Compare the past tense with the past progressive tense below.

> (1) Larry worked at the bookstore.
>
> (2) Larry was working at the bookstore.

■ Sentence (1) is in the past tense. Which word tells you this?

___worked___

■ Sentence (2) is also in the past tense. Which word tells you this?

___was___

■ Notice that the main verb in sentence (2), *working,* has no tense. Only the helping verb *was* shows tense.

PRACTICE 1

Change each one-word past tense verb in the left-hand column to a two-part past progressive verb in the right-hand column. Do this by filling in the missing helping verb (*was* or *were*).

Past Tense	**Past Progressive Tense**
EXAMPLES: I flew.	I ___was___ flying.
He wore my sweater.	He ___was___ wearing my sweater.
1. Elsa and I set goals together.	1. Elsa and I ___were___ setting goals together.
2. You wrote rapidly.	2. You ___were___ writing rapidly.
3. He planned the wedding.	3. He ___was___ planning the wedding.
4. Our work began to pay off.	4. Our work ___was___ beginning to pay off.
5. We posed for the photographer.	5. We ___were___ posing for the photographer.
6. Maryann smiled.	6. Maryann ___was___ smiling.
7. Sal did his Elvis impression.	7. Sal ___was___ doing his Elvis impression.
8. I spoke Portuguese to Manuel.	8. I ___was___ speaking Portuguese to Manuel.
9. Frank got lazy.	9. Frank ___was___ getting lazy.
10. You probably wondered why.	10. You ___were___ probably wondering why.

PRACTICE 2

Below are sentences in the past tense. Rewrite each sentence in the past progressive tense by changing the verb to *was* or *were* plus the *-ing* form of the main verb.

EXAMPLE: You cooked dinner.

You were cooking dinner.

1. The two linebackers growled at each other.

   The two linebackers were growling at each other.

2. Leroy examined his bank receipt.

   Leroy was examining his bank receipt.

3. We watched the news.

   We were watching the news.

4. Marsha read the *Wall Street Journal*.

   Marsha was reading the Wall Street Journal.

5. He acted like a patient, not a doctor!

   He was acting like a patient, not a doctor!

PART C   Using the Progressive Tenses

As you read these sentences, do you hear the differences in meaning?

> (1) Lenore *plays* the piano.
>
> (2) Al *is playing* the piano.

■ Which person is definitely at the keyboard right now?

■ If you said Al, you are right. He is *now in the process of playing* the piano. Lenore, on the other hand, *does* play the piano; she may also paint, write novels, and play center field, but we do not know from the sentence what she *is doing right now.*

■ The present progressive verb *is playing* tells us that the action is *in progress.*

Here is another use of the present progressive tense:

> (3) Tony *is coming* here later.

■ The present progressive verb *is coming* shows *future* time: Tony is going to come here.

(4) Linda *washed* her hair last night.

(5) Linda *was washing* her hair when we arrived for the party.

■ In sentence (4), *washed* implies a completed action.

■ The past progressive verb in sentence (5) has a special meaning: that Linda was *in the process* of washing her hair when something else happened (we arrived).

■ To say, "Linda *washed* her hair *when* we arrived for the party" means that first we arrived, and then Linda started washing her hair.

Writers in English use the progressive tenses *much less often* than the present tense and past tense. Use the progressive tense only when you want to emphasize that something is or was in the process of happening.

Use the *present progressive tense (am, is, are + -ing)* **to show that an action is in progress now or that it is going to occur in the future.**

Use the *past progressive tense (was, were + -ing)* **to show that an action was in progress at a certain time in the past.**

PRACTICE

Read each sentence carefully. Then circle the verb or verbs that best express the meaning of the sentence.

EXAMPLE: Right now, we (write, (are writing)) letters.

1. Last week, we ((saw), were seeing) a fantastic play, *Chicago*.
2. Darrell ((loves), is loving) to solve problems.
3. Where is Ellen? She (drives, (is driving)) to Omaha.
4. Most mornings we ((get), are getting) up at 7 A.M.
5. Believe it or not, Leroy (does, (is doing)) the laundry right now.
6. My dog Gourmand ((eats), is eating) anything at all.
7. At this very moment, Gourmand (eats, (is eating)) the sports page.
8. Max (fried, (was frying)) onions when the smoke alarm ((went), was going) off.
9. Please don't bother me now; I (study, (am studying)).
10. Newton (sat, (was sitting)) under a tree when he ((discovered), was discovering) gravity.
11. When Soo-Ling lived in Nevada, she ((drove), was driving) through the desert every day.
12. The *Andrea Doria*, a huge pleasure ship ((sank), was sinking) on July 25, 1956.
13. Right now, she (takes, (is taking)) a nap.

14. Through a scheduling error, runner Eddie Hart (missed, was missing) his race at the 1972 Olympics.

15. The last time I (saw, was seeing) Sandy, he (headed, was heading) toward the Lone Star Café.

PART D Avoiding Incomplete Progressives

Now that you can write both present and past progressive verbs, here is a mistake you should not make:

> We having fun. *(incomplete)*

■ Can you see what is missing?

■ All by itself, the *-ing* form *having* is not a verb. It has to have a helping verb.

■ Because the helping verb is missing, *we having fun* has no time. It could mean *we are having fun* or *we were having fun*.

■ *We having fun* is not a sentence. It is a fragment of a sentence.*

PRACTICE

Each group of words below is incomplete. Put an X over the exact spot where a word is missing. Then, in the Present Progressive column, write the word that would complete the sentence in the *present progressive tense*. In the Past Progressive column, write the word that would complete the sentence in the *past progressive tense*.

	Present Progressive	Past Progressive
EXAMPLE: He ̽ having fun.	is	was
	(He is having fun.)	(He was having fun.)
1. Mario ̽ balancing his checkbook.	is	was
2. Fran and I ̽ watching the sunrise.	are	were
3. You ̽ taking a computer course.	are	were
4. A big log ̽ floating down the river.	is	was
5. Those women always ̽ playing poker.	are	were
6. The tulips ̽ blooming.	are	were
7. I ̽ trying to give up caffeine.	am	was

---

*For more on this type of fragment, see Chapter 7, Part B.

	Present Progressive	Past Progressive
8. Fights about money ^X getting me down.	are	were
9. Jean and Marie ^X opening a café.	are	were
10. Thick fog ^X blanketing the city.	is	was
11. He ^X fixing up old cars.	is	was
12. That child ^X reading already.	is	was
13. Your ice cream ^X melting.	is	was
14. Her skills ^X improving.	are	were
15. They ^X discussing the terms of the new contract.	are	were

PRACTICE: WRITING ASSIGNMENT

Write a brief account that begins, "We are watching an amazing scene on TV. A man is ripping open an enormous brown box. . . . " Write four or five more sentences describing the unfolding action in the present progressive tense—as if the action is taking place now. Then read over what you have written, checking the verbs.

Now rewrite the whole account in the past progressive tense. The new version will begin, "We were watching an amazing scene on TV. A man was ripping open an enormous brown box. . . . "

✔ Chapter Highlights

■ **The progressive tenses combine** *to be* **with the** *-ing* **verb form:**

present progressive tense: I *am reading*. He *is reading*.
past progressive tense: I *was reading*. He *was reading*.

■ **The** *-ing* **verb form must have a helping verb to be complete:**

She playing the tuba. *(incorrect)*
She *is playing* the tuba. *(correct)*

■ **The present progressive tense shows that an action is in progress now:**

Aunt Belle *is waxing* her van.

■ **The present progressive tense can also show that an action will take place in the future:**

Later today, Aunt Belle *is driving* us to the movies.

■ **The past progressive tense shows that an action was in progress at a certain time in the past:**

Aunt Belle *was waxing* her van when she heard thunder.

Chapter Review

Proofread this paragraph for incomplete progressive verbs. Then write any missing verbs above the lines.

(1) One of the most important scientific projects in history is going on right

are

now. (2) Scientists studying the role of human genes in everything from hair color to

intelligence to a tendency toward obesity. (3) This huge effort is called the Human

Genome Project. (4) Its goal is to map every gene in the human body—three billion

are

elements in all. (5) Scientists finding the genes that cause or contribute to many

is

diseases. (6) This valuable information leading to new cures and to other discov-

eries—like bacteria that eat up oil spills and then die. (7) On the other hand,

are

ethical problems arising. (8) Some insurance companies are refusing to insure

healthy people who carry certain genes. (9) In the future, will employers be al-

lowed to use genetic tests the way some now use lie detectors or drug tests?

(10) Will parents try to plan the physical traits or intelligence of their babies?

are

(11) Because of questions like these, some critics calling genetic research "more a

Pandora's box than a magic bullet."

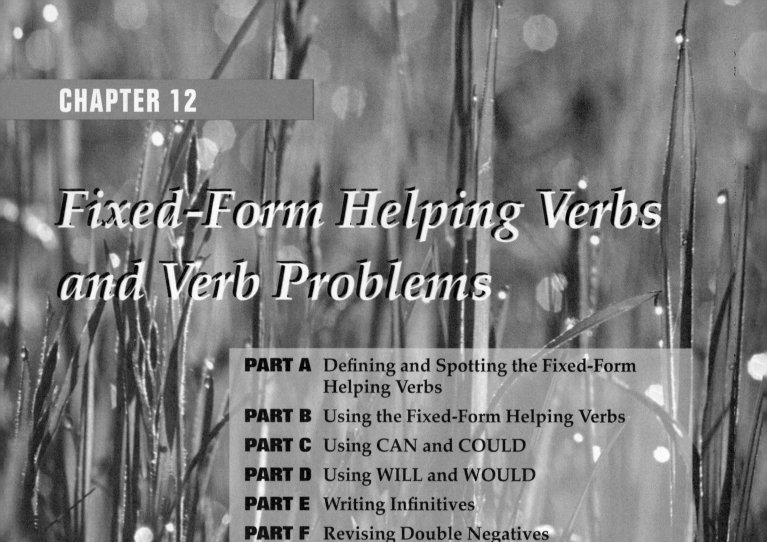

CHAPTER 12

Fixed-Form Helping Verbs and Verb Problems

PART A — Defining and Spotting the Fixed-Form Helping Verbs

You already know the common—and changeable—helping verbs: *to have, to do,* and *to be.* Here are some helping verbs that do not change:

Fixed-Form Helping Verbs	
can	could
will	would
may	might
shall	should
must	

The fixed-form helping verbs do not change, no matter what the subject is. They always keep the same form.

PRACTICE

Fill in each blank with a fixed-form helping verb.

1. You _____*can*_____ do it!

2. This _____*must*_____ be the coldest day of the year.

3. I _____*will*_____ row while you watch for crocodiles.

4. Rico _____*might*_____ go to medical school.

5. In South America, the elephant beetle _____*may*_____ grow to twelve inches in length.

6. If the committee _____*can*_____ meet today, we _____*will*_____ have a new budget on time.

7. This computer _____*should*_____ last another few years.

8. Violent films _____*may*_____ cause children to act out violently.

9. You _____*should*_____ have no difficulty finding a sales position.

10. Janice _____*may*_____ teach users to do research on the Internet.

PART B   Using the Fixed-Form Helping Verbs

> (1) Al will stay with us this summer.
> (2) Susan can shoot a rifle well.

- *Will* is the fixed-form helping verb in sentence (1). What main verb does it

   help? _____*stay*_____

- *Can* is the fixed-form helping verb in sentence (2). What main verb does it

   help? _____*shoot*_____

- Notice that *stay* and *shoot* are the simple forms of the verbs. They do not show tense by themselves.

When a verb has two parts—a fixed-form helping verb and a main verb—the main verb keeps its simple form.

PRACTICE

In the left column, each sentence contains a verb made up of some form of *to have* (the changeable helping verb) and a past participle (the main verb).

Each sentence in the right column contains a fixed-form helping verb and a blank. Write the form of the main verb from the left column that correctly completes each sentence.

Have + Past Participle	Fixed-Form Helping Verb + Simple Form

EXAMPLES: I have talked to him.   I may ____talk____ to him.

She has taken so long.   She will ____take____ so long.

1. Irena has written a song.   1. Irena must ____write____ a song.
2. We have begun.   2. We can ____begin____.
3. Joy has arrived.   3. Joy will ____arrive____.
4. He has slept all day.   4. He could ____sleep____ all day.
5. I have gone there.   5. I will ____go____ there.
6. We have seen an eclipse.   6. We might ____see____ an eclipse.
7. It has drizzled.   7. It may ____drizzle____.
8. Fred has fastened his seat belt.   8. Fred could ____fasten____ his seat belt.
9. Has he studied?   9. Should he ____study____?
10. Della has been promoted.   10. Della might ____be____ promoted.

PART C   Using CAN and COULD

(1) He said that I *can* use any tools in his garage.
(2) He said that I *could* use any tools in his garage.

■ What is the tense of sentence (1)? ____present____

■ What is the tense of sentence (2)? ____past____

■ What is the helping verb in (1)? ____can____

■ What is the helping verb in (2)? ____could____

■ As you can see, *could* may be used as the past tense of *can*.

> **Present tense:** Today, I *can* touch my toes.
>
> **Past tense:** Yesterday, I *could* touch my toes.

Can **means** *am/is/are able.* **It may be used to show present tense.**
Could **means** *was/were able* **when it is used to show the past tense of** *can.*

> (3) If I went on a diet, I *could* touch my toes.
>
> (4) Rod wishes he *could* touch his toes.

■ In sentence (3), the speaker *could* touch his toes *if.* . . . Touching his toes is a possibility, not a certainty.

■ In sentence (4), Rod *wishes* he *could* touch his toes, but probably he cannot. Touching his toes is a wish, not a certainty.

Could **also means** *might be able,* **a possibility or a wish.**

PRACTICE 1

Fill in the present tense helper *can* or the past tense *could,* whichever is needed. To determine whether the sentence is present or past, look at the other verbs in the sentence, or look for words like *now* and *yesterday.*

1. When I am rested, I _____*can*_____ study for hours.

2. When I was rested, I _____*could*_____ study for hours.

3. Renard claims that he _____*can*_____ fly a plane.

4. Renard claimed that he _____*could*_____ fly a plane.

5. A year ago, Zora _____*could*_____ jog for only five minutes at a time.

6. Now Zora _____*can*_____ jog for nearly an hour at a time.

7. If you're so smart, how come you _____*can*_____ never find your own socks?

8. If you were so smart, how come you _____*could*_____ never find your own socks?

9. When the air was clear, you _____*could*_____ see the next town.

10. When the air is clear, you _____*can*_____ see the next town.

PRACTICE 2

Circle either *can* or *could.*

1. Sue thinks that she (**can,** could) carry a tune.

2. Yesterday, we (can, **could**) not go to the town meeting.

3. I wish I (can, **could**) play with the Lakers.

4. You should meet Tony: he (**can,** could) lift a two-hundred-pound weight.

5. Nobody I know (can, could) change a flat tire.

6. Until the party, everyone thought that Harry (can, could) cook.

7. She (can, could) ice skate better now than she (can, could) last year.

8. On the night that Smithers disappeared, the butler (can, could) not be found.

9. When my brother was younger, he (can, could) name every car on the road.

10. I hope that the snow leopards (can, could) survive in captivity.

PRACTICE 3

On separate paper, write five sentences using *can* to show present tense and five sentences using *could* to show past tense.

PART D   Using WILL and WOULD

> (1) You know you *will* do well in that class.
> (2) You knew you *would* do well in that class.

■ Sentence (1) says that *you know* now (present tense) that you *will* do well in the future. *Will* points to the future from the present.

■ Sentence (2) says that *you knew* then (past tense) that you *would* do well after that. *Would* points to the future from the past.

Would **may be used as the past tense of** *will,* **just as** *could* **may be used as the past tense of** *can.*

> (3) *If* you studied, you *would* pass physics.
> (4) Juanita wishes she *would* get an A in French.

■ In sentence (3), the speaker *would* pass physics *if.* . . . Passing physics is a possibility, not a certainty.

■ In sentence (4), Juanita *wishes* she *could* get an A, but this is a wish, not a certainty.

Would **can also express a possibility or a wish.**

PRACTICE 1

Fill in the present tense *will* or the past tense *would.*

1. The meteorologist predicts that it _____*will*_____ snow Friday.

2. The meteorologist predicted that it _____*would*_____ snow Friday.

3. Hernan said that he _____*would*_____ move to Florida.

4. Hernan says that he _____*will*_____ move to Florida.

5. Roberta thinks that she _____*will*_____ receive financial aid.

6. Roberta thought that she _____*would*_____ receive financial aid.

7. I _____*will*_____ marry you if you propose to me.

8. Unless you stop adding salt, no one _____*will*_____ want to eat that chili.

9. Hugo thinks that he _____*will*_____ be a country western star someday.

10. Because she hated blind dates, she said that she _____*would*_____ never go on another one.

PRACTICE 2

Circle either *will* or *would*.

1. You (**will**, would) find the right major once you start taking courses.

2. When the house is painted, you (**will**, would) see how lovely the old place looks.

3. Yolanda wishes that her neighbor (will, **would**) stop raising ostriches.

4. The instructor assumed that everyone (will, **would**) improve.

5. They insisted that they (will, **would**) pick up the check.

6. The whole town assumed that they (will, **would**) live happily ever after.

7. When you get off the bus, you (**will**, would) see a diner.

8. If I had a million dollars, I (will, **would**) buy a big house on the ocean.

9. Your dinner (**will**, would) be ready in fifteen minutes.

10. Because we hated waiting in long lines, we decided that we (will, **would**) shop somewhere else.

PART E   Writing Infinitives

Every verb can be written as an *infinitive*. An infinitive has two parts: *to + the simple form of the verb*—*to kiss, to gaze, to sing, to wonder, to help.* Never add endings to the infinitive form of a verb: no *-ed*, no *-s*, no *-ing.*

(1) Roberta has *to finish* dental school this summer.
(2) Neither dictionary seems *to contain* the words I need.

■ In sentences (1) and (2), the infinitives are *to finish* and *to contain.*

■ *To* is followed by the simple form of the verb: *finish, contain.*

Don't confuse an infinitive with the preposition *to* followed by a noun or a pronoun.

> (3) Robert spoke *to Sam*.
>
> (4) I gave the award *to her*.

■ In sentences (3) and (4), the preposition *to* is followed by the noun *Sam* and the pronoun *her*.

■ *To Sam* and *to her* are prepositional phrases, not infinitives.*

PRACTICE 1

Find the infinitives in the following sentences, and write them in the blanks at the right.

Infinitive

EXAMPLE: Many people don't realize how hard
it is to write a funny essay.

to write

1. Our guests started to leave at midnight.

to leave

2. Barbara has decided to become a landscape
gardener.

to become

3. Hal has to get a B on his final exam, or he will not
transfer to Wayne State.

to get

4. It is hard to think with that radio blaring!

to think

5. The man wanted to buy a silver watch to give
to his son.

to buy, to give

PRACTICE 2

Write an infinitive in each blank in the following sentences. Use any verb that makes sense. Remember that the infinitive is made up of *to* plus the simple form of the verb.

1. They began _____ *to dance* _____ in the cafeteria.

2. Few people know how _____ *to skate* _____ well.

3. Would it be possible for me _____ *to leave* _____ now?

4. Try not _____ *to disturb* _____ that hornets' nest.

5. I enjoy people who like _____ *to eat* _____.

6. He hopes _____ *to become* _____ an operating-room nurse.

7. They wanted _____ *to build* _____ a better relationship.

———

*For more work on prepositions, see Chapter 6, Part C, and Chapter 23.

8. _____*To continue*_____ or not _____*to continue*_____ : this is the question.

9. Len learned how _____*to freewrite*_____ yesterday.

10. It will be hard _____*to tutor*_____ that child, but you can do it.

PRACTICE 3

The verbs below are listed in the present, past, past participle, or -*ing* form. Put each one in the infinitive form. Then create a sentence using the infinitive.

	Word	Infinitive	Sentence
EXAMPLE:	helping	to help	I want to help you.
1.	shouting	to shout	The crowd began to shout.
2.	drove	to drive	I want to drive a Jaguar.
3.	wiggles	to wiggle	The baby likes to wiggle his toes.
4.	heard	to hear	I expect to hear from you.
5.	tried	to try	She has to try harder.
6.	found	to find	I have to find the exit.
7.	directing	to direct	She wants to direct the choir.
8.	rumble	to rumble	The thunder continues to rumble.
9.	decided	to decide	To decide is difficult.
10.	discovers	to discover	We hope to discover new lands.

PART F   Revising Double Negatives

The most common *negatives* are *no, none, not, nowhere, no one, nobody, never,* and *nothing.*

The negative *not* is often joined to a verb to form a contraction: *can't, didn't, don't, hasn't, haven't,* and *won't,* for example.

However, a few negatives are difficult to spot. Read these sentences:

(1) There are hardly any beans left.
(2) By noon, we could scarcely see the mountains on the horizon.

■ The negatives in these sentences are *hardly* and *scarcely.*

■ They are negatives because they imply that there are *almost* no beans left and that we *almost couldn't* see the mountains.

Use only one negative in each idea. The double negative is an error you should avoid.

> (1) **Double negative:** I *can't* eat *nothing*.

- There are two negatives in this sentence—*can't* and *nothing*—instead of one.
- Double negatives cancel each other out.

To revise a double negative, simply drop one of the negatives.

> (2) **Revised:** I *can't* eat anything.
> (3) **Revised:** I can eat *nothing*.

- In sentence (2), the negative *nothing* is changed to the positive *anything*.
- In sentence (3), the negative *can't* is changed to the positive *can*.

When you revise double negatives that include the words *hardly* and *scarcely*, keep those words and change the other negatives to positives.

> (4) **Double negative:** They couldn't hardly finish their papers on time.

- The two negatives are *couldn't* and *hardly*.

> (5) **Revised:** They could hardly finish their papers on time.

- Change *couldn't* to *could*.

PRACTICE

Revise the double negatives in the following sentences.

EXAMPLE: I don't have no more homework to do.

Revised: *I don't have any more homework to do.*

1. I can't hardly wait for Christmas vacation.

   Revised: *I can hardly wait for Christmas vacation.*

2. Ms. Chandro hasn't never been to Los Angeles before.

   Revised: *Ms. Chandro has never been to Los Angeles before.*

3. Sonia was so tired that she couldn't do nothing.

   Revised: *Sonia was so tired that she couldn't do anything.*

4. Nat won't talk to nobody until he's finished studying.

   Revised: *Nat won't talk to anybody until he's finished studying.*

5. Yesterday's newspaper didn't contain no ads for large-screen television sets.

   Revised: *Yesterday's newspaper didn't contain any ads for large-screen television sets.*

6. I don't have no credit cards with me.

Revised: _I don't have any credit cards with me._

7. If Harold were smart, he wouldn't answer no one in that tone of voice.

Revised: _If Harold were smart, he wouldn't answer anyone in that tone of voice._

8. Kylie claimed that she hadn't never been to a rodeo before.

Revised: _Kylie claimed that she had never been to a rodeo before._

9. Some days, I can't seem to do nothing right.

Revised: _Some days, I can't seem to do anything right._

10. Umberto searched, but he couldn't find his gold bow tie nowhere.

Revised: _Umberto searched, but he couldn't find his gold bow tie anywhere._

PRACTICE: WRITING ASSIGNMENT

Review this chapter briefly. What part was most difficult for you? Write a paragraph in which you explain that difficult material to someone who is having the same trouble you had. Your purpose is to make the lesson crystal-clear to him or her.

✔ Chapter Highlights

- **Fixed-form verbs do not change, no matter what the subject is:**

  I *can.*

  He *can.*

  They *can.*

- **The main verb after a fixed-form helping verb keeps the simple form:**

  I will *sleep.*

  She might *sleep.*

  Sarita should *sleep.*

- **An infinitive has two parts, *to* + the simple form of a verb:**

  to dance

  to exclaim

  to read

- **Do not write double negatives:**

  I didn't order no soup. *(incorrect)*

  I didn't order any soup. *(correct)*

  They couldn't hardly see. *(incorrect)*

  They could hardly see. *(correct)*

Chapter Review

Proofread the following essay for errors in fixed-form verbs, infinitives, and double negatives. Cross out each incorrect word, and correct the error above the line.

The Great Houdini

(1) Harry Houdini began to study magic as a child. (2) He became very famous as an escape artist. (3) He could free himself from ropes, chains, and locked con-
could
tainers. (4) Nobody ~~couldn't~~ keep Harry where he didn't want to be. (5) He could get out of any jail. (6) Once, the head of Scotland Yard handcuffed Houdini's arms around a thick post and then locked him in a prison cell. (7) Houdini managed
to free
~~free~~ himself immediately. (8) Another time, some of the best locksmiths in Europe
to open
attempted to trick him with a foolproof lock. (9) Houdini was able ~~open~~ it in
would
seconds. (10) In one of the master's favorite stunts, the police ~~will~~ first put him in a straitjacket and bind him with ropes and chains; then they would hang him by
could
his feet. (11) Even in that position, Houdini ~~can~~ wriggle free.
amaze
(12) Houdini continued to ~~amazing~~ people with his incredible feats. (13) He once jumped in midair from one airplane to another while handcuffed. (14) He leaped from a bridge into San Francisco Bay with his hands tied behind his back and a seventy-five-pound ball and chain tied to his feet. (15) People expected to
find
~~found~~ him dead, but he survived the ordeal. (16) In the most daring feat of all, he asked to be sealed in a coffin and lowered into a swimming pool. (17) He stayed locked up underwater for ninety minutes and then emerged in perfect health. (18)
will   *ever*
No doubt, Houdini's fame ~~would~~ last. (19) Probably, we won't ~~never~~ see another escape artist as daring as he.

UNIT 3   WRITING ASSIGNMENTS

As you complete each writing assignment, remember to perform these steps:

- Write a clear, complete topic sentence.
- Use freewriting, brainstorming, or clustering to generate ideas.
- Arrange your best ideas in a plan.
- Revise for support, unity, coherence, and exact language.
- Proofread for grammar, punctuation, and spelling errors.

Writing Assignment 1: *Retell an early experience.* Choose an incident from your childhood or adolescence that deeply affected you—for instance, an experience that determined your career choice (or lack of choice). First, using past tense verbs, tell exactly what happened. Then discuss the meaning of this experience for you. Let the reader know precisely why it was so important. You may want to let a classmate read your paper and offer suggestions before you write your final draft. Check all verb endings.

Writing Assignment 2: *Describe the moments just before a big event.* In the Unit 3 Review, read paragraph A, which uses lively verbs to describe a runner's intense moments just before a race. This writer uses the present tense, as if the action is happening now. Describe the moments just before some important event—the birth of a child, the opening of an important letter, the arrival of a blind date, the verdict of a jury (or of the person to whom you just proposed). Decide whether present or past tense would be best, and choose varied, interesting verbs. As you revise, make sure the verbs are correct.

Writing Assignment 3: *Tell a family story.* Many of us heard family stories as we were growing up—how our great-grandmother escaped from Poland, how Uncle Chester took his sister for a joy ride in the Ford when he was six. Assume that you have been asked to write such a story for a scrapbook that will be given to your grandmother on her eightieth birthday. Choose a story that reveals something important about a member of your family. As you revise, make sure that all your verbs are correct.

Writing Assignment 4: *Write to Abby.* Think of a problem with love, marriage, parents, or school that might prompt you or someone you know to write to "Dear Abby." Then as if you are the person with the problem, write a letter. In your first sentence, state the problem clearly. Then explain it. Remember, you are confused and don't know what to do. You want to give Abby enough information so that she can answer you wisely. Proofread your letter carefully. Don't let grammatical errors or incorrect verbs stand between you and happiness!

UNIT 3 REVIEW

Transforming

A. Rewrite this paragraph, changing every *I* to *she*, every *me* to *her*, and so forth. Keep all verbs in the present tense. Be sure all verbs agree with the new subjects, and make any other necessary changes.

(1) The race is about to begin. (2) ~~My~~ *Her* heart pounds as ~~I peel~~ *she peels* off ~~my~~ *her* sweatpants and jacket and ~~drop~~ *drops* them on the grass. (3) ~~I step~~ *She steps* onto the new, all-weather track and ~~enter my~~ *enters her* assigned lane. (4) Next ~~I check my~~ *she checks her* track shoes for loose laces. (5) By now, the athletes around ~~me~~ *her* are stretching backwards, forwards, and sideways. (6) ~~I extend~~ *She extends* one leg, then the other, and ~~bend~~ *bends* low, giving ~~my~~ *her* hamstrings a final stretch. (7) Although ~~I~~ never ~~come~~ *she comes* eye to eye with ~~my~~ *her* opponents, ~~I feel~~ *she feels* their readiness as they exhale loudly. (8) Their energy charges the air like electricity. (9) ~~I plant my~~ *She plants her* feet in the blocks. (10) Off to one side, a coach starts to speak. (11) ~~My~~ *Her* mind is flashing. (12) How will ~~my~~ *her* opponents kick off? (13) How will they start?

(14) The seconds swell, thick and dreamlike. (15) The gun sounds.

Sheila Grant, student

B. Rewrite this paragraph, changing the verbs from present tense to past tense.

(1) It ~~is~~ *was* the morning of April 18, 1906. (2) Alfred Hunt ~~sleeps~~ *slept* peacefully in the Palace Hotel in San Francisco. (3) At 5:12 A.M., a violent jolt suddenly ~~shakes~~ *shook* his room and ~~sends~~ *sent* him rolling from bed. (4) The shaking ~~lasts~~ *lasted* for forty-five seconds. (5) During the calm of the next ten seconds, Hunt ~~staggers~~ *staggered* to the window. (6) Another tremor ~~rocks~~ *rocked* the city for twenty-five more seconds. (7) Hunt ~~watches~~ *watched* in terror. (8) The whole city ~~looks~~ *looked* like breaking waves. (9) Buildings ~~reel~~ *reeled* and ~~tumble~~ *tumbled* to the ground. (10) Then fires ~~break~~ *broke* out and ~~start~~ *started* to spread. (11) Hunt quickly ~~dresses, throws~~ *dressed, threw* open his door, and ~~runs~~ *ran* downstairs into the street. (12) Crowds of rushing people ~~block~~ *blocked* his path. (13) Some people ~~carry~~ *carried* screaming children while others ~~struggle~~ *struggled* under loads of furniture and other valuable objects. (14) It ~~takes~~ *took* Hunt four hours to push through the four blocks from his hotel to the safety of the Oakland ferry. (15) Later, he ~~will~~ *would* learn that the great San Francisco earthquake ~~has~~ *had* destroyed 520 city blocks and ~~has~~ *had* killed more than seven hundred people.

Proofreading

The following essay contains a number of past tense errors and past participle errors. First, proofread for verb errors, underlining all incorrect verbs. Then correct any errors above the lines.

They Made Computer History

(1) Charles Babbage is sometimes called the grandfather of the computer, and
known
Ada Lovelace is knowed as the first computer programmer. (2) Ada met Charles
was
in June 1833. (3) She was only eighteen; he were over forty. (4) Together, they
made
make computer history.

(5) Ada Lovelace was the only legal child of Lord Byron, the great English

poet. (6) However, she never knew her father. (7) He had separated from her
left
mother thirty-six days after her birth and then had leaved England forever.
raised
(8) Ada's mother raise her with a strong hand, but she encouraged her daughter's

natural talent for mathematics. (9) Ada was taught at home. (10) She also wrote to

famous mathematicians and scientists, among them Charles Babbage.
designed
(11) By the time he met Ada Lovelace, Babbage had already design a machine

that could perform any mathematical operation. (12) He called it the analytical
promised
engine. (13) The British government had promise him money to build it. (14) Ada
gave
give him both money and support. (15) She also created the system of punch

cards for feeding information into the machine. (16) Some people said that she
wanted
want to use the machine to win at the horse races. (17) However, the analytical
built
engine was never build. (18) No one at that time could make the necessary parts.

(19) The analytical engine was almost forgotten until 1937 when Howard H.
used
Aiken discovered Babbage's plans. (20) Aiken use them to help design the first
became
modern computer. (21) In the 1980s, ADA become the name of a programming

language.

Tell a Lively Story

A *narrative* tells a story. It presents the most important events in the story, usually in time order. Here, a student explains her main idea with a single example, a childhood narrative.

In your group or class, read this narrative essay aloud if possible. As you read, underline any words or details that strike you as vivid or powerful.

Happy in Butterfly Heaven

(1) When I was a child on our farm in South Carolina, my family always supported my expansive imagination. For example, one year, I had a favorite butterfly named Mr. Jonce Browne, and I named his wife Mrs. Sadie Caesar. I would play with them in the fields, flapping my arms and darting my head until I felt I had turned into a butterfly. One day I found Mr. Jonce Brown stiff and brittle in a spider web next to the barn. When I told Papa the tragic news, he said, "Give him a proper burial because Mrs. Sadie Caesar will be too busy taking care of her children."

(2) Mama gave me a wooden matchbox for a casket. Two of my sisters and three brothers made funeral arrangements. They dug a tiny grave, and we all picked wild flowers. My brother Emiza gave the eulogy from a milk crate. "We gather here today to put to rest a good butterfly papa." My sisters Gertrude and Jeanie jumped up and down flinging their arms and yelling, "Yes! He was a good papa!"

(3) The preacher started clapping his hands and flinging his arms. He rolled his eyes upward and raised his voice two octaves as he went on about the deceased's great qualities. "He never failed to bring home pretzels for his children!" I started waving my arms as I told how he always brought me balloons. "And yo-yos for me," my brother Jeff hollered.

(4) By this time, sweat was rolling down the preacher's face. He yelled and screamed, shaking his head. Spit was flying everywhere. Suddenly he squealed a high note that made my ears ring. My brother James started singing, "When the saints go marching in." We all sang as we covered the grave and put flowers on top. I felt assured that Mr. Jonce Browne was happy in butterfly heaven, knowing how much we all liked him.

Stelline Hill, student

1. How effective is Ms. Hill's essay?

   <u>Y</u> Clear thesis statement?   <u>Y</u> Rich supporting details?

   <u>Y</u> Logical organization?   <u>Y</u> Effective conclusion?

2. Underline the thesis statement (main idea sentence) for the whole essay. The rest of the paper—a childhood narrative—develops this idea.

3. How would you describe the writer's tone? Is she totally serious, or is she having some fun here? Do you find this subject appropriate for a college paper, or is it too childish?

4. On paper, as in life, this student shows a lively imagination. Discuss your underlinings with a group or with the class. How many of the words you liked are verbs or verb forms? Ms. Hill uses many different action verbs to help the reader see and hear the story, especially in paragraphs (3) and (4). Can you identify them?

5. Would you suggest any changes or revisions?

6. Proofread for grammar and spelling. Do you notice any error patterns (two or more errors of the same type) that this student should watch out for? *No errors*

Writing and Revising Ideas

1. Write a lively story about one way your family supported you (or failed to).

2. Use narration to develop this topic or thesis sentence: Country (or city) living has great advantages (or disadvantages).

For help writing your paragraph or essay, see Chapter 4, Part C, and Chapter 5. As you revise, make sure your main idea is clear and that your paper explains it. To add punch to your writing as you revise, replace *is, was, has,* and *had* with action verbs whenever possible.

Joining Ideas Together

Too many short, simple sentences can make your writing sound monotonous. This unit will show you five ways to create interesting sentences. In this unit, you will

✔ Join ideas through *coordination* and *subordination*

✔ Spot and correct run-ons or comma splices

✔ Use semicolons and conjunctive adverbs correctly

✔ Join ideas with *who*, *which*, and *that*

✔ Join ideas by using *-ing* modifiers

Here, writer Brent Staples uses several methods of joining ideas as he describes his first passionate kiss (at least, *he* was passionate). If possible, read the paragraph aloud.

I stepped outside and pulled the door closed behind me, and in one motion encircled her waist, pulled her to me, and whispered breathlessly that I loved her. There'd been no rehearsing this; the thought, deed, and word were one. "You do? You love me?" This amused her, but that didn't matter; I had passion enough for the two of us. When I closed in for the kiss, she turned away her lips and offered me her cheek. I kissed it feverishly and with great force. We stood locked this way until I came up for air. Then she peeled me from her and went inside for the flour.

Brent Staples, *Parallel Time*

- Mr. Staples mixes simple sentences with sentences that join ideas in different ways. Sentences 1, 2, and 5, for example, combine ideas in ways you will learn in this unit.

- How do you think the writer now feels about this incident from his youth? Does his tone seem angry, frustrated, or amused? Which sentences tell you?

Writing Ideas

- Your first crush or romantic encounter
- A time you discovered that your loved one's view of the relationship was very different from your view

CHAPTER 13

Coordination

As a writer, you will sometimes want to join short, choppy sentences to form longer sentences. One way to join two ideas is to use a comma and a *coordinating conjunction.*

> (1) This car has many special features, and it costs less than $12,000.
>
> (2) The television picture is blurred, but we will watch the football game anyway.
>
> (3) She wants to practice her Italian, so she is going to Italy.

■ Can you break sentence (1) into two complete and independent ideas or thoughts? What are they? Underline the subject and verb in each.

■ Can you do the same with sentences (2) and (3)? Underline the subjects and verbs.

■ In each sentence, circle the word that joins the two parts of the sentence together. What punctuation mark comes before that word?

■ *And, but,* and *so* are called *coordinating conjunctions* because they coordinate, or join together, ideas. Other coodinating conjunctions are *for, nor, or,* and *yet.*

To join two complete and independent ideas, use a coordinating conjunction preceded by a comma.

Now let's see just how coordinating conjunctions connect ideas:

Coordinating Conjunctions		
and	*means*	in addition
but, yet	*mean*	in contrast
for	*means*	because
nor	*means*	not either
or	*means*	either, a choice
so	*means*	as a result

BE CAREFUL: *Then, also,* and *plus* are not coordinating conjunctions. By themselves, they cannot join two ideas.

Incorrect: He studied, then he went to work.

Correct: He studied, and then he went to work.

PRACTICE 1

Read these sentences for meaning. Then punctuate them correctly, and fill in the coordinating conjunction that best expresses the relationship between the two complete thoughts. REMEMBER: Do you want to *add, contrast, give a reason, show a result,* or *indicate a choice?* Some sentences may take more than one conjunction. Punctuate correctly!

1. President John F. Kennedy established the Peace Corps in 1961 *1961,*

   ___*but*___ he didn't live long enough to see the program grow.

2. The first group of Peace Corps volunteers was made up of fifty-two people in their early twenties *twenties,* ___*so*___ the group was both small and young.

3. Since then, more than 140,000 people of all ages have participated in the program *program,* ___*and*___ they have worked in more than 125 different countries.

4. The Peace Corps has grown greatly *greatly,* ___*but*___ its goals have remained the same.

5. Americans and people in other countries learn about each other's cultures *cultures,*

   ___*and*___ volunteers help improve living conditions.

6. In the early days, most volunteers taught school *school,* ___*or*___ they worked on health projects.

7. However, many different kinds of projects have been added *added,* _____*for*_____ nations now need new kinds of assistance.

8. For example, Eastern European countries are developing free markets *markets,* _____*so*_____ Peace Corps volunteers are helping them run small businesses.

9. Businesspeople in former Soviet Union provinces learn how to prepare budgets *budgets,* budgets _____*but*_____ meeting Americans interests them too.

10. In 1996, most of the first group of Peace Corps volunteers met for a thirty-fifth reunion *reunion,* reunion _____*and*_____ many said those years had been the most meaningful ones of their lives.

PRACTICE 2

Every one of these thoughts is complete by itself, but you can join them together to make more interesting sentences. Combine pairs of these thoughts, using *and, but, for, nor, or, so,* or *yet,* and write six new sentences on the lines that follow. Punctuate correctly.

teeth fascinate Jack

mimes performed in the store window

in the 1840s, American women began to fight for the right to vote

I will write my essay at home tonight

the ancient Chinese valued peaches

a curious crowd gathered on the sidewalk

they are the best Ping-Pong players on the block

he has decided to become a dentist

I will write it tomorrow in the computer lab

they did not win that right until 1920

they can't beat my cousin from Cleveland

they believed that eating peaches made a person immortal

1. *Teeth fascinate Jack, so he decided to become a dentist.*

2. *I will write my essay at home tonight, or I will write it tomorrow in the computer lab.*

3. *In the 1840s, American women began to fight for the right to vote, yet they did not win that right until 1920.*

4. *Mimes performed in the store window, and a curious crowd gathered on the sidewalk.*

5. *They are the best Ping-Pong players on the block, but they can't beat my cousin from Cleveland.*

6. *The ancient Chinese valued peaches, for they believed that eating peaches made a person immortal.*

PRACTICE 3

Finish these sentences by adding a second complete idea after the coordinating conjunction.

1. I usually vacation in the Caribbean, but *this year I'm staying home.*

2. Please help Yolanda carry her packages, or *ask Brittany to help her.*

3. Yuri has lived in the United States for ten years, so *his English is quite good.*

4. Len has been married three times, and *now he's a widower.*

5. These are my favorite sneakers, for *I was wearing them the day I met you.*

6. He loves to tell people what to do, so *a coaching job suits him well.*

7. She carries her math book everywhere, yet *she never opens it.*

8. This curry had better be hot, or *I'm taking my business elsewhere.*

9. I like owning a car, for *it allows me to drive to the country on weekends.*

10. I like owning a car, but *I hate the repair bills.*

PRACTICE 4

On separate paper, write seven sentences of your own using each of the coordinating conjunctions—*and, but, for, nor, or, so,* and *yet*—to join two independent ideas. Punctuate correctly.

PRACTICE: WRITING ASSIGNMENT

Whether you are a teenager, a young adult, middle-aged, elderly, single, or part of a couple, there are characters in TV sitcoms who are supposed to represent you. Do these characters correctly portray the kind of person you are, or are you seeing one or more irritating exaggerations?

Write a letter of praise or complaint to a network that broadcasts one of these sitcoms. Make clear why you think a certain character does or does not correctly portray someone like you. Use examples and specific details. As you write, avoid choppy sentences by joining ideas with coordinating conjunctions.

✔ Chapter Highlights

■ **A comma and a coordinating conjunction join two independent ideas:**

The fans booed, *but* the umpire paid no attention.

$$
\boxed{\text{Independent idea}}
\left\{
\begin{array}{l}
\text{, and} \\
\text{, but} \\
\text{, for} \\
\text{, nor} \\
\text{, or} \\
\text{, so} \\
\text{, yet}
\end{array}
\right\}
\boxed{\text{independent idea.}}
$$

■ Note: *Then, also,* and *plus* are not coordinating conjunctions.

Chapter Review

Read this paragraph of short, choppy sentences. Then rewrite it, using different coordinating conjunctions to combine some pairs of sentences. Keep some short sentences for variety. Copy your revised paragraph on a fresh sheet of paper. Punctuate with care.

(1) In 1929, Alice Orr answered a want ad for bronco riders for a Wild West show. (2) She was hired ~~immediately.~~ *immediately, and her* (3) ~~Her~~ new job launched a remarkable career. (4) Orr became an international rodeo star. (5) She was an expert in every rodeo ~~event.~~ *event, but her* (6) ~~Her~~ specialty was saddle bronc riding. (7) That tough competition has since been dropped from women's ~~rodeos.~~ *rodeos, yet* (8) Orr won four world champi-onships in it. (9) Orr was also concerned about working conditions for rodeo ~~competitors.~~ *competitors, so she* (10) ~~She~~ helped establish a professional rodeo association. (11) In the 1940s, Orr and her husband put on rodeos ~~themselves.~~ *themselves, and she* (12) ~~She~~ would demonstrate her world-famous saddle bronc riding. (13) Orr retired from rodeos in her ~~fifties.~~ *fifties,* (14) ~~She~~ *but she* did movie stunt work until she was eighty. (15) When Alice Orr died in 1995 at the age of 93, many people still remembered her as queen of the bronco riders.

CHAPTER 14

Subordination

> **PART A** Defining and Using Subordinating Conjunctions
>
> **PART B** Punctuating Subordinating Conjunctions

PART A   Defining and Using Subordinating Conjunctions

Another way to join ideas together is with a *subordinating conjunction*.
    Read this paragraph:

> A great disaster happened in 1857. The S.S. *Central America* sank. This steamship was carrying six hundred wealthy passengers from California to New York. Many of them had recently struck gold. Battered by a storm, the ship began to flood. Many people on board bailed water. Others prayed and quieted the children. Thirty hours passed. A rescue boat arrived. Almost two hundred people were saved. The rest died. Later, many banks failed. Three tons of gold had gone down with the ship.

This could have been a good paragraph, but notice how dull the writing is because the sentences are short and choppy.
    Here is the same paragraph rewritten to make it more interesting:

> A great disaster happened in 1857 *when* the S.S. *Central America* sank. This steamship was carrying six hundred wealthy passengers from California to New York. Many of them had recently struck gold. Battered by a storm, the ship began to flood. Many people on board bailed water *while* others prayed and quieted the children. *After* thirty hours passed, a rescue boat arrived. Almost two hundred people were saved *although* the rest died. Later, many banks failed *because* three tons of gold had gone down with the ship.

■ Note that the paragraph now reads more smoothly and is more interesting because the following words were used to join some of the choppy sentences: *when, while, after, although,* and *because.*

■ *When, while, after, although,* and *because* are part of a large group of words called *subordinating conjunctions.* As you can see from the paragraph, these conjunctions join ideas.

BE CAREFUL: Once you add a subordinating conjunction to an idea, that idea can no longer stand alone as a complete and independent sentence. It has become a subordinate or dependent idea; it must rely on an independent idea to complete its meaning.*

(1) Because he is tired, *he will take a nap.*

(2) As I left the room, *the waiter dropped a tray of desserts.*

(3) If you know Spanish, *will you translate this letter for me?*

■ Note that each of these ideas is dependent and must be followed by something else—a complete and independent thought.

■ Sentence (1), for example, could be completed like this: Because he is tired, *he won't go out.*

■ Add an independent idea to complete each dependent idea on the lines above.

Below is a partial list of subordinating conjunctions.

Common Subordinating Conjunctions

after	even though	when
although	if	whenever
as	since	where
as if	so that	whereas
as though	though	wherever
because	unless	whether
before	until	while

PRACTICE 1

Read these sentences for meaning. Then fill in the subordinating conjunction that best expresses the relationship between the two ideas.

1. _____*While*_____ the animal world is filled with exciting journeys, perhaps none is more amazing than the flight of monarch butterflies.

2. _____*Although*_____ monarchs are only five inches across and weigh only a fiftieth of an ounce, they travel thousands of miles: north to south and back again.

———

*For more work on sentence fragments of this type, see Chapter 7, Part C.

3. _____*When*_____ summer changes to fall, millions of these beautiful black-and-orange butterflies begin to migrate to warmer climates.

4. Monarchs have to migrate _____*because*_____ they need warm sunshine to stay alive.

5. The monarch butterflies that live west of the Rocky Mountains fly to the California coast _____*whereas*_____ those that live east of the Rockies go south.

6. For years, scientists wondered where eastern monarchs went _____*after*_____ they left Canada and the northern United States.

7. Researchers at the University of Toronto eventually began tagging the butterflies _____*before*_____ the monarchs migrated south.

8. Volunteers throughout the United States and Mexico would contact the university _____*whenever*_____ they saw a tagged monarch.

9. People continued to search _____*until*_____ they finally tracked the butterflies to several sites in the forests of central Mexico.

10. At those sites, millions of butterflies cover the giant fir trees _____*so that*_____ no green from the trees is visible.

11. _____*Whenever*_____ the butterflies leave the trees to find water, they fill the sky, sometimes blocking out the sun completely.

12. _____*As*_____ visitors from all over the world arrive at the monarch sanctuary in El Rosario, they marvel at the incredible beauty of this butterfly world.

13. Unfortunately, _____*since*_____ an unusual cold spell in Mexico in 1995 killed up to 15 percent of the monarch population, monarchs have been in danger.

14. Another threat to their existence is logging _____*because*_____ monarchs need the fir trees to keep themselves warm and dry.

15. Some experts have predicted that these wonderful butterflies will be extinct within twenty years _____*if*_____ logging in the Mexican forests continues at 1996 levels.

PRACTICE 2

Now that you understand how subordinating conjunctions join thoughts together, try these sentences. Here you have to supply one idea. Make sure that the ideas you add have subjects and verbs.

1. The cafeteria food improved when _*the college hired a new food manager.*_

   _____

2. Because Mark and Joel both love basketball, _*they often attend local games.*_

   _____

3. If _the newspaper doesn't stop printing negative advertising,_
   I'll cancel my subscription.

4. When _Jason accidentally spilled his coffee,_
   Harriet pretended not to have noticed.

5. The history class seemed sad after _Professor Wilde announced that he was_

   retiring.

6. I was repairing the roof while _John was ironing clothes._

7. Before _you write that article,_
   you had better get all the facts.

8. After _I swim twenty laps,_
   I always feel wonderful.

PART B   Punctuating Subordinating Conjunctions

As you may have noticed in the preceding exercises, some sentences with subordinating conjunctions use a comma while others do not. Here is how it's done.

> (1) Because it rained very hard, we had to leave early.
> (2) We had to leave early because it rained very hard.

■ Sentence (1) has a comma because the dependent idea comes before the independent idea.

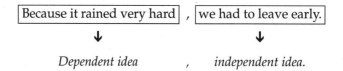

Dependent idea   ,   independent idea.

■ Sentence (2) has no comma because the dependent idea follows the independent idea.

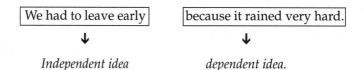

Independent idea   dependent idea.

Use a comma after a dependent idea; do not use a comma before a dependent idea.

PRACTICE 1

If a sentence is punctuated correctly, write *C* in the blank. If not, punctuate it correctly by adding a comma.

1. Whenever Americans get hungry *hungry,* they want to eat quickly. _____

2. When McDonald's opened in 1954 *1954,* it started a trend that still continues. _____

3. Whether you are talking about hamburgers or pizza *pizza,* fast food is big business—more than $90 billion a year. _____

4. Fast food is appealing because it is cheap, tasty, and—of course—fast. *C*

5. Although it has many advantages *advantages,* fast food also presents some health hazards. _____

6. While the industry is booming *booming,* many people are worried about the amount of fat in fast foods. _____

7. Although some nutritionists recommend only thirty-five grams of fat a *day,* day you often eat more than that in just one fast-food meal. _____

8. If you order a Big Mac, fries, and a chocolate shake *shake,* you take in forty-five grams of fat. _____

9. That goes up to sixty-three grams whenever you go for a Burger King double whopper with cheese. *C*

10. Fortunately, fast-food restaurants are now providing low-fat items so that they can attract health-conscious customers. *C*

11. For instance, a McGrilled Chicken Classic has only three grams of fat, whereas a Burger King chunky chicken salad has only four. *C*

12. While Wendy's provides salad bars in all its locations *locations,* Taco Bell offers light Mexican entrées. _____

13. If you like seafood *seafood,* you can eat baked lemon crumb fish with only one gram of fat at Long John Silver's. _____

14. Although you may not think of baked potatoes or fresh vegetables as fast *food,* food many fast-food restaurants are offering these dishes. _____

15. Restaurants will continue to offer low-fat meals only if people will continue to order them. *C*

Combine each pair of sentences by using a subordinating conjunction. Write each combination two ways: once with the subordinating conjunction at the beginning of the sentence and once with the conjunction in the middle of the sentence. Punctuate correctly.

EXAMPLE: Marriage exists in all societies.

Every culture has unique wedding customs.

Although marriage exists in all societies, every culture has unique

wedding customs.

Every culture has unique wedding customs although marriage exists

in all societies.

1. Young couples in India marry.
   The ceremony may last for days.

   When young couples in India marry, the ceremony may last for days.

   The ceremony may last for days when young couples in India marry.

2. The wedding takes place at the bride's home.
   Everyone travels to the groom's home for more celebrating.

   After the wedding takes place at the bride's home, everyone travels to

   the groom's home for more celebrating.

   Everyone travels to the groom's home for more celebrating after the

   wedding takes place at the bride's home.

3. They are often included in Korean wedding processions.
   Ducks mate for life.

   Because ducks mate for life, they are often included in Korean

   wedding processions.

   Ducks are often included in Korean wedding processions because they

   mate for life.

4. Iroquois brides gave grain to their mothers-in-law.
   Mothers-in-law gave meat to the bride.

   Whereas Iroquois brides gave grain to their mothers-in-law,

   mothers-in-law gave meat to the brides.

   Iroquois brides gave grain to their mothers-in-law whereas

   mothers-in-law gave meat to the brides.

5. The food was exchanged.
   The bride and groom were considered married.

   When the food was exchanged, the bride and groom were considered

   married.

   The bride and groom were considered married when the food was

   exchanged.

6. The tradition went out of style.
   Finnish brides and grooms used to exchange wreaths.

   Until the tradition went out of style, Finnish brides and grooms used to

   exchange wreaths.

   Finnish brides and grooms used to exchange wreaths until the tradition

   went out of style.

7. The bride, groom, and bridal party dance special dances.
   A Zulu wedding is not complete.

   Unless the bride, groom, and bridal party dance special dances, a Zulu

   wedding is not complete.

   A Zulu wedding is not complete unless the bride, groom, and bridal

   party dance special dances.

8. The bride dances wildly and gloriously.
   She stabs at imaginary enemies with a knife.

   As the bride dances wildly and gloriously, she stabs at imaginary

   enemies with a knife.

   The bride stabs at imaginary enemies with a knife as she dances wildly

   and gloriously.

9. The wedding ring is a very old symbol.

   The elaborate wedding cake is even older.

   Although the wedding ring is a very old symbol, the elaborate

   wedding cake is even older.

   The wedding ring is a very old symbol although the elaborate

   wedding cake is even older.

10. The ring symbolizes the oneness of the new couple.

    The cake represents fertility.

    Whereas the ring symbolizes the oneness of the new couple, the cake

    represents fertility.

    The cake represents fertility whereas the ring symbolizes the oneness of

    the new couple.

PRACTICE 3

Now try writing sentences of your own. Fill in the blanks, being careful to punctuate correctly. Do not use the comma when the independent idea precedes the dependent idea.

1. _____ because

   _____ .

2. Although _____

   _____ .

3. Since _____

   _____ .

4. _____ whenever

   _____ .

5. Unless _____

   _____ .

PRACTICE: WRITING ASSIGNMENT

Imagine that you are a teacher planning a lesson on courtesy for a class of young children. Use a personal experience, either positive or negative, to illustrate your point. Brainstorm, freewrite, or cluster to generate details for the lesson. Then write what—and how—you plan to teach. Keeping in mind that you are trying to reach young children, make sure that the significance of the experience you will describe is clear. Join ideas together with subordinating conjunctions, being careful about punctuation.

   Form small groups to evaluate one another's lessons. Which are most convincing? Why? Would children learn more from examples of good behavior or from examples of bad behavior?

✔ Chapter Highlights

■ **A subordinating conjunction joins a dependent idea and an independent idea:**

When I registered, all the math courses were closed.

All the math courses were closed *when* I registered.

■ **Use a comma after a dependent idea.**

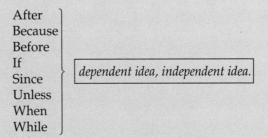

■ **Do not use a comma before a dependent idea.**

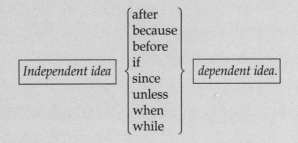

Chapter Review

Read this paragraph of short, choppy sentences. Then rewrite it in the blank lines, using different subordinating conjunctions to combine pairs of sentences. Keep some short sentences for variety. Punctuate with care.

(1) Bill Gates is greatly admired for his technological and business skills. (2) The chairman of Microsoft Corporation was born in 1955 in Seattle, Washington. (3) He started a computer company. (4) He was fourteen years old. (5) The successful company lost business. (6) Clients learned that it was run by high school students. (7) Gates attended Harvard University for two years. (8) He dropped out to create computer software. (9) In 1975, he and a friend established the now world-famous Microsoft Corporation. (10) The new company attracted attention. (11) It produced an operating system for IBM's personal computer.

(12) By 1997, eight out of ten computers were starting up with Microsoft operating systems. (13) Microsoft Corporation has also led the market in word-processing software and other on-line programs. (14) Gates is a billionaire several times over. (15) He is not satisfied. (16) There are new fields like interactive television and telecommunications satellites to explore.

(1) Bill Gates is greatly admired for his technological and business skills. (2) The chairman of Microsoft Corporation was born in 1955 in Seattle, Washington. (3) He started a computer company when he was fourteen years old. (4) The successful company lost business after clients learned that it was run by high school students.

(5) Although Gates attended Harvard University for two years, he dropped out to create computer software. (6) In 1975, he and a friend established the now world-famous Microsoft Corporation. (7) The new company attracted attention because it produced an operating system for IBM's personal computer. (8) By 1997, eight out of ten computers were starting up with Microsoft operating systems. (9) Microsoft Corporation has also led the market in word-processing software and other on-line programs. (10) Although Gates is a billionaire several times over, he is not satisfied. (11) There are new fields like interactive television and telecommunications satellites to explore.

CHAPTER 15

Avoiding Run-ons and Comma Splices

Now that you have had practice in joining ideas together, here are two errors to watch out for: the *run-on* and the *comma splice*.

Run-on: Herb talks too much nobody seems to mind.

■ There are two complete ideas here: *Herb talks too much* and *nobody seems to mind*.

■ A run-on incorrectly runs together two complete ideas without using a conjunction or punctuation.

Comma splice: Herb talks too much, nobody seems to mind.

■ A comma splice incorrectly joins two complete ideas with a comma but no conjunction.

Here are three ways to correct a run-on and a comma splice.

1. Write two separate sentences, making sure that each is complete.

Herb talks too much. Nobody seems to mind.

2. Use a comma and a coordinating conjunction (*and, but, for, nor, or, so, yet*).*

Herb talks too much, *but* nobody seems to mind.

---

*For more work on coordinating conjunctions, see Chapter 13.

3. Use a subordinating conjunction (for example, *although, because, if, since,* or *when*).*

> *Although* Herb talks too much, nobody seems to mind.

PRACTICE 1

Many of these sentences contain run-ons or comma splices. If a sentence is correct, write *C* in the right-hand column. If it contains a run-on or a comma splice, write either *RO* or *CS*. Then correct the error in any way you wish. Use each method at least once.

EXAMPLE:
Because several   addictions,
Several celebrities have admitted their addictions public awareness of
addiction has increased.   *RO*

1. Many famous people have struggled with alcoholism or drug abuse
                                                                abuse, but
   some have overcome those problems.   *RO*

2. Often politicians, athletes, and actors hide their addiction and their
                        for
   recovery, they do not want to risk ruining their careers.   *CS*

3. Other celebrities choose to go public in their battles with
   alcohol or drugs.   *C*

4. They feel that their struggles may help others, they want to act as
                                            so
   positive role models.   *CS*

5. One such person is Betty Ford, a former First Lady with her family's
                                        Lady. With
   help, she became sober at age sixty.   *RO*
   Because her   successful,
6. Her recovery was successful she agreed to help several friends
   create a treatment center.   *RO*

7. The center opened in 1982 in Rancho Mirage, California.   *C*

8. At the Betty Ford Center, alcoholics and addicts receive counseling
                                        and
   and support for their new way of life, thousands have been treated
   there.   *CS*

9. Film star Elizabeth Taylor first entered the Betty Ford Center in
                                    and
   1983 to deal with alcohol dependency, she returned in 1988 to deal
   with painkiller dependency.   *CS*
   Although
10. NBA forward Lloyd Daniels was forced by his coach to admit his
                        problems. Now
    drinking and drug problems now he takes his recovery very
    seriously.   *RO*

---

*For more work on subordinating conjunctions, see Chapter 14.

11. Today people may become addicted when they are very young *young. The* the actress Drew Barrymore is just one example. *RO*

12. At age six, Barrymore acted in *E.T.: The Extra-Terrestrial* *, but* by age nine she was addicted to drugs and alcohol. *RO*

13. Her mother forced her into treatment when she was thirteen, *and* the two tried to keep Drew's problems a secret. *CS*

14. When a gossip magazine ran a story about her drug treatment, Barrymore decided to write a book about her addiction. *C*

15. Alcohol and drugs harm millions of Americans, *but* when someone recovers, his or her triumph can give others the courage to seek help. *CS*

PRACTICE 2

Correct each run-on or comma splice in two ways. Be sure to punctuate correctly.

EXAMPLE: Technology will change the way we shop will we like the new way?

a. *Technology will change the way we shop. Will we like the new way?*

b. *Technology will change the way we shop, but will we like the new way?*

1. For instance, you want to purchase a car, you may walk up to an outdoor booth.

   a. *For instance, when you want to purchase a car, you may walk up to an outdoor booth.*

   b. *For instance, you want to purchase a car, so you may walk up to an outdoor booth.*

2. You select the options on a computer screen, you press an order entry key.

   a. *After you select the options on a computer screen, you press an order entry key.*

   b. *You select the options on a computer screen, and you press an order entry key.*

3. A factory assembles your car it is later delivered to your local dealer.

   a. *A factory assembles your car, and it is later delivered to your local dealer.*

   b. *A factory assembles your car. It is later delivered to your local dealer.*

4. You go to a store to buy jeans, none are on the shelf.

  a. *When you go to a store to buy jeans, none are on the shelf.*

  b. *You go to a store to buy jeans, but none are on the shelf.*

5. Instead, you look at different styles on-screen you make your choice.

  a. *Instead, as you look at different styles on-screen, you make your choice.*

  b. *Instead, you look at different styles on-screen, and you make your choice.*

6. Taking measurements is not new now they can be taken by a three-dimensional camera.

  a. *Although taking measurements is not new, now they can be taken by a three-dimensional camera.*

  b. *Taking measurements is not new, but now they can be taken by a three-dimensional camera.*

7. Your measurements have been taken electronically your jeans will fit perfectly.

  a. *Because your measurements have been taken electronically, your jeans will fit perfectly.*

  b. *Your measurements have been taken electronically, so your jeans will fit perfectly.*

8. Your selection and measurements are transmitted to a factory your jeans are made to order.

  a. *Your selection and measurements are transmitted to a factory. Your jeans are made to order.*

  b. *Your selection and measurements are transmitted to a factory, and your jeans are made to order.*

9. You want to experiment with changing your hairstyle, a computer screen will show you with long, short, or differently colored hair.

   a. *If you want to experiment with changing your hairstyle, a computer*

   screen will show you with long, short, or differently colored hair.

   b. *You want to experiment with changing your hairstyle. A computer*

   screen will show you with long, short, or differently colored hair.

10. You can leave the way you came in you can leave with a new look.

    a. *Although you can leave the way you came in, you can leave with a new look.*

    b. *You can leave the way you came in, or you can leave with a new look.*

PRACTICE: WRITING ASSIGNMENT

On the first day of the term, teachers generally announce their rules: rules about how homework should be handed in or how many absences are allowed. This writing assignment is your chance to think about rules that *students* might expect *instructors* to follow. In small groups, discuss what rules instructors should follow in order to help students learn. List at least five rules.

Then let each group member choose one rule to write about, using examples from his or her classroom experiences to explain why that rule is important. Finally, exchange papers with a group-mate, checking each other's work for run-ons and comma splices.

✔ Chapter Highlights

Avoid run-ons and comma splices:

Her house faces the ocean the view is breathtaking. *(run-on)*

Her house faces the ocean, the view is breathtaking. *(comma splice)*

Use these techniques to avoid run-ons and comma splices.

■ **Write two complete sentences:**

Her house faces the ocean. The view is breathtaking.

■ **Use a coordinating conjunction:**

Her house faces the ocean, *so* the view is breathtaking.

■ **Use a subordinating conjunction:**

Because her house faces the ocean, the view is breathtaking.

Chapter Review

Run-ons and comma splices are most likely to occur in paragraphs or longer pieces of writing. Proofread each paragraph for run-ons and comma splices. Correct the run-ons and the comma splices in any way that makes sense: Make two separate sentences, add a coordinating conjunction, or add a subordinating conjunction. Then write a revised version of the paragraph on a separate sheet of paper. Punctuate with care.

A. (1) More than 750,000 people traveled to Graceland last *year it* is the most visited home in America except for the White House. (2) In case you didn't know, Graceland was the home of rock-and-roll legend Elvis *Presley. He* bought it in 1957 at the age of twenty-two when he suddenly became rich and famous. (3) It was opened to the public in 1982, five years after Elvis died there. (4) The eighteen-room Memphis mansion was Elvis's home for twenty years, *so* visitors can see what was considered luxury living in the 1960s and '70s. (5) Vinyl beanbag chairs, mirrored ceilings, and shag carpeting were high fashion then. (6) However, many visitors travel to the singer's home to honor the man rather than to see the house. (7) For some, a trip to Graceland has become a spiritual *experience. During* Elvis Presley's "Death Week," tens of thousands arrive from all over the world to honor their idol.

B. (1) José Clemente Orozco was a brilliant twentieth-century Mexican painter. (2) He became interested in art when he was seven years *old. On* his way to school, Orozco watched printmaker José Guadalupe Posada. (3) He begged his mother to let him take art classes. (4) Orozco became the youngest student to study drawing at the Academia de San *Carlos, but* he was soon able to draw better than older students. (5) At seventeen, Orozco lost his left hand in an *accident, yet* the young artist continued to take classes. (6) In his late thirties, he began to paint large, colorful murals on building *walls. These* murals made him famous. (7) Although Orozco was driven out of Mexico several times for publicly criticizing the government, he won praise and *awards, and* his work helped draw international attention to Mexican art.

C. (1) The U.S. government first investigated unidentified flying objects, or UFOs, during the 1940s. (2) In 1947, President Truman formed a secret panel of scientists and military officers to research ~~UFOs, that~~ *UFOs. That* same year, one of the most bizarre cases occurred. (3) Between June 27 and July 2, more than a dozen witnesses in western states saw bright, disk-shaped objects in the sky. (4) On July 2, a sheep rancher named William Brazel heard a huge ~~explosion~~ *explosion, and* the next day he found the wreckage of a crash. (5) He notified local Air Force officials, who issued a press release about the discovery of an alien ~~spaceship both~~ *spaceship. Both* national and international newspapers carried the story. (6) Near Roswell, New Mexico, unusual tinfoil-like metal and the bodies of space aliens were supposedly ~~found,~~ *found, but* almost immediately, the Air Force changed its story and denied its own report.

(7) In 1995 and 1996, film footage broadcast on TV claimed to be a record of an autopsy performed on an alien from the Roswell crash. (8) The film's photographer insists that the film is authentic, *but* it has been a center of controversy since its showing. (9) The film is of poor ~~quality, the~~ *quality. The* photographer seems to avoid showing the alien clearly. (10) It has been examined by experts from various fields, including specialists in anatomy and in film special effects. (11) ~~Many~~ *Although many* of the experts suggest that the film is a fake, others are sure that it is genuine. (12) Kodak agreed to examine the film for authenticity, *yet* the film was not sent to Kodak's laboratory. (13) The matter still remains a mystery.

D. (1) What do you do every night before you go to sleep and every morning when you wake up? (2) You probably brush your teeth, *but* most people in the United States did not start brushing their teeth until after the 1850s. (3) People living in the nineteenth century did not have ~~toothpaste,~~ *toothpaste.* Dr. Washington Wentworth Sheffield developed a tooth-cleaning substance, which soon became widely available. (4) With the help of his son, this Connecticut dentist changed our daily habits by making the first ~~toothpaste it~~ *toothpaste. It* was called Dr. Sheffield's Creme Dentifrice. (5) ~~The~~ *Because the* product was not marketed cleverly enough, the idea of using toothpaste caught on slowly. (6) Then toothpaste was put into tin ~~tubes~~ *tubes, and* everyone wanted to try this new product. (7) Think of life without tubes of mint-flavored ~~toothpaste~~ *toothpaste, and* then thank Dr. Sheffield for his idea.

E. (1) The first semester of college is difficult for many students they must take on many new responsibilities. *because*

(2) For instance, they must create their own schedules. (3) New students get to select their ~~courses in~~ addition, they have to decide when they will take them. *courses. In*

(4) Students also must purchase their own textbooks. ~~textbooks, colleges~~ do not distribute textbooks each term as high schools do. *textbooks. Colleges*

(5) No bells ring to announce when classes begin and ~~end~~ students are supposed to arrive on time. *end, yet*

(6) Furthermore, many professors do not call the ~~roll~~ they expect students to attend classes regularly and know the assignments. *roll, for*

(7) Above all, new students must be self-disciplined. (8) No one stands over them telling them to do their homework or to visit the writing lab for extra ~~help, they~~ must balance the temptation to have fun and the desire to build a successful future. *help. They*

CHAPTER 16

Semicolons

So far you have learned to join ideas together in two ways.

Coordinating conjunctions (*and, but, for, nor, or, so, yet*) can join ideas:

(1) This is the worst food we have ever tasted, *so* we will never eat in this restaurant again.

Subordinating conjunctions (for example, *although, as, because, if,* and *when*) can join ideas:

(2) *Because* this is the worst food we have ever tasted, we will never eat in this restaurant again.

Another way to join ideas is with a semicolon:

(3) This is the worst food we have ever tasted; we will never eat in this restaurant again.

A *semicolon* joins two related independent ideas without a conjunction; do not capitalize the first word after a semicolon.

Use the semicolon for variety. In general, use no more than one or two semicolons in a paragraph.

Each independent idea below is the first half of a sentence. Add a semicolon and a second complete idea, one that can stand alone.

EXAMPLE: Ken was a cashier at Food City ____; *now he manages the store.* _____

_____

1. My cat spotted a mouse ____; *both of them ran in opposite directions.* ____

_____

2. The garage was filled with used tires ____; *the yard was littered with fenders and* hubcaps.

3. Beatrice has an unlisted phone number ____; *I have it programmed into my phone.*

_____

4. The man browsed the sale table ____; *he purchased two ties and a belt.* ____

_____

5. I felt sure someone had been in the room ____; *my coat was not where I had left it.*

_____

6. P.J. is majoring in philosophy ____; *he loves to think.* ____

_____

7. Roslyn's first car had a stick shift ____; *her second one has an automatic* transmission.

8. The batter takes a hard swing at the ball ____; *he misses it for strike three.*

_____

BE CAREFUL: Do not use a semicolon between a dependent idea and an independent idea.

Although he is never at home, he is not difficult to reach at the office.

■ You cannot use a semicolon in this sentence because the first idea (*although he is never at home*) cannot stand alone.

■ The word *although* requires that another idea be added in order to make a complete sentence.

PRACTICE 2

Which of these ideas can be followed by a semicolon and an independent thought? Check them (✔).

1. Mr. Horgan squinted through his glasses ✔
2. The library has installed new computers ✔
3. After he finishes cleaning the fish ____
4. When I left, she was laughing ✔
5. My answer is simple ✔
6. Because I could not find my car keys ____
7. The rain poured down in buckets ✔
8. When the health fair is over ____
9. Unless you arrive early ____
10. The town of Montclair recycles its newspapers and glass ✔

   Now copy the sentences you have checked, add a semicolon, and complete each sentence with a second independent idea. You should have checked sentences 1, 2, 4, 5, 7, and 10.

1. *Mr. Horgan squinted through his glasses; the print was just too small.*

2. *The library has installed new computers; we can find information faster now.*

4. *When I left, she was laughing; she had just finished reading the comics.*

5. *My answer is simple; I will not go.*

7. *The rain poured down in buckets; everyone left the stands.*

10. *The town of Montclair recycles its newspapers and glass; other towns should follow its lead.*

PRACTICE: WRITING ASSIGNMENT

Many people find that certain situations make them nervous or anxious—for example, giving a speech or meeting strangers at a social gathering. Have you ever conquered such an anxiety yourself or even learned to cope with it successfully?

Write to someone who has the same fear you have had; encourage him or her with your success story, explaining how you managed the anxiety. Describe what steps you took.

Use one or two semicolons in your paper. Make sure that semicolons join together two independent ideas.

✔ Chapter Highlights

■ **A semicolon joins two independent ideas:**

I like hiking; she prefers fishing.

■ **Do not capitalize the first word after a semicolon.**

| Independent idea | ; | independent idea. |

Chapter Review

Proofread for incorrect semicolons or capital letters. Make any corrections above the lines.

(1) The Swiss Army knife is carried in the pockets and purses of millions of travelers, campers, and just plain folks. (2) Numerous useful gadgets are folded into its famous red handle; *these* These include knife blades, tweezers, scissors, toothpick, screwdriver, bottle opener, fish scaler, and magnifying glass. (3) Because the knife contains many tools; *tools,* it is also carried by explorers, mountain climbers, and astronauts. (4) Lives have been saved by the Swiss Army knife. (5) It once opened the iced-up oxygen system of someone climbing Mount Everest; *it* It saved the lives of scientists stranded on an island who used the tiny saw on the knife to cut branches for a fire. (6) The handy Swiss Army knife was created for Swiss soldiers in 1891; *1891 and* and soon became popular all over the world. (7) It comes in many models and colors *colors; many* many people prefer the classic original. (8) The Swiss Army knife deserves its reputation for beautiful design and usefulness; a red one is on permanent display in New York's famous Museum of Modern Art.

CHAPTER 17

Conjunctive Adverbs

PART A Defining and Using Conjunctive Adverbs

PART B Punctuating Conjunctive Adverbs

PART A — Defining and Using Conjunctive Adverbs

Another excellent method of joining ideas is to use a semicolon and a special kind of adverb. This special adverb is called a *conjunctive adverb* because it is part *conjunction* and part *adverb*.

> (1) (a) He received an A on his term paper; *furthermore,*
>
>   (b) the instructor exempted him from the final.

■ *Furthermore* adds idea (b) to idea (a).

■ The sentence might have been written, "He received an A on his term paper, *and* the instructor exempted him from the final."

■ But *furthermore* is stronger, more emphatic.

■ Note the punctuation.

> (2) (a) Jane has never studied finance; *however,*
>
>   (b) she plays the stock market like a pro.

■ *However* contrasts ideas (a) and (b).

■ The sentence might have been written, "Jane has never studied finance, *but* she plays the stock market like a pro."

■ But *however* is stronger, more emphatic.

■ Note the punctuation.

> (3) (a) The complete dictionary weighs thirty pounds; *therefore,*
>
>   (b) I bring my pocket edition to school.

■ *Therefore* shows that idea (a) is the cause of idea (b).

■ The sentence might have been written, "*Because* the complete dictionary weighs thirty pounds, I bring my pocket edition to school."

■ But *therefore* is stronger, more emphatic.

■ Note the punctuation.

A *conjunctive adverb* **may be used with a semicolon only when both ideas are independent and can stand alone.**

Here are some common conjunctive adverbs and their meanings:

Common Conjunctive Adverbs		
consequently	*means*	as a result
furthermore	*means*	in addition
however	*means*	in contrast
instead	*means*	in place of
meanwhile	*means*	at the same time
nevertheless	*means*	in contrast
otherwise	*means*	as an alternative
therefore	*means*	for that reason

Conjunctive adverbs are also called *transitional expressions*. They help the reader see the transitions, or changes, in meaning from one idea to the next.

PRACTICE

Add an idea after each conjunctive adverb. The idea you add must make sense in terms of the entire sentence, so keep in mind the meaning of each conjunctive adverb. If necessary, refer to the chart.

EXAMPLE: Several students had questions about the final; therefore, _they stayed after class to chat with the instructor._

1. Anthony ran to get help; meanwhile, _the rest of us just stood there in shock._

2. Anna says whatever is on her mind; consequently, _she sometimes offends people_

3. I refuse to wear those red cowboy boots again; furthermore, _I won't wear the ten-gallon hat._

4. Travis is a good role model; otherwise, *his little son might not be so polite.*

5. Kim wanted to volunteer at the hospital; however, *she couldn't find time to* *take the training course for volunteers.*

6. My mother carried two bulky pieces of luggage off the plane; furthermore, *she had her coat and a tennis racket under her arm.*

7. My parents love to read mysteries; however, *my brother and I read only* *nonfiction.*

8. The gas gauge on my car does not work properly; therefore, *I record my* *mileage every time I fill the gas tank.*

PART B   Punctuating Conjunctive Adverbs

Notice the punctuation pattern:

> Complete idea; conjunctive adverb, complete idea.

■ The conjunctive adverb is preceded by a semicolon.

■ It is followed by a comma.

PRACTICE 1

Punctuate these sentences correctly.

1. Within the next eight years, employment will increase by 14 percent therefore *percent; therefore,*

   17.7 million jobs will be added to the job market.

2. Ninety-five percent of the increase will be in salaried employment however *employment; however,*

   the number of self-employed workers will increase by 950,000.

3. Service jobs will account for most of the new jobs furthermore business, *jobs; furthermore,*

   health, and education services will account for 70 percent of the growth in

   service jobs.

4. Two of the industries that produce goods—manufacturing and mining—will

   decline meanwhile other goods-producing industries—construction and *decline; meanwhile,*

   agriculture—will grow.

5. One of the two fastest-growing job areas will be health services therefore *services; therefore,*

   personal care assistants and similar help will be in great demand.

6. Scientific research and computer applications are thriving in business and
   industry; consequently,
   industry consequently it isn't surprising that computer technology is the

   other of the two fastest-growing job areas.

7. Education is usually important in getting a high-paying *job; nevertheless,* job nevertheless

   occupations such as carpentry and police work offer higher-than-average

   earnings without requiring a college degree.

8. Work that requires the least education and training will provide the most
   openings; however,
   openings however it offers the lowest pay.

9. For more information about the future job market, go to your college
   library; otherwise,
   library otherwise you can go to your town library.

10. Studying the *Occupational Outlook Handbook* can give you valuable career
    information; furthermore,
    information furthermore it may help you find a rewarding career.

PRACTICE 2

Combine each set of sentences into one, using a conjunctive adverb. Choose a conjunctive adverb that expresses the relationship between the two ideas. Punctuate with care.

1. (a) Marilyn fell asleep on the train.

   (b) She missed her stop.

   Combination: *Marilyn fell asleep on the train; therefore, she missed her stop.*

   _____

2. (a) Last night, Channel 20 televised a special about gorillas.

   (b) I did not get home in time to see it.

   Combination: *Last night, Channel 20 televised a special about gorillas;*

   however, I did not get home in time to see it.

3. (a) Roberta wrote her nephew every month.

   (b) She received answers infrequently.

   Combination: *Roberta wrote her nephew every month; nevertheless, she*

   received answers infrequently.

4. (a) It takes me almost an hour to get to the factory each morning.

   (b) The employers make working there a pleasure.

   Combination: *It takes me almost an hour to get to the factory each morning;*

   however, the employers make working there a pleasure.

5. (a) Luke missed work on Monday.

   (b) He did not proofread the quarterly report.

   Combination: *Luke missed work on Monday; consequently, he did not*

   proofread the quarterly report.

BE CAREFUL: Never use a semicolon and a conjunctive adverb when the conjunctive adverb does not join two independent ideas.

(1) *However,* I don't like him.
(2) I don't, *however,* like him.
(3) I don't like him, *however.*

■ Why aren't semicolons used in sentences (1), (2), and (3)?

■ These sentences contain only one independent idea; therefore, a semicolon cannot be used.

Never use a semicolon to join two ideas if one of the ideas is subordinate to the other.

(4) If I were you, *however,* I would never talk to him again.

■ Are the two ideas in sentence (4) independent?

■ *If I were you* cannot stand alone as an independent idea; therefore, a semicolon cannot be used.

PRACTICE 3

On separate paper, write four sentences, using a different conjunctive adverb in each one. Make sure both ideas in each sentence are independent.

PRACTICE: WRITING ASSIGNMENT

Reread Practice 1 in Part B, and choose a career or a general area of work that you are interested in. Then assume that you are writing to a job counselor requesting information. You want him or her to get a clear sense of who you are and what kind of work might be right for you. Mention any relevant past experience you may have had or even family members or friends who are doing similar work and have encouraged you.

Use one or two semicolons with conjunctive adverbs in your letter. Be sure that the semicolons and the conjunctive adverbs join two independent ideas.

✔ Chapter Highlights

■ **A semicolon and a conjunctive adverb join two independent ideas:**

We can't go rowing now; *however,* we can go on Sunday.

Lou earned an 83 on the exam; *therefore,* he passed physics.

$$\boxed{Independent\ idea} \left\{ \begin{array}{l} ;\ consequently, \\ ;\ furthermore, \\ ;\ however, \\ ;\ instead, \\ ;\ meanwhile, \\ ;\ nevertheless, \\ ;\ therefore, \end{array} \right\} \boxed{independent\ idea.}$$

■ **Use a semicolon** *only* **when the conjunctive adverb joins two independent ideas:**

I wasn't sorry; however, I apologized. *(two independent ideas)*

I apologized, however. *(one independent idea)*

If you wanted to go, however, you should have said so. *(one dependent idea + one independent idea)*

Chapter Review

Proofread the following paragraph for conjunctive adverb errors and punctuation errors. Then correct each error above the line.

(1) You might not know that the largest museum of Native American culture in the world is in New York ~~City~~ City; however, it is. (2) The National Museum of the American Indian houses more than one million ~~items~~ items; furthermore, it has more than eighty thousand photographs and forty thousand books. (3) The collection includes objects from such tribes as the Navajo, Algonquin, Hopi, Creek, Cherokee, and Seminole. (4) Among the items are textiles from Peru, baskets from the American Southwest, gold work from Colombia, and painted garments from the North American Plains tribes. (5) Many objects in the collection are on ~~display nevertheless~~ display; nevertheless, the museum needs more space in which to exhibit its treasures. (6) It will be ~~moved;~~ moved, therefore, to Washington, D.C. (7) In 2002, it will open on the last available site on the National Mall, next to the National Air and Space Museum.

CHAPTER 18

Relative Pronouns

PART A Defining and Using Relative Pronouns

PART B Punctuating Ideas Introduced by WHO, WHICH, or THAT

PART A   Defining and Using Relative Pronouns

To add variety to your writing, you sometimes may wish to use *relative pronouns* to combine two sentences.

(1) My father is eighty years old.
(2) He collects stamps.

■ Sentences (1) and (2) are grammatically correct.

■ They are so short, however, that you may wish to combine them.

(3) My father, who is eighty years old, collects stamps.

■ Sentence (3) is a combination of (1) and (2).

■ *Who* has replaced *he,* the subject of sentence (2). *Who* introduces the rest of the idea, *is eighty years old.*

■ *Who* is called a *relative pronoun* because it *relates* "is eighty years old" to "my father."*

BE CAREFUL: An idea introduced by a relative pronoun cannot stand alone as a complete and independent sentence. It is dependent; it needs an independent idea (like "My father collects stamps") to complete its meaning.

---

*For work on subject-verb agreement with relative pronouns, see Chapter 8, Part G.

Here are some more combinations:

> (4) He gives great singing lessons.
> (5) All his pupils love them.
> (6) He gives great singing lessons, *which* all his pupils love.

> (7) I have a large dining room.
> (8) It can seat twenty people.
> (9) I have a large dining room *that* can seat twenty people.

■ As you can see, *which* and *that* also can be used as relative pronouns.

■ In sentence (6), what does *which* relate or refer to? <u>great singing lessons</u>

■ In sentence (9), what does *that* relate or refer to? <u>a large dining room</u>

When *who, which,* and *that* are used as relative pronouns, they usually come directly after the words they relate to.

My father, who . . .

. . . singing lessons, which . . .

. . . dining room that . . .

BE CAREFUL: *Who, which,* and *that* cannot be used interchangeably.

Who **refers to people.**

Which **refers to things.**

That **refers to people or things.**

PRACTICE

Combine each set of sentences into one sentence. Make sure to use *who, which,* and *that* correctly.

EXAMPLE: a. The garden is beginning to sprout.

b. I planted it last week.

Combination: <u>The garden that I planted last week is beginning to sprout.</u>

1. a. My uncle is giving me diving lessons.

b. He was a state champion.

Combination: <u>My uncle, who was a state champion, is giving me diving lessons.</u>

_____

2. a. Our marriage ceremony was quick and sweet.

   b. It made our nervous parents happy.

   Combination: _Our marriage ceremony, which was quick and sweet, made our_

   nervous parents happy.

3. a. The manatee is a sea mammal.

   b. It lives along the Florida coast.

   Combination: _The manatee is a sea mammal that lives along the Florida coast._

4. a. Donna's house has a terrace.

   b. The terrace overlooks the bay.

   Combination: _Donna's house has a terrace that overlooks the bay._

5. a. This shopping mall has two hundred stores.

   b. It is a joy to shop in.

   Combination: _This shopping mall, which has two hundred stores, is a joy to shop in._

6. a. Hockey is a fast-moving game.

   b. It often becomes violent.

   Combination: _Hockey, which is a fast-moving game, often becomes violent._

7. a. Andrew Jackson was the seventh American president.

   b. He was born in South Carolina.

   Combination: _Andrew Jackson, who was born in South Carolina, was the_

   seventh American president.

8. a. At the beach, I always use sunscreen.

   b. It prevents burns and lessens the danger of skin cancer.

   Combination: _At the beach, I always use sunscreen, which prevents burns and_

   lessens the danger of skin cancer.

PART B Punctuating Ideas Introduced by WHO, WHICH, or THAT

Ideas introduced by relative pronouns can be one of two types, either *restrictive* or *nonrestrictive*. Punctuating them must be done carefully.

Restrictive

> Never eat peaches *that are green*.

■ What is the relative clause in this sentence? ___*that are green*___

■ Can you leave out *that are green* and still keep the basic meaning of the sentence?

■ *No!* You are not saying *don't eat peaches;* you are saying don't eat *certain kinds* of peaches—*green* ones.

■ Therefore, *that are green* is *restrictive;* it restricts the meaning of the sentence.

A *restrictive clause* **is not set off by commas; it is necessary to the meaning of the sentence.**

Nonrestrictive

> My guitar, *which is a Martin,* was given to me as a gift.

■ In this sentence, the relative clause is ___*which is a Martin*___.

■ Can you leave out *which is a Martin* and still keep the basic meaning of the sentence?

■ *Yes! Which is a Martin* merely adds a fact. It does not change the basic idea of the sentence, that *my guitar was given to me as a gift.*

■ Therefore, *which is a Martin* is called *nonrestrictive* because it does not restrict or change the meaning of the sentence.

A *nonrestrictive clause* **is set off by commas; it is not necessary to the meaning of the sentence.**

Note: *Which* **is often used as a nonrestrictive relative pronoun.**

PRACTICE 1

Punctuate correctly. Write a *C* next to each correct sentence.

1. People who need help are often embarrassed to ask for it. ___*C*___

2. Ovens that clean themselves are the best kind. ___*C*___

3. Paint that contains lead can be dangerous to children. ___*C*___

4. This silver ~~coin~~ *coin,* which is a rare ~~one~~ *one,* comes from Korea. ___

5. Edward's *watch,* watch which tells the time and the *date,* date was a

   gift from his wife.   _____

6. *Carol,* Carol who is a flight *attendant,* attendant has just left for Pakistan.   _____

7. Joel *Upton,* Upton who is a dean of *students,* students usually sings in the

   yearly talent show.   _____

8. Exercise that causes severe exhaustion is dangerous.   ___*C*___

PRACTICE 2

Complete each sentence by completing the relative clause.

EXAMPLE: Boxing is a sport that ___*upsets me*_____.

1. My aunt, who ___*doesn't even like animals*_____, rescued a cat last week.

2. A family that ___*works as a team*_____
   can solve its problems.

3. I never vote for candidates who ___*promise too much*_____.

4. This T-shirt, which *says, "All this and brains, too,"* was a gift from my husband.

5. Chicago, which ___*has a great aquarium*_____,
   is fun to visit.

6. James, who ___*wants to be a pilot*_____,
   just enlisted in the Air Force.

7. I cannot resist stores that ___*have bargain basements*_____.

8. The fireworks, which ___*were spectacular*_____, began at nine o'clock.

PRACTICE 3

On separate paper, write four sentences using restrictive relative clauses and four using nonrestrictive relative clauses. Punctuate with care.

PRACTICE: WRITING ASSIGNMENT

In small groups, discuss a change that you would like to see made in your neighborhood—an additional traffic light or more police patrols. Your task is to write a flier that will convince neighbors that this change is important; your purpose is to win them over to your side. The flier might note, for instance, that a child was killed at a certain intersection or that you know of several burglaries that could have been prevented.

   Each member of the group should write his or her own flier, including one or two sentences with relative pronouns and correct punctuation. Then read the fliers aloud; decide which one is the most effective and why. Be prepared to defend your choice. Finally, exchange papers with a partner and check for the correct use of relative pronouns.

✔ Chapter Highlights

■ **Relative pronouns** (*who, which,* **and** *that*) **can join two independent ideas:**

> We met Krizia Stone, *who* runs an advertising agency.

> Last night, I had a hamburger *that* was too rare.

> My favorite radio station, *which* is WQDF, plays mostly jazz.

■ **Restrictive relative clauses change the meaning of the sentence. They are not set off by commas:**

> The uncle *who is helping me through college* lives in Texas.

> The car *that we saw Ned driving* was not his.

■ **Nonrestrictive relative clauses do not change the meaning of the sentence. They are set off by commas:**

> My uncle, *who lives in Texas,* owns a supermarket.

> Ned's car, *which is a 1985 Mazda,* was at the repair shop.

Chapter Review

Proofread the following paragraph for relative pronoun errors and punctuation errors. Then correct each error above the line.

(1) Charles Anderson is best known as the trainer of the Tuskegee ~~Airmen~~ *Airmen,* who were the first African American combat pilots. (2) During a time when African Americans were prevented from becoming pilots, Anderson was fascinated by planes. (3) He learned about flying from books. (4) At age twenty-two, he bought a used ~~plane which,~~ *plane, which* became his teacher. (5) Eventually he met ~~someone, who~~ *someone who* helped him become an expert flyer. (6) Battling against discrimination, Anderson became the first African American to earn an air transport pilot's license. (7) He and another pilot made the first round-trip flight across America by black Americans. (8) In 1939, Anderson started a civilian pilot training program at Tuskegee Institute, in Alabama. (9) One day Eleanor Roosevelt, ~~which~~ *who* was First Lady at the ~~time~~ *time,* insisted on flying with him. (10) Soon afterward, Tuskegee Institute was chosen by the Army Air Corps for a special program. (11) ~~Anderson~~ *Anderson, who* who was chief flight ~~instructor~~ *instructor,* gave America's first African American World War II pilots their initial training. (12) During the war, the Tuskegee Airmen showed great skill and ~~heroism which~~ *heroism, which* were later recognized by an extraordinary number of honors and awards.

CHAPTER 19

-ING Modifiers

PART A Using -ING Modifiers
PART B Avoiding Confusing Modifiers

PART A   Using -ING Modifiers

Another way to join ideas together is with an *-ing* modifier, or present participle.

> (1) Beth was learning to ski. She broke her ankle.
> (2) Learning to ski, Beth broke her ankle.

■ It seems that *while* Beth was learning to ski, she had an accident. Sentence (2) emphasizes this time relationship and also joins two short sentences in one longer one.

■ Remember that in sentence (2), *learning*, without its helping verb *was*, is no longer a verb. Instead, *learning to ski* refers to or modifies *Beth*, the subject of the new sentence.

> Learning to ski, Beth broke her ankle.

■ Note that a comma follows the introductory *-ing* modifier, setting it off from the independent idea.

PRACTICE

Combine the two sentences in each pair, using the *-ing* modifier to connect them. Drop unnecessary words. Draw an arrow from the *-ing* word to the word or words it refers to.

EXAMPLE: Tom was standing on the deck. He waved good-bye to his family.

Standing on the deck, Tom waved good-bye to his family.

1. Kyla was searching for change. She found her lost earring.

   Searching for change, Kyla found her lost earring.

2. Herb was singing in the shower. He woke the neighbors.

   Singing in the shower, Herb woke the neighbors.

3. They were hiking cross-country. They made many new friends.

   Hiking cross-country, they made many new friends.

4. She was visiting Santa Fe. She decided to move there.

   Visiting Santa Fe, she decided to move there.

5. You are loading your camera. You spot a grease mark on the lens.

   Loading your camera, you spot a grease mark on the lens.

6. Seth was mumbling to himself. He named the fifty states.

   Mumbling to himself, Seth named the fifty states.

7. Judge Smithers was pounding his gavel. He called a recess.

   Pounding his gavel, Judge Smithers called a recess.

8. The students enjoyed the evening together. They were listening to classical guitar and eating grapes.

   Listening to classical guitar and eating grapes, the students enjoyed the

   evening together.

PART B   Avoiding Confusing Modifiers

Be sure that your *-ing* modifiers say what you mean!

(1) Hanging by the toe from the dresser drawer, Joe found his sock.

■ Probably the writer did not mean that Joe spent time hanging by his toe. What, then, was hanging by the toe from the dresser drawer?

■ *Hanging* refers to the *sock*, of course, but the order of the sentence does not show this. We can clear up the confusion by turning the ideas around.

Joe found his sock hanging by the toe from the dresser drawer.

Read your sentences in the previous exercise to make sure the order of the ideas is clear, not confusing.

(2) Visiting my cousin, our house was robbed.

■ Does the writer mean that *our house* was visiting my cousin? Whom or what, then, does *visiting my cousin* refer to?

■ *Visiting* seems to refer to *I*, but there is no *I* in the sentence. To clear up the confusion, we would have to add or change words.

Visiting my cousin, I learned that our house was robbed.

PRACTICE 1

Rewrite the following sentences to clarify any confusing *-ing* modifiers.

1. Huffing and puffing, Ari's last race was run.

   Rewrite: _Huffing and puffing, Ari ran his last race._

2. Leaping from tree to tree, Professor Fernandez spotted a monkey.

   Rewrite: _Professor Fernandez spotted a monkey leaping from tree to tree._

3. Painting for three hours straight, the bathroom and the hallway were finished by Theresa.

   Rewrite: _Painting for three hours straight, Theresa finished the bathroom and_

   the hallway.

4. My son spotted our dog playing baseball in the schoolyard.

   Rewrite: _Playing baseball in the schoolyard, my son spotted our dog._

5. Lying in the driveway, Tonia discovered her calculus textbook.

   Rewrite: _Tonia discovered her calculus textbook lying in the driveway._

PRACTICE 2

On separate paper, write three sentences of your own, using *-ing* modifiers to join ideas.

PRACTICE: WRITING ASSIGNMENT

Some people feel that much popular music degrades women and encourages drug abuse and violence. Others feel that popular songs expose many of the social ills we suffer from today. What do you think?

Prepare to take part in a debate to defend or criticize popular music. Your job is to convince the other side that your view is correct. Use specific song titles and artists as examples to support your argument.

Use one or two *-ing* modifiers to join ideas together. Remember to punctuate correctly.

✔ Chapter Highlights

■ **An *-ing* modifier can join two ideas:**

(1) Sol was cooking dinner.

(2) He started a small fire.

(1) + (2) *Cooking* dinner, Sol started a small fire.

■ **Avoid confusing modifiers:**

I finally found my cat riding my bike. *(incorrect)*

Riding my bike, I finally found my cat. *(correct)*

Chapter Review

Proofread the following paragraph for comma errors and confusing modifiers. Then correct each error above the line.

(1) What happened in the shed behind Patrick O'Leary's house to start the Great Chicago Fire of 1871? (2) No one knows for sure. (3) S̶m̶o̶k̶i̶n̶g̶ ̶i̶n̶ ̶t̶h̶e̶ ̶s̶h̶e̶d̶,̶ *Some* s̶o̶m̶e̶ people say the fire was started by careless b̶o̶y̶s̶. *boys smoking in the shed.* (4) In another story, poker-playing youngsters accidentally kicked over an oil lamp. (5) However, the blame usually is placed on Mrs. O'Leary's cow. (6) At 8:45 P.M., swinging a lantern at her s̶i̶d̶e̶ *side,* Mrs. O'Leary went out to milk the unruly cow. (7) T̶h̶e̶ cow tipped the l̶a̶n̶t̶e̶r̶n̶ ̶s̶w̶i̶t̶c̶h̶i̶n̶g̶ ̶i̶t̶s̶ ̶t̶a̶i̶l̶. *Switching its tail, the lantern.* (8) Recalling the i̶n̶c̶i̶d̶e̶n̶t̶ ̶M̶r̶s̶. *incident, Mrs.* Nellie Hayes branded the cow theory "nonsense." (9) In fact, she said that the O'Learys' neighbors were having a party on the hot night of October 7. (10) Looking for some fresh m̶i̶l̶k̶ *milk,* a thirsty guest walked into the shed and dropped a lighted candle along the way. (11) Whatever happened, the fire was the greatest calamity of nineteenth-century America. (12) Killing three hundred people and destroying more than three square miles of b̶u̶i̶l̶d̶i̶n̶g̶s̶ ̶i̶t̶ *buildings, it* left ninety thousand people homeless.

UNIT 4   WRITING ASSIGNMENTS

As you complete each writing assignment, remember to perform these steps:

- Write a clear, complete topic sentence.

- Use freewriting, brainstorming, or clustering to generate ideas.

- Arrange your best ideas in a plan.

- Revise for support, unity, coherence, and exact language.

- Proofread for grammar, punctuation, and spelling errors.

Writing Assignment 1: *Be a witness.* You have just witnessed a fender-bender involving a car and an ice cream truck. No one was hurt, but the insurance company has asked you to write an eyewitness report. First, visualize the accident and how it occurred. Then jot as many details as possible to make your description of the accident as vivid as possible. Use subordinating conjunctions that indicate time (*when, as, before, while,* and so on) to show the order of events. Use as many techniques for joining ideas together as you can, being careful about punctuation. Proofread for run-ons and comma splices.

Writing Assignment 2: *Explain an accomplishment.* Suppose that the admissions committee of a college or graduate school needs to decide if you are the kind of person who can and will get difficult work done. Write a letter to prove that you are an achiever, someone with a major accomplishment under your belt. Discuss how you felt after the accomplishment and how the success has made you feel about the future. Use as many techniques for joining ideas together effectively as you can. Proofread for run-ons and comma splices.

Writing Assignment 3: *Define a person of faith.* How would you define a person of faith? Is it someone who goes regularly to a house of worship? Perhaps you feel it is someone who always volunteers for community service—in day-care centers or nursing homes. Use a person in the news, a friend, or a family member as an example of a person of faith. Give specific instances from his or her life and activities that show faith at work. Use as many techniques for joining ideas as you can. Proofread for run-ons and comma splices.

Writing Assignment 4: *React to a quotation.* From the Quotation Bank section "Work and Success," choose a quotation that you strongly agree or disagree with. For instance, is it true that "a good reputation is more valuable than money" or that "eighty percent of success is showing up"? What do you think? In your first sentence, repeat the quotation, explaining whether you do or don't agree with it. Then brainstorm, freewrite, or cluster to generate examples and facts supporting your view. Use your own or other people's experiences to strengthen your argument. Use as many techniques for joining ideas as you can. Proofread for run-ons and comma splices.

UNIT 4 REVIEW

Five Useful Ways to Join Ideas

In this unit, you have combined simple sentences by means of a **coordinating conjunction**, a **subordinating conjunction**, a **semicolon**, and a **semicolon** and **conjunctive adverb.** Here is a review chart of the sentence patterns discussed in this unit.

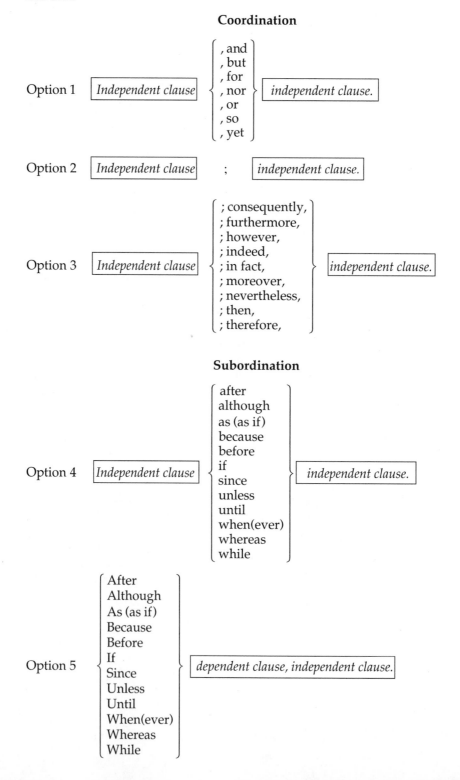

Coordination

Option 1 · Independent clause {, and / , but / , for / , nor / , or / , so / , yet} independent clause.

Option 2 · Independent clause ; independent clause.

Option 3 · Independent clause {; consequently, / ; furthermore, / ; however, / ; indeed, / ; in fact, / ; moreover, / ; nevertheless, / ; then, / ; therefore,} independent clause.

Subordination

Option 4 · Independent clause {after / although / as (as if) / because / before / if / since / unless / until / when(ever) / whereas / while} independent clause.

Option 5 · {After / Although / As (as if) / Because / Before / If / Since / Unless / Until / When(ever) / Whereas / While} dependent clause, independent clause.

Proofreading

We have changed the student composition below so that it contains run-ons, comma splices, and misused semicolons. Proofread for these errors. Then correct them above the lines in any way you choose.

Managing Time in College

(1) When I started college, time was a problem. (2) I was always desperately reading an assignment just before class or racing to get to work on time. (3) The stress became too much. (4) It took a ~~while~~ *while, but* now I know how to manage my time. (5) The secret of my success is flexible planning.

(6) At the beginning of each semester, I mark a calendar with all the due dates for the ~~term these~~ *term. These* include deadlines for assignments, papers, and tests. (7) I also write in social events and ~~obligations, therefore;~~ *obligations; therefore,* I know at a glance when I need extra time during the next few months.

(8) Next, I make out a model weekly study schedule. (9) First, I block in the hours when I have to sleep, eat, work, go to class, and tend to my ~~family then~~ *family. Then* I decide what time I will devote to study and relaxation. (10) Finally, I fill in the times I will study each subject, making sure I plan at least one hour of study time for each hour of class time. (11) Generally, I plan some time just before or after a ~~class that~~ *class. That* way I can prepare for a class or review my notes right after a lecture. (12) In reality, I don't follow this schedule ~~rigidly,~~ *rigidly;* I vary it according to the demands of the week and day. (13) In addition, I spend more time on my harder subjects and less time on the easy ones. (14) I also try to study my harder subjects in the ~~morning;~~ *morning* when I am most awake.

(15) I find that by setting up a model schedule but keeping it flexible, I can accomplish all I have to do with little worry. (16) This system may not help ~~everyone,~~ *everyone; however,* it has certainly worked for me.

Jesse Rose, student

Combining

Read each pair of sentences below to determine the relationship between them. Then join each pair in *two* different ways, using the conjunctions shown. Punctuate correctly.

1. The tide had not yet come in.
   We went swimming.

   (although) _____ *Although the tide had not yet come in, we went swimming.*
   _____

   (but) _____ *The tide had not yet come in, but we went swimming.*
   _____

2. Fans love watching Michael Jordan.
   He seems to fly.

   (for) _____ *Fans love watching Michael Jordan, for he seems to fly.*
   _____

   (because) _____ *Fans love watching Michael Jordan because he seems to fly.*
   _____

3. Alexis plays the trumpet very well.
   She hopes to have her own band someday.

   (and) _____ *Alexis plays the trumpet very well, and she hopes to have her*
   _____ *own band someday.*

   (furthermore) _____ *Alexis plays the trumpet very well; furthermore, she hopes to*
   _____ *have her own band someday.*

4. The lecture starts in five minutes.
   We had better get to our seats.

   (because) _____ *Because the lecture starts in five minutes, we had better get to*
   _____ *our seats.*

   (so) _____ *The lecture starts in five minutes, so we had better get to*
   _____ *our seats.*

5. He knows how to make money.
   He doesn't know how to save it.

   (although) _____ *Although he knows how to make money, he doesn't know how*
   _____ *to save it.*

   (however) _____ *He knows how to make money; however, he doesn't know how*
   _____ *to save it.*

Revising

Read through this paragraph of short, choppy sentences. Then revise it, combining some sentences. Use one coordinating conjunction, one subordinating conjunction, and any other ways you have learned to join ideas together. Keep some short sentences for variety. Make corrections above the lines, and punctuate with care.

(1) Nature lovers should watch out for a common danger, poison ivy.

harmless, but its

(2) Poison ivy looks ~~harmless.~~ (3) ~~Its~~ leaves, stems, and roots contain an allergy-

potent; one

producing oil. (4) This oil is very ~~potent.~~ (5) ~~One~~ drop can affect more than five

Because most   *oil, it*

hundred people. (6) ~~Most~~ people develop skin reactions from the ~~oil.~~ (7) ~~It~~ is best

to avoid any contact with poison ivy. (8) The potency of poison ivy lasts a long

jar that

time. (9) In fact, scientists once found a ~~jar.~~ (10) ~~The jar~~ had been buried for ten

artifact, they

centuries. (11) Handling this ~~artifact.~~ (12) ~~They~~ developed skin rashes. (13) Then

they realized the jar had been coated with poison ivy sap one thousand years

earlier! (14) Outdoor enthusiasts should learn to recognize poison ivy and

avoid it.

Describe a Detour off the Main Highway

When a writer really cares about a subject, often the reader will care too. In your group or class, read this student's paragraph, aloud if possible. As you read, underline any words or details that strike you as vivid or powerful.

> Sometimes detours off the main highway can bring wonderful surprises, and last week this happened to my husband and me. On the Fourth of July weekend, we decided to drive home the long way *way,* taking the old dirt farm road. When we pulled over to admire the afternoon light gleaming on a field of wet corn, we saw a tiny farm stand under a tree. No one was in sight, but a card table covered with a red checked cloth held pints of tomatoes, jars of jam, and a handwritten price list. Next to these was a vase full of red poppies and tiny American flags. We bought tomatoes *tomatoes,* leaving our money in the tin box stuffed with dollar bills. Driving home *home,* we both felt so happy, as if we had been given a great gift.
>
> *Kim Lee, student*

1. How effective is Ms. Lee's paragraph?

   __Y__ Clear topic sentence?   __Y__ Rich supporting details?

   __Y__ Logical organization?   __Y__ Effective conclusion?

2. Discuss your underlinings with one another, explaining as specifically as possible why a particular word or sentence is effective. For instance, the "red poppies and tiny American flags" are so exact that you can see them.

3. This student supports her topic sentence with a single *example*, one brief story told in detail. If you were to support the same topic sentence, what example from your own life might you use?

4. The concluding sentence tells the reader that she and her husband felt they had been given a "great gift." What was that gift? Is it clear?

5. Proofread for grammar and spelling. Do you notice any error patterns (two or more errors of the same type) that this student should watch out for? *She omits the comma when she joins ideas with an -ing modifer.*

About her writing process, Ms. Lee writes:

> I wrote this paper in my usual way—I sort of plan, and then I freewrite on the subject. I like freewriting—I pick through it for certain words or details, but of course it is also a mess. From my freewriting I got "light gleaming on a field of wet corn" and the last sentence, about the gift.

Writing and Revising Ideas

1. Develop the topic sentence "Sometimes detours off the main highway can bring wonderful [disturbing] surprises."

2. Use one example to develop the topic sentence "The best [worst] gifts

   are often _____."

As you plan your paragraph, try to angle the subject toward something that interests *you*—chances are, it will interest your readers too. Consider using one good example to develop your paragraph. As you revise, make sure that the body of your paragraph perfectly fits the topic sentence.

Choosing the Right Noun, Pronoun, Adjective, Adverb, or Preposition

Choosing the right *form* of many words in English can be tricky. This unit will help you avoid some common errors. In this unit, you will

✔ Learn about singular and plural nouns

✔ Choose correct pronouns

✔ Use adjectives and adverbs correctly

✔ Choose the right prepositions

Here, two researchers set forth new findings about happiness. If possible, read the paragraph aloud.

In study after study, four traits characterize happy people. First, especially in individualistic Western cultures, they like themselves. They have high self-esteem and usually believe themselves to be *more ethical, more intelligent, less prejudiced, better able* to get along with others, and *healthier* than the average person. Second, happy people typically feel personal control. Those with little or no control over their lives—such as prisoners, nursing home patients, severely impoverished groups or individuals, and citizens in totalitarian regimes—suffer lower morale and worse health. Third, happy people are usually optimistic. Fourth, most happy people are extroverted. Although one might expect that introverts would live more happily in the serenity of their less stressed . . . lives, extroverts are happier—whether alone or with others.

David G. Myers and Ed Diener, "The Pursuit of Happiness," *Scientific American*

■ This well-organized paragraph tells us that happy people think they are more *ethical*, more *intelligent*, less *prejudiced*, better *able* . . . , and *healthier*. Do you know why these words—adjectives—are correct as written?

■ If you don't know the useful words *extrovert* and *introvert*, look them up. Which refers to you?

■ Analyze how happy you are based on the four traits.

■ Describe an extrovert or introvert you have observed.

Nouns

PART A Defining Singular and Plural

A *noun* names a person, a place, a thing, or an idea. Nouns may be singular or plural.

Singular **means one.** *Plural* **means more than one.**

Singular	Plural
a reporter	the reporters
a pear	pears
the boss	the bosses

■ Nouns usually add *-s* or *-es* to form the plural.

Some nouns form their plurals in other ways. Below is a partial list:

Singular	Plural
child	children
foot	feet
goose	geese
man	men
mouse	mice
tooth	teeth
woman	women

■ Many nouns ending in *-f* or *-fe* change their endings to *-ves* in the plural:

Singular	Plural
half	halves
knife	knives
leaf	leaves
life	lives
scarf	scarves
shelf	shelves
wife	wives
wolf	wolves

Add *-es* to most nouns that end in *o*.

echo + *es* = echoes	potato + *es* = potatoes
hero + *es* = heroes	veto + *es* = vetoes

Here are some exceptions to memorize:

pianos	solos
radios	sopranos

Other nouns do not change at all to form the plural. Below is a partial list:

Singular	Plural
deer	deer
fish	fish
moose	moose
sheep	sheep

Hyphenated nouns usually form plurals by adding *-s* or *-es* to the first word:

Singular	Plural
brother-in-law	brothers-in-law
maid-of-honor	maids-of-honor
mother-in-law	mothers-in-law
runner-up	runners-up

If you are ever unsure about the plural of a noun, check a dictionary. For example, if you look up the noun *woman* in the dictionary, you will find an entry like this:

woman\women

The first word listed, *woman*, is the singular form of the noun; the second word, *women*, is the plural.

Some dictionaries list the plural form of a noun only if the plural is unusual. If no plural is listed, the noun probably adds *-s* or *-es*.

PRACTICE 1

Make the following nouns plural.* If you are not sure of a particular plural, check the charts.

Singular	Plural
1. necktie	neckties
2. hero	heroes
3. man	men
4. half	halves
5. purse	purses
6. deer	deer
7. runner-up	runners-up
8. woman	women
9. radio	radios
10. tooth	teeth
11. brother-in-law	brothers-in-law
12. birdcage	birdcages
13. knife	knives
14. potato	potatoes
15. mouse	mice
16. child	children
17. pot	pots
18. wife	wives
19. place	places
20. maid-of-honor	maids-of-honor

REMEMBER: Do not add an *-s* **to words that form plurals by changing an internal letter or letters. For example, the plural of** *man* **is** *men,* **not** *mens;* **the plural of** *woman* **is** *women,* **not** *womens;* **the plural of** *foot* **is** *feet,* **not** *feets.*

---

*For help with spelling, see Chapter 31.

© 1998 Houghton Mifflin Company

PRACTICE 2

Proofread the following paragraph for incorrect plural nouns. Cross out errors, and correct them above the lines.

(1) Last summer, my friend Jake and I took our families, including our
mothers-in-law,
~~mother-in-laws~~, to Yellowstone National Park. (2) While the adults looked for
children
ward to seeing hot springs and geysers, the ~~childs~~ were most excited about seeing

the wildlife. (3) Yellowstone, which is located primarily in Wyoming, is one of

the world's greatest wildlife sanctuaries. (4) The animals that live there include
wolves, sheep, moose,   deer.   fish.
~~wolfes, sheeps, mooses,~~ and ~~deers~~. (5) Yellowstone's streams are filled with ~~fishs~~.
                                                geese.   sisters-in-
(6) Among its two hundred species of birds are Canada ~~gooses~~. (7) Our ~~sister-in-~~
law
~~laws~~ were most impressed by Old Faithful, the geyser that erupts almost hourly.
wives
(8) Our ~~wifes~~ enjoyed fishing in many of Yellowstone's lakes and streams. (9) We
            men   women
easily understood why so many ~~mens~~ and ~~womans~~ go to this beautiful place.

(10) However, most of the three million tourists who visit each year arrive in cars

and race through the park's 2.2 million acres in just three days. (11) Those with
            lives
more time in their ~~lifes~~ and more willingness to experience discomfort can avoid
        passers-by.
being ~~passer bys~~. (12) They can leave the cars, crowds, and hotels behind, camp

in the wild, and have an even deeper experience of this gorgeous wilderness.

PART B Signal Words: Singular and Plural

A *signal word* **tells you whether a singular or a plural noun usually follows.**

These signal words tell you that a *singular noun* usually follows:

Signal Words

a(n)
another
a single
each   } motorboat
every
one

These signal words tell you that a *plural noun* usually follows:

Signal Words

all
both
few
many   ⎫
several   ⎬ motorboats
some
two (or more) ⎭

PRACTICE 1

In the blank following each signal word, write either a singular or a plural noun. Use as many different nouns as you can think of.

EXAMPLES: a single *stamp*

most *fabrics*

1. a(n) *map*

2. some *people*

3. few *words*

4. nine *pens*

5. one *angel*

6. several *attorneys*

7. each *moment*

8. another *tent*

9. a single *governor*

10. every *relative*

11. both *situations*

12. most *statues*

PRACTICE 2

Read the following essay for incorrect singular or plural nouns following signal words. Cross out errors, and correct them above the lines.

The Best Medicine

(1) Many ~~researcher~~ *researchers* believe that laughter is good for people's health. (2) In fact, some ~~doctor~~ *doctors* have concluded that laughter actually helps patients heal faster. (3) To put this theory into practice, several ~~hospital~~ *hospitals* have introduced humor routines into their treatment programs. (4) One ~~programs~~ *program* is a children's clown care unit that operates in seven New York City hospitals. (5) Thirty-five ~~clown~~ *clowns* from the Big Apple Circus go to the hospitals three times every ~~weeks.~~ *week.* (6) Few ~~child~~ *children* can keep from laughing at the "rubber chicken soup" and "red nose transplant" routines.

(7) Although the program hasn't been studied scientifically, many ~~observer~~ *observers* have witnessed its positive effects. (8) However, some ~~specialist~~ *specialists* are conducting strictly scientific research on health and laughter. (9) One study, carried out at Loma Linda University in California, has shown the positive effects of laughter on the immune system. (10) Another ~~tests,~~ *test,* done at the College of William and Mary in Virginia, has confirmed the California findings. (11) Other studies in progress are suggesting that all physiological ~~system~~ *systems* may be affected positively by laughter. (12) Finally, research also is backing up a ~~claims~~ *claim* made by Norman Cousins, author of the book *Anatomy of an Illness.* (13) While he was fighting a life-threatening ~~diseases,~~ *disease,* Cousins maintained that hearty laughter took away his pain. (14) Several recent ~~study~~ *studies* have shown that pain does become less intense when the sufferer responds to comedy.

PRACTICE 3

On separate paper, write three sentences using signal words that require singular nouns. Then write three sentences using signal words that require plural nouns.

PART C   Signal Words with OF

Many signal words are followed by *of . . .* or *of the . . . .* Usually, these signal words are followed by a *plural* noun (or a collective noun) because you are really talking about one or more from a larger group.*

many of the
a few of the } houses are . . .
lots of the

one of the } houses is . . .
each of the

BE CAREFUL: The signal words *one of the* and *each of the* are followed by a *plural* noun, but the verb is *singular* because only the signal word (*one, each*) is the real subject.**

---

*For more work on collective nouns, see Chapter 21, Part C.
**For more work on this type of construction, see Chapter 8, Part G.

> (1) *One* of the apples *is* spoiled.
> (2) *Each* of the trees *grows* quickly.

- In sentence (1), *one* is the subject, not *apples*.
- In sentence (2), *each* is the subject, not *trees*.

PRACTICE 1

Fill in your own nouns in the following sentences. Use a different noun in each sentence.

1. Many of the _____*students*_____ enrolled in Chemistry 202.

2. Larry lost one of his _____*sandals*_____ at the beach.

3. This is one of the _____*suggestions*_____ that everyone liked.

4. Each of the _____*protesters*_____ carried a sign.

5. You are one of the few _____*parents*_____ who can do somersaults.

6. Lots of the _____*guests*_____ gave long, dull speeches.

PRACTICE 2

Use a different noun in each sentence. Write five sentences using signal words with *of*.

EXAMPLE: (many of those . . .) _*I planted many of those flowers myself.*_

_____

1. (one of my . . .) _____

_____

2. (many of the . . .) _____

_____

3. (lots of the . . .) _____

_____

4. (each of these . . .) _____

_____

5. (a few of your . . .) _____

_____

PRACTICE 3

Read the following essay for correct plural nouns after signal words with *of*. Cross out errors, and correct them above the lines.

The Fender Sound

(1) If you are a fan of popular music or blues, the guitar sound you have been listening to was created by Leo Fender. (2) Leo Fender invented the modern amplified guitar, the instrument of choice for many of today's pop ~~star.~~ *stars.* (3) The instrument that Fender introduced in the 1940s had an incredible sound—clear, crisp, and clean. (4) Buddy Holly, the Beatles, Jimi Hendrix, and B. B. King were just a few of the ~~performer~~ *performers* who bought and loved a Fender guitar.

(5) Unfortunately, by the time Fender sold his invention to CBS, the famous Fender guitars had declined in quality and were selling very poorly. (6) William Schultz, who worked for CBS at the time, felt that he could turn things around; however, few of the ~~musician~~ *musicians* who had played the original Fenders believed he could succeed. (7) He did.

(8) The Telecaster and the Stratocaster have become two of the most famous instruments in music history. (9) Approximately 335,000 are sold a year; each of these ~~instrument~~ *instruments* is considered a classic. (10) The next time you attend a concert, listen for the Fender sound.

PRACTICE: WRITING ASSIGNMENT

For some families, shopping—whether for food, clothing, or a television set—is a delightful group outing, a time to be together and share. For other families, it is an ordeal, a time of great stress, with arguments about what to purchase and how much to spend.

Describe a particularly delightful or awful family shopping experience. Your first sentence might read, "Shopping for _____ was (is) a(n) _____ experience." Explain what made it so good or so bad: Was it what you were shopping for or where you were shopping? Were there arguments? Why?

Check your work for the correct use of singular and plural nouns. Be especially careful of nouns that follow signal words.

✔ Chapter Highlights

- **Most plural nouns are formed by adding *-s* or *-es* to the singular noun:**

  egg/eggs, watch/watches

- **Some plurals are formed in other ways:**

  child/children, woman/women, wolf/wolves

- **Some nouns ending in *o* add *-es*; others add *-s*:**

  echo/echoes, solo/solos

- **Some nouns have identical singular and plural forms:**

  fish/fish, deer/deer

- **Hyphenated nouns usually add *-s* or *-es* to the first word:**

  sister-in-law/sisters-in-law

- **Signal words indicate whether a singular or a plural noun usually follows:**

  another musician, many of the musicians

Chapter Review

Proofread the following essay for incorrect singular and plural nouns. Cross out any errors, and correct them above the lines.

The Effects of Alcohol on Pregnancy

(1) All ~~mother-to-bes~~ *mothers-to-be* who drink alcohol run the risk of harming an innocent ~~children.~~ *child.* (2) When a pregnant ~~women~~ *woman* takes a drink, the alcohol goes straight

from her bloodstream into the bloodstream of her child. (3) When she has several ~~drink,~~ *drinks,* the blood-alcohol level of her child rises as high as her own.

(4) Newborns can be harmed by alcohol in many ~~way.~~ *ways.* (5) Some ~~infant~~ *infants* are

born addicted to alcohol. (6) Other children are born mentally retarded. (7) In fact, most ~~doctor~~ *doctors* believe that exposure to alcohol before birth is one of the major ~~cause~~ *causes* of mental retardation. (8) In the worst cases, babies are born with a disease called fetal alcohol syndrome. (9) These unfortunate children not only are men-

tally retarded but also can have many physical ~~deformity~~ *deformities* as well. (10) In milder

cases, the children's problems don't show up until they go to school. (11) For

instance, they may have poor memories and short attention spans. (12) Later,

they may have trouble holding a ~~jobs~~ *job.*

(13) Too many young ~~life~~ *lives* have been ruined before birth because of alcohol

consumption. (14) All unborn ~~child~~ *children* need and deserve a chance to have a healthy,

normal ~~futures~~ *future.* (15) If you are a ~~women~~ *woman* who is expecting a baby, stop drinking

alcohol now!

CHAPTER 21

Pronouns

PART A — Defining Pronouns and Antecedents

Pronouns take the place of or refer to nouns or other pronouns. The word or words that a pronoun refers to are called the *antecedent* of the pronoun.

(1) *Bob* said that *he* was tired.

- *He* refers to *Bob*.
- *Bob* is the antecedent of *he*.

(2) *Sonia* left early, but I did not see *her* until later.

- *Her* refers to *Sonia*.
- *Sonia* is the antecedent of *her*.

(3) *Robert and Tyrone* have been good friends ever since *their* college days.

■ *Their* refers to *Robert and Tyrone*.

■ *Robert and Tyrone* is the antecedent of *their.*

A pronoun must agree with its antecedent. In sentence (1), the antecedent *Bob* requires the singular, masculine pronoun *he.* In sentence (2), the antecedent *Sonia* requires the singular, feminine pronoun *her.* In sentence (3), the antecedent *Robert and Tyrone* requires the plural pronoun *their.*

PRACTICE 1

In each of these sentences, a pronoun is circled. In the columns on the right, write the pronoun and its antecedent as shown in the example.

	Pronoun	Antecedent
EXAMPLE: Susan B. Anthony promoted women's rights before (they) were popular.	they	rights
1. Susan B. Anthony deserves praise for (her) accomplishments.	her	Susan B. Anthony
2. Anthony became involved in the antislavery movement because of (her) principles.	her	Anthony
3. She helped President Lincoln develop (his) plans to free the slaves during the Civil War.	his	President Lincoln
4. Eventually, Anthony realized that women wouldn't be fully protected by law until (they) could vote.	they	women
5. When Anthony voted in the presidential election of 1872, (she) was arrested.	she	Anthony
6. She was found guilty and given a $100 fine, but she refused to pay (it.)	it	fine
7. The judge did not sentence Anthony to jail because a sentence would have given (her) grounds for an appeal.	her	Anthony

	Pronoun	Antecedent

8. If the Supreme Court had heard her appeal, (it) might have ruled that women had the right to vote.

it — *Supreme Court*

9. Audiences in England and Germany showed (their) appreciation of Anthony's work with standing ovations.

their — *audiences*

10. Unfortunately, women in the United States had to wait until 1920 before (they) could legally vote.

they — *women*

PRACTICE 2

Read this paragraph for meaning; then write the antecedent of each boxed pronoun above it.

(1) In 1935, a Hungarian journalist got tired of the ink blotches *journalist* [his] fountain pen made. (2) So László Biro and *Biro* [his] brother developed a pen with a rolling ball at the point. (3) *pen* [It] wrote without making blotches. (4) *Biro and his brother* [Their] pen wasn't the first ballpoint, but it was the first one that worked well. (5) The new pens got a big boost during World War II. (6) Pilots needed a pen *pilots* [they] could use at high altitudes. (7) Only ballpoints did the job. (8) In 1945, a department store in New York City introduced these pens to *department store* [its] shoppers. (9) The store sold ten thousand ballpoints the first day. (10) *ballpoints* [They] cost $12.50 each! (11) Today, people buy almost two *billion* ballpoints a year, for as little as ten cents apiece.

PART B   Referring to Indefinite Pronouns

Indefinite pronouns do not point to a specific person.

anybody
anyone
each
everybody   Indefinite pronouns are usually *singular*.
everyone   A pronoun that refers to an indefinite
no one   pronoun should also be singular.
nobody
somebody
someone

(1) *Everyone* should do what *he* or *she* can to help.

■ *Everyone* is a singular antecedent and must be used with the singular pronoun *he* or *she.*

(2) *Each* wanted to read *his* or *her* composition aloud.

■ *Each* is a singular antecedent and must be used with the singular pronoun *his* or *her.*

(3) If *someone* smiles at you, give *him* or *her* a smile in return.

■ *Someone* is a singular antecedent and must be used with the singular pronoun *him* or *her.*

In the past, writers used *he, his,* or *him* to refer to both men and women. Now, however, many writers use *he or she, his or her,* or *him or her.* Of course, if *everyone* is a woman, use *she* or *her;* if *everyone* is a man, use *he, his,* or *him.**

Someone left *her* purse in the classroom.

Someone left *his* necktie on the bus.

Someone left *his or her* glasses on the back seat.

It is often best to avoid the repetition of *his or her* and *he or she* by changing the indefinite pronoun to a plural.

(4) *Everyone* in the club agreed to pay *his or her* dues on time.

or

(5) The club *members* agreed to pay *their* dues on time.

PRACTICE 1

Fill in the blanks with the correct pronouns. Then write the antecedent of each pronoun in the column on the right.

Antecedent

EXAMPLE: Everyone should do ____his or her____ best.   ____everyone____

1. The average citizen does not take ____his or her____

     right to vote seriously enough.   ____citizen____

2. If a person chooses a career in accounting,

     ____he or she____ must enjoy working with numbers.   ____person____

*For more work on pronoun reference, see Chapter 25, "Consistent Person."

3. Each player gave _____*her*_____ best in the women's basketball finals.

_____*player*_____

4. Anyone can learn to drive if _____*he or she*_____ has a patient instructor.

_____*anyone*_____

5. Fred and Nina always do _____*their*_____ housecleaning on Tuesday.

_____*Fred and Nina*_____

6. Someone left _____*his or her*_____ fingerprints on the windshield.

_____*someone*_____

7. The sales managers asked me to attend _____*their*_____ meeting tomorrow.

_____*managers*_____

8. Everyone should see _____*his or her*_____ dentist at least once a year.

_____*everyone*_____

9. No one wanted to devote _____*his or her*_____ time to the library fundraiser.

_____*no one*_____

10. Everybody is welcome to try _____*his or her*_____ luck in the lottery.

_____*everybody*_____

PRACTICE 2

Some of the following sentences contain errors in pronoun reference. Revise the incorrect sentences. Place a C in the blank next to each correct sentence.

EXAMPLE: Everyone must provide ~~their~~ *his or her* lunch. _____

1. Somebody left ~~their~~ *his or her* bag of popcorn on the seat. _____
2. A person should not try to impose ~~their~~ *his or her* ideas on others. _____
3. Everybody can take ~~their~~ *his or her* choice of two dishes from column A and one from column B. _____
4. No one works harder at ~~their~~ *his or her* paramedic job than my brother-in-law. _____
5. Each state has ~~their~~ *its* own flag. _____
6. Anyone can conquer his or her fear of speaking in public. _____*C*_____

PRACTICE 3

On separate paper, write three sentences using indefinite pronouns as antecedents.

PART C   Referring to Collective Nouns

Collective nouns imply more than one person but are generally considered *singular.* Here is a partial list:

Common Collective Nouns		
board	family	panel
class	flock	school
college	government	society
committee	group	team
company	jury	tribe

(1) The *jury* meets early today because *it* must decide on a verdict.

■ *Jury* is a singular antecedent and is used with the singular pronoun *it.*

(2) *Society* must protect *its* members from violence.

■ *Society* is a singular antecedent and is always used with the singular pronoun *it.*

■ Use *it* or *its* when referring to collective nouns.

■ Use *they* or *their* only when referring to collective nouns in the plural (*schools, companies,* and so forth).

PRACTICE 1

Write the correct pronoun in the blank. Then write the antecedent of the pronoun in the column on the right.

Antecedent

EXAMPLE: The committee sent _____its_____ recommendations to the president of the college.

committee

1. Wanda's company will have _____its_____ annual picnic next week.

company

2. The two teams picked up _____their_____ gloves and bats and walked off the field.

teams

3. My high school class will soon have _____its_____ tenth reunion.

class

4. The city is doing _____its_____ best to build a new stadium.

city

5. Many soap operas count on _____their_____ viewers' enjoyment of "a good cry."

soap operas

6. Each group has _____*its*_____ insiders and outsiders.   _____*group*_____

7. The panel made _____*its*_____ report public.   _____*panel*_____

8. This college needs to increase _____*its*_____ course
offerings in African-American studies.   _____*college*_____

PRACTICE 2

Some of the following sentences contain errors in pronoun reference. Cross out the incorrect pronoun, and write the correct pronoun above the line. Place a *C* in the blank next to each correct sentence.

its
EXAMPLES: The committee will present ~~their~~ report today.   _____

The jury has reached its verdict.   *C*

its
1. The computer company retrains ~~their~~ employees for new jobs.   _____

its
2. Central Technical College wants to double ~~their~~ enrollment by 2000.   _____

its
3. That rock group has changed ~~their~~ name again.   _____

4. The plumbing crew did its best to finish by 4 a.m.   *C*

its
5. The telephone company plans to raise ~~their~~ rates again.   _____

6. The Robinson family moved into its new apartment last week.   *C*

PRACTICE 3

On separate paper, write three sentences using collective nouns as antecedents.

PART D   Referring to Special Singular Constructions

each of . . .
either of . . .
every one of . . .   Each of these constructions is *singular.*
neither of . . .   Pronouns that refer to them must also
one of . . .   be singular.

---

(1) *Each* of the women did *her* work.

- *Each* is a singular antecedent and is used with the singular pronoun *her.*
- Do not be confused by the prepositional phrase *of the women.*

---

(2) *Neither* of the men finished *his* meal.

- *Neither* is a singular antecedent and is used with the singular pronoun *his.*
- Do not be confused by the prepositional phrase *of the men.*

(3) *One* of the bottles is missing from *its* place.

■ *One* is a singular antecedent and is used with the singular pronoun *its.*

■ Do not be confused by the prepositional phrase *of the bottles.**

PRACTICE 1

Fill in the blanks with the correct pronouns. Then write the antecedent of each pronoun in the column on the right.

Antecedent

EXAMPLE: Each of my nephews did _____*his*_____ homework.   _____*each*_____

1. One of the hikers filled _____*his or her*_____ canteen.   _____*one*_____

2. Every one of the women scored high on _____*her*_____ entrance examination.

  _____*every one*_____

3. Each of the puzzles has _____*its*_____ own solution.   _____*each*_____

4. Either of them should be able to learn _____*his or her*_____ lines before opening night.

  _____*either*_____

5. Neither of the dental technicians has had _____*his or her*_____ lunch yet.

  _____*neither*_____

6. Each of the photographers takes pride in _____*his or her*_____ work.

  _____*each*_____

7. Lin Li and her mother opened _____*their*_____ boutique in 1993.

  _____*Lin Li and her mother*_____

8. One of the ambulances has a dent in _____*its*_____ hood.   _____*one*_____

PRACTICE 2

Some of the following sentences contain errors in pronoun reference. Cross out the incorrect pronoun, and write the correct pronoun above it. Place a C in the blanks next to the correct sentences.

EXAMPLE: One of my uncles made ~~their~~ *his* opinion known.   _____

1. One of the women at the hardware counter hasn't made ~~their~~ *her* purchase yet.   _____

2. Each of the birds has ~~their~~ *its* distinctive mating ritual.   _____

—————
*For more work on these special constructions, see Chapter 8, Part G.

3. Many Asian cooks use cilantro in their dishes.   *C*

                                          his or her
4. I hope that neither of the senators will change ~~their~~ vote.

5. Both supermarkets now carry Superfizz Carrot Juice for their health-

    conscious customers.   *C*

                                his
6. Neither of the men found ~~their~~ job challenging.

7. One of the ski sweaters was still in its box.   *C*

                                    his or her
8. Each of the children has ~~their~~ own bedroom.

PRACTICE 3

On separate paper, write three sentences that use the special singular constructions as antecedents.

PART E   Avoiding Vague and Repetitious Pronouns

Vague Pronouns

Be sure that all pronouns *clearly* refer to their antecedents. Be especially careful of the pronouns *they* and *it*. If *they* or *it* does not refer to a *specific* antecedent, change *they* or *it* to the exact word you have in mind.

> (1) **Vague pronoun:** At registration, they said I should take Math 101.
> (2) **Revised:** At registration, an adviser said I should take Math 101.

- In sentence (1), who is *they?* The pronoun *they* does not clearly refer to an antecedent.
- In sentence (2), the vague *they* has been replaced by *an adviser.*

> (3) **Vague pronoun:** On the beach, it says that no swimming is allowed.
> (4) **Revised:** On the beach, a sign says that no swimming is allowed.

- In sentence (3), what is *it?* The pronoun *it* does not clearly refer to an antecedent.
- In sentence (4), the vague *it* has been replaced by *a sign.*

Repetitious Pronouns

Don't repeat a pronoun directly after its antecedent. Use *either* the pronoun *or* the antecedent—not both.

> (1) **Repetitious pronoun:** The doctor, he said that my daughter is in perfect health.

■ The pronoun *he* unnecessarily repeats the antecedent *doctor,* which is right before it.

> (2) **Revised:** *The doctor* said that my daughter is in perfect health.
>
> *or*
>
> *He* said that my daughter is in perfect health.

■ Use either *the doctor* or *he,* not both.

PRACTICE

Rewrite the sentences that contain vague or repetitious pronouns. If a sentence is correct, write *C.*

EXAMPLE: Dyslexia, it is a learning disorder that makes reading difficult.

Revised: ___Dyslexia is a learning disorder that makes reading difficult.___

1. Many dyslexic persons, they have achieved success in their chosen professions.

   Revised: ___Many dyslexic persons have achieved success in their chosen professions.___

2. For example, Albert Einstein, he was dyslexic.

   Revised: ___For example, Albert Einstein was dyslexic.___

3. His biography, it says that he couldn't interpret written words the way others could.

   Revised: ___His biography says that he couldn't interpret written words the way others could.___

4. His elementary school teachers, they claimed he was a slow learner.

   Revised: ___His elementary school teachers claimed he was a slow learner.___

5. However, this slow learner, he changed the way science looked at time and space.

   Revised: _However, this slow learner changed the way science looked_

   at time and space.

6. Even politics has had its share of dyslexic leaders.

   Revised: _C_

   _____

7. American history, it teaches us that President Woodrow Wilson and Vice President Nelson Rockefeller, they were both dyslexic.

   Revised: _American history teaches us that President Woodrow Wilson_

   and Vice President Nelson Rockefeller were both dyslexic.

8. Authors can have this problem too; the well-known mystery writer Agatha Christie, she had trouble reading.

   Revised: _Authors can have this problem too; the well-known mystery writer_

   Agatha Christie had trouble reading.

9. Finally, several magazines, they report that Cher, the famous singer and actress, is dyslexic.

   Revised: _Finally, several magazines report that Cher, the famous singer_

   and actress, is dyslexic.

10. This show-business personality, she wasn't able to read until she was eighteen years old.

    Revised: _This show business personality wasn't able to read until she_

    was eighteen years old.

PART F — Using Pronouns as Subjects, Objects, and Possessives

Pronouns have different forms, depending on how they are used in a sentence. Pronouns can be *subjects* or *objects* or *possessives*. They can be in the *subjective case*, *objective case*, or *possessive case*.

Pronouns as Subjects

A pronoun can be the *subject* of a sentence:

> (1) *He* loves the summer months.
> (2) By noon, *they* reached the top of the hill.

■ In sentences (1) and (2), the pronouns *he* and *they* are subjects.

Pronouns as Objects

A pronoun can be the *object* of a verb:

> (1) Graciela kissed *him.*
> (2) Sheila moved *it* to the corner.

■ In sentence (1), the pronoun *him* tells whom Graciela kissed.

■ In sentence (2), the pronoun *it* tells what Sheila moved.

■ These objects answer the questions *kissed whom?* or *moved what?*

A pronoun can also be the *object* of a preposition, a word like *to, for,* or *at.**

> (3) The umpire stood between *us.*
> (4) Near *them,* the children played.

■ In sentences (3) and (4), the pronouns *us* and *them* are the objects of the prepositions *between* and *near.*

Sometimes the prepositions *to* and *for* are understood, usually after words like *give, send, tell,* and *bring.*

> (5) I gave *her* the latest sports magazine.
> (6) Carver bought *him* a cowboy hat.

■ In sentence (5), the preposition *to* is understood before the pronoun *her:* I gave *to* her. . . .

■ In sentence (6), the preposition *for* is understood before the pronoun *him:* Carver bought *for* him. . . .

Pronouns That Show Possession

A pronoun can show *possession* or ownership.

> (1) Bill took *his* report and left.
> (2) The climbers spotted *their* gear on the slope.

■ In sentences (1) and (2), the pronouns *his* and *their* show that Bill owns *his* report and that the climbers own *their* gear.

*See the list of prepositions on page 281.

The chart below can help you review all the pronouns discussed in this part.

<table>
<tr><td colspan="7" align="center">**Pronoun Case Chart**</td></tr>
<tr><td colspan="3" align="center">**Singular Pronouns**</td><td></td><td colspan="3" align="center">**Plural Pronouns**</td></tr>
<tr><td>Subjective</td><td>Objective</td><td>Possessive</td><td></td><td>Subjective</td><td>Objective</td><td>Possessive</td></tr>
<tr><td>1st person: I</td><td>me</td><td>my (mine)</td><td></td><td>we</td><td>us</td><td>our (ours)</td></tr>
<tr><td>2nd person: you</td><td>you</td><td>your (yours)</td><td></td><td>you</td><td>you</td><td>your (yours)</td></tr>
<tr><td>3rd person: he</td><td>him</td><td>his</td><td></td><td>they</td><td>them</td><td>their (theirs)</td></tr>
<tr><td>she</td><td>her</td><td>her (hers)</td><td></td><td></td><td></td><td></td></tr>
<tr><td>it</td><td>it</td><td>its</td><td></td><td></td><td></td><td></td></tr>
</table>

PRACTICE

In the sentences below, underline the pronouns. Then, over each pronoun, write an *S* if the pronoun is in the subjective case, an *O* if it is in the objective case, and a *P* if it is in the possessive case.

                  S   *O*   *P*
EXAMPLE: I sent them my résumé.

1. My best friend and I had our first job interviews the same day.

2. To prepare, we had attended a job interviewing workshop.

3. Until then, I hadn't realized the importance of a first impression.

4. Our workshop leader explained that we had to make a good first impression

   or we wouldn't get a chance to make a second.

5. A few days before my interview, I had my hair cut.

6. Tom helped me decide what to wear, and I helped him.

7. We looked very professional when we headed for the Astra Insurance

   Company.

8. I chew gum occasionally, and so does Tom, but we left our gum at home.

9. Tom was offered a job in customer service because he was polite and

   professional.

10. He asked thoughtful questions about the responsibilities of the job before he

    accepted it.

11. I was offered a trainee position in the accounting department.

12. To celebrate, we took our families out to dinner.

PART G   ## Choosing the Correct Case After AND or OR

When nouns or pronouns are joined by *and* or *or,* be careful to use the correct pronoun case after the *and* or the *or.*

> (1) **Incorrect:** *Bob* and *me* have to leave soon.

■ In sentence (1), the pronoun *me* should be in the *subjective case* because it is part of the subject of the sentence.

> (2) **Revised:** *Bob* and *I* have to leave soon.

■ Change *me* to *I.*

> (3) **Incorrect:** The dean congratulated *Charles* and *she.*

■ In sentence (3), the pronoun *she* should be in the *objective case* because it is the object of the verb *congratulated.*

■ The dean congratulated *whom?* The dean congratulated *her.*

> (4) **Revised:** The dean congratulated *Charles* and *her.*

■ Change *she* to *her.*

> (5) **Incorrect:** Is that letter for *me* or *he?*

■ In sentence (5), both objects of the preposition *for* must be in the *objective case.*

What should *he* be changed to? _____ *him* _____

   One simple way to make sure that you have the right pronoun case is to leave out the *and* or the *or,* and the word before it. You probably would not write these sentences:

> (6) **Incorrect:** *Me* have to leave soon.
> (7) **Incorrect:** The dean congratulated *she.*
> (8) **Incorrect:** Is that letter for *he?*

The sentences above look and sound strange, and you would know that they have to be corrected.

PRACTICE 1

Circle the correct pronoun in the parentheses. If the pronoun is a *subject*, use the *subjective case*. If it is the *object* of a verb or a preposition, use the *objective case*.

1. Frieda and (**I**, me) were born in Bogotá, Colombia.

2. My brother gave Kylee and (I, **me**) a ride to the subway.

3. For (we, **us**), there is nothing like lemonade on a hot day.

4. If it were up to Angelo and (she, **her**), they would spend all their time searching for out-of-print LPs.

5. My supervisor took Pete and (I, **me**) out to lunch.

6. I'm going to the movies tonight with Yolanda and (she, **her**).

7. The foreman chose Ellen and (he, **him**).

8. Between you and (I, **me**), I don't like spinach.

9. Robert and (**he**, him) have decided to go to Rocky Mountain National Park with Jacinto and (I, **me**).

10. Either (**he**, him) or (**she**, her) must work overtime.

PRACTICE 2

Revise the sentences in which the pronouns are in the wrong case. Write a C in the blanks next to correct sentences.

1. Jeannie and ~~me~~ *I* love watching James Bond films. _____

2. ~~Her~~ *She* and ~~me~~ *I* have seen every Bond film from *Dr. No* to *Goldeneye*. _____

3. Between you and ~~I,~~ *me,* I like the first Agent 007, Sean Connery, better. _____

4. However, I am not sure whether ~~him~~ *he* or Roger Moore made more

   Bond films. _____

5. Talking about these movies used to keep Jeannie and me up half the

   night. *C*

6. ~~Us~~ *We* and our friends used to argue about the role of women in these

   films. _____

7. Those stereotyped Bond "girls" always bothered us: sexy, but either

   dumb or deadly. *C*

8. Most Bond fans and ~~us~~ *we* agree that the heroine in *Goldeneye* was much

   more real than the women in the earlier films. _____

PART H   Choosing the Correct Case in Comparisons

Pronouns in comparisons usually follow *than* or *as.*

> (1) Ferdinand is taller *than* I.
> (2) These guidelines help you as much *as* me.

- In sentence (1), the comparison is completed with a pronoun in the subjective case, *I.*

- In sentence (2), the comparison is completed with a pronoun in the objective case, *me.*

> (1) Ferdinand is taller than I . . . (am tall).
> (2) These guidelines help you as much as . . . (they help) . . . me.

- A comparison is really a kind of shorthand that omits repetitious words.

By completing the comparison mentally, you can choose the correct case for the pronoun.

> BE CAREFUL: The case of the pronoun you place after *than* or *as* can change the meaning of the sentence.

> (3) Diana likes Tom more than *I* . . . (more than *I* like him).
>
> *or*
>
> (4) Diana likes Tom more than *me* . . . (more than she likes *me*).

- Sentence (3) says that Diana likes Tom more than I like Tom.

- Sentence (4) says that Diana likes Tom more than she likes me.*

PRACTICE 1

Circle the correct pronoun in these comparisons.

1. Rena exercises more often than (I, me).
2. The verdict surprised you more than it did (he, him).
3. Barbara looks as old as (I, me).
4. She ran a better campaign for the local school board than (he, him).
5. Stan cannot memorize vocabulary words faster than (he, him).
6. The ringing of a telephone disturbs her more than it disturbs (they, them).
7. They may think they are sharper than (she, her), but wait until they tangle with her and find out the truth.
8. I hate doing laundry more than (they, them).
9. Sometimes our children are more mature than (we, us).
10. Learning English often seems easier for me than for (he, him).

---

*For more work on comparisons, see Chapter 22, Part C.

PRACTICE 2

Revise only those sentences in which the pronoun after the comparison is in the wrong case. Write a *C* in the blanks next to the correct sentences.

1. Raoul moved to San Diego six months earlier than ~~them~~. *they.* ____

2. Jean can sing Haitian folk songs better than ~~me~~. *I.* ____

3. Nobody, but nobody, can whistle louder than she. *C*

4. Sarah was surprised that Joyce paid more than she for a ticket. *C*

5. In a crowd, you would notice her faster than you would him. *C*

6. Before switching jobs, I wanted to know if Rose would be as good a boss as ~~him~~. *he.* ____

7. The night shift suits her better than ~~I~~. *me.* ____

8. Antoinette is six feet tall; no one on the loading dock is taller than ~~her~~. *she.* ____

PRACTICE 3

On separate paper, write three sentences using comparisons that are completed with pronouns. Choose case carefully.

PART I Using Pronouns with -SELF and -SELVES

Pronouns with *-self* and *-selves* are used in two ways.

> (1) José admired *himself* in the mirror.

■ In sentence (1), José did something to *himself;* he admired *himself.* In this sentence, *himself* is called a *reflexive* pronoun.

> (2) The teacher *herself* thought the test was too difficult.

■ In sentence (2), *herself* emphasizes the fact that the teacher—much to her surprise—found the test too hard. In this sentence, *herself* is called an *intensive* pronoun.

This chart will help you choose the right reflexive or intensive pronoun.

	Antecedent	Reflexive or Intensive Pronoun
Singular	I _____	myself
	you _____	yourself
	he _____	himself
	she _____	herself
	it _____	itself
Plural	we _____	ourselves
	you _____	yourselves
	they _____	themselves

Note that in the plural *-self* is changed to *-selves.*

PRACTICE 1

Write the correct reflexive or intensive pronoun in each sentence. Be careful to match the pronoun with the antecedent.

EXAMPLES: I could have kicked _____myself_____.

Roberta _____herself_____ made this bracelet.

1. Dimitri cooked the black beans _____himself_____.

2. She _____herself_____ was surprised to discover that she had a green thumb.

3. We gave _____ourselves_____ a party after we graduated.

4. Rick, look at _____yourself_____ in the mirror!

5. Don't bother; Don and André will hang the pictures _____themselves_____.

6. The trainer _____herself_____ was amazed at the progress the athletes had made.

7. Sonia found _____herself_____ in a difficult situation.

8. These new lamps turn _____themselves_____ on and off.

9. The oven cleans _____itself_____.

10. We _____ourselves_____ decided to rearrange the furniture.

PRACTICE 2

On separate paper, write three sentences using either a reflexive or an intensive pronoun in each.

PRACTICE: WRITING ASSIGNMENT

In small groups, discuss the factors that seem absolutely necessary for a successful marriage or long-term relationship. As a group, brainstorm for four or five key factors.

Now imagine that a friend with very little experience has asked you for written advice about relationships. Each member of the group should choose just one of the factors and write a letter to this person. Explain in detail why this factor—for example, honesty or mutual respect—is so important to a good relationship.

Read the finished letters to one another. Which letters give the best advice or are the most convincing? Why? Exchange letters with a partner, checking for the correct use of pronouns.

✔ Chapter Highlights

■ **A pronoun takes the place of or refers to a noun or another pronoun:**

Louise said that *she* would leave work early.

■ **The word that a pronoun refers to is its antecedent:**

I have chosen *my* seat for the concert.
(*I* is the antecedent of *my*.)

■ **A pronoun that refers to an indefinite pronoun or a collective noun should be singular:**

Everyone had cleared the papers off *his* or *her* desk.

The *committee* will give *its* report Friday.

■ **A pronoun after *and* or *or* is usually in the subjective or objective case:**

Dr. Smythe and *she* always work as a team. (*subjective*)

The bus driver wouldn't give the map to Ms. Tallon or *me*. (*objective*)

■ **Pronouns in comparisons usually follow *than* or *as*:**

Frank likes Sally more than *I*.
(*subjective*: . . . more than I like Sally)

Frank likes Sally more than *me*.
(*objective*: . . . more than he likes me)

■ **A pronoun ending in *-self* (singular) or *-selves* (plural) may be used as a reflexive or an intensive pronoun. A reflexive pronoun shows that someone did something to himself or to herself; an intensive pronoun shows surprise:**

On his trip, Martin bought nothing for *himself*.

The musicians *themselves* were almost late for the street fair.

Chapter Review

Proofread the following essay for pronoun errors. Cross out any incorrect, vague, or repetitious pronouns, and make corrections above the lines. Use nouns to replace vague pronouns.

A New Beginning

(1) Martha Andrews/~~she~~ was a good student in high school. (2) After graduation, she found a job as a bank teller in order to save money for college. (3) She liked her job because she knew her regular customers and enjoyed handling *their* ~~his or her~~ business. (4) When she was nineteen, Patrick Kelvin, another teller, and *she* ~~her~~ fell in love and married. (5) By the time she was twenty-two, she had become the mother of three children. (6) Martha's plans for college faded.

(7) As her fortieth birthday approached, Martha began thinking about going to college in order to study accounting; however, she had many fears. (8) Would she remember how to study after so many years? (9) Would the younger students *she?* be smarter than ~~her?~~ (10) Would she feel out of place with them? (11) Worst of all, her husband/~~he~~ worried that Martha would neglect him. (12) He thought that *his or her* everyone who went to college forgot ~~their~~ family. (13) He also feared that Martha *he.* would be more successful than ~~him.~~

himself,
(14) One of Martha's children, who attended college ~~hisself,~~ encouraged her. (15) With his help, Martha got the courage to visit Middleton College. (16) In the *an adviser* admissions office, ~~they~~ told her that older students were valued at Middleton. *they* (17) Older students often enriched classes because ~~he or she~~ brought a wealth of life experiences with them. (18) Martha also learned that the college had a special *its* program to help ~~their~~ older students adjust to school.

she
(19) Martha enrolled in college the next fall. (20) To their credit, ~~her~~ and her husband soon realized that they had made the right decision.

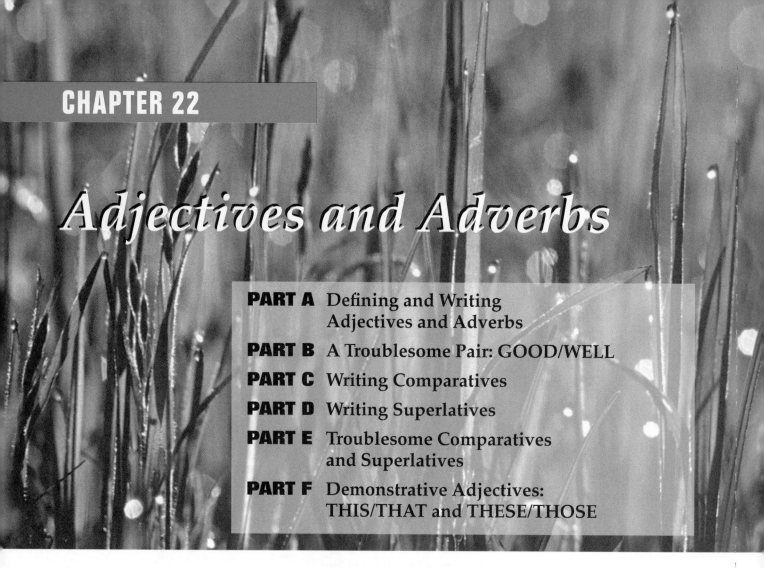

CHAPTER 22

Adjectives and Adverbs

PART A Defining and Writing Adjectives and Adverbs

Adjectives and adverbs are two kinds of descriptive words. An *adjective* describes a noun or a pronoun. It tells *which one, what kind,* or *how many.*

> (1) The *red* coat belongs to me.
>
> (2) He looks *healthy.*

■ In sentence (1), the adjective *red* describes the noun *coat.*

■ In sentence (2), the adjective *healthy* describes the pronoun *he.*

An *adverb* describes a verb, an adjective, or another adverb. Adverbs often end in *-ly*. They tell *how, to what extent, why, when,* or *where.*

> (3) Laura sings *loudly.*
> (4) My biology instructor is *extremely* short.
> (5) Lift this box *very* carefully.

■ In sentence (3), *loudly* describes the verb *sings.* How does Laura sing? She sings *loudly.*

■ In sentence (4), *extremely* describes the adjective *short.* How short is the instructor? *Extremely* short.

■ In sentence (5), *very* describes the adverb *carefully.* How carefully should you lift the box? *Very* carefully.

PRACTICE 1

Complete each sentence with an appropriate adjective from the list below.

funny	yellow	sarcastic	energetic
old	tired	bitter	little

1. Janet is _____*energetic*_____ .

2. She always carries a(n) _____*yellow*_____ duffel bag.

3. _____*Sarcastic*_____ remarks will be his downfall.

4. My daughter collects _____*old*_____ movie posters.

5. This coffee tastes _____*bitter*_____ .

PRACTICE 2

Complete each sentence with an appropriate adverb from the list below.

quietly	loudly	wildly	convincingly
sadly	quickly	constantly	happily

1. The waiter _____*quickly*_____ cleaned the table.

2. Mr. Huff whistles _____*constantly*_____ .

3. The lawyer spoke _____*convincingly*_____ .

4. He gazed _____*sadly*_____ at his empty wallet.

5. _____*Quietly*_____ , he entered the rear door of the church.

Many adjectives can be changed into adverbs by adding an *-ly* ending. For example, *glad* becomes *gladly, thoughtful* becomes *thoughtfully,* and *wise* becomes *wisely.*

Be especially careful of the adjectives and adverbs in this list; they are easily confused.

Adjective	Adverb	Adjective	Adverb
awful	awfully	quiet	quietly
bad	badly	real	really
poor	poorly	sure	surely
quick	quickly		

> (6) This chair is a *real* antique.
> (7) She has a *really* bad sprain.

■ In sentence (6), *real* is an adjective describing the noun *antique.*

■ In sentence (7), *really* is an adverb describing the adjective *bad.* How bad is the sprain? The sprain is *really* bad.

PRACTICE 3

Change each adjective in the left-hand column into its adverb form.*

Adjective	Adverb
EXAMPLE: You are polite.	You answer _____politely_____.
1. She is honest.	1. She speaks _____honestly_____.
2. They are quiet.	2. They play _____quietly_____.
3. It is easy.	3. It turns _____easily_____.
4. We are careful.	4. We decide _____carefully_____.
5. He is creative.	5. He thinks _____creatively_____.
6. She was quick.	6. She acted _____quickly_____.
7. It is perfect.	7. It fits _____perfectly_____.
8. It is real.	8. It is _____really_____ hot.
9. He is poor.	9. He plays _____poorly_____.
10. We are joyful.	10. We watch _____joyfully_____.

_____

*For more work on spelling, see Chapter 31, Part E.

PRACTICE 4

Circle the adjective or adverb form of the word in parentheses.

EXAMPLE: The office is (**quiet,** quietly) on a snowy Sunday afternoon.

1. On the couch, a young man snores (noisy, **noisily**).
2. A (**tired,** tiredly) young woman slumps in a chair.
3. (Sudden, **Suddenly**), the telephone rings.
4. Grunting (sleepy, **sleepily**), the man rolls over.
5. By the time he answers the phone, he is (full, **fully**) awake.
6. He takes notes (hasty, **hastily**) and nods to his partner.
7. She puts on her (**official,** officially) jacket and grabs her bag of tools.
8. This is another (**typical,** typically) call for two (high, **highly**) skilled technicians.
9. The man rereads his notes aloud while the panel truck moves (quick, **quickly**) through the streets.
10. In a (**calm,** calmly) voice, the man describes the problem to his partner.
11. Sam and Terri Phillips have been (anxious, **anxiously**) awaiting their arrival.
12. They point (sad, **sadly**) to the blank TV screen and say, "The game starts in exactly one hour."
13. The technicians examine the set (careful, **carefully**); the problem is not a (**serious,** seriously) one.
14. In fifty-five minutes, the screen is (bright, **brightly**) lit, and the game is about to begin.
15. "Another job well done," they (happy, **happily**) whisper to each other as they leave.

PRACTICE 5

On separate paper, write sentences using the following adjectives and adverbs: *quick/quickly, bad/badly, happy/happily, real/really, easy/easily.*

EXAMPLE: (*sweet*) He is a sweet child.
(*sweetly*) He sings sweetly.

PART B   A Troublesome Pair: GOOD/WELL

Unlike most adjectives, *good* does not add *-ly* to become an adverb; it changes to *well*.

> (1) **Adjective:** Peter is a *good* student.
> (2) **Adverb:** He writes *well*.

■ In sentence (1), the adjective *good* describes or modifies *student*.

■ In sentence (2), the adverb *well* describes or modifies *writes*.

Note, however, that *well* can be used as an adjective to mean *in good health*—for example, *He felt well after his long vacation.*

PRACTICE

Write either *good* or *well* in each sentence.

EXAMPLE: Charles plays ball very _____*well*_____.

1. Lorelle is a _____*good*_____ pilot.

2. She handles a plane _____*well*_____.

3. How _____*well*_____ do you understand virtual reality?

4. Pam knows my bad habits very _____*well*_____.

5. It is a _____*good*_____ thing we ran into each other.

6. He works _____*well*_____ in a quiet room.

7. How _____*well*_____ or how badly did you do at the tryouts?

8. Were the cherry tarts _____*good*_____ or tasteless?

9. Aretha Franklin is a _____*good*_____ singer of soul music.

10. These plants don't grow very _____*well*_____ in the sunlight.

11. Carole doesn't look as though she takes _____*good*_____ care of herself.

12. He asked _____*good*_____ questions at the meeting, and she

    answered them _____*well*_____.

PART C   Writing Comparatives

> (1) John is *tall.*
>
> (2) John is *taller* than Mike.

■ Sentence (1) describes John with the adjective *tall,* but sentence (2) *compares* John and Mike in terms of how tall they are: John is the *taller* of the two.

Taller **is called the** *comparative* of *tall.*

Use the comparative when you want to compare two people or things.

To Form Comparatives

Add *-er* to adjectives and adverbs that have *one syllable:**

short	shorter
fast	faster
thin	thinner

Place the word *more* before adjectives and adverbs that have *two or more syllables:*

foolish	more foolish
rotten	more rotten
happily	more happily

PRACTICE 1

Write the comparative form of each word. Either add *-er* to the word or write *more* before it. Never add both *-er* and *more!*

EXAMPLES: _____ dumb *er* _____

_____*more*_____ willing _____

1. _____ fast *er* _____   5. _____ fat *(t)er* _____

2. ___*more*___ interesting _____   6. ___*more*___ foolish _____

3. ___*more*___ hopeful _____   7. ___*more*___ valuable _____

4. _____ quick *er* _____   8. _____ cold *er* _____

_____

*For more work on spelling, see Chapter 31, Part C.

Here is one important exception to the rule that two-syllable words use *more* to form the comparative:

> To show the comparative of two-syllable adjectives ending in *-y*, change the *y* to *i* and add *-er*.*
>
> cloudy   cloudier
>
> sunny   sunnier

PRACTICE 2

Write the comparative form of each adjective.

EXAMPLE: happy ___*happier*___.

1. shiny ___*shinier*___
2. friendly ___*friendlier*___
3. lazy ___*lazier*___
4. easy ___*easier*___

5. heavy ___*heavier*___
6. lucky ___*luckier*___
7. skinny ___*skinnier*___
8. crazy ___*crazier*___

PRACTICE 3

The following sentences use both *more* and *-er* incorrectly. Decide which one is correct, and write your revised sentences on the lines provided.

REMEMBER: Write comparatives with either *more* or *-er*—not both!

EXAMPLES: Jan is more younger than her brother.

Jan is younger than her brother.

He looks more intelligenter with glasses than without.

He looks more intelligent with glasses than without.

1. No one can set up a stereo system more faster than she.

   No one can set up a stereo system faster than she.

2. The trail was more rockier than we expected.

   The trail was rockier than we expected.

3. The people in my new neighborhood are more friendlier than those in my old one.

   The people in my new neighborhood are friendlier than those in my old one.

4. Magda has a more cheerfuler personality than her sister.

   Magda has a more cheerful personality than her sister.

_____

*For more work on spelling, see Chapter 31, Part F.

5. When the children are in bed and the house is more quieter, I can study.

   When the children are in bed and the house is quieter, I can study.

6. The audience at this theater is more noisier than usual.

   The audience at this theater is noisier than usual.

7. His jacket is more newer than Rudy's.

   His jacket is newer than Rudy's.

8. If today is more warmer than yesterday, we'll picnic on the lawn.

   If today is warmer than yesterday, we'll picnic on the lawn.

PRACTICE 4

On separate paper, write sentences using the comparative form of the following adjectives or adverbs: *dark, noisy, handsome, slowly, wet.*

EXAMPLE: *(funny)* This play is funnier than the one we saw last week.

PART D Writing Superlatives

(1) Tim is the *tallest* player on the team.
(2) Juan was voted the *most useful* player.

- In sentence (1), Tim is not just *tall* or *taller than* someone else; he is the *tallest* of all the players on the team.
- In sentence (2), Juan was voted the *most useful* of all the players.

Tallest **and** *most useful* **are called** *superlatives.*

Use the superlative when you wish to compare more than two people or things.

To Form Superlatives
Add *-est* to adjectives and adverbs of *one syllable:*
short　　　　　shortest
Place the word *most* before adjectives and adverbs that have *two or more syllables:*
foolish　　　　most foolish
Exception: With two-syllable adjectives ending in *-y*, change the *y* to *i* and add *-est.**
happy　　　　happiest

*For more work on spelling, see Chapter 31, Part F.

PRACTICE 1

Write the superlative form of each word. Either add -*est* to the word or write *most* before it, not both.

EXAMPLES: _____ tall _*est*_

*most* ridiculous _____

1. _____ loud *est* _____   6. _____ wild *est* _____
2. _*most*_ colorful _____   7. _*most*_ intelligent _____
3. _____ brave _*bravest*_   8. _*most*_ frightening _____
4. _____ thick *est* _____   9. _____ green *est* _____
5. _*most*_ brilliant _____   10. _____ hazy _*haziest*_

PRACTICE 2

The following sentences use both *most* and -*est* incorrectly. Decide which one is correct, and write your revised sentences on the lines provided.
REMEMBER: Write superlatives with either *most* or -*est*—not both!

EXAMPLES: Jane is the most youngest of my three children.

Jane is the youngest of my three children.

He is the most skillfulest guitarist in the band.

He is the most skillful guitarist in the band.

1. This mattress feels like the most comfortablest one in the store.

   This mattress feels like the most comfortable one in the store.

2. The World Trade Center towers are the most tall buildings in New York City.

   The World Trade Center towers are the tallest buildings in New York City.

3. My baby makes the most oddest gurgling noises I have ever heard.

   My baby makes the oddest gurgling noises I have ever heard.

4. Jackie always makes us laugh, but she is most funniest when she hasn't had enough sleep.

   Jackie always makes us laugh, but she is funniest when she hasn't had

   enough sleep.

5. When I finally started college, I was the most eagerest student on campus.

   When I finally started college, I was the most eager student on campus.

6. Professor Deitz conducts the most strangest experiments in the chemistry lab.

   Professor Deitz conducts the strangest experiments in the chemistry lab.

7. My daughter is the most thoughtfulest teenager I know.

   My daughter is the most thoughtful teenager I know.

8. He thinks that the most successfulest people are just lucky.

   He thinks that the most successful people are just lucky.

PART E   Troublesome Comparatives and Superlatives

These comparatives and superlatives are some of the trickiest you will learn:

		Comparative	Superlative
Adjective:	good	better	best
Adverb:	well	better	best
Adjective:	bad	worse	worst
Adverb:	badly	worse	worst

PRACTICE

Fill in the correct comparative or superlative form of the word in parentheses. REMEMBER: *Better* and *worse* compare *two* persons or things. *Best* and *worst* compare three or more persons or things.

EXAMPLES: Is this theme _____*better*_____ (good) than my last one?
(Here two themes are compared.)

It was the _____*worst*_____ (bad) movie I have ever seen.
(Of *all* movies, it was the *most* awful.)

1. He likes jogging _____*better*_____ (well) than running.

2. I like country and western music _____*best*_____ (well) of all.

3. My uncle's arthritis is _____*worse*_____ (bad) now than it was last month.

4. That is the _____*worst*_____ (bad) joke I have ever heard!

5. The volleyball team played _____*worse*_____ (badly) than it did last year.

6. He plays the piano _____*better*_____ (well) than he plays the guitar.

7. The traffic is _____*worse*_____ (bad) on Fridays than on Mondays.

8. That was the _____*worst*_____ (bad) storm Kansas has had in years.

9. Sales are _____*better*_____ (good) this year than last.

10. He is the _____*best*_____ (good) mechanic in the shop.

11. He is also the _____*worst*_____ (bad) slob.

12. Do you take this person for _____*better*_____ (good) or for _____*worse*_____ (bad)?

PART F Demonstrative Adjectives: THIS/THAT and THESE/THOSE

This, that, these, and *those* are called *demonstrative adjectives* because they point out, or demonstrate, which noun is meant.

> (1) I don't trust *that* wobbly front wheel.
> (2) *Those* toys are not as safe as their makers claim.

■ In sentence (1), *that* points to a particular wheel, the wobbly front one.

■ In sentence (2), *those* points to a particular group of toys.

Demonstrative adjectives are the only adjectives that change to show singular and plural:

Singular	Plural
this book	these books
that book	those books

This and *that* are used before singular nouns; *these* and *those* are used before plural nouns.

PRACTICE

In each sentence, circle the correct form of the demonstrative adjective in parentheses.

1. (This, **These**) corn flakes taste like cardboard.
2. Mr. Lathorpe is sure (**this**, these) address is correct.
3. You can find (that, **those**) maps in the reference room.
4. Can you catch (**that**, those) waiter's eye?
5. I can't imagine what (that, **those**) gadgets are for.
6. I like (this, **these**) leather gloves best of all.
7. The learning center is in (**that**, those) gray building.
8. (These, **This**) biography tells the story of Charles Curtis, the first Native American elected to the Senate.

PRACTICE: WRITING ASSIGNMENT

Sports figures and entertainers can be excellent role models. Sometimes, though, they can be bad examples and teach the wrong lessons. For example, some athletes and entertainers have been convicted of drug possession, spousal abuse, or assault.

Assume that you are concerned that your child or sibling is being negatively influenced by one of these figures. Write a "fan letter" to this person explaining the bad influence he or she is having on young people—in particular, your child or sibling. Convince him or her that being in the spotlight is a serious responsibility and that a positive change in behavior could help many young fans.

Brainstorm, freewrite, or cluster to generate ideas and examples to support your concern. Check your letter for the correct use of adjectives and adverbs.

✔ Chapter Highlights

■ **Most adverbs are formed by adding -*ly* to an adjective:**

quick/quickly, bright/brightly, *but* good/well

■ **Comparative adjectives and adverbs compare two persons or things:**

I think Bill Cosby is *funnier* than Eddie Murphy.

Laura can balance a checkbook *more quickly* than I can.

■ **Superlative adjectives and adverbs compare more than two persons or things:**

Last winter, Ingrid had the *worst* cold of her life.

That was the *most carefully* prepared speech I have ever heard.

■ **The adjectives *good* and *bad* and the adverbs *well* and *badly* require special care in the comparative and the superlative:**

good/better/best
bad/worse/worst

well/better/best
badly/worse/worst

■ **Demonstrative adjectives can be singular or plural:**

this/that (chair)

these/those (chairs)

Chapter Review

Proofread these paragraphs for adjective and adverb errors. Cross out any errors, and then correct them above the lines.

A. (1) The most ~~famousest~~ *famous* comet, Halley's comet, appears ~~regular~~ *regularly* every

seventy-six years. (2) This mass of gas and dust has caused panic and fear

because its appearance has often coincided with the ~~baddest~~ *worst* events in history.

(3) During the Middle Ages, people believed that Halley's comet was a ~~surely~~ *sure*

omen of destruction. (4) The ~~most silly~~ *silliest* notions about Halley's comet came about

during its 1910 appearance when people bought pills and bottled oxygen to pro-

tect themselves. (5) Although that sounds ~~real~~ *really* foolish, they believed that

poisonous gas was contained in the comet's ~~brilliantly~~ *brilliant* tail. (6) Despite the

~~most wildest~~ *wildest* superstitions, Halley's comet has given us ~~more better~~ *better* information

about comets and our solar system.

B. (1) It is ~~awful~~ *awfully* easy to forget that artificial satellites have been circling the

Earth for only forty or so years. (2) The first and probably ~~bestest~~ *best* known artificial

satellite was *Sputnik I,* launched by the former Soviet Union in 1957. (3) The next

year, the United States sent a satellite to gather ~~real~~ *really* important information about

radiation around the equator. (4) Now more than five thousand artificial satellites

orbit the Earth. (5) As they move ~~quiet~~ *quietly* across the night sky, we take them for

granted.

(6) We also take for granted the ways in which many of ~~this~~ *these* satellites make

our lives ~~more easier~~ *easier.* (7) Because of communications satellites, for example, a

caller in the United States can get through ~~quick~~ *quickly* to someone in Brazil—or even

Senegal. (8) Weather satellites help weather stations receive ~~more earlier~~ *earlier* warn-

ings about hurricanes. (9) Navigation satellites guide ships when visibility is

poor. (10) Other satellites design more ~~accurater~~ *accurate* maps of the Earth to help find

scarce minerals. (11) Soon satellites may enable scientists to forecast earthquakes.

(12) These forecasts will help authorities prepare for the ~~baddest~~ *worst* effects of the

quakes. (13) Within thirty years, this list of practical uses will probably grow

much ~~more longer~~ *longer.*

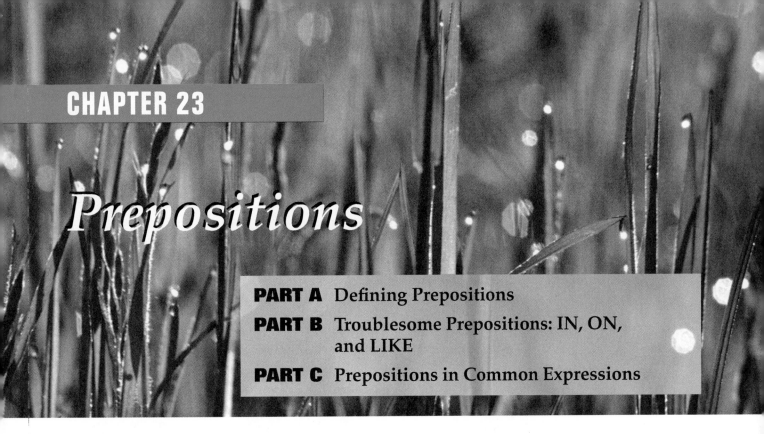

CHAPTER 23

Prepositions

PART A Defining Prepositions

PART B Troublesome Prepositions: IN, ON, and LIKE

PART C Prepositions in Common Expressions

PART A — Defining Prepositions

A preposition is a word like *at, from, in,* or *of.* Below is a partial list of common prepositions:*

Common Prepositions		
about	beside	off
above	between	on
across	by	over
after	during	through
against	except	to
along	for	toward
among	from	under
around	in	until
at	into	up
before	like	with
behind	of	without

A preposition is usually followed by a noun or pronoun. The noun or pronoun is called the *object* of the preposition. Together, the preposition and its object are called a *prepositional phrase.* Here are some prepositional phrases:

---

*For more work on prepositions, see Chapter 6, Part C.

Prepositional Phrase	=	Preposition	+	Object
after the movie		after		the movie
at Kean College		at		Kean College
beside them		beside		them
between you and me		between		you and me

Below are some sentences with prepositional phrases:

(1) Ms. Kringell arrived *at noon*.

(2) A man *in a gray suit* bought three lottery tickets.

(3) The huge moving van sped *through the tunnel*.

■ In sentence (1), the prepositional phrase *at noon* tells when Ms. Kringell arrived. It describes *arrived*.

■ In sentence (2), the prepositional phrase *in a gray suit* describes how the man was dressed. It describes *man*.

■ What is the prepositional phrase in sentence (3)? _____*through the tunnel*_____

Which word does it describe? _____*sped*_____

PRACTICE

Underline the prepositional phrases in the following sentences.

1. Bill collected some interesting facts <u>about human biology.</u>

2. Human eyesight is sharpest <u>at midday.</u>

3. <u>In extreme cold,</u> shivering produces heat, which can save lives.

4. A pound <u>of body weight</u> equals 3,500 calories.

5. Each <u>of us</u> has a distinguishing odor.

6. Fingernails grow fastest <u>in summer.</u>

7. One <u>of every ten people</u> is left-handed.

8. The human body contains approximately ten pints <u>of blood.</u>

9. Beards grow more rapidly than any other hair <u>on the human body.</u>

10. Most people <u>with an extra rib</u> are men.

PART B Troublesome Prepositions: IN, ON, and LIKE

IN/ON for Time

Use *in* before seasons of the year, before months not followed by specific dates, and before years that do not include specific dates.

> (1) *In the summer,* most of us like to laze around in the sun.
>
> (2) No classes will meet *in January*.
>
> (3) Rona was a student at Centerville Business School *in 1996*.

Use *on* before days of the week, before holidays, and before months if a date follows.

> (4) *On Thursday,* the gym was closed for renovations.
>
> (5) The city looked deserted *on Christmas Eve*.
>
> (6) We hope to arrive in Burlington *on October 3*.

PRACTICE

Writer either *in* or *on* in the following sentences.

EXAMPLE: Professor Bradshaw will talk about the War Between the States _____*on*_____ Monday.

1. South Carolina seceded from the United States _____*in*_____ December 1860.

2. President Lincoln sat in the White House _____*on*_____ Christmas Eve wondering what would happen next.

3. _____*In*_____ the winter of 1861, other southern states from Virginia to Texas joined South Carolina to form the Confederate States of America.

4. The war actually began _____*on*_____ April 12, 1861, when the Confederates fired on Fort Sumter, South Carolina.

5. After four years of fierce fighting, the war finally ended _____*in*_____ 1865.

IN/ON for Place

In means *inside of.*

> (1) Raoul slept *in the spare bedroom*.
>
> (2) The exchange student spent the summer *in Sweden*.

On means *on top of* or *at a particular place*.

> (3) The spinach pie *on the table* is for tonight's book discussion group.
> (4) Dr. Helfman lives *on Marblehead Road*.

PRACTICE

Write either *in* or *on* in the following sentences.

EXAMPLE: Here's how you can make raspberry sherbet right _____*in*_____ your own kitchen.

1. Set out all the ingredients you need _____*on*_____ a counter top: 3/4 cup of sugar, 1 cup warm water, 1/2 cup light corn syrup, 1/4 cup lemon juice, 1 container of strained raspberries, and 2 egg whites.

2. Dissolve the sugar _____*in*_____ the warm water; then add the corn syrup, lemon juice, and raspberries, and freeze the mixture until the edges are hard.

3. _____*In*_____ a separate container, beat the egg whites until they are stiff.

4. Whip the partly frozen mixture _____*in*_____ a chilled bowl so that it is smooth but not melted.

5. After folding in the egg whites quickly, place the mixture _____*on*_____ a

    shelf _____*in*_____ your refrigerator freezer until the sherbet is firm.

LIKE

Like is a preposition that means *similar to*. Therefore, it is followed by an object (usually a noun or a pronoun).

> (1) *Like you*, I prefer watching films on a VCR rather than going to a crowded movie theater.

Do not confuse *like* with *as* or *as if*. *As* and *as if* are subordinating conjunctions.* They are followed by a subject and a verb.

> (2) *As the instructions explain*, insert flap B into slit B before folding the bottom in half.
> (3) Robert sometimes acts *as if he has never made a mistake*.

———

*For more work on subordinating conjunctions, see Chapter 14.

PRACTICE

Write *like*, *as*, or *as if* in the following sentences.

EXAMPLE: George grinned _____*as*_____ he approached the door.

1. _____*Like*_____ his friends, Kirk plays basketball at least once a week.

2. Joyce came home _____*as*_____ I was leaving, but she persuaded me to stay a bit longer.

3. Mr. Porter acts _____*as if*_____ he is in charge.

4. Penny's voice sounds _____*like*_____ her mother's.

5. _____*As*_____ the weather forecaster predicted, six inches of snow fell overnight.

PART C   Prepositions in Common Expressions

Prepositions often are combined with other words to form certain expressions—groups of words, or phrases, in common use. These expressions can sometimes be confusing. Below is a list of some troublesome expressions. If you are in doubt about others, consult a dictionary.

Common Expressions with Prepositions

Expression	Example
acquainted with	He became *acquainted with* his duties.
addicted to	I am *addicted to* chocolate.
agree on (a plan)	They finally *agreed on* a sales strategy.
agree to (another's proposal)	Did she *agree to* their demands?
angry about or at (a thing)	The subway riders are *angry about* (or *at*) the delays.
angry with (a person)	The manager seems *angry with* Jake.
apply for (a position)	You should *apply for* this job.
approve of	Does he *approve of* the proposed budget?
consist of	The plot *consisted of* both murder and intrigue.
contrast with	The red lettering *contrasts* nicely *with* the gray stationery.
convenient for	Is Friday *convenient for* you?
correspond with (write)	My daughter *corresponds with* a pen pal in India.
deal with	How do you *deal with* friends who always want to borrow your notes?
depend on	He *depends on* your advice.
differ from (something)	A diesel engine *differs from* a gasoline engine.

Common Expressions with Prepositions (*continued*)

Expression	Example
differ with (a person)	On that point, I *differ with* the medical technician.
displeased with	She is *displeased with* all the publicity.
fond of	We are all *fond of* Sam's grandmother.
grateful for (something)	Jim was *grateful for* the two test review sessions.
grateful to (someone)	We are *grateful to* the plumber for repairing the leak on Sunday.
identical with	This watch is *identical with* hers.
interested in	George is *interested in* modern art.
interfere with	Does the party *interfere with* your study plans?
object to	She *objects to* the increase in the state sales tax.
protect against	This vaccine *protects* people *against* the flu.
reason with	Don't *reason with* a hungry pit bull.
reply to	Did the newspaper editor *reply to* your letter?
responsible for	Omar is *responsible for* marketing.
shocked at	We were *shocked at* the damage to the buildings.
similar to	That popular song is *similar to* another one I know.
specialize in	The shop *specializes in* clothing for large men.
succeed in	Gandhi *succeeded in* freeing India from British rule.
take advantage of	Let's *take advantage of* that two-for-one paperback book sale.
worry about	I no longer *worry about* my manager's moods.

PRACTICE

Circle the correct expressions in these sentences.

1. The amazing career of Albert Goodwill Spalding (consisted of, consisted in) baseball and business success.

2. At first, his mother did not (approve in, approve of) his playing professional ball.

3. Spalding obeyed his mother and (applied for, applied to) a "regular" job.

4. Eventually (displeased with, displeased at) the work he found, Spalding signed up with the Boston Red Stockings in 1871.

5. Over the next five years, the Boston team came to (depend on, depend with) his unusual underhand pitching style.

6. In fact, he was the first pitcher ever to (succeed in, succeed on) winning two hundred games.

7. Spalding soon became more (interested in, interested with) designing baseballs than in playing.

8. Pitchers were (grateful for, grateful to) him for marketing the ball he had designed for his own pitching use; it became the official ball of the National League.

9. Spalding became (fond for, fond of) designing other kinds of balls; for example, he designed the first basketball.

10. He also (dealt on, dealt with) the problem of what to use as goals in this new ball game.

11. He (took advantage of, took advantage for) peach baskets, and the new game was called "basketball."

12. By the 1890s, Spalding had been (responsible for, responsible to) developing one of the world's largest sporting goods companies.

PRACTICE: WRITING ASSIGNMENT

A friend or relative of yours has come to spend a holiday week in your city. He or she has never been there before and wants advice on sightseeing. In complete sentences, write directions for one day's sightseeing. Make sure to explain why you think this person would enjoy visiting each particular spot.

Organize your directions according to time order: that is, what to do first, second, and so on. Use transitional expressions like *then*, *after*, and *while* to indicate time order.

Be especially careful of the prepositions *in* and *on*. Try to work in a few of the expressions listed in Part C.

✔ Chapter Highlights

■ **Prepositions are words like** *at, from, in,* **and** *of.* **A prepositional phrase contains a preposition and its object:**

The tree *beneath my window* has lost its leaves.

■ **Be careful of prepositions** like *in, on,* **and** *like:*

I expect to graduate *in* June.
I expect to graduate *on* June 10.

The Packards live *in* Tacoma.
The Packards live *on* Farnsworth Avenue.

Like my father, I am a Dodgers fan.

■ **Prepositions are often combined with other words to form fixed phrases:**

convenient for, different from, reason with

Chapter Review

Proofread this essay for preposition errors. Cross out the errors, and correct them above the lines.

Taking a Stand

(1) Important events often begin with a person who decides to take a stand.
(2) ~~At~~ *On* Thursday, December 1, 1955, Rosa Parks helped inspire the civil rights movement simply by sitting down.

(3) ~~On~~ *In* 1955, city buses in Montgomery, Alabama, were segregated.
(4) African-American riders had to sit in the back of the bus. (5) The African-American community and its leaders were angry ~~with~~ *about* segregation. (6) They also knew that the city depended ~~at~~ *on* its African-American riders for income. (7) They were waiting to take advantage ~~about~~ *of* the right occasion to organize a bus boycott. (8) Rosa Parks gave them that occasion.

(9) Rosa Parks was a forty-three-year-old tailor's assistant. (10) ~~At~~ *On* that December afternoon, she was tired after a hard day's work. (11) When she was told to give her seat to a white man, she objected ~~from~~ *to* moving. (12) She was arrested.

(13) African-American community leaders organized a boycott, and the buses stayed empty for more than a year. (14) To deal ~~about~~ *with* the lack of transportation, African Americans organized a system of car pools or just walked. (15) At last, ~~in~~ *on* December 20, 1956, an order from the United States Supreme Court declared Montgomery's bus laws unconstitutional. (16) The next day, Rosa Parks was photographed inside one of the first integrated buses ~~on~~ *in* the city. (17) Her simple act of courage helped change the course of American history.

UNIT 5 WRITING ASSIGNMENTS

As you complete each writing assignment, remember to perform these steps:

- Write a clear, complete topic sentence.

- Use freewriting, brainstorming, or clustering to generate ideas.

- Arrange your best ideas in a plan.

- Revise for support, unity, coherence, and exact language.

- Proofread for grammar, punctuation, and spelling errors.

Writing Assignment 1: *Explain your job.* Explain what you do—your duties and responsibilities—to someone who knows nothing about your kind of work but is interested in it. In your first sentence, sum up the work you do. Then name the equipment you use and tell how you spend an average working day. Explain the rewards and drawbacks of your job. Finally, proofread for the correct use of nouns, pronouns, adjectives, adverbs, and prepositions.

Writing Assignment 2: *Give an award.* When we think of awards, we generally think of awards for the most home runs or the highest grade average. However, Cal Ripkin, Jr. of the Baltimore Orioles became famous because he played in a record number of consecutive games. In other words, his award was for *showing up,* for *being there,* for *constancy.* Write a speech for an awards dinner in honor of someone who deserves recognition for this kind of constancy. Perhaps your parents deserve the award, or your spouse, or the law enforcement officer on the beat in your neighborhood. Be specific in explaining why this person deserves the award. You might try a humorous approach. Proofread your speech for the correct use of nouns, pronouns, adjectives, adverbs, and prepositions.

Writing Assignment 3: *Discuss your future.* Imagine yourself ten years from now; how will your life be different? Pick one major way in which you expect it will have changed. You may want to choose a difference in your income, your marital status, your idea of success, or anything else that is important to you. Your first sentence should state this expected change. Then explain why this change will be important to you. Proofread for the correct use of nouns, pronouns, adjectives, adverbs, and prepositions.

Writing Assignment 4: *Answer a personal advertisement.* The following personal advertisement appears in a local newspaper: "35-year-old medical technician would like to meet someone for serious relationship and marriage. Likes cats and outdoors, especially hiking. Not much on sports. Favorite music: rock and jazz. Loves movies, except violent ones; prefers adventure, like Indiana Jones. Wants large family. Occasional churchgoer." First decide whether you are writing to a man or a woman. Then answer this ad. Cover hobbies, interests, things you like and do not like, and so on. Explain why you feel the medical technician and you would or would not be a good match. Note possible areas of conflict. Proofread for the correct use of nouns, pronouns, adjectives, adverbs, and prepositions.

UNIT 5 REVIEW

Proofreading

Proofread the following paragraph for incorrect use of nouns, pronouns, adjectives, adverbs, and prepositions. Cross out any errors, and then correct them above the lines.

The Last Frontier

(1) When the government of Brazil opened the Amazon rain forest for settle-
in *it*
ment ~~on~~ the 1970s, ~~they~~ created the last frontier on earth. (2) Many concerned
men *women* *disaster*
~~man~~ and ~~woman~~ everywhere now fear that the move has been a ~~disasters~~ for the

land and for the people.
largest
(3) The ~~most large~~ rain forest in the world, the Amazon rain forest has been
really hard. *easier*
hit ~~real hard.~~ (4) The government built highways to make it ~~more easy~~ for poor
interested in
people to get to the land, but the roads also made investors ~~interested to~~ the
trees.
forest. (5) Lumber companies chopped down millions of ~~tree.~~ (6) Ranchers and
themselves
settlers ~~theirselves~~ burned the forest to make room for cattle and crops. (7) All
these
~~this~~ activities have taken their toll: in one area, which is the size of Colorado,

three-quarters of the rain forest has already been destroyed. (8) Many kinds of

plants and animals have been lost forever.
forest are
(9) The Indians of the rain ~~forest, they~~ are also threatened by this wholesale

destruction. (10) Ranchers, miners, loggers, and settlers have moved onto Indian

lands. (11) Contact with the outside world has changed the Indians' traditional
tribes
way of life. (12) A few Indian ~~tribe~~ have made economic and political gains;

however, many tribes have totally disappeared.
settlers *well*
(13) Many of the ~~settler~~ are not doing very ~~good~~ either. (14) People have
rapidly,
poured into the region too ~~rapid,~~ and the government is unable to provide the

needed services. (15) Small villages have become crowded cities, diseases (espe-
Worst
cially malaria) have spread, and lawlessness is common. (16) ~~Worse~~ of all, the soil
land is
beneath the rain forest is not fertile. (17) After a few years, the settlers' ~~land, it is~~
advantage of
worthless. (18) As the settlers go into debt, businesses take ~~advantage for the~~
quickly *badly.*
situation by buying land ~~quick~~ and exploiting it ~~bad.~~

(19) Can the situation in the rain forest improve? (20) Although the Brazilian

government has been trying to preserve ~~those~~ *that* forest, thousands of fires are still

set every year to clear land for cattle grazing, planting, and building. (21) On the

more hopeful side, however, scientists have discovered fruits in the rain forest

that are ~~extreme~~ *extremely* high in vitamins and proteins. (22) Those fruits would be much

better crops for the rain forest than the corn, rice, and beans that farmers are

growing now. (23) The world watches ~~nervous.~~ *nervously.* (24) Will the Earth's ~~preciousest~~ *most precious*

rain forest survive?

Transforming

Change the subject of this paragraph from singular to plural, changing every *the
dog* to *dogs*, every *it* to *they*, and so forth. Make all necessary verb and other
changes. Make your revisions above the lines.

(1) ~~The Saint Bernard is a~~ *Saint Bernards are* legendary ~~dog~~ *dogs* famous for ~~its~~ *their* many acts of

bravery. (2) Bred in the wild mountains of Switzerland, ~~it~~ *they* can find paths in the

worst snowstorms, smell human beings buried in snow, and detect avalanches

before they occur. (3) ~~This~~ *These* powerful yet sensitive ~~creature works~~ *creatures work* in rescue patrols.

(4) When ~~a Saint Bernard finds~~ *Saint Bernards find* a hurt traveler, ~~it lies~~ *they lie* down next to the sufferer to

keep him or her warm and ~~licks~~ *lick* the person's face to restore consciousness.

(5) ~~Another dog goes~~ *Other dogs go* back to headquarters to sound the alarm and guide a rescue

party to the scene. (6) In all, ~~the Saint Bernard has~~ *Saint Bernards have* saved more than two thousand

lives. (7) Oddly enough, though ~~this dog has~~ *these dogs have* been known for about three

hundred years, ~~the Saint Bernard~~ *Saint Bernards* did not get ~~its~~ *their* name until about a hundred

years ago. (8) ~~The Saint Bernard was~~ *Saint Bernards were* named for a shelter in the Swiss Alps.

(9) Monks of the shelter of Saint Bernard used ~~this dog~~ *these dogs* in rescue patrols.

UNIT 5 WRITERS' WORKSHOP

Tell How Someone Changed Your Life

Strong writing flows clearly from point to point so that a reader can follow easily. In your class or group, read this essay, aloud if possible. As you read, pay special attention to organization.

Stephanie

(1) There are many people who are important to me. However, the most important person is Stephanie. Stephanie is my daughter. She has changed my life completely. She has changed my life in a positive way.

(2) Stephanie is only five years old, but she has taught me the value of education. When I found out that I was pregnant, my life changed in a positive way. Before I got pregnant, I didn't like school. I went to school just to please my mom, but I wasn't learning anything. When I found out that I was pregnant, I changed my mind about education. I wanted to give my baby the best of this world. I knew that without a good education, I wasn't going anywhere, so I decided to get my life together.

(3) Stephanie taught me not to give up. I remember when she was trying to walk, and she fell down. She didn't stop but kept on going until she learned how to walk.

(4) In conclusion, you can learn a lot from babies. I learned not to give up. Stephanie is the most important person in the whole world to me. She has changed me in the past, and she will continue to change me in the future.

Claudia Huezo, student

1. How effective is this essay?

    __Y__ Clear thesis statement?   __N__ Good support?

    __Y__ Logical organization?   __Y__ Effective conclusion?

2. Ms. Huezo has organized her essay very well: introduction and thesis statement, two supporting paragraphs, conclusion. Is the main idea of each supporting paragraph clear? Does each have a good topic sentence?

3. Is each supporting paragraph developed with enough facts and details? If not, what advice would you give the writer for revising, especially paragraph (3)? *Aim for less repetition, more fresh facts and details.*

4. This student has picked a wonderful subject and writes clearly—two excellent qualities. However, did you find any places where short, choppy, or repetitious sentences could be improved?

   If so, point out one or two places where Ms. Huezo might cross out or rewrite repetitious language (where she says the same thing twice in the same words). Point out one or two places where she might combine short sentences for variety.*

5. Proofread for grammar and spelling. Do you spot any error patterns this student should watch out for? *No grammar errors*

Writing and Revising Ideas

1. Tell how someone changed your life.

2. Discuss two reasons why education is (is not) important.

Before you write, plan or outline your paragraph or essay so that it will be clearly organized (see Chapter 3, Part E, and Chapter 4, Parts B and C). As you revise, pay special attention to the order of ideas and to clear, concise writing without needless repetition.

Cross out paragraph 2, sentence 2, and paragraph 4, sentence 2. Combine paragraph 1, sentences 2 and 3. Combine paragraph 1, sentences 4 and 5.

Revising for Consistency and Parallelism

This unit will teach you some easy but effective ways to add style to your writing. In this unit, you will

✔ Make sure your verbs and pronouns are consistent

✔ Use a secret weapon of many writers—parallel structure

✔ Vary the lengths and types of your sentences

This writer uses balanced sentences to make her point about date rape. If possible, read her paragraph aloud.

Women charge that date rape is the hidden crime; men complain it is hard to prevent a crime they can't define. Women say it isn't taken seriously; men say it is a concept invented by women who like to tease but not take the consequences. Women say the date-rape debate is the first time the nation has talked frankly about sex; men say it is women's unconscious reaction to the excesses of the sexual revolution. Meanwhile, men and women argue among themselves about the "gray area" that surrounds the whole murky arena of sexual relations, and there is no consensus in sight.

Nancy Gibbs, "When Is It Rape?" *Time*

- This writer presents the differing ideas of many men and women by balancing their points of view in sentence after sentence, a technique you will learn in this unit.

- Note that she increases the force of the paragraph by placing the topic sentence last.

Writing Ideas

- Date rape
- Another issue on which men and women disagree

CHAPTER 24

Consistent Tense

Consistent tense means using the same verb tense whenever possible within a sentence or paragraph. As you write and revise, avoid shifting from one tense to another—for example, from present to past—without a good reason for doing so.

(1) **Inconsistent tense:**	We *were* seven miles from shore. Suddenly, the sky *turns* dark.	
(2) **Consistent tense:**	We *were* seven miles from shore. Suddenly, the sky *turned* dark.	
(3) **Consistent tense:**	We *are* seven miles from shore. Suddenly, the sky *turns* dark.	

- The sentences in (1) begin in the past tense with the verb *were* but then shift into the present tense with the verb *turns.* The tenses are inconsistent because both actions are occurring at the same time.

- The sentences in (2) are consistent. Both verbs, *were* and *turned,* are in the past tense.

- The sentences in (3) are also consistent. Both verbs, *are* and *turns,* are in the present tense.

Of course, you should use different verb tenses in a sentence or paragraph if they convey the meaning you want to convey.

(4) Two years ago, I *wanted* to be a chef, but now I *am studying* forestry.

- The verbs in sentence (4) accurately show the time relationship: In the past, I *wanted* to be a chef, but now I *am studying* forestry.

As you proofread your papers for tense consistency, ask yourself: Have I unthinkingly moved from one tense to another, from past to present, or from present to past?

PRACTICE

Underline the verbs in these sentences. Then correct any inconsistencies above the line.

got
EXAMPLE: As soon as I <u>get</u> out of bed, I <u>did</u> fifty pushups.

or

do
As soon as I <u>get</u> out of bed, I <u>did</u> fifty pushups.

appeared
1. We <u>were walking</u> near the lake when a large moose <u>appears</u> just ahead.

asked
2. When Bill <u>ask</u> the time, the cab driver <u>told</u> him it was after six.

was
3. The man behind me <u>was slurping</u> soda and <u>crunching</u> candy. I <u>am getting</u>

angrier by the minute.

welcomed
4. Dr. Choi smiled and <u>welcomes</u> the next patient.

5. The Oklahoma prairie <u>stretches</u> for miles, flat and rusty red. Here and there,
breaks
an oil rig <u>broke</u> the monotony.

went
6. They <u>were strolling</u> down Main Street when the lights <u>go</u> out.

described
7. My cousins <u>questioned</u> me for hours about my trip. I <u>describe</u> the flight, my

impressions of Paris, and every meal I <u>ate</u>.

approached
8. We started cheering as he <u>approaches</u> the finish line.

doesn't
9. If Terry <u>takes</u> short naps during the day, she <u>didn't</u> feel tired in the evening.

marched   *accompanied*
10. Yesterday, we <u>march</u> in the New Year's Day parade. Colorful floats <u>accompany</u>

us. At the end of the route, Grinley's Department Store <u>served</u> hot chocolate

to all of us.

PRACTICE: WRITING ASSIGNMENT

Suppose that you have been asked for written advice on what makes a successful family. Your adult child, an inexperienced friend, or a sibling has asked you to write down some words of wisdom on what makes a family work. Using your own family as an example, write your suggestions for making family life as nurturing, cooperative, and joyful as possible. You may draw on your family's experience to give examples of pitfalls to avoid or of positive behaviors and attitudes.

Revise for consistent tense.

✔ Chapter Highlights

■ **In general, use the same verb tense within a sentence or a paragraph:**

She *sings* beautifully, and the audience *listens* intently.

or

She *sang* beautifully, and the audience *listened* intently.

■ **However, at times different verb tenses are required because of meaning:**

He *is* not *working* now, but he *spent* sixty hours behind the counter last week.

Chapter Review

Read each of these paragraphs for consistent tense. Correct any inconsistencies by changing the tense of the verbs. Write your corrections above the lines.

A. (1) Teaching children self-confidence is vital to their success in childhood
know
and adulthood. (2) With self-confidence, children ~~knew~~ they are worthwhile

persons with worthwhile goals. (3) Parents can teach their children self-
need *draw,*
confidence in several ways. (4) First, children ~~needed~~ praise. (5) When they ~~drew,~~

for example, parents can tell them how beautiful their drawings are. (6) The
have
praise lets them know they ~~had~~ talents that other people admire. (7) Second, chil-
require *find*
dren ~~required~~ exposure to many different experiences. (8) They soon ~~found~~ that
realize
they need not be afraid to try new things. (9) They ~~realized~~ they can succeed as
discover
well at chess as they do at basketball. (10) They ~~discovered~~ that a trip to a

museum to examine medieval armor is fascinating, or that they enjoy taking a
is
class in pottery. (11) Finally, it ~~was~~ very important to treat children individually.
do
(12) Sensitive parents ~~did~~ not compare their children's successes or failures with

those of their brothers or sisters, relatives, or friends. (13) Of course, parents should

inform children if their behavior or performance in school needs improvement.
help
(14) Parents ~~helped~~ children do better, however, by showing them how much they

have accomplished so far and suggesting how much they can and will accom-

plish in the future.

© 1998 Houghton Mifflin Company

B. (1) Last summer, we visited one of the world's oddest museums, the home of someone who never existed. (2) Early one afternoon, we walked along the real Baker Street in London, England. (3) Suddenly, it ~~looms~~ *loomed* in front of us: number 221B, Mrs. Hudson's boarding house, home of the famous but fictitious detective Sherlock Holmes. (4) Once inside the perfect reproduction of Holmes's rooms, we ~~are~~ *were* astonished to find all of Holmes's belongings, including his violin, his walking stick, and his chemistry set. (5) We ~~learn~~ *learned* that the founders of the museum had searched the country for Victorian objects and furniture like those in the Holmes stories. (6) They ~~succeed~~ *succeeded* beyond any Sherlock Holmes fan's wildest dreams. (7) They ~~locate~~ *located* a Persian slipper like the one in which Holmes stored pipe tobacco. (8) They even ~~uncover~~ *uncovered* a gold and emerald tie pin like the one Queen Victoria gave Holmes. (9) The museum also had quarters for Holmes's friend and assistant, Dr. Watson. (10) For him, the founders ~~buy~~ *bought* nineteenth-century medical supplies and surgical instruments. (11) After we ~~return~~ *returned* home that summer, I reread several Sherlock Holmes stories. (12) In my mind's eye, I ~~see~~ *saw* Holmes's rooms and belongings more vividly than ever before. (13) Of course, Holmes would have predicted that. (14) "Elementary," he would have said.

C. (1) Almost every major city in the world has a subway system. (2) Underground trains speed through complex networks of tunnels and ~~carried~~ *carry* millions of passengers every day.

(3) Subway systems sometimes differ because of their locations. (4) In Mexico City, for example, subway cars ~~traveled~~ *travel* through suspended tunnels capable of absorbing earthquake shocks. (5) Residents of Haifa, Israel, use an unusually short, straight subway that ~~ran~~ *runs* up and down inside a mountain. (6) The train ~~brought~~ *brings* people from Haifa's lower port city up—a thousand feet— to the upper residential city. (7) In Hong Kong, the world's first completely air- conditioned subway system ~~offered~~ *offers* relief from extremely hot and humid outdoor temperatures. (8) Cities like San Francisco, of course, expand the defi- nition of subway to cover underwater as well as underground transportation.

includes
(9) The San Francisco Bay Area Rapid Transit (BART) system ~~included~~ several

miles of track under San Francisco Bay.

(10) Some subway systems are famous for their artwork. (11) With paintings
look
and walls of precious marble, many Moscow subway stations ~~looked~~ like
seem
museums. (12) Several stations in Stockholm, Sweden, ~~seemed~~ like elegant caverns

because of granite carvings and rock in its natural state. (13) With colorful designs

and all kinds of special effects, subways stations from Montreal to Tokyo
resemble
~~resembled~~ modern art galleries.
do
(14) Subways, therefore, ~~did~~ more than provide an efficient means of public

transportation. (15) They are also creative solutions to special problems as well as

expressions of art and culture.

CHAPTER 25

Consistent Person

Consistent person means using the same person or personal pronoun throughout a sentence or a paragraph. As you write and revise, avoid confusing shifts from one person to another. For example, don't shift from *first person (I, we)* or *third person (he, she, it, they)* to *second person (you).**

(1) **Inconsistent person:**		College *students* soon see that *you* are on *your* own.
(2) **Consistent person:**		College *students* soon see that *they* are on *their* own.
(3) **Consistent person:**		In college, *you* soon see that *you* are on *your* own.

- ■ Sentence (1) shifts from the third person plural *students* to the second person *you* and *your.*

- ■ Sentence (2) uses the third person plural consistently. *They* and *their* now clearly refer to *students.*

- ■ Sentence (3) is also consistent, using the second person *you* and *your* throughout.

PRACTICE

Correct any inconsistencies of person in these sentences. If necessary, change the verbs to make them agree with any new subjects. Make your corrections above the lines.

EXAMPLE: Each hiker should bring ~~your~~ ^{his or her} own lunch.

1. Belkys treats me like family when I visit her. She always makes ~~you~~ ^{me} feel

   at home.

2. I love to go dancing. ~~You~~ ^I can exercise, work off tension, and have fun, all at

   the same time.

----

*For more work on pronouns, see Chapter 21.

3. If a person has lived in a city, ~~you~~ *he or she* may find the country a welcome change.

4. When Lee and I ride our bikes to work at 6 A.M., ~~you~~ *we* can see the city waking up.

5. Every mechanic should make sure ~~they have~~ *he or she has* a good set of tools.

6. People who want to buy cars today are often stopped by high prices. ~~You~~ *They* aren't sure how to get the most for ~~your~~ *their* money.

7. A working mother must schedule ~~your~~ *her* time carefully.

8. Many people mistakenly think that ~~your~~ *their* votes don't really count.

9. A teacher's attitude affects the performance of ~~their~~ *his or her* students.

10. It took me three years to decide to enroll in college; in many ways, ~~you~~ *I* really didn't know what ~~you~~ *I* wanted to do when ~~you~~ *I* was graduated from high school.

PRACTICE: WRITING ASSIGNMENT

In small groups, write as many endings as you can think of for this sentence: "You can (or cannot) tell much about a person by . . ." You might write, "the way he or she dresses," "the way he or she styles his or her hair," or "the kind of movies he or she likes." Each group member should write down every sentence.

Now, choose one sentence and write a short paragraph supporting it. Let each group member write about a different sentence. Use people in the news or friends as examples to prove your point. As you write, be careful to use the first, second, or third person correctly. Now, exchange papers, checking each other's work for consistent person.

 ## Chapter Highlights

■ **Use the same personal pronoun throughout a sentence or a paragraph:**

When *you* apply for a driver's license, *you* may have to take a written test and a driving test.

When a *person* applies for a driver's license, *he or she* may have to take a written test and a driving test.

Chapter Review

Correct the inconsistencies of person in these paragraphs. Then make any other necessary changes. Write your corrections above the lines.

A. (1) When exam time comes, do you become anxious because you aren't sure how to study for tests? (2) ~~They~~ *You* may have done all the work for ~~their~~ *your* courses, but you still don't feel prepared. (3) Fortunately, ~~he~~ *you* can do some things to make taking tests easier. (4) ~~They~~ *You* can look through the textbook and review the material ~~one has~~ *you have* underlined. (5) You might read the notes you have taken in class and highlight or underline main points. (6) ~~A person~~ *You* can think about some questions the professor may ask and then try writing answers. (7) Sometimes, ~~they~~ *you* can find other people from your class and form a study group to compare class notes. (8) The night before a test, ~~they~~ *you* shouldn't drink too much coffee. (9) ~~They~~ *You* should get a good night's sleep so that your mind will be as sharp for the exam as your pencil.

B. (1) The sport of mountain biking began in northern California in the 1970s. (2) Some experienced cyclists began using ~~his or her~~ *their* old one-speed fat-tire bikes to explore dirt roads and trails. (3) ~~You~~ *They* began by getting car rides up one of the mountains and pedaling their bikes down. (4) Then they began cycling farther up the mountain until ~~he and she~~ *they* were pedaling to the top. (5) Those cyclists eventually started designing bikes to fit ~~our~~ *their* sport. (6) By the end of the 1970s, road bike manufacturers decided ~~you~~ *they* would join the action. (7) By 1986, mountain biking had become a national craze, and sales of mountain bikes were exceeding sales of road bikes.

(8) Today, mountain bikers pay about $1,000 for bikes that have everything ~~we~~ *they* need for riding on rough trails: front-wheel shock absorbers, twenty-four gears that shift easily, a lightweight frame, flexible wheels, and even a full suspension frame. (9) Cyclists ride ~~your~~ *their* bikes everywhere; some of their favorite places are South Dakota's Badlands, Colorado's ski resorts, and Utah's Canyonlands National Park. (10) ~~You~~ *They* compete in mountain bike races all over the world. (11) To top this off, in 1996 some of ~~you~~ *them* competed in the first Olympic mountain bike race, outside Atlanta, Georgia. (12) The course, which had tightly spaced trees and large rocks, included steep climbs and sharp descents with surprise jumps. (13) What were those early "inventors" thinking as ~~he and she~~ *they* watched that race?

CHAPTER 26

Parallelism

PART A Defining and Writing Parallels
PART B Using Parallelism for Special Writing Effects

PART A   Defining and Writing Parallels

Which sentence in each pair sounds better to you?

> (1) Jennie is an artist, spends time at athletics, and flies planes.
>
> (2) Jennie is *an artist, an athlete,* and *a pilot.*
>
> (3) He slowed down and came sliding. The winning run was scored.
>
> (4) He *slowed* down, *slid,* and *scored* the winning run.

■ Do sentences (2) and (4) sound smoother and clearer than sentences (1) and (3)?

■ Sentences (2) and (4) balance similar words or phrases to show similar ideas.

This technique is called *parallelism* **or** *parallel structure.* **The italicized parts of (2) and (4) are** *parallel.* **When you use parallelism, you repeat similar grammatical structures in order to express similar ideas.**

■ In sentence (2), can you see how *an artist, an athlete,* and *a pilot* are parallel? All three words in the series are singular nouns.

■ In sentence (4), can you see how *slowed, slid,* and *scored* are parallel? All three words in the series are verbs in the past tense.

Now let's look at two more pairs of sentences. Note which sentence in each pair contains parallelism.

(5) The car was big, had beauty, and it cost a lot.

(6) The car was *big, beautiful,* and *expensive.*

(7) They raced across the roof, and the fire escape is where they came down.

(8) They raced *across the roof* and *down the fire escape.*

■ In sentence (6), how are *big, beautiful,* and *expensive* parallel words?

All three words are adjectives.

■ In sentence (8), how are *across the roof* and *down the fire escape* parallel phrases?

Both are prepositional phrases.

Certain special constructions require parallel structure:

(9) The room is *both* light *and* cheery.

(10) You *either* love geometry *or* hate it.

(11) Tanya *not only* plays the guitar *but also* sings.

(12) Richard would *rather* fight *than* quit.

Each of these constructions has two parts:

both . . . and	not only . . . but also
(n)either . . . (n)or	rather . . . than . . .

The words, phrases, or clauses following each part must be parallel:

light . . . cheery	plays . . . sings
love . . . hate	fight . . . quit

Parallelism is an excellent way to add smoothness and power to your writing. Use it in pairs or series of ideas, balancing a noun with a noun, an *-ing* verb with an *-ing* verb, a prepositional phrase with a prepositional phrase.

PRACTICE 1

Circle the element that is *not* parallel in each list.

EXAMPLE: blue

red

(colored like rust)

purple

1. broiling

   frying

   (baker)

   cooking

2. under the porch

   in the attic

   (the basement stairs)

   behind the back door

3. (painting the kitchen)
   cans of paint
   several brushes
   one roller

4. goodness
   strength
   love
   (wise)

5. standing on tiptoes
   (toward the audience)
   smiling with anticipation
   leaning against the table

6. music shops
   clothing stores
   (buying a birthday present)
   gift boutiques

7. topped with whipped cream
   (bananas and ice cream)
   sprinkled with pecans
   covered with chocolate sauce

8. We shop for fruits at the market.
   We buy enough to last all week.
   (We are baking a cake tonight.)
   We cook special meals often.

PRACTICE 2

Rewrite each sentence, using parallelism to accent the similar ideas.

EXAMPLE: How can you recognize and you can be helpful to someone who is on drugs?

Rewrite: _How can you recognize and help someone who is on drugs?_

1. A person on drugs may become unusually nervous, irritable, or there may be anger.

   Rewrite: _A person on drugs may become unusually nervous, irritable, or angry._

2. He or she might neglect chores, be forgetting dates, and the person might skip work or classes also.

   Rewrite: _He or she might neglect chores, forget dates, and skip work or classes._

3. New friends may appear whose names and where they are living are kept secret.

   Rewrite: _New friends may appear whose names and addresses are kept secret._

4. Other signs include reckless driving. Health may become poor, and sloppy physical appearance is also a sign.

Rewrite: *Other signs include reckless driving, poor health, and sloppy physical*

appearance.

5. Heavy drug users may experience deep depression and are having wild hallucinations.

Rewrite: *Heavy drug users may experience deep depression and wild*

hallucinations.

6. Many drug users will deny their problem rather than admitting to having it.

Rewrite: *Many drug users will deny their problem rather than admit it.*

7. However, wisely and thoughtful friends and relatives can try to help.

Rewrite: *However, wise and thoughtful friends and relatives can try to help.*

8. They can approach the person with compassion rather than accusingly.

Rewrite: *They can approach the person with compassion rather than with*

accusations.

9. They might not only express their concern but also be making suggestions about treatment programs.

Rewrite: *They might not only express their concern but also make suggestions*

about treatment programs.

10. Groups that use the twelve-step method or when the program uses the "tough love" approach have the most successful programs.

Rewrite: *Groups that use the twelve-step method or the "tough love" approach*

have the most successful programs.

Fill in the blanks in each sentence with parallel words or phrases of your own. Be creative. Take care that your sentences make sense and that your parallels are truly parallel.

EXAMPLE: I feel _____ *rested* _____ and _____ *happy* _____ .

1. Ethan's favorite colors are _____ *yellow* _____ and _____ *green* _____ .

2. The day of the storm, we _____ *sat by the window* _____ , and they _____ *played cards* _____ .

3. Her attitude was strange. She acted as if _____ *she was always right* _____ and as if _____ *everyone else was always wrong* _____ .

4. I like people who _____ *like to hike* _____ and who _____ *like to sing* _____ .

5. Some married couples _____ *spend most of their time together* _____ , while others _____ *pursue separate interests* _____ .

6. Harold _____ *flies a plane* _____ , but I just _____ *fly my kite* _____ .

7. To reach the lake, walk _____ *through the clearing* _____ and _____ *into the woods* _____ .

8. _____ *Playing the piano* _____ and _____ *lying on the beach* _____ relax me.

9. We found _____ *delicate shells* _____ , _____ *smooth stones* _____ , and _____ *broken glass* _____ on the beach.

10. He would like to _____ *work in a hospital* _____ or to _____ *teach physical education* _____ .

PART B   Using Parallelism for Special Writing Effects

By rearranging the order of a parallel series, you can sometimes add a little drama or humor to your sentences. Which of these two sentences is more dramatic?

> (1) Bharati is a wife, a mother, and a black belt in karate.
> (2) Bharati is a wife, a black belt in karate, and a mother.

■ If you chose sentence (1), you are right. Sentence (1) saves the most surprising item—*a black belt in karate*—for last.

■ Sentence (2), on the other hand, does not build suspense but gives away the surprise in the middle.

You can also use parallelism to set up your readers' expectations and then surprise them with humor.

> (3) The handsome cowboy saddled up, leaped on his horse, and slid off.

PRACTICE

On separate paper, write five sentences of your own using parallel structure. In one or two of your sentences, arrange the parallel elements to build toward a dramatic or humorous conclusion. For ideas, look at Practice 3 in Part A, but create your own sentences.

PRACTICE: WRITING ASSIGNMENT

Write a one-paragraph newspaper advertisement to rent or sell your house or apartment. Using complete sentences, let the reader know the number of rooms, their size, and their appearance, and why someone would be happy there. Emphasize your home's good points, such as "lots of light" or "closet space galore," but don't hide the flaws. If possible, minimize them while still being honest.

You may want to begin with a general description, such as "This apartment is a plant lover's dream." Be careful, though: if you describe only the good features or exaggerate, readers may think, "It's too good to be true." Use parallel structure to help your sentences read more smoothly.

✔ Chapter Highlights

- **Parallelism balances similar words or phrases to express similar ideas:**

  He left the gym *tired, sweaty,* and *satisfied.*

  Tami not only *finished the exam in record time* but also *answered the question for extra credit.*

  To celebrate his birthday, Roger *went to a dance, took in a show,* and *ate a late dinner.*

Chapter Review

This essay contains both correct and faulty parallel structures. Revise any faulty parallelism. Write your corrections above the lines.

Chinese Medicine in the United States

(1) When diplomatic relations between the United States and mainland China were restored in 1972, acupuncture was one import that sparked America's imagination and ~~made people interested~~ *interest.* (2) In the United States today, the most popular form of Chinese medicine is acupuncture.

(3) Acupuncture involves the insertion of thin, sterile, ~~made of~~ stainless steel needles at specific points on the body. (4) Chinese medical science believes that the *chi,* or life force, can be redirected by inserting and ~~by the manipulation of~~ *manipulating* these needles. (5) They are inserted to just below the skin and are either removed quickly or ~~leave them~~ *left* in for up to forty minutes. (6) In addition, the acupuncturist can twirl them, heat them, or ~~charging~~ *charge* them with a mild electrical current.

(7) Acupuncture can reduce pain for those suffering from allergies, arthritis, backache, or ~~with a~~ toothache. (8) It has also helped in cases of chronic substance abuse, anxiety, and ~~for depressed people~~ *depression.*

(9) Chinese medicine has grown in popularity and ~~become important~~ *importance* in America. (10) Thirty-five schools in the United States teach Chinese acupuncture. (11) Forty-four states have passed laws that regulate or ~~for licensing~~ *license* the practice of acupuncture. (12) Since 1974, the government has authorized several studies of acupuncture's effectiveness and ~~how reliable it is~~ *reliability.* (13) Although research has failed to explain how acupuncture works, it has confirmed that it does work.

(14) The studies also suggest that acupuncture should continue to be tested and ~~using it~~ *used.*

UNIT 6   WRITING ASSIGNMENTS

As you complete each writing assignment, remember to perform these steps:

■ Write a clear, complete topic sentence.

■ Use freewriting, brainstorming, or clustering to generate ideas.

■ Arrange your best ideas in a plan.

■ Revise for support, unity, coherence, and exact language.

■ Proofread for grammar, punctuation, and spelling errors.

Writing Assignment 1: *Explain your attitude toward writing.* From the "Writing" section of the Quotation Bank, pick a quotation that accurately describes how you feel about writing. For example, do you "think best with a pencil in your hand," or is writing "the hardest work in the world not involving heavy lifting"? Use the quotation as your first sentence; then explain how and why it describes your experience of writing. Refer to papers or letters you have written to illustrate your explanation. Revise for consistent tense and person; use parallelism to make your sentences smooth.

Writing Assignment 2: *Review a restaurant.* You have been asked to review the food, service, and atmosphere at a local restaurant. Your review will appear in a local newspaper and will have an impact on the success or failure of this eating establishment. Name what you ordered, how it tasted, and why you would or would not recommend this dish. Note the service: was it slow, efficient, courteous, rude, or generally satisfactory? Is the restaurant one in which customers can easily carry on a conversation, or is there too much noise? Is the lighting good or poor? Include as much specific detail as you can. Revise for consistent tense and person.

Writing Assignment 3: *Write a letter to the editor.* Your city wishes to put a homeless shelter in your neighborhood, next to an elementary school. Residents are being asked to voice their opinions about the proposed shelter. You have decided to write your reactions. Your chances of being published are good, so you want your argument to be persuasive. Give one or two reasons for locating—or not locating—the shelter near your school. Use your experience or the experience of others to support your points. Revise for consistent tense and person; use parallelism to make your sentences smooth.

Writing Assignment 4: *Evaluate a textbook.* A publisher has asked you to evaluate this textbook, *Grassroots,* or a text you use in a different course. The publisher wants an honest evaluation so that the new edition can be even better than the present one. Rate the textbook on clarity and organization: that is, does it explain the subject matter well, and does one chapter naturally follow from another? You also might want to consider whether the material is shown in a way that is pleasing to the eye. Most important, does the book help you learn? Revise for consistent tense and person; use parallelism to make your sentences smooth.

UNIT 6   REVIEW

Proofreading

A. We have changed this student's composition so that it contains inconsistent tense and faulty parallelism. Proofread for these errors, and correct them above the lines.

Inspiration

(1) When I was a freshman in high school, I ~~have~~ *had* a serious problem with English. (2) All day long, my head was filled with ideas for compositions, but when I arrived in English class, my mind ~~goes~~ *went* blank. (3) I feared that my teacher ~~thinks~~ *thought* I was just another lazy student. (4) In fact, I almost gave up; thank goodness, I didn't!

(5) Then, by the strangest twist of fate, I ~~find~~ *found* out why my mind ~~goes~~ *went* blank and why my compositions were never finished. (6) One day, the English class moved from the basement to the third floor of the building. (7) The moment I stepped into the new room and ~~the window was seen,~~ *saw the window,* I ~~know~~ *knew* what had bothered me all semester—no light, no fresh air, and ~~the fact that there wasn't a sense of~~ *no* space. (8) I ~~select~~ *selected* a seat near the window and looked over my shoulder at the tall oak tree that stretched past the third-floor window. (9) When I ~~pick~~ *picked* up my pen, the writing began to flow. (10) If I ran out of things to say, I just ~~glance~~ *glanced* over my shoulder at the tree and at the sky—and I ~~would be~~ *was* inspired to continue my essay.

Christopher Moore, student

B. Proofread the following essay for inconsistent person and faulty parallelism. Correct the errors above the lines.

Touring Boston

(1) Boston offers visitors a rich variety of places to see and things to ~~be doing.~~ *do.* (2) For instance, the Freedom Trail takes visitors through the downtown area. (3) There ~~you~~ *they* can find the sites of important historic events, like the Old North Church. (4) The church has copies of the lanterns that were used during the Revolutionary War to signal that British troops were coming. (5) If the guard in

the steeple signaled once, the British were coming by land. (6) If he signaled

twice, they were coming ~~on their way~~ by sea. (7) Paul Revere waited nearby in

carried

his home. (8) He watched for the signal and ~~was carrying~~ the news to the patriots

in Lexington.

    (9) In addition, the Black Heritage Trail takes visitors to sites important to

They

the development of Boston's black community. (10) ~~He or she~~ can stop at the

African Meeting House, the oldest black church in New England. (11) At the

meeting house, William Lloyd Garrison founded the New England Anti-Slavery

they

Society in 1832. (12) On Boston Common, ~~you~~ can see the Boston Massacre

monument. (13) Black citizens of Boston erected this monument. (14) It commem-

orates the death of Crispus Attucks, a former slave and ~~he was also~~ the first casu-

alty of the Boston Massacre. (15) Boston is clearly a city filled with history.

Shift Your Audience and Purpose

Playing with the idea of audience and purpose can produce some interesting writing—such as writing to your car to persuade it to keep running until finals are over. Likewise, writing as if you are someone else can be a learning experience.

In your class or group, read this unusual essay, aloud if possible.

A Fly's-Eye View of My Apartment

(1) Hey, are you guys ready? Today is Armageddon!* When you enter this door, remember, you're not getting out alive. She's a pretty tough lady. Oh, and don't forget to eat all you can. The kids are always dropping crumbs. You can make it through the night if you stay on the ceilings. Whatever you do, stay out of the peach room that is always humid. Once the door is shut, you're trapped. Try not to be noticed on the cabinets in the room where the smells come from. There is nothing interesting in the room with the big screen, but the room with the large bed can be rather stimulating if you stay on the walls.

(2) She won't get tired of us until about 6 P.M.; that is usually around dinnertime. She switches around, using different swatters, so you never really know what to look for. When you hear the gospel music, start looking out. She gets an enormous amount of energy from this music, and her swats are accurate, which means they're deadly. It kills me how she becomes so baffled about how we get in since she has screens on the windows. Little does she know that it's every time she opens the front door.

(3) Well, I think she's ready to leave for work. I hear the lock. To a good life, fellows. See you in heaven—and remember to give her hell!

Tanya Peck, student

1. How effective is Ms. Peck's essay?

     __Y__ Interesting subject?   __Y__ Good supporting details?

     __Y__ Logical organization?   __Y__ Effective conclusion?

2. This writer cleverly plays with the notions of speaker, audience, and purpose. Who is Ms. Peck pretending to be as she writes? Whom is she addressing and for what purpose? *She is a fly addressing flies about to enter Ms. Peck's apartment.*

---

*Armaggedon: a final battle between forces of good and evil.

3. The writer/speaker refers to the "pretty tough lady" of the house. Who is that lady? How do you know?

4. She divides her essay into two main paragraphs and a brief conclusion. Because of her unusual subject, the paragraphs do not have topic sentences. However, does each paragraph have a clear main idea? What is the main idea of paragraph (1)? of paragraph (2)? *(1) A guide to the rooms; (2) advice about the homeowner*

5. Underline any details or sentences that you especially liked—for example, in paragraph (2), the clever idea that the fly realizes that gospel music (for some mysterious reason) energizes the woman with the swatter. Can you identify the rooms described in paragraph (1)?

6. The essay concludes by playing with the terms *heaven* and *hell.* Do you find this effective—or offensive? Are these words connected to *Armageddon* in the introduction? How?

7. Proofread for any grammar or spelling errors. *No errors*

Writing and Revising Ideas

1. Write a _____ 's-eye view of your home (dog, cat, flea, canary, goldfish, ant, roach).

2. Describe an important moment in history as if you were there.

Before you write, read about audience and purpose in Chapter 1. Prewrite and plan to get an engaging subject. As you revise, pay special attention to keeping a consistent point of view; really try to imagine what that person (or other creature) would say in these circumstances.

Mastering Mechanics

Even the best ideas may lose their impact if the writer doesn't know how to capitalize and punctuate correctly. In this unit, you will

✔ Learn when—and when not—to capitalize

✔ Recognize when—and when not—to use commas

✔ Find out how to use apostrophes

✔ Learn how to quote the words of others in your writing

Correct punctuation adds to the power of this writer's fresh look at an old subject. If possible, read his paragraphs aloud.

Adolescence is a cruel word. Its cruelty lies hidden in its vaguely official, diagnostic air. To say people are "adolescent," "going through adolescence," or worse, "being adolescent" is to dismiss their feelings, minimize their troubles, and (if you're the parent) protect yourself from their uncompromising rage. The words *teenager* and *teen* are worse. They reek of cuteness. But we all know that being a teen doesn't feel cute.

People that age hardly ever use those words. They tend to call themselves "kids" when pushed, as in, "What makes you think you know so much about kids—you sure don't know much about *me!*" Or they dress up and act out and give themselves better words: "punk," "gothic," "rapper," . . ., "low-rider," "homeboy," "soc," "hippie," "freak"—words to remind us just how volatile, how dangerous, how "freaked out," "awesome," "bummed," "bitchin'," "groovy," "wasted," and "bad" those years really are.

Michael Ventura, "The Age of Endarkenment," *UTNE Reader*

■ This writer contrasts two sets of names for the same period of life: the first paragraph looks at the "cruel" adult words, and the second paragraph looks at the colorful—and disturbing—words that young people use about themselves.

■ Do you think that teenagers have more rage than people of other ages?

■ A term currently used by teenagers

■ Any jargon—specialized words—from your job: for instance, terms from sales, fast food, computer or car repair, or patient care

Here are the basic rules of capitalization:

1. nationality, race, language, religion

 Capitalize → American, African American, French, English, Protestant, Jewish, Catholic, Muslim, Buddhist, and so forth

This group is *always capitalized.*

2. names of persons, countries, states, cities, places, streets, bodies of water, and so forth

 Capitalize → Bill Morse, New Zealand, California, Denver, Central Park, Jones Street, Pacific Ocean, and so forth

but → a large state, a town, the lake, and so forth

If you name a specific person, state, city, street, or body of water, *capitalize;* if you don't, use small letters.

3. buildings, organizations, institutions

 Capitalize → World Trade Center, Paradise Theater, National Organization for Women, Johnson City Library, Smithson University, and so forth

but → a tall building, an expensive theater, a feminist group, an old school, and so forth

If you name a specific building, group, or institution, *capitalize;* if you don't, use small letters.

4. historical events, periods, documents

 Capitalize → the Spanish-American War, the Renaissance, the Constitution, and so forth

but → a terrible war, a new charter, and so forth

If you name a specific historical event, period, or document, *capitalize;* if you don't, use small letters.

318

5. months, days, holidays Capitalize → June, Monday, the Fourth of July, and so forth

but → summer, fall, winter, spring

Always capitalize months, days, and holidays; use small letters for the seasons.

6. professional and civil titles Capitalize → Dr. Smith, Professor Greenstein, Judge Alvarez, and so forth

but → the doctor, the professor, the judge, and so forth

If you name the doctor, judge, and so forth, *capitalize;* if you don't, use small letters.

7. family names Capitalize → Uncle Joe, Grandmother Stein, Cousin Beverly, Mother, Grandfather, and so forth

but → an uncle, the aunt, our cousin, my mother, her grandfather, and so forth

If you name a relative or use *Mother, Father, Grandmother,* or *Grandfather* as a name, *capitalize;* however, if these words are preceded by the word *a, an,* or *the,* a possessive pronoun, or an adjective, use small letters.

8. brand names Capitalize → Greaso hair oil, Quick drafting ink, and so forth

Capitalize the brand name but not the type of product.

9. geographic locations Capitalize → the East, the Northwest, the South, and so forth

but → east on the boulevard

If you mean a geographic location, *capitalize;* if you mean a direction, use small letters.

10. academic subjects Capitalize → Mathematics 51, Sociology 11, English Literature 210, and so forth

but → a tough mathematics course, an A in sociology, a course in English literature, and so forth

If you use the course number, *capitalize;* if you don't, use small letters. However, always capitalize languages and countries.

11. titles of books, poems, plays, films Capitalize → *A Farewell to Arms,* "Ode to a Bat," *Major Barbara, Jurassic Park,* and so forth

Capitalize titles except for short words or prepositions; however, always capitalize the *first* and *last* words of the title.

PRACTICE

Capitalize where necessary.

EXAMPLE: The S͟smithsonian consists of thirteen museums and the N͟national Z͟zoo.

1. Judy and I took the children and A͟aunt M͟mae to W͟washington last summer during
   the week of I͟independence D͟day.

2. We spent one full day visiting the museums.

3. Carl and Luke liked the N͟national A͟air and S͟space M͟museum best.

4. They thought that the tiny craft flown by O͟orville and W͟wilbur W͟wright at
   K͟kitty H͟hawk, N͟north C͟carolina, in 1903, looked like a model plane.

5. We all marveled that C͟charles L͟lindbergh would dare to fly a plane as small
   as the *S͟spirit of S͟saint L͟louis* across the A͟atlantic O͟ocean.

6. There was a great difference between those early planes and the model of
   the *V͟voyager* spacecraft; this modern spacecraft was designed to explore
   J͟jupiter, S͟saturn, and U͟uranus.

7. Next, we walked along C͟constitution A͟avenue to the N͟national M͟museum of
   A͟american H͟history.

8. There I saw my favorite car, the 1903 W͟winton that made the first trip across
   the U͟united S͟states.

9. We also saw the flag that inspired F͟francis S͟scott K͟key to write "T͟the S͟star S͟spangled
   B͟banner."

10. This was the same flag that M͟mrs. P͟pickersgill sewed to fly over Fort McHenry
    in C͟chesapeake B͟bay during 1812.

11. Some of the other treasures we viewed there were P͟president W͟washington's
    wooden false teeth, a pair of ruby slippers from the film *T͟the W͟wizard of O͟oz,* and
    a copy of T͟thomas P͟paine's book *C͟common S͟sense.*

12. Finally, my family and I went to the N͟national M͟museum of N͟natural H͟history to
    stare at the A͟african B͟bull elephant and bengal tiger on display.

13. Exhausted, we returned to the R͟ramada I͟inn, flopped into bed, and watched
    a rerun of *S͟star T͟trek.*

14. The next day, thursday, we visited the white house and the library of
    congress.
    T   *W*   *H*   *L*
    C

15. We never saw any of the art museums that are also part of the smithsonian,
    S

    but we will be back soon.

PRACTICE: WRITING ASSIGNMENT

Is your family vacation usually a disaster or a success? Describe a particularly memorable vacation—either bad or good—in which you learned something about how to plan or enjoy a vacation.

In your first sentence, tell what you learned. Explain what went right and what went wrong. Be sure to name the places you visited and the sights you saw. You will probably wish to arrange events in time order. Proofread for correct capitalization.

✔ Chapter Highlights

- **Capitalize nationalities, languages, races, and religions:**

  Asian, French, Caucasian, Baptist

- **Capitalize specific countries, states, cities, organizations, and buildings:**

  Belgium, Utah, Akron, United Nations, the White House

- **Capitalize months, days, and holidays, but not seasons:**

  November, Friday, Labor Day, summer

- **Capitalize professional titles only when a person is named:**

  Mayor Alexander, the mayor, Superintendent Alicia Morgan

- **Capitalize brand names, but not the type of product:**

  Dawn dishwashing detergent

- **Capitalize geographic locations, but not directions:**

  the West, west of the city

- **Capitalize academic subjects only when they are followed by a course number:**

  History 583, psychology

- **Capitalize titles of books, poems, plays, and films:**

  Lord of the Flies, "The Raven," *Rent, Autobiography of My Mother*

Chapter Review

Proofread the following essay for errors in capitalization; correct the errors above the lines.

The Strange Career of Deborah Sampson

(1) Few *s*Soldiers have had a stranger army career than Deborah Sampson. (2) Sampson disguised herself as a man so that she could fight in the *R*revolutionary *W*war. (3) Born on *D*december 17, 1760, she spent her early years in a *t*Town near *P*plymouth, *M*massachusetts. (4) Her *f*Father left his large family, however, and went to sea when Sampson was seven years old. (5) After living with a *c*Cousin and then with the widow of a *m*Minister, *S*sampson became a servant in a wealthy family.

(6) Household tasks and hard outdoor work built up her physical strength. (7) She was taller than the average *m*Man and more muscular than the average *w*Woman. (8) Therefore, she was able to disguise herself successfully. (9) Sampson enlisted in the *C*continental *A*army on *M*may 20, 1782, under the name of *R*robert *S*shurtleff. (10) Sampson fought in several *b*Battles and was wounded at least twice.

(11) One story says that she took a bullet out of her own leg with a penknife to avoid seeing a *d*Doctor. (12) However, after the surrender of the *B*british, Sampson's regiment was sent to *P*philadelphia, where she was hospitalized with a high fever and lost consciousness. (13) At the *h*Hospital, *D*dr. Barnabas Binney made the discovery that ended Sampson's army life. (14) She was honorably discharged by *G*general *H*henry *K*knox at *W*west *P*point on *O*october 28, 1783.

(15) Officially female again, Sampson returned to Massachusetts and eventually married a *f*Farmer named *B*benjamin *G*gannett. (16) The story of Sampson's adventures spread; in 1797, a book titled *T*the *F*female *R*review was published about her. (17) When Sampson decided to earn money by telling her own story, she became the first *A*american woman to be paid as a *p*Public *s*Speaker. (18) She gave her first talk at the *F*federal *S*street *T*theatre in *B*boston in *M*march 1802 and toured until *S*september. (19) Her health was poor, however, and she could not continue her appearances.

                        P   R   *G*
(20) In 1804, paul revere, who was a neighbor of the gannetts, wrote to a
                U   S   C   *s*
member of the united states congress. (21) He asked for a pension for this Soldier

who had never been paid and was still suffering from her war wounds. (22)
                        D   S   G
Congress granted deborah sampson gannett a pension of four dollars a month.
                                              S   *A*
(23) Deborah Sampson died in sharon, Massachusetts, in april 1827. (24) Her
                p   *p*
story inspired the People of her own time and continues to inspire People today.
                                              S   W   T   *P*
(25) Two plays have been written about her: *she was there* and *portrait of*
D   *V*   *D*
deborah. (26) On veterans day in 1989, a life-size bronze statue was dedicated in
                        S   P   L
front of the sharon public library to honor her.

Commas

The comma is a pause. It gives your reader a chance to stop for a moment to think about where your sentence has been and where it is going, and to prepare to read on.

Although this chapter will cover some basic uses of the comma, always keep this generalization in mind: If there is no reason for a comma, leave it out!

PART A   Commas after Items in a Series

(1) I like apples, oranges, and pears.

■ What three things do I like? _____apples_____, _____oranges_____, and

_____pears_____

Use commas to separate three or more items in a series.

(2) We will walk through the park, take in a film, and visit a friend.

■ What three things will we do? _____*walk through the park*_____,

_____*take in a film*_____, and _____*visit a friend*_____

> (3) She loves to explore new ~~cultures~~ *cultures,* sample different ~~foods~~ *food,* and learn foreign languages.

■ In sentence (3), what are the items in the series?

_____*explore new cultures*_____, _____*sample different foods*_____,

and _____*learn foreign languages*_____

■ Punctuate sentence (3).

However, if you want to join three or more items with *and* or *or* between the items, do not use commas.

> (4) She plays tennis *and* golf *and* softball.

■ Note that commas are not used in sentence (4).

PRACTICE 1

Punctuate these sentences correctly.

1. I can't find my shoes my socks or my hat!
   shoes, socks,
2. Sylvia Eric and James have just completed a course in welding.
   Sylvia, Eric,
3. Over lunch, they discussed new accounts marketing strategy and motherhood.
   accounts, strategy,
4. Francine went to the wrestling match Harry visited the antique automobile
   show and Isaac caught a cold.
   match, show,
5. On Sunday, we repaired the porch cleaned the basement and shingled the roof.
   porch, basement,
6. The exhibit will include photographs diaries and love letters.
   photographs, diaries,
7. Body building tennis and roller blading have become very popular in the past
   ten years.
   building, tennis,
8. Paula hung her coat on the hook Henry draped his jacket over her coat and
   hook, coat,

   Sonia threw her scarf on top of the pile.

PRACTICE 2

On separate paper, write three sentences, each containing three or more items in a series. Punctuate correctly.

PART B   Commas after Introductory Phrases

> (1) By the end of the season, our local basketball team will have won thirty games straight.

■ *By the end of the season* introduces the sentence.

An introductory phrase is usually followed by a comma.

> (2) On Thursday we left for Hawaii.

However, a very short introductory phrase, like the one in sentence (2), need not be followed by a comma.

PRACTICE 1

Punctuate these sentences correctly. One sentence is already punctuated correctly.

1. During the *rainstorm,* rainstorm we huddled in a doorway.
2. Every Saturday at 9 *p.m.,* p.m. she carries her telescope to the roof.
3. After their last *trip,* trip Fred and Nita decided on separate vacations.
4. The phone system must be installed by Friday.
5. By the light of the *moon,* moon we could make out a dim figure.
6. During the coffee *break,* break George reviewed his psychology homework.
7. In the deep end of the *pool,* pool he found three silver dollars.
8. In almost no *time,* time they had changed the tire.

PRACTICE 2

On separate paper, write three sentences using introductory phrases. Punctuate correctly.

PART C   Commas for Direct Address

> (1) Bob, you must leave now.
> (2) You must, Bob, leave now.
> (3) You must leave now, Bob.
> (4) Don't be surprised, old buddy, if I pay you a visit very soon.

■ In sentences (1), (2), and (3), Bob is the person spoken to; he is being *addressed directly.*

■ In sentence (4), *old buddy* is being *addressed directly.*

The person addressed directly is set off by commas wherever the direct address appears in the sentence.

PRACTICE 1

Circle the person or persons directly addressed, and punctuate the sentences correctly.

1. I am happy to inform you, (Mr. Forbes), that you are the father of twins.
2. We will meet in an hour, (Florence).
3. It appears, (my friend), that you have won two tickets to the opera.
4. Get out of my roast, (you mangy old dog).
5. (Tom), it's probably best that you sell the old car at a loss.
6. If I were you, (Hilda), I would start my own mail order business.
7. (Bruce), it's time you learned to operate the lawn mower!
8. I am pleased to announce, (ladies and gentlemen), that Madonna is our surprise guest tonight.

PRACTICE 2

On separate paper, write three sentences using direct address. Punctuate correctly.

PART D   Commas to Set Off Appositives

(1) The Rialto, a new theater, is on Tenth Street.

■ *A new theater* describes *the Rialto.*

(2) An elderly man, my grandfather walks a mile every day.

■ What group of words describes *my grandfather?* ___*an elderly man*___

(3) They bought a new painting, a rather beautiful landscape.

■ What group of words describes *a new painting?*

   a rather beautiful landscape
   _____

■ *A new theater, an elderly man,* and *a rather beautiful landscape* are called *appositives.*

An *appositive* is usually a group of words that describes a noun or pronoun. It can occur at the beginning, middle, or end of a sentence. An appositive is usually set off by commas.

PRACTICE 1

Circle the appositive, and punctuate correctly.

1. That door the one with the X on it leads backstage.

2. A short man he decided not to pick a fight with the basketball player.

3. Hassim my friend from Morocco will be staying with me this week.

4. She expects to go to Midvale Technical College a fine institution.

5. George Eliot a nineteenth-century novelist was a woman named Mary Ann Evans.

6. A very close race the election for mayor wasn't decided until 2 a.m.

7. On Thanksgiving my favorite holiday my whole family gets together for a wonderful feast.

8. Dr. Simpson a specialist in ethnic music always travels with a tape recorder.

PRACTICE 2

On separate paper, write three sentences using appositives. Punctuate correctly.

PART E Commas for Parenthetical Expressions

(1) By the way, I think that you're beautiful.
(2) I think, by the way, that you're beautiful.
(3) I think that you're beautiful, by the way.

■ *By the way* modifies or qualifies the entire sentence or idea.

■ It is called a *parenthetical expression* because it is a side remark, something that could be placed in parentheses: *(By the way) I think that you're beautiful.*

Set off a parenthetical expression with commas.

Below is a partial list of parenthetical expressions:

as a matter of fact	in fact
believe me	it seems to me
I am sure	it would seem
I assure you	to tell the truth

PRACTICE 1

Circle the parenthetical expressions in the sentences below; then punctuate correctly.

1. (Believe me) Sonia has studied hard for her driver's test.
2. She possesses (it would seem) an uncanny gift for gab.
3. It was (I assure you) an accident.
4. (To tell the truth) I am not pleased with my sandwich.
5. His supervisor (by the way) will never admit when he is wrong.
6. A well-prepared résumé (as a matter of fact) can help you get a job.
7. He is (in fact) a black belt.
8. (To begin with) I don't like westerns.

PRACTICE 2

On separate paper, write three sentences using parenthetical expressions. Punctuate them correctly.

PART F   Commas for Dates

(1) I arrived on Tuesday, March 20, 1997, and found that I was in the wrong city.

■ Note that commas separate the different parts of the date.
■ Note that a comma follows the last item in the date.

(2) She saw him on Wednesday and spoke with him.

However, a one-word date (*Wednesday* or *1995*) **preceded by a preposition** (*in, on, near,* or *from,* for example) **is not followed by a comma unless there is some other reason for it.**

PRACTICE 1

Punctuate these sentences correctly. Not every sentence requires additional punctuation.

1. By Tuesday *Tuesday,* October 6 *6,* he had outlined the whole history text.
2. Thursday *Thursday,* May 8 *8,* is Hereford's birthday.

9, 1945,
3. She was born on January 9 1945 in a small New England town.

4, 1976,
4. He was born on July 4 1976 the two-hundredth anniversary of the Declaration

of Independence.

5. Do you think we will have finished the yearbook by May?

24, 1848,
6. On January 24 1848 James Wilson Marshall found gold in California.

7. I saw six films between Tuesday and Sunday.

8. This book was due back in the library more than five years ago—on March
13,
13 1992.

PRACTICE 2

On separate paper, write three sentences using dates. Punctuate correctly.

PART G   Commas for Addresses

> (1) We just moved from 11 Landow Street, Wilton, Connecticut, to 73 James Street, Charleston, West Virginia.

■ Commas separate different parts of an address.
■ A comma generally follows the last item in an address, usually a state (*Connecticut*).

> (2) Julio Smith *from* Queens was made district sales manager.

However, a one-word address preceded by a preposition (*in, on, at, near,* or *from,* for example) is not followed by a comma unless there is another reason for it.

> (3) Julio Smith, Queens, was made district sales manager.

Commas are required to set off a one-word address if the preposition before the address is omitted.

PRACTICE 1

Punctuate these sentences correctly. Not every sentence requires additional punctuation.

Street, London,
1. Their address is 6 Great Ormond Street London England.
Seattle, Washington,
2. Seattle Washington faces the Cascade Mountains.

3. That package must be sent to 30 West Overland Street Phoenix Arizona.
   Street, Phoenix,

4. She lives near Valentine Avenue, around the corner from the park.

5. His father now lives in Waco Texas but his sister has never left Vermont.
   Waco, Texas,

6. How far is Kansas City Kansas from Independence Missouri?
   City, Kansas, Independence,

7. My old apartment at 98 Underhill Avenue Fargo North Dakota was much
   Avenue, Fargo, Dakota,

   larger than the one I have now.

8. Foster's Stationery 483 Heebers Street Plainview sells special calligraphy pens.
   Stationery, Street, Plainview,

PRACTICE 2

On separate paper, write three sentences using addresses. Punctuate correctly.

PART H   Commas for Coordination and Subordination

Chapters 13 and 14 covered the use of commas with coordinating and subordinating conjunctions. Below is a brief review.

> (1) Enzio enjoys most kinds of music, but heavy metal gives him a headache.
>
> (2) Although the weather bureau had predicted rain, the day turned out bright and sunny.
>
> (3) The day turned out bright and sunny although the weather bureau had predicted rain.

- In sentence (1), a comma precedes the coordinating conjunction *but*, which joins together two independent ideas.

- In sentence (2), a comma follows the dependent idea because it precedes the independent idea.

- Sentence (3) does not require a comma because the independent idea precedes the subordinate one.

Use a comma before coordinating conjunctions—*and, but, for, nor, or, so,* **or** *yet—* **that join two independent ideas.**

Use a comma after a dependent idea only when the dependent idea precedes the independent one; do not use a comma if the dependent idea follows the independent one.

PRACTICE 1

Punctuate correctly. Not every sentence requires additional punctuation.

waste,

EXAMPLE: Because scrapped cars create millions of tons of waste recycling auto parts has become an important issue.

parts,

1. Today new cars are made from many old parts and manufacturers are trying to increase the use of recycled materials from old cars.

2. Scrapped cars can be easily recycled because they consist mostly of metals.

crushed,

3. After these cars are crushed magnets draw the metals out of them.

4. However, the big problem in recycling cars is the plastic they contain.

recycled,

5. Although plastic can be recycled the average car contains about twenty different kinds of plastic.

time,

6. Separating the different types of plastic takes much time but companies are developing ways to speed up the process.

7. Still, new cars need to be made differently before recycling can truly succeed.

easily,

8. Their parts should detach easily and they should be made of plastics and metals that can be separated from each other.

auto parts,

9. As we develop more markets for the recycled auto parts new cars may soon be 90 percent recycled and recyclable.

benefit,

10. Our environment will benefit and brand-new cars will really be more than fifty years old!

PRACTICE 2

On separate paper, write three sentences, one with a coordinating conjunction, one beginning with a subordinating conjunction, and one with the subordinating conjunction in the middle.

PRACTICE: WRITING ASSIGNMENT

The twentieth century is often called the age of invention because of its rapid advances in technology, communication, and medicine. Which modern invention has meant the most to you *personally,* and why? You might choose something as common as disposable diapers or as sophisticated as a special feature of a personal computer.

In the first sentence, name the invention. Then, as specifically as possible, discuss why it means so much to you. Proofread for the correct use of commas.

✔ Chapter Highlights

■ **Commas separate three or more items in a series:**

He bought a ball, a bat, and a fielder's glove.

■ **Unless it is very short, an introductory phrase is followed by a comma:**

By the end of January, I'll be in Australia.

■ **Commas set off the name of a person directly addressed:**

I think, Aunt Betty, that your latest novel is a winner.

■ **Commas set off appositives:**

My boss, the last person in line in the cafeteria, often forgets to eat lunch.

■ **Commas set off parenthetical expressions:**

My wife, by the way, went to school with your sister.

■ **Commas separate the parts of a date or an address, except for a one-word date or address preceded by a preposition:**

On April 1, 1997, I was in a terrible blizzard.

I live at 48 Trent Street, Randolph, Michigan.

She works in Tucson as a plumber.

■ **A comma precedes a coordinating conjunction that joins two independent ideas:**

We had planned to see a movie together, but we couldn't agree on one.

■ **If a dependent idea precedes the independent idea, it is followed by a comma; if the independent idea comes first, it is not followed by a comma:**

Although I still have work to do, my project will be ready on time.

My project will be ready on time although I still have work to do.

Chapter Review

Proofread the following essay for comma errors—either missing commas or commas used incorrectly. Correct any errors right on the page.

Sitting Bull

(1) Sitting ~~Bull~~ *Bull,* the great Sioux ~~chief~~ *chief,* was born about 1830. (2) From the stories of the tribal ~~elders~~ *elders,* he learned that a Sioux must be ~~brave strong generous~~ *brave, strong, generous,* and wise. (3) He also learned that a Sioux had/to earn his adult name.

(4) When he was ~~fourteen~~ *fourteen,* he earned the name Sitting Bull. (5) Armed with only a coup stick, a long wooden pole, he rode into battle against the Crow tribes. (6) He was the first Sioux to touch a Crow with his coup stick. (7) This act was considered as brave as killing an enemy. (8) After that battle, his father gave him his adult ~~name~~ *name,* a ~~bow arrows~~ *bow, arrows,* a ~~spear~~ *spear,* and other weapons.

(9) When he was thirty-five years ~~old~~ *old,* Sitting Bull became the chief of the Hunkpapa Sioux. (10) He led/his people/across the Great Plains. (11) He saw greedy men taking away native ~~lands~~ *lands,* ruining native holy ~~places~~ *places,* and destroying the buffalo.

(12) The destruction of the buffalo was disastrous for the Sioux. (13) The Sioux used every part of the ~~buffalo~~ *buffalo,* the "giver of life." (14) They made leather clothes from the ~~hide~~ *hide,* they ate the ~~meat~~ *meat,* and they used the tendons for bow strings. (15) In ~~fact~~ *fact,* they even used buffalo droppings for fuel. (16) Without the ~~buffalo~~ *buffalo,* the Sioux could barely survive. (17) They had to fight to protect their land and their "giver of life."

(18) On June ~~25 1876~~ *25, 1876,* the Sioux fought their famous battle against General George Custer and his army. (19) In less than half an ~~hour~~ *hour,* Custer and all his men had been killed. (20) This battle became known as "Custer's Last Stand." (21) It also was the Sioux tribes' last stand against the United States cavalry. (22) Despite their great ~~victory~~ *victory,* most of the Sioux were forced to settle on reservations. (23) Even Sitting Bull/lived on Standing Rock Reservation.

(24) Sitting Bull was killed on December ~~15 1890~~ *15, 1890,* and buried in Fort ~~Yates~~ *Yates,* North Dakota. (25) More than sixty years later, his remains were reburied in ~~Mobridge~~ *Mobridge,* South Dakota. (26) Sitting Bull is remembered still for his ~~leadership~~ *leadership,* for his ~~courage~~ *courage,* and for his wisdom.

© 1998 Houghton Mifflin Company

CHAPTER 29

Apostrophes

PART A   Using the Apostrophe for Contractions

A *contraction* **is a way of combining two words and making one word out of them.**

$$do + not = don't$$

■ Note that the *o* of *not* is omitted in the contraction. An apostrophe (') replaces the omitted letter *o*.

$$should + not = shouldn't \ (o \text{ omitted})$$

$$I + have = I've \ (ha \text{ omitted})$$

BE CAREFUL: *Won't* is an odd contraction because it cannot be broken into parts in the same way the previous contractions can.

$$will + not = won't$$

PRACTICE 1

Write these words as contractions.

1. you + are = _____you're_____

2. who + is = _____who's_____

3. are + not = _____aren't_____

4. they + are = _____they're_____

5. can + not = _____can't_____

6. it + is = _____it's_____

7. I + am = _____I'm_____

8. will + not = _____won't_____

335

PRACTICE 2

Insert the missing apostrophes in these contractions.

Won't
1. Wont you go with us?
What's
2. Whats in the locked box?
don't
3. I dont know the answer.
You're
4. Youre gorgeous.
Who's
5. Whos appearing at the Blue Bongo?
Aren't
6. Arent we early?
we're
7. Now were in trouble.

can't
8. They just cant agree.
It's
9. Its too early to leave.
Shouldn't
10. Shouldnt we eat soon?
Didn't
11. Didnt he mention his name?
doesn't
12. She doesnt like blues; they
don't
dont like classical music.

PRACTICE 3

On separate paper, write five sentences using an apostrophe in a contraction.

PART B   Defining the Possessive

A *possessive* is a way of showing that someone or something owns someone or something else.

PRACTICE

In the following phrases, who owns what?

EXAMPLE: "The hat of the man" means ___the man owns the hat___.

1. "The camera of Judson" means ___Judson owns the camera___.

2. "The hopes of the people" means ___the people have hopes___.

3. "The thought of the woman" means ___the woman owns the thought___.

4. "The trophies of the home team" means ___the home team owns trophies___.

5. "The reputation of that man" means ___that man has a reputation___.

PART C   Using the Apostrophe to Show Possession (in Words That Do Not Already End in -*S*)

(1) the hands of my father	becomes	(2) my father's hands

- In phrase (1), who owns what? ___My father owns the hands.___

- In phrase (1), what is the *owner word*? ___father___

- How does the owner word show possession in phrase (2)?

  ___Father ends in 's.___

■ Note that what is owned, *hands*, follows the owner word.

If the *owner word* (possessive) does not end in -*s*, add an apostrophe and an -*s* to show possession.

PRACTICE 1

Change these phrases into possessives with an apostrophe and an -*s*. (Note that the owner words do not end in -*s*.)

EXAMPLE: the friend of my cousin =   *my cousin's friend*

1. the eyes of Rona =   *Rona's eyes*

2. the voice of the coach =   *the coach's voice*

3. the ark of Noah =   *Noah's ark*

4. the prices of today =   *today's prices*

5. the jacket of someone =   *someone's jacket*

PRACTICE 2

Add an apostrophe and an -*s* to show possession in these phrases.

    Judy's
1. Judy briefcase

    diver's
2. the diver tanks

    Edison's
3. Edison invention

    Bill's
4. Bill decision

    somebody's
5. somebody umbrella

    everyone's
6. everyone dreams

    daughter's
7. your daughter sandwich

    yesterday's
8. yesterday fashion

    woman's
9. that woman talent

    anyone's
10. anyone guess

PRACTICE 3

On separate paper, write five sentences. In each, use an apostrophe and an -*s* to show ownership. Use owner words that do not already end in -*s*.

PART D   Using the Apostrophe to Show Possession (in Words That Already End in -*S*)

(1) the uniforms of the pilots   becomes   (2) the pilots' uniforms

■ In phrase (1), who owns what?   *The pilots own the uniforms.*

■ In phrase (1), what is the owner word?   *pilots*

■ How does the owner word show possession in phrase (2)?

    Pilots ends in '

■ Note that what is owned, *uniforms*, follows the owner word.

If the owner word (possessive) ends in -s, add an apostrophe after the -s to show possession.*

PRACTICE 1

Change these phrases into possessives with an apostrophe. (Note that the owner words already end in -s.)

EXAMPLE: the helmets of the players = _____ the players' helmets _____

1. the farm of my grandparents = _____ my grandparents' farm _____

2. the kindness of my neighbors = _____ my neighbors' kindness _____

3. the dunk shots of the basketball players = _____ the basketball players' dunk shots

4. the music of The Smashing Pumpkins = _____ The Smashing Pumpkins' music

5. the trainer of the horses = _____ the horses' trainer _____

PRACTICE 2

Add either 's or ' to show possession in these phrases. BE CAREFUL: Some of the owner words end in -s and some do not.

models'	*family's*
1. the models faces	7. my family history
model's	*parents'*
2. the model face	8. your parents garden
writer's	*men's*
3. the writer ideas	9. the men locker room
children's	*students'*
4. the children room	10. the students exams
runner's	*contestants'*
5. the runner time	11. several contestants answers
Boris'/Boris's	*Jones'/Jones's*
6. Boris radio	12. Mr. Jones band

PRACTICE 3

Rewrite each of the following pairs of short sentences as *one* sentence by using a possessive.

EXAMPLE: Joan has a friend. The friend comes from Chile.

Joan's friend comes from Chile.

1. Rusty has a motorcycle. The motorcycle needs new brakes.

Rusty's motorcycle needs new brakes.

2. Nurse Johnson had evidence. The evidence proved that the doctor was not careless.

Nurse Johnson's evidence proved that the doctor was not careless.

3. Ahmad has a salary. The salary barely keeps him in peanut butter.

Ahmad's salary barely keeps him in peanut butter.

_____

*Some writers add an 's to one-syllable proper names that end in -s: *James's* book.

4. Lee has a job. His job in the Complaint Department keeps him on his toes.

   Lee's job in the Complaint Department keeps him on his toes.

5. José has a bad cold. It makes it hard for him to sleep.

   José's bad cold makes it hard for him to sleep.

6. Ms. Rose has a class. Her class will meet every other week.

   Ms. Rose's class will meet every other week.

7. Lucy had a day off. The day off gave her a chance to weed the garden.

   Lucy's day off gave her a chance to weed the garden.

8. My sisters have a day-care center. The day-care center is open seven days a week.

   My sisters' day-care center is open seven days a week.

9. The twins have a goal. Their goal is to learn synchronized swimming.

   The twins' goal is to learn synchronized swimming.

10. Darren has a thank-you note. The thank-you note says it all.

    Darren's thank-you note says it all.

PRACTICE 4

On separate paper, write six sentences that use an apostrophe to show ownership—three using owner words that do not end in -s and three using owner words that do end in -s.

BE CAREFUL: Apostrophes show possession by nouns. As the following chart indicates, possessive pronouns do not have apostrophes.

Possessive Pronouns	
Singular	**Plural**
my book, mine	our book, ours
your book, yours	your book, yours
his book, his	their book, theirs
her book, hers	
its book, its	

Do not confuse *its* (possessive pronoun) with *it's* (contraction for *it is* or *it has*) or *your* (possessive pronoun) with *you're* (contraction for *you are*).*

REMEMBER: Use apostrophes for contractions and possessive nouns only. Do not use apostrophes for plural nouns, verbs, or possessive pronouns.

PRACTICE: WRITING ASSIGNMENT

Assume that you are writing to apply for a position as a teacher's aide. You want to convince the school principal that you would be a good teacher, and you decide

---

*See Chapter 32 for work on words that look and sound alike.

to do this by describing a time that you taught a young child—your own child, a younger sibling, or a friend's child—to do something new.

In your topic sentence, briefly state who the child was and what you taught him or her. What made you want to teach this child? Was the experience easier or harder then you expected? How did you feel afterward? Proofread for the correct use of apostrophes.

 Chapter Highlights

■ **An apostrophe can indicate a contraction:**

We're glad you could come.

They *won't* be back until tomorrow.

■ **A word that does not end in -s takes an 's to show possession:**

Is that *Barbara's* coat on the sofa?

I like *Clint Eastwood's* movies.

■ **A word that ends in -s takes just an ' to show possession:**

That store sells *ladies'* hats with feathers.

I depend on my *friends'* advice.

Chapter Review

Proofread this essay for apostrophe errors—missing apostrophes and apostrophes used incorrectly. Correct the errors above the lines.

The Magic Fastener

(1) ~~Its~~ *It's* hard to remember the world without Velcro. (2) Shoelaces had to be tied; ~~jackets'~~ *jackets* had to be zipped and ~~did'nt~~ *didn't* make so much noise when they were loosened. (3) We have a Swiss ~~engineers'~~ *engineer's* curiosity to thank for ~~todays~~ *today's* changes.

(4) On a hunting trip in 1948, Georges de Mestral became intrigued by the seedpods that clung to his clothing. (5) He knew that they ~~we're~~ *were* hitching rides to new territory by fastening onto him, but he ~~could'nt~~ *couldn't* tell how they were doing it.

(6) He examined the seedpods to find that their tiny hooks were catching onto the threads of his jacket.

(7) The idea of Velcro was born, but the actual product ~~wasnt~~ *wasn't* developed overnight. (8) It took eight more ~~years'~~ *years* before Georges de ~~Mestrals~~ *Mestral's* invention was ready for the market. (9) Today, Velcro is used on clothing, on space suits, and even in artificial hearts. (10) Velcro can not only help keep a skier warm but can also save a ~~persons'~~ *person's* life.

© 1998 Houghton Mifflin Company

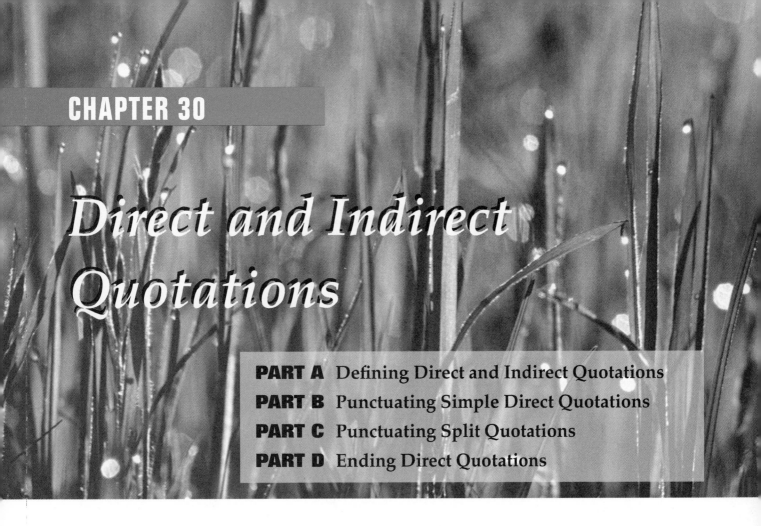

CHAPTER 30

Direct and Indirect Quotations

PART A   Defining Direct and Indirect Quotations

> (1) John said that he was going.
>
> (2) John said, "I am going."

■ Which sentence gives the *exact words* of the speaker, John?

sentence (2)

■ Why is sentence (2) called a *direct quotation?*

It gives the speaker's exact words.

■ Why is sentence (1) called an *indirect quotation?*

It only reports the speaker's words without giving his exact words.

■ Note that the word *that* introduces the *indirect quotation.*

PRACTICE

Write *D* in the blank at the right if the sentence uses a *direct quotation*. Write *I* in the blank at the right if the sentence uses an *indirect quotation*.

1. I insisted that I was first.   *I*

2. Rita asked, "Which is my chair?"   *D*

3. Ruth insisted that one turkey would feed the whole family.   *I*

4. The students shouted, "Get out of the building! It's on fire!"   *D*

5. "This is silly," she said, sighing.   *D*

6. I suggested that Bill continue practicing.   *I*

PART B Punctuating Simple Direct Quotations

Note the punctuation:

> (1) Rafael whispered, "I'll always love you."

- ■ Put a comma before the direct quotation.
- ■ Put quotation marks around the speaker's exact words.
- ■ Capitalize the first word of the direct quotation.
- ■ Put the period *inside* the end quotation marks.

Of course, the direct quotation may come first in the sentence:

> (2) "I'll always love you," Rafael whispered.

- ■ List the rules for a direct quotation written like the sentence above:

    Put quotation marks around the speaker's exact words.

    Capitalize the first word of the direct quotation.

    Put the comma inside the end quotation marks.

PRACTICE

Rewrite these simple direct quotations, punctuating them correctly.

1. He yelled answer the phone!

    Rewrite: *He yelled, "Answer the phone!"*

2. The usher called no more seats in front.

    Rewrite: *The usher called, "No more seats in front."*

3. It's raining we muttered angrily.

   Rewrite: ___"It's raining," we muttered angrily.___

4. Examining the inside cover, Bob said, this book was printed in 1879.

   Rewrite: ___Examining the inside cover, Bob said, "This book was printed in 1879."___

5. Something is doing the backstroke in my soup the man said.

   Rewrite: ___"Something is doing the backstroke in my soup," the man said.___

PART C   Punctuating Split Quotations

Sometimes one sentence of direct quotation is split into two parts:

> (1) "Because it is 2 a.m.," he said, "you had better go."

- ■ *He said* is set off by commas.
- ■ The second part of the quotation—*you had better go*—begins with a small letter because it is part of one directly quoted sentence.

> (2) "Because it is 2 a.m. . . . you had better go."

A direct quotation can also be broken into separate sentences:

> (3) "It is a long ride to San Francisco," he said. "We should leave early."

- ■ Because the second part of the quotation is a separate sentence, it begins with a capital letter.
- ■ Note the period after *said*.

   BE CAREFUL: If you break a direct quotation into separate sentences, be sure that both parts of the quotation are complete sentences.

PRACTICE 1

Rewrite these split direct quotations, punctuating them correctly.

1. Before the guests arrive she said let's relax.

   Rewrite: ___"Before the guests arrive," she said, "let's relax."___

2. Don't drive so fast he begged I get nervous.

   Rewrite: ___"Don't drive so fast," he begged. "I get nervous."___

3. Although my new phone looks terrific he said it has a funny ring.

   Rewrite: ___"Although my new phone looks terrific," he said, "it has a funny ring."___

4. Being the youngest in the family she said has its advantages.

Rewrite: *"Being the youngest in the family," she said, "has its advantages."*

5. This catalog is fantastic the clerk said and you can have it for free.

Rewrite: *"This catalog is fantastic," the clerk said, "and you can have*

it for free."

PRACTICE 2

On separate paper, write three sentences using split quotations.

PART D   Ending Direct Quotations

A sentence can end in any of three ways:

■ with a period (.)

■ with a question mark (?)

■ with an exclamation point (!)

The period is *always* placed inside the end quotation marks:

> (1) He said, "My car cost five thousand dollars."

The question mark and the exclamation point go before or after the quotation marks—depending on the sense of the sentence.

> (2) He asked, "Where are you?"
> (3) Did he say, "I am thirty-two years old"?
> (4) She yelled, "Help!"

■ The question mark in sentence (2) is placed before the end quotation marks because the direct quotation is a question.

■ The question mark in sentence (3) is placed after the end quotation marks because the direct quotation itself *is not a question.*

Note that sentence (2) can be reversed:

> (5) "Where are you?" he asked.

■ Can you list the rules for the exclamation point used in sentence (4)?

Place the exclamation point inside the end quotation marks.

Place the quotation marks around the speaker's exact words.

■ Note that sentence (4) can be reversed:

> (6) "Help!" she yelled.

PRACTICE

Rewrite these direct quotations, punctuating them correctly.

1. Barbara asked is that your station wagon.

   Rewrite: _Barbara asked, "Is that your station wagon?"_

2. Did Shenoya make the team he inquired.

   Rewrite: _"Did Shenoya make the team?" he inquired._

3. Be careful with that mirror she begged the movers.

   Rewrite: _"Be careful with that mirror!" she begged the movers._

4. The truck driver shouted give me a break.

   Rewrite: _The truck driver shouted, "Give me a break!"_

5. The man thought how can I leave without being seen.

   Rewrite: _The man thought, "How can I leave without being seen?"_

PRACTICE: WRITING ASSIGNMENT

Write a note to someone with whom you have had an argument. Your goal is to get back on friendly terms with this person. In your first sentence, state this goal, asking for his or her open–minded attention. Then tell him or her why you think a misunderstanding occurred, and explain how you think conflict might be avoided in the future. Refer to the orginal argument by using both direct and indirect quotations. Check for the correct use of quotation marks; be careful with *all* punctuation.

✔ Chapter Highlights

■ **A direct quotation requires quotation marks:**

Benjamin Franklin said, "There never was a good war or a bad peace."

■ **Both parts of a split quotation require quotation marks:**

"It isn't fair," she argued, "for us to lose the money for the after-school programs."

■ **When a direct quotation is split into separate sentences, begin the second sentence with a capital letter:**

"It's late," he said. "Let's leave in the morning."

■ **Always place the period inside the end quotation marks:**

He said, "Sometimes I talk too much."

■ **A question mark or exclamation point can be placed before or after the end quotation marks, depending on the meaning of the sentence:**

She asked, "Where were you when we needed you?"

Did she say, "Joe looks younger without his beard"?

Chapter Review

Proofread this essay for direct and indirect quotations. Punctuate the quotations correctly, and make any other necessary changes above the lines.

Satchel Paige

(1) Some people say that the great pitcher Leroy Paige was called Satchel because of his big feet. (2) Paige himself ~~said~~ *said, "I* I got the nickname as a boy in Mobile before my feet ~~grew~~. *grew."* (3) He earned money by carrying bags, called satchels, at the railroad station. (4) ~~I~~ *"I* figured out a way to make more money by carrying several bags at a time on a ~~pole~~ *pole,"* he said. (5) Other boys began shouting at him that he looked like a satchel tree. (6) The name stuck.

(7) Unfortunately, for most of Paige's long pitching career, major league baseball excluded African-American players. (8) However, Satchel Paige pitched impressively in the black leagues and in tours against white teams. (9) In 1934, he won a thirteen-inning, one-to-nothing pitching duel against the white pitcher Dizzy Dean and a team of major league all-stars. (10) ~~My~~ *"My* fast ~~ball~~ *ball,"* admitted ~~Dean~~ *Dean,* ~~looks~~ *"looks* like a change of pace alongside of that little bullet old Satchel shoots up to the ~~plate!~~ *plate!"*

(11) After Jackie Robinson broke the major league color barrier in 1948, Satchel Paige took his windmill windup to the Cleveland Indians. (12) He became the oldest rookie in major league history. (13) Some people said that he was too old, but his record proved them wrong. (14) His plaque in the Baseball Hall of Fame ~~reads he~~ *reads, "He* helped pitch the Cleveland Indians to the 1948 ~~pennant~~. *pennant."*

(15) Satchel Paige pitched off and on until he was sixty years old.

(16) When people asked how he stayed young, he gave them his famous rules. (17) Everyone remembers the last one. (18) ~~Don't~~ *"Don't* look ~~back~~ *back,"* he said. (19) ~~Something~~ *"Something* might be gaining on ~~you~~. *you."*

UNIT 7   WRITING ASSIGNMENTS

As you complete each writing assignment, remember to perform these steps:

- Write a clear, complete topic sentence.
- Use freewriting, brainstorming, or clustering to generate ideas.
- Arrange your best ideas in a plan.
- Revise for support, unity, coherence, and exact language.
- Proofread for grammar, punctuation, and spelling errors.

Writing Assignment 1: *Write a letter to compliment or to complain.* Write a letter to a store manager or a dean, praising an especially helpful salesperson or a particularly good teacher. Or write the opposite: a letter of complaint about a salesperson or an instructor. State your compliment or complaint, describing what occurred and explaining why you are pleased or displeased. Remember, how well your letter is written will contribute to the impression you make. Proofread carefully for the correct use of capitals, commas, apostrophes, and quotation marks.

Writing Assignment 2: *Write a letter to the editor.* Recently, large sums of money fell off an armored truck and into the street. As the money scattered in the wind, people collected the bills and put them in their handbags, shopping bags, and pockets. Part of the money was turned in at the local police station, but most was kept by those who had found it. Write a letter to a newspaper, explaining why you feel the money should have been returned or why you would claim, "Finders keepers." Be honest: What do you think you would have done? Proofread carefully for the correct use of capitals, commas, apostrophes, and quotation marks.

Writing Assignment 3: *Write a TV or radio commercial.* Interested in a career in advertising, you have been asked to write a short commercial to show your skills. Pick a product or service that you really like. You might want to get other people to buy a particular kind of paper towel, athletic shoe, or weed killer. Your commercial can be serious or funny, using hard sell or soft. It is up to you. Proofread carefully for the correct use of capitals, commas, apostrophes, and quotation marks.

Writing Assignment 4: *Revise a quotation.* Pick a quotation from the Quotation Bank and alter it to express something new. For example, you might want to change "Insanity is hereditary—you get it from your children" to "Insanity is learned—you get it from going to school." Be as serious or as humorous as you would like. Prove that your quotation is valid, arguing from your own or others' experience. Proofread carefully for the correct use of capitals, commas, apostrophes, and quotation marks.

UNIT 7 REVIEW

Proofreading

A. Proofread the following business letter for incorrect or missing capitals, commas, apostrophes, and quotation marks. Correct all errors above the lines. BE CAREFUL: There are errors lurking everywhere.

Somers Street
99 ~~somers street~~
Ohio
Northfield, ~~ohio~~ 44056
February
~~february~~ 28, 1996

Weird Walt's
~~weird walts~~ Discount Store
Office
Main ~~office~~
Akron,
~~akron,~~ Ohio 44313
Sir
Dear ~~sir~~ or Madam:

February 20, 1996,
On ~~february 20 1996~~ I ordered a Zenith nineteen-inch color television with

Avenue, Medina, Ohio.
remote control from your store at 1101/Lakeland ~~avenue medina ohio.~~ The

model number is 19K44P. When the delivery man brought the set to my home

yesterday, he seemed impatient. He urged me to sign before I had a chance to
box, *it,*
open the ~~box~~ unpack ~~it~~ or examine the equipment. In fact, he said, "Listen,
mister, I'm *not."* *dismay,*
~~mister Im~~ leaving now whether you open this box or ~~not.~~ To my ~~dismay~~ I later

discovered that the handheld remote control was missing.
possible,
As soon as ~~possible~~ please send me this remote control. I want to use my
Zenith *now,* *Walt's*
new ~~zenith~~ properly. For years ~~now~~ I have been a loyal customer of Weird ~~walt's~~
Thank you.
and would appreciate your prompt attention in this matter. ~~thank You.~~
yours,
Sincerely ~~your's,~~
Rainford
Milton ~~rainford~~

B. Proofread the following essay for incorrect or missing capitals, commas, apostrophes, and quotation marks. Correct the errors above the lines.

The Liberator of South America

1805,
(1) One day in ~~1805~~ Simón Bolívar made a vow. (2) He vowed that he
wouldn't *Spanish*
~~wouldnt~~ rest until South America was free from ~~spanish~~ oppression. (3) This
history. *Bolívar,*
promise changed his life and Latin American ~~history~~ (4) ~~Bolívar~~ surprisingly
enough,
~~enough~~ spent the first twenty-two years of his life as a rich aristocrat. (5) When he

died at ~~fifty-seven~~ *fifty-seven,* he was known as the ~~george~~ *George* Washington of ~~south america.~~ *South America.*

(6) Bolívar was born in ~~caracas, Venezuela~~ *Caracas, Venezuela,* on July ~~24~~ *24,* 1783. (7) ~~after~~ *After* he became an orphan at the age of ~~nine~~ *nine,* his uncle provided him with a tutor *tutor,* Simón ~~Rodriguez~~ *Rodriguez.* (8) A fierce ~~patriot~~ *patriot,* Rodriguez wanted South ~~American's~~ *Americans* to rule themselves. (9) ~~However~~ *However,* young Simón Bolívar ~~was'nt~~ *wasn't* very interested in his ~~tutors~~ *tutor's* ideas about independence. (10) ~~Bolívars~~ *Bolívar's* uncle sent Simón to ~~europe~~ *Europe* to help further the young ~~mans~~ *man's* education. (11) ~~during~~ *During* his travels in Spain, Bolívar

realized that Latin America was destined to be independent of Spain.

(12) Bolívar returned to Venezuela and joined those fighting Spain. (13) His troops were ~~defeated~~ *defeated,* but Bolívar would not admit to failure. (14) In a famous letter that he wrote in 1814, he declared, ~~"the~~ *"The* bonds that unite us to Spain have been ~~cut".~~ *cut."* (15) Finally, the tide turned against Spain. (16) The ~~spaniards~~ *Spaniards* were driven out of ~~Colombia Venezuela Ecuador~~ *Colombia, Venezuela, Ecuador,* Peru, and ~~Bolivia~~ *Bolivia.* (17) Bolívar, leader of much of South ~~America~~ *America,* wanted to unite the people under one government. (18) His idea may have been a good ~~one~~ *one,* yet each area preferred to become a separate nation. (19) Although his plan for a united country ~~failed~~ *failed,* Bolívar is still remembered as South ~~Americas~~ *America's* greatest hero.

Explain a Cause or an Effect

Examining causes and effects is a useful skill, both in college and at work. This student's thoughtful essay looks at the effects of school pressure to "speak like an American." In your group or class, read it aloud if possible. As you read, pay attention to the causes and effects he describes.

In America, Speak Like an American

(1) Many teachers tell immigrant students to lose their accents and "speak like an American." They mean well. They want the children to succeed. However, this can also encourage children to be ashamed of who they are and give up their heritage.

(2) When I was in fourth grade, I was sent to a class for "speech imperfections." Apparently, I had a Spanish accent. The class wasn't so bad. It
bad, it taught us to say "chair" instead of "shair" and "school" instead of "eschool." It was so important for me to please the teacher, I did practically everything she asked. She told us things like "The bums on
accents. That's
the street have accents, that's why they're not working." I abandoned my roots and my culture and embraced "America." I learned of Stonewall Jackson and William Shakespeare. Soon Ponce de León and Gonzalo de Barca were just memories at the back of my mind. I listened to country music and rock because this was "American."

(3) I can't remember when it happened, but suddenly I found myself listening to Spanish love songs. They were great! They were so
and
sincere, the lyrics were beautiful. While turning the radio dial one day, I stopped at a Hispanic radio station. It was playing salsa. Holy smokes, I thought to myself. All the instruments were synchronized so tightly. The horn section kept accenting the singer's lines. All of a sudden, my hips started swaying, my feet started tapping, and I stood up. And
music. I
then the horror. I couldn't dance to this music, I had never learned how. There I was, a Puerto Rican boy, listening to Puerto Rican music, but unable to dance the typical Puerto Rican way.

(4) Anger flared through me as I remembered my fourth grade
parents. In
teacher. I was also upset with my parents, in their zeal to have me excel, they kept me from my roots as a first-generation Hispanic American. But that was years ago. I have searched for my Latin

heritage. I've found beautiful music, wonderful literature, and great foods. I now associate with "my people" as well as with everyone else, and I am learning the joys of being Sam Rodriguez, Puerto Rican.

Sam Rodriguez, student

1. How effective is Mr. Rodriguez's essay?

   ___*Y*___ Clear main idea?   ___*Y*___ Good supporting details?

   ___*Y*___ Logical organization?   ___*Y*___ Effective conclusion?

2. Does the essay have a *thesis statement*, one sentence that states the main idea of the entire essay? Which sentence is it? *Paragraph 1, sentence 1*

3. In paragraph (2), the writer says that he "abandoned [his] roots." In his view, what caused him to do this?

4. Underline the lines and ideas you find especially effective, and share them with your group or class. Try to understand exactly why you like a word or sentence. For example, in paragraph (3), we can almost experience the first time the writer really *hears* salsa—the instruments, the horns accenting the singer's lines, his tapping feet and swaying hips.

5. As the writer gets older, he realizes he has lost too much of his heritage. At first he is angry (short-term effect), but what long-term effect does this new understanding have on him?

6. What order does this writer follow throughout the essay? *Time order*

7. This fine essay is finished and ready to go, but the student makes the same punctuation error four different times. Can you spot and correct the error pattern that he needs to watch out for? *Four comma splices*

Writing and Revising Ideas

1. What does it mean to "become American"?

2. Write about a time you gave up something important and what caused you to do this.

Plan carefully, outlining your paragraph or essay before you write. State your main idea clearly and plan your supporting ideas or paragraphs. As you revise, pay special attention to clear organization and convincing, detailed support.

Improving Your Spelling

Some people are naturally better spellers than others, but anyone can *become* a better speller. In this unit, you will

✔ Master six basic spelling rules

✔ Learn to avoid common look alike/sound alike errors

No spelling errors mar this writer's memory of summer mornings years ago. If possible, read the paragraph aloud.

Summer, when I was a boy in Brooklyn, was a string of <u>intimacies</u>, a sum of small knowings, and almost none of them cost money. Nobody ever <u>figured</u> out a way to charge us for morning, and morning then was the <u>beginning</u> of everything. I was an altar boy in the years after the war, up in the morning before most other people for the long walk to the church on the hill. And I would watch the sun rise in Prospect Park—first a rumor, then a <u>heightened</u> light, something unseen and immense melting the hard early darkness; then suddenly there was a molten ball, <u>screened</u> by the trees, about to climb to a scalding noon. The sun would dry the dew on the grass of the park, soften the tar, bake the rooftops, brown us on the <u>beaches</u>, make us sweat, force us out of the tight, small flats of the tenements.

Pete Hamill, "Spaldeen Summers"

■ Through his choice and arrangement of words, this writer helps us see and feel the park at sunrise. He also has avoided the six most common types of spelling errors. The underlined words are all spelled correctly. If you don't know why, read on.

Writing Ideas

■ Morning in a particular place (a desert, a suburb, an all-night bar, a mountain top, and so forth)

■ An experience of "awe" or wonder

CHAPTER 31

Spelling

PART A   Suggestions for Improving Your Spelling

One important ingredient of good writing is accurate spelling. No matter how interesting your ideas are, your writing will not be effective if your spelling is incorrect.

Tips for Improving Your Spelling

1. Look closely at the words on the page.

2. Use any tricks you can to remember the right spelling: for example, "the *a*'s in *separate* are separated by an *r*," or "*dessert* has two *s*'s because you want two *desserts*."

3. Use a dictionary. Even professional writers frequently check spelling in a dictionary. As you write, underline the words you are not sure of, and look them up when you write your final draft. If locating words in the dictionary is a real problem for you, consider a "poor speller's dictionary." Ask your professor to recommend one.

4. Keep a list of the words you misspell. Look over your list whenever you can, and keep it handy as you write.

5. Look over corrected papers for misspelled words (often marked *sp*). Add these words to your list.

6. Test yourself. Use flash cards or have a friend dictate words from your list or from this chapter.

7. Read through Chapter 32, "Look-alikes/Sound-alikes," for commonly confused words (*their, there,* and *they're,* for instance). The practices in that chapter will help you eliminate some common spelling errors from your writing.

8. Review the basic spelling rules explained in this chapter. Take time to learn the material; don't rush through the entire chapter all at once.

PART B   Spotting Vowels and Consonants

To learn some basic spelling rules, you must know the difference between vowels and consonants.

The vowels are *a, e, i, o,* **and** *u.*

The consonants are *b, c, d, f, g, h, j, k, l, m, n, p, q, r, s, t, v, w, x,* **and** *z.*

The letter *y* **can be either a vowel or a consonant, depending on its sound.**

> happy, shy

■ In each of these words, *y* is a vowel because it has a vowel sound: an *ee* sound in *happy* and an *i* sound in *shy.*

> young, yawn

■ In each of these words, *y* is a consonant because it has the consonant sound of *y.*

PRACTICE

Write *V* for vowel or *C* for consonant in the space over each letter. Be careful of the *y.*

EXAMPLES:

$$\overset{C}{h}\overset{V}{o}\overset{C}{p}\overset{V}{e}\overset{C}{d}$$

$$\overset{C}{s}\overset{C}{t}\overset{V}{a}\overset{C}{r}$$

1. $\overset{C}{t}\overset{C}{h}\overset{V}{e}\overset{C}{r}\overset{V}{e}$ 2. $\overset{C}{r}\overset{V}{e}\overset{C}{l}\overset{C}{y}$ 3. $\overset{C}{y}\overset{V}{a}\overset{C}{m}\overset{C}{s}$

4. $\overset{C}{j}\overset{V}{u}\overset{C}{m}\overset{C}{p}$ 5. $\overset{C}{h}\overset{V}{i}\overset{C}{d}\overset{C}{d}\overset{V}{e}\overset{C}{n}$ 6. $\overset{C}{s}\overset{V}{i}\overset{C}{l}\overset{C}{v}\overset{V}{e}\overset{C}{r}$

PART C   Doubling the Final Consonant (in Words of One Syllable)

When you add a suffix or ending that begins with a vowel (like *-ed, -ing, -er, -est*) to a word of one syllable, double the final consonant *if* the last three letters of the word are consonant-vowel-consonant, or *cvc*.

mop + ed = mopped

swim + ing = swimming

thin + est = thinnest

burn + er = burner

■ *Mop, swim,* and *thin* all end in *cvc;* therefore, the final consonants are doubled.

■ *Burn* does not end in *cvc;* therefore, the final consonant is not doubled.

PRACTICE 1

Which of the following words double the final consonant? Check to see whether the word ends in *cvc*. Double the final consonant if necessary; then add the suffixes *-ed* and *-ing.*

	Word	Last Three Letters	-ed	-ing
EXAMPLES:	drop	cvc	dropped	dropping
	boil	vvc	boiled	boiling
1.	plan	cvc	planned	planning
2.	brag	cvc	bragged	bragging
3.	rip	cvc	ripped	ripping
4.	sail	vvc	sailed	sailing
5.	stop	cvc	stopped	stopping
6.	peel	vvc	peeled	peeling

PRACTICE 2

Which of the following words double the final consonant? Check for *cvc*. Then add the suffixes *-er* or *-est*.

	Word	Last Three Letters	-er	-est
EXAMPLES:	wet	cvc	wetter	wettest
	cool	vvc	cooler	coolest
1.	tall	vcc	taller	tallest
2.	short	vcc	shorter	shortest
3.	fat	cvc	fatter	fattest
4.	slim	cvc	slimmer	slimmest
5.	red	cvc	redder	reddest
6.	green	vvc	greener	greenest

PRACTICE 3

Which of the following words double the final consonant? Check for *cvc*. Then add the suffixes *-ed* or *-ing*.

Basketball's Clown Princes

(1) The Harlem Globetrotters, organized in 1927, are the longest-

__running__ exhibition basketball team, but success and recognition
run + ing

did not come easily. (2) __Donning__ red, white, and blue uniforms and
Don + ing

__bumping__ over rough roads in an old beat-up car, the Globetrotters
bump + ing

__toured__ the Midwest, picking up games against local amateur teams.
tour + ed

(3) Although it had a __winning__ first season, __beating__ its oppo-
win + ing   beat + ing

nents in 101 out of 117 games, the team __earned__ only about $75 a game.
earn + ed

(4) At first, it __looked__ just like the other touring teams of that day,
look + ed

playing aggressive, straightforward basketball.

(5) When Inman Jackson joined it in 1929, however, he ___*added*___
add + ed

his sense of humor to the team. (6) He introduced ___*spinning*___ the ball on the
spin + ing

tip of one finger, ___*flipping*___ the ball between the players in outrageous fake-
flip + ing

out plays, and drop-kicking the ball toward the basket. (7) The Globetrotters soon

___*learned*___ that if they could entertain and amuse as well as win, they could
learn + ed

gain a ___*bigger*___ audience than any other team. (8) They ___*capped*___
big + er   cap + ed

their fourteenth season by winning the world championship against the Chicago

Bruins in overtime after being five points behind late in the game. (9) From then

on, the Globetrotters were ___*booked*___ into the best arenas, ___*paired*___
book + ed   pair + ed

against the best teams, and treated like a first-class team.

(10) In recent years the team has ___*starred*___ in two feature films, faced
star + ed

numerous college all-star teams, toured the world several times, raised a fortune

for charity, and been the subject of a children's animated TV series. (11) The key to

the Harlem Globetrotters' ___*greatest*___ success has been its determination
great + est

in developing its unique style of brilliantly skillful basketball and hilarious

___*clowning*___.
clown + ing

PART D   Doubling the Final Consonant (in Words of More Than One Syllable)

When you add a suffix that begins with a vowel to a word of more than one syllable, double the final consonant *if*

(1) the last three letters of the word are *cvc, and*

(2) the accent or stress is on the *last* **syllable.**

> begin + ing = beginning
> patrol + ed = patrolled

■ *Begin* and *patrol* both end in *cvc.*

■ In both words, the stress is on the last syllable: *be-gin´, pa-trol´.* (Pronounce the words aloud, and listen for the correct stress.)

■ Therefore, *beginning* and *patrolled* double the final consonant.

> gossip + ing = gossiping
>
> visit + ed = visited

■ *Gossip* and *visit* both end in *cvc*.

■ However, the stress is *not* on the last syllable: *goś-sip, viś-it*.

■ Therefore, *gossiping* and *visited* do not double the final consonant.

PRACTICE 1

Which of the following words double the final consonant? First, check for *cvc*. Then check for the final stress, and add the suffixes *-ed* and *-ing*

Word	Last Three Letters	-ed	-ing
EXAMPLES: repel	cvc	repelled	repelling
enlist	vcc	enlisted	enlisting
1. occur	cvc	occurred	occurring
2. happen	cvc	happened	happening
3. polish	vcc	polished	polishing
4. admit	cvc	admitted	admitting
5. offer	cvc	offered	offering
6. prefer	cvc	preferred	preferring
7. enter	cvc	entered	entering
8. travel	cvc	traveled	traveling
9. wonder	cvc	wondered	wondering
10. omit	cvc	omitted	omitting

PRACTICE 2

Which of the following words double the final consonant? First check for *cvc*. Then check for the final stress, and add the suffixes *-ed* and *-ing*.

Martial Arts Magic

(1) Jackie Chan, the martial arts film star and director, ___*labored*___ long
labor + ed

and hard for his success in movies. (2) When he was a child, his parents

___*enrolled*___ him in the Peking Opera Academy. (3) Unlike western opera,
enroll + ed

Chinese opera is more like a circus that features acrobats, jugglers, and contortionists. (4) Throughout his film career, Chan has ____depended____ on the tumbling
and gymnastic skills that he learned in those years at the academy. (5)
depend + ed

When he graduated from the academy, Chinese opera was out of fashion, and he
was ____compelled____ to take a job ____performing____ stunts in martial arts films. (6)
compel + ed   *perform + ing*

He ____obtained____ small parts in two of Bruce Lee's films and much larger parts
obtain + ed

in many other, unsuccessful pictures.

(7) Following Lee's death, a producer ____predicted____ that Jackie Chan
predict + ed

would be the new Bruce Lee and signed him to a multipicture contract. (8) After

more unsuccessful films, Chan ____admitted____ to himself that he was getting
admit + ed

nowhere and considered retiring from movies entirely. (9) By a stroke of luck,

another producer ____borrowed____ him to star in the martial arts comedy *Snake in*
borrow + ed

the Eagle's Shadow. (10) Instead of trying to turn Chan into a poor copy of Bruce

Lee, this producer ____permitted____ him to create a comic underdog character.
permit + ed

(11) The film was a huge success in Asia, and audiences ____demanded____ more
demand + ed

martial arts comedies and more Jackie Chan movies.

(12) Once Chan was a hit in the Far East, he ____committed____ his time and
commit + ed

energy to breaking into the American film industry. (13) After several unsuccessful
attempts in the 1980s, he eventually had a worldwide crossover hit with

Rumble in the Bronx (with Toronto standing in for New York) in 1994.

(14) Following the success of *Rumble in the Bronx*, Chan announced that he

____preferred____ to make films in Hollywood and ____intended____ to leave
prefer + ed   *intend + ed*

the Far East. (15) Since that announcement, he has____astonished____ audiences
astonish + ed

with hits like *Operation Condor* and ____conferred____ with stars like Sylvester
confer + ed

Stallone and Steven Segal about future projects.

PART E   Dropping or Keeping the Final *E*

When you add a suffix that begins with a vowel (like *-able, -ence,* **or** *-ing),* **drop the final** *e.*

When you add a suffix that begins with a consonant (like *-less, -ment,* **or** *-ly),* **keep the final** *e.*

> write + ing = writing
>
> pure + ity = purity

■ *Writing* and *purity* both drop the final *e* because the suffixes *-ing* and *-ity* begin with vowels.

> hope + less = hopeless
>
> advertise + ment = advertisement

■ *Hopeless* and *advertisement* keep the final *e* because the suffixes *-less* and *-ment* begin with consonants.

Here are some exceptions to memorize:

argument	manageable
awful	noticeable
courageous	truly
judgment	

PRACTICE 1

Add the suffix shown to each word.

EXAMPLES: come + ing = ___coming___

rude + ness = ___rudeness___

1. pleasure + able = ___pleasurable___
2. guide + ance = ___guidance___
3. manage + ment = ___management___
4. motive + ation = ___motivation___
5. sincere + ly = ___sincerely___
6. desire + able = ___desirable___
7. argue + ment = ___argument___
8. home + less = ___homeless___

9. response + ible = ___responsible___
10. divide + ing = ___dividing___
11. awe + ful = ___awful___
12. manage + er = ___manager___
13. judge + ment = ___judgment___
14. fame + ous = ___famous___
15. grieve + ance = ___grievance___

Add the suffix shown to each word in parentheses. Write the correctly spelled word in each blank.

A Precious Resource

(1) Many people have _____*pleasurable*_____ memories of _____*receiving*_____ their
             (pleasure + able)   (receive + ing)

first library card or _____*choosing*_____ books for the first time at a local public
             (choose + ing)

library. (2) _____*Widely*_____ recognized as a _____*priceless*_____ resource, the public
      (Wide + ly)   (price + less)

library is _____*defined*_____ just as you might expect: as a collection of books and
      (define + ed)

other materials supported by the public for public use.

(3) Several New England towns claim the honor of _____*contributing*_____ the first
                                   (contribute + ing)

public money for a library. (4) However, the first such library of meaningful size

and influence—the first _____*famous*_____ public library— _____*originated*_____ in
             (fame + ous)   (originate + ed)

Boston, Massachusetts in 1854. (5) The Boston Public Library, with its

_____*useful*_____ reference collection and its policy of _____*circulating*_____ popular
  (use + ful)   (circulate + ing)

books, set the pattern for all public libraries _____*ultimately*_____ _____*created*_____ in
                            (ultimate + ly) (create + ed)

the United States and Canada. (6) By the end of the nineteenth century, many

state legislatures felt _____*responsible*_____ for _____*raising*_____ taxes to support
              (response + ible)   (raise + ing)

libraries. (7) They _____*recognized*_____ that public libraries had an _____*extremely*_____
             (recognize + ed)   (extreme + ly)

_____*valuable*_____ role in _____*providing*_____ people with the best possible means of
 (value + able)   (provide + ing)

_____*continuing*_____ their education. (8) Although public libraries today have much
(continue + ing)

the same goal, they now offer a _____*truly*_____ _____*admirable*_____ number of
                          (true + ly) (admire + able)

resources and services. (9) These include story hours for children, book discussion clubs for adults, lectures, art exhibits, literacy classes, and most recently,

_____computer_____ training and _____guidance_____ .
(compute + er)   (guide + ance)

(10) Technology, of course, has _____completely_____ transformed the
                                                (complete + ly)

_____management_____ of the public library, as well as the way the library is
(manage + ment)

_____used_____ . (11) The most _____noticeable_____ changes— today's computerized
(use + ed)   (notice + able)

catalogs and searchable databases—would _____surely_____ have been beyond
                                                            (sure + ly)

the wildest dreams of even the most _____sincerely_____ enthusiastic early
                                                    (sincere + ly)

public library supporters.

PART F   Changing or Keeping the Final Y

When you add a suffix to a word that ends in -*y*, change the *y* to *i* if the letter before the *y* is a consonant.

> **Keep the final *y* if the letter before the *y* is a vowel.**

> happy + ness = happiness
>
> delay + ed = delayed

- The *y* in *happiness* is changed to *i* because the letter before the *y* is a consonant, *p*.
- However, the *y* in *delayed* is not changed to *i* because the letter before it is a vowel, *a*.

> **When you add -*ing* to words ending in *y*, always keep the *y*.**

> copy + ing = copying
>
> delay + ing = delaying

Here are some exceptions to memorize:

> day + ly = daily   pay + ed = paid
>
> lay + ed = laid   say + ed = said

When the final *y* is changed to *i*, add *-es* instead of *-s*.

fly + es = flies

marry + es = marries

candy + es = candies

PRACTICE 1

Add the suffix shown to each of the following words.

EXAMPLES: marry + ed = _married_

buy + er = _buyer_

1. cry + ed = _cried_

2. mercy + ful = _merciful_

3. worry + ing = _worrying_

4. say + ed = _said_

5. juicy + er = _juicier_

6. enjoy + able = _enjoyable_

7. clumsy + ness = _clumsiness_

8. wealthy + est = _wealthiest_

9. day + ly = _daily_

10. occupy + ed = _occupied_

PRACTICE 2

Add the suffixes in parentheses to each word.

1. lonely (er) _lonelier_

(est) _loneliest_

(ness) _loneliness_

2. beauty (fy) _beautify_

(ful) _beautiful_

(es) _beauties_

3. angry (er) _angrier_

(est) _angriest_

(ly) _angrily_

4. study (es) _studies_

(ous) _studious_

(ing) _studying_

5. busy (ness) _business_

(er) _busier_

(est) _busiest_

6. try (es) _tries_

(ed) _tried_

(al) _trial_

PRACTICE 3

Add the suffix in parentheses to each word.

Winter Blues

(1) Although Kim _____*tried*_____ to ignore her feelings, she always felt
        try (ed)

_____*hungrier*_____, _____*sleepier*_____, _____*angrier*_____, and _____*lonelier*_____ during
    hungry (er)   sleepy (er)   angry (er)   lonely (er)

the winter months of the year. (2) As part of her _____*denial*_____, she would go
                                                      deny (al)

about her _____*business*_____ as usual, but she knew that she was no longer
            busy (ness)

_____*enjoying*_____ her _____*beautiful*_____ surroundings or feeling _____*happiness*_____.
    enjoy (ing)   beauty (ful)   happy (ness)

(3) Then one day she read a magazine article that discussed several

_____*studies*_____ of a medical condition called "seasonal affective disorder," or
    study (es)

SAD. (4) Kim immediately _____*identified*_____ many _____*similarities*_____ between her
                              identify (ed)   similarity (es)

own yearly mood changes and the symptoms that people with SAD

_____*displayed*_____. (5) She learned that winter SAD is brought on _____*primarily*_____
    display (ed)   primary (ly)

by a lack of exposure to light. (6) The article _____*said*_____ that insufficient sun-
                                                    say (ed)

shine, inadequate artificial light at home or at work, and even _____*mercilessly*_____
                                                                   mercy (lessly)

cloudy weather could trigger SAD.

(7) _____*Happily*_____, Kim discovered that three or four different kinds of
        Happy (ly)

treatment are available. (8) The most severe cases—people who sleep more than

fourteen hours a day and still feel fatigued, for example—are usually cured by

_____*daily*_____ light therapy, which can be administered by a light-therapy
    day (ly)

clinic or by the patient under a doctor's supervision. (9) Medication, exercise, and

changes in diet are also effective in many cases. (10) Although Kim had

_____*delayed*_____ treatment for so long, she didn't waste any time _____*pitying*_____
    delay (ed)   pity (ing)

herself. (11) She immediately telephoned the Center for Environmental

_____*Therapies*_____ in Colorado and the Depression and Related Affective Disorders
Therapy (es)

Association in Maryland for a list of SAD clinics and for more information and

support. (12) Within a short time, she had received information from both

_____*agencies*_____ about a light-therapy clinic near her, and she was beginning to
agency (es)

experience her _____*healthiest*_____ winter in years.
healthy (est)

PART G   Choosing *IE* or *EI*

Write *i* before *e*, except after *c*, or in any *ay* sound like *neighbor*:

> niece, believe
> conceive
> weigh

- *Niece* and *believe* are spelled *ie*.
- *Conceive* is spelled *ei* because of the preceding *c*.
- *Weigh* is spelled *ei* because of its *ay* sound.

However, words with a *shen* sound are spelled with an *ie* after the *c*: *ancient, conscience, efficient, sufficient.*

Here are some exceptions to memorize:

either	seize
foreign	society
height	their
neither	weird

PRACTICE 1

Pronounce each word out loud. Then fill in the blanks with either *ie* or *ei*.

1. f _i__e_ ld
2. w _e__i_ ght
3. n _e__i_ ther
4. th _e__i_ r
5. ch _i__e_ f

6. soc _i__e_ ty
7. rec _e__i_ ve
8. br _i__e_ f
9. h _e__i_ ght
10. ach _i__e_ ve

PRACTICE 2

In the following sentences, write either *ie* or *ei* in the blanks.

(1) The story is anc _i_ _e_ nt history, but I can't bel _i_ _e_ ve how easy it is for parents to rel _i_ _e_ ve a child's gr _i_ _e_ f. (2) My n _i_ _e_ ce Paula was staying with me while her mother and father took a br _i_ _e_ f vacation. (3) She was _e_ _i_ ght years old and a bundle of energy. (4) All day Saturday, we played baseball in a n _e_ _i_ ghbor's f _i_ _e_ ld, so we were tired at the end of the afternoon—at least I was! (5) That night there was a f _i_ _e_ rce storm. (6) My ch _i_ _e_ f fear was that the lights would go out because I knew that Paula was afraid of the dark. (7) At the h _e_ _i_ ght of the storm, I effic _i_ _e_ ntly got out a flashlight and candles. (8) That's all Paula needed to see! (9) She immediately burst into worr _i_ _e_ d tears. (10) I tr _i_ _e_ d to calm her; I cut us each a p _i_ _e_ ce of p _i_ _e_ . (11) However, n _e_ _i_ ther I nor my dog, who climbed into her lap, could console her. (12) Suddenly the phone rang; Paula ran to it and picked up the rec _e_ _i_ ver. (13) Her parents were calling, and just hearing th _e_ _i_ r voices made her feel much better. (14) Within seconds, she was her cheery, fr _i_ _e_ ndly self again. (15) I just stared in amazement.

PART H Commonly Misspelled Words

Below is a list of commonly misspelled words. They are words that you probably use daily in speaking and writing. Each word has a trouble spot, the part of the word that is often spelled incorrectly. The trouble spot is in bold type.

Two tricks to help you learn these words are (1) to copy each word twice, underlining the trouble spot, and (2) to copy the words on flash cards and have someone else test you.

If possible, consult this list while or after you write.

1. a**cr**oss	10. cons**cie**nce	19. eig**ht**h
2. add**r**ess	11. crow**ded**	20. emba**rr**ass
3. **answ**er	12. def**i**nite	21. envir**on**ment
4. arg**u**ment	13. d**e**scribe	22. exa**gg**erate
5. ath**l**ete	14. desp**er**ate	23. famil**iar**
6. begi**nn**ing	15. di**ff**erent	24. finall**y**
7. behav**ior**	16. dis**app**oint	25. govern**m**ent
8. calen**dar**	17. dis**app**rove	26. gra**mm**ar
9. car**eer**	18. do**e**sn't	27. h**ei**ght

28. **ill**egal	44. opin**ion**	60. ridi**cul**ous
29. immed**iately**	45. optimist	61. sep**ar**ate
30. import**ant**	46. particular	62. simi**lar**
31. int**eg**ration	47. **per**form	63. **sin**ce
32. int**ell**igent	48. **per**haps	64. spe**ech**
33. int**er**est	49. perso**nn**el	65. stren**gth**
34. int**er**fere	50. pos**sess**	66. suc**cess**
35. jew**el**ry	51. possible	67. **sur**prise
36. jud**gm**ent	52. **pre**fer	68. **tau**ght
37. knowle**dge**	53. **pre**ju**d**ice	69. temperature
38. main**tain**	54. privil**ege**	70. tho**rough**
39. mathematics	55. prob**ably**	71. **thou**ght
40. meant	56. **p**s**y**cholog**y**	72. tire**d**
41. nec**ess**ary	57. **pur**sue	73. until
42. nerv**ous**	58. reference	74. wei**ght**
43. oc**cas**ion	59. **rhy**th**m**	75. wri**tt**en

Success can be defined in many different ways. In a small group, discuss what the term *success* means to you. Is it a rewarding career, a happy family life, lots of money . . . ? Offer as many different definitions of success as you can.

Now pick the definition that most appeals to you and write a paragraph explaining what success is. You may wish to use people in the news or friends to support your main idea. Proofread your work for accurate spelling, especially the words covered in this chapter. Finally, exchange papers and read each other's work. Did your partner find any spelling errors that you missed?

✔ Chapter Highlights

- **Double the final consonant in one-syllable words that end in** *cvc:*

  hop/hopped, swim/swimming

- **Double the final consonant in words of more than one syllable if they end in** *cvc* **and if the stress is on the last syllable:**

  begin/beginning, prefer/preferred

- **Keep the final** *e* **when adding a suffix that begins with a consonant:**

  hope/hopeful, time/timely

- **Drop the final** *e* **when adding a suffix that begins with a vowel:**

  hope/hoping, time/timer

- **Keep the final** *y* **when adding a suffix if the letter before the** *y* **is a vowel:**

  buy/buying, delay/delayed

- **Change the** *y* **to** *i* **when adding a suffix if the letter before the** *y* **is a consonant:**

  happy/happiest, pity/pitiful

- **Write** *i* **before** *e,* **except after** *c,* **or in any** *ay* **sound like** *neighbor:*

  believe, niece, *but* receive, weigh

- **Remember that there are exceptions to all of these rules. Check a dictionary whenever you are uncertain.**

Chapter Review

Proofread this essay for spelling errors. Correct the errors above the lines.

The Discovery of Penicillin

(1) Penicillin was discovered almost by accident. (2) During World War I, Alexander Fleming, a Scottish scientist, was working without ~~succes~~ *success* on the problem of infected wounds. (3) The antiseptics used then to cleanse wounds ~~probaly~~ *probably* did more harm than good. (4) They killed germs but ~~ocassionally~~ *occasionally* harmed the ~~pateint.~~ *patient* (5) Despite his hard work, Fleming made little progress.

(6) In 1928, however, his luck changed. (7) He returned to his laboratory
disappointed
after a vacation. (8) At first he was ~~disapointed~~ to find that some of his bacteria
noticeable
samples were spoiled. (9) One of the spoiled cultures had a ~~noticable~~ mold on it.
surprise,
(10) To his ~~supprise,~~ the mold had killed all the bacteria! (11) He named the

bacteria-killing mold penicillin.
truly   *beginning*
(12) This might have ~~truely~~ been the ~~begining~~ of the age of miracle drugs if
stopped   *Fortunately*
Fleming had not ~~stoped~~ his research. (13) ~~Fortunatly,~~ Howard Florey and Ernst
seized   *their discoveries,*
Chaim ~~siezed~~ the opportunity to perfect the drug. (14) For ~~thier discoverys,~~

Fleming, Florey, and Chaim were awarded the Nobel Prize for medicine in 1945.
saving
(15) Penicillin saved many lives in World War II and has gone on ~~saveing~~ them

ever since.

Personal Spelling List

Keep a list of words that *you* misspell. Add words to your list from corrected papers and from the exercises in this chapter. First, copy each word as you misspelled it, underlining the trouble spot; then write the word correctly. Use the following form. Study your list often.

	As I Wrote It	**Correct Spelling**
1.		
2.		
3.		
4.		
5.		
6.		
7.		
8.		
9.		
10.		
11.		
12.		
13.		
14.		

As I Wrote It   **Correct Spelling**

15. _____   _____

16. _____   _____

17. _____   _____

18. _____   _____

19. _____   _____

20. _____   _____

21. _____   _____

22. _____   _____

23. _____   _____

24. _____   _____

25. _____   _____

26. _____   _____

27. _____   _____

28. _____   _____

29. _____   _____

30. _____   _____

31. _____   _____

32. _____   _____

33. _____   _____

34. _____   _____

35. _____   _____

36. _____   _____

37. _____   _____

38. _____   _____

39. _____   _____

40. _____   _____

Look-alikes/ Sound-alikes

A/An/And

A is used before a word beginning with a consonant or a consonant sound.

> (1) *a* man
> (2) *a* house
> (3) *a* union (the *u* in *union* is pronounced like the consonant *y*)

An is used before a word beginning with a vowel (*a, e, i, o, u*) or a silent *h*.

> (4) *an* igloo
> (5) *an* apple
> (6) *an* hour (the *h* in *hour* is silent)

And joins words or ideas together.

> (7) Edward *and* Ralph are taking the same biology class.
> (8) He is very honest, *and* most people respect him.

PRACTICE 1

Fill in *a*, *an*, or *and*.

EXAMPLE: Choosing __*a*__ career is __*an*__ important step for __*a*__ college student.

1. Don Miller has used each summer vacation to try out __*a*__ different career choice.

2. Last summer, he worked in __*a*__ law office.

3. He filled in for __*an*__ administrative assistant on leave.

4. He found the work __*and*__ the atmosphere very stimulating.

5. In fact, he had never liked __*a*__ job so much.

6. Because Don was eager to learn, __*a*__ young lawyer let him proofread some important documents.

7. The lawyer was impressed by how carefully Don worked __*and*__

   suggested that Don consider __*a*__ law career.

8. Don returned to school in the fall __*and*__ spent time researching his new career.

9. He talked to his adviser about becoming __*a*__ paralegal.

10. __*A*__ paralegal investigates the facts of cases, prepares documents, __*and*__ does other background work for lawyers.

11. His adviser could see that Don had both __*an*__ interest in law __*and*__ the ability to succeed.

12. With his adviser's help, Don found __*a*__ course of study to prepare for his career.

13. Next summer, he hopes to work for __*a*__ public interest law firm

    __*and*__ to learn about environmental law.

14. He is happy to have found __*a*__ worthwhile career __*and*__ looks forward to the future.

PRACTICE 2

On separate paper, write two sentences using *a*, two using *an*, and two using *and*.

Accept/Except

Accept means "to receive."

> (1) Please *accept* my apologies.
> (2) I *accepted* his offer of help.

Except means "other than" or "excluding."

> (3) Everyone *except* Ron thinks it's a good idea.

PRACTICE 1

Fill in *accept* or *except*.

1. Did Steve _____*accept*_____ the collect call from his brother?

2. Mr. Francis will _____*accept*_____ the package in the mailroom.

3. Did Meg _____*accept*_____ Ron's explanation?

4. The athlete proudly _____*accepted*_____ his award.

5. Every toddler _____*except*_____ my daughter enjoyed the piñata party.

6. _____*Except*_____ for Governor Salinas, all the visiting politicians stayed at the Beagle Hotel.

7. The tornado left every building standing, _____*except*_____ for the barn.

8. _____*Except*_____ for Jean, we all had tickets for the movie.

PRACTICE 2

On separate paper, write two sentences using *accept* and two using *except*.

Been/Being

Been is the past participle form of *to be*. *Been* is usually used after the helping verb *have, has,* or *had.*

> (1) I *have been* to that restaurant before.
> (2) She *has been* in Akron for ten years.

■ *Being* is the *-ing* form of *to be*. *Being* is usually used after the helping verbs *is, are, am, was,* and *were.*

> (3) They *are being* helped by the salesperson.
> (4) Rhonda *is being* courageous and independent.

PRACTICE 1

Fill in *been* or *being*.

1. Shirley has _____*been*_____ very quiet all evening.

2. What good films are _____*being*_____ shown on television tonight?

3. We have _____*been*_____ working on the jigsaw puzzle for two hours.

4. I haven't _____*been*_____ in such a good mood for a week.

5. This building is ____being____ turned into a community center.

6. His last offer has ____been____ on my mind all day.

7. Which elevator is ____being____ inspected now?

8. Because you are ____being____ honest with me, I admit that I have

____been____ seeing someone else.

PRACTICE 2

On separate paper, write two sentences using *been* and two using *being*.

Buy/By

Buy means "to purchase."

(1) She *buys* new furniture every five years.

By means "near," "before," or "by means of."

(2) He walked right *by* and didn't say hello.
(3) *By* sunset, we had finished the harvest.
(4) We prefer traveling *by* bus.

PRACTICE 1

Fill in *buy* or *by*.

1. Did you ____buy____ that computer, or did you rent it?

2. These quilted potholders were made ____by____ hand.

3. He stood ____by____ the cash register and waited his turn to

____buy____ a cheeseburger.

4. She finds it hard to walk ____by____ a bookstore without going in to browse.

5. It's expensive to ____buy____ imported cheeses.

6. Please answer this letter ____by____ October 10.

7. Pat trudged through the storm to ____buy____ a Sunday paper.

8. The dishes ____by____ the sink need to be put away.

PRACTICE 2

On separate paper, write two sentences using *buy* and two using *by*.

Fine/Find

Fine means "good" or "well." It can also mean "a penalty."

> (1) He wrote a *fine* analysis of the short story.
> (2) She paid a $10 *fine*.

Find means "to locate."

> (3) I can't *find* my red suspenders.

PRACTICE 1

Fill in *fine* or *find*.

1. You will have to pay a _____*fine*_____ if you drive without a seat belt.

2. As soon as we _____*find*_____ your lost suitcase, we'll send it to you.

3. Can you _____*find*_____ me one of these in an extra-large size?

4. Harold made a _____*fine*_____ impression on the assistant buyer.

5. It's _____*fine*_____ weather for handball.

6. My father gave me good advice: "When you _____*find*_____ good friends, stick with them."

PRACTICE 2

On separate paper, write two sentences using *fine* and two using *find*.

It's/Its

It's is a contraction of *it is* or *it has*. If you cannot substitute *it is* or *it has* in the sentence, you cannot use *it's*.

> (1) *It's* a ten-minute walk to my house.
> (2) *It's* been a nice party.

Its is a possessive and shows ownership.

> (3) The bear cub rolled playfully on *its* side.
> (4) Industry must do *its* share to curb inflation.

PRACTICE 1

Fill in *it's* or *its*.

1. If _____*it's*_____ not too much trouble, drop the package off on your way home.

2. _____*It's*_____ been hard for him to accept the fact that he can no longer play ball.

3. The *Daily News* reporter was lucky because the jury reached _____*its*_____ verdict just before her deadline.

4. _____*It's*_____ been a long time since I had a real vacation.

5. If _____*it's*_____ a good idea, I'm all for it.

6. _____*It's*_____ a chocolate cake with your social security number in pink frosting.

7. My family is at _____*its*_____ best when there is work to be done.

8. _____*It's*_____ amazing how devious Ray is.

9. Although I hate shoveling the walk, I am happy _____*it's*_____ been a good year for winter sports.

10. I can't open this window because _____*it's*_____ been nailed shut.

PRACTICE 2

On separate paper, write two sentences using *it's* and two using *its*.

Know/Knew/No/New

Know means "to have knowledge or understanding." *Knew* is the past tense of the verb *to know*.

> (1) Carl *knows* he has to finish by 6 p.m.
> (2) The police officer *knew* the quickest route to the pier.

No is a negative.

> (3) He is *no* longer dean of academic affairs.

New means "fresh" or "recent."

> (4) I like your *new* belt.

PRACTICE 1

Fill in *know*, *knew*, *no*, or *new*.

1. We will need _____*new*_____ wiring to handle those powerful air conditioners.

2. She didn't _____*know*_____ the lid was loose.

3. Tim has _____*no*_____ time to recheck his answers to the quiz.

4. I _____*know*_____ I need to find _____*new*_____ jokes because no one laughs when I tell my old ones.

5. Because she _____*knew*_____ the answer, she won a pool table and a complete set of china.

6. How _____*new*_____ are automated teller machines?

7. Because you really _____*know*_____ the _____*new*_____ material, why don't you take the final early?

8. Charlene thinks there's _____*no*_____ way we can do it, but I

   _____*know*_____ we'll be speaking Italian by June.

9. Rosalyn _____*knew*_____ that she would win the fifty-yard freestyle.

10. We have _____*no*_____ way of knowing how well you scored on the civil service examination.

11. He didn't _____*know*_____ whether the used equipment came with a guarantee.

12. I wish I _____*knew*_____ then what I _____*know*_____ now.

PRACTICE 2

On separate paper, write two sentences using *know*, two using *knew*, two using *no*, and two using *new*.

Lose/Loose

Lose means "to misplace" or "not to win."

(1) Be careful not to *lose* your way on those back roads.
(2) George hates to *lose* at cards.

Loose means "ill fitting" or "too large."

(3) That's not my size; it's *loose* on me.

PRACTICE 1

Fill in *lose* or *loose*.

1. Because the plug is _____*loose*_____ in the socket, the television keeps blinking on and off.

2. A professional team has to learn how to win and how to _____*lose*_____ gracefully.

3. If Irene doesn't tighten that _____*loose*_____ hubcap, she will _____*lose*_____ it.

4. I like wearing _____*loose*_____ clothing in the summer.

5. Before finals, I always _____*lose*_____ my appetite.

6. Act now, or you will _____*lose*_____ your opportunity to get that promotion.

7. This belt is too _____*loose*_____.

8. I'm surprised you didn't _____*lose*_____ those _____*loose*_____ quarters.

PRACTICE 2

On separate paper, write two sentences using *lose* and two using *loose*.

Mine/Mind

Mine is a possessive and shows ownership.

> (1) This is your umbrella, but where is *mine?*

   Mind means "intelligence." It can also be a verb meaning "to object" or "to pay attention to."

> (2) What's on your *mind?*
> (3) I don't *mind* if you come late.

PRACTICE 1

Fill in *mine* or *mind.*

1. Her road test is tomorrow; _____*mine*_____ was yesterday.

2. Will Doris _____*mind*_____ if we spend the evening talking about our days in boot camp?

3. Sherlock put his _____*mind*_____ to work and solved the mystery.

4. I really _____*mind*_____ when you crack your knuckles in church.

5. Don't interrupt him; he really _____*minds*_____ when someone breaks his train of thought.

6. My _____*mind*_____ is made up; I want to switch my major from accounting to marketing.

7. Don't _____*mind*_____ him; he always snores in public.

8. Camping out in the woods wasn't his idea; it was _____*mine*_____.

PRACTICE 2

On separate paper, write two sentences using *mine* and two using *mind*.

Past/Passed

Past is that which has already occurred; it is over with.

> (1) His *past* work has been satisfactory.
> (2) Never let the *past* interfere with your hopes for the future.

Passed is the past tense of the verb *to pass*.

> (3) She *passed* by and nodded hello.
> (4) The wild geese *passed* overhead.

PRACTICE 1

Fill in *past* or *passed*.

1. He asked for the butter, but I absentmindedly _____*passed*_____ him the mayonnaise.

2. Forget about failures in the _____*past*_____, and look forward to success in the future.

3. The police car caught up to the truck that had _____*passed*_____ every other car on the road.

4. I have _____*passed*_____ this same corner every Saturday morning for a year.

5. I am sure we _____*passed*_____ through this town an hour ago.

6. In the _____*past*_____, Frieda and Carolyn used to talk on the phone once a week.

7. Is your _____*past*_____ catching up with you?

8. Don knew he had _____*passed*_____ the test, but he had never received such a high grade in the _____*past*_____.

PRACTICE 2

On separate paper, write two sentences using *past* and two using *passed*.

Quiet/Quit/Quite

Quiet means "silent, still."

> (1) The woods are *quiet* tonight.

Quit means "to give up" or "to stop doing something."

> (2) Last year, I *quit* smoking.

Quite means "very" or "exactly."

> (3) He was *quite* tired after playing handball for two hours.
> (4) That's not *quite* right.

PRACTICE 1

Fill in *quiet*, *quit*, or *quite*.

1. When it comes to expressing her feelings, Tonya is _____*quite*_____ vocal.

2. I can't concentrate when my apartment is too _____*quiet*_____.

3. Taking care of children can be _____*quite*_____ tiring.

4. Please be _____*quiet*_____; I'm trying to listen to the news.

5. If she _____*quits*_____ now, she will risk losing her vacation pay.

6. Dwight asked the crew to be absolutely _____*quiet*_____ while the magicians performed.

7. Don't _____*quit*_____ when the going gets rough; just increase your efforts and succeed.

8. I have the general idea, but I don't _____*quite*_____ understand all the details.

9. City people are surprised by the _____*quiet*_____ nights in the country.

10. She _____*quit*_____ pushing when people in the line began to stare at her.

PRACTICE 2

On separate paper, write two sentences using *quiet*, two using *quit*, and two using *quite*.

Rise/Raise

Rise means "to get up by one's own power." The past tense of *rise* is *rose*. The past participle of *rise* is *risen.*

> (1) The sun *rises* at 6 a.m.
> (2) Daniel *rose* early yesterday.
> (3) He *has risen* from the table.

Raise means "to lift an object" or "to grow or increase." The past tense of *raise* is *raised*. The past participle of *raise* is *raised.*

(4) *Raise* your right hand.

(5) She *raised* the banner over her head.

(6) We have *raised* $1,000.

PRACTICE 1

Fill in *rise* or *raise*.

1. When the moon _____*rises*_____, we'll be able to see the path better.

2. During the meeting, she _____*raised*_____ the possibility of a strike.

3. The jet _____*rose*_____ off the runway and roared into the clouds.

4. Bud would like to _____*rise*_____ early, but usually he wakes, turns over, and goes back to sleep.

5. The butcher _____*raised*_____ his prices again.

6. He couldn't _____*rise*_____ from his chair because of the chewing gum stuck to his pants.

7. A flock of birds _____*rose*_____ out of the salt marsh.

8. I felt foolish when I accidentally _____*raised*_____ my voice in the quiet concert hall.

9. The loaves of homemade bread have _____*risen*_____.

10. He _____*rose*_____ to his feet and shuffled out the door.

PRACTICE 2

On separate paper, write two sentences using some form of *rise* and two using some form of *raise*.

Sit/Set

Sit means "to seat oneself." The past tense of *sit* is *sat*. The past participle of *sit* is *sat*.

(1) *Sit* up straight!

(2) He *sat* down on the porch and fell asleep.

(3) She has *sat* reading that book all day.

    Set means "to place" or "to put something down." The past tense of *set* is *set*. The past participle of *set* is *set*.

(4) Don't *set* your books on the dining room table.

(5) She *set* the package down and walked off without it.

(6) He had *set* the pot on the stove.

PRACTICE 1

Fill in *sit* or *set*.

1. Marcy _____*set*_____ her glasses on the seat next to her.

2. Please _____*sit*_____ there; the dentist will see you in ten minutes.

3. _____*Set*_____ the cans of paint in the corner.

4. I always _____*sit*_____ in the front row.

5. Please _____*set*_____ that box of clothes by the door.

6. _____*Sit*_____ down, and let me _____*set*_____ this Hawaiian feast before you.

7. I would have _____*set*_____ your bracelet on the counter, but I was afraid someone might walk off with it.

8. Rather than _____*sit*_____ in the first row, I will stand in the back.

PRACTICE 2

On separate paper, write two sentences using some form of *sit* and two using *set*.

Suppose/Supposed

Suppose means "to assume" or "to guess." The past tense of *suppose* is *supposed.* The past participle of *suppose* is *supposed.*

(1) Brad *supposes* that the teacher will give him an A.
(2) We all *supposed* she would win first prize.
(3) I had *supposed* Dan would win.

■ *Supposed* means "should have"; it is followed by *to.*

(4) He is *supposed to* meet us after class.
(5) You were *supposed to* wash and wax the car.

REMEMBER: When you mean *ought* or *should,* always use the *-ed* ending—*supposed.*

PRACTICE 1

Fill in *suppose* or *supposed*.

1. How do you _____*suppose*_____ he will get himself out of this mess?

2. My father-in-law was _____*supposed*_____ to arrive last night.

3. I _____*suppose*_____ I'll find my car keys in my other pants.

4. Why do you _____*suppose*_____ that cereal is so expensive?

5. You are not _____*supposed*_____ to open the presents until your birthday.

6. Diane was _____*supposed*_____ to check the bus schedule.

7. What do you _____*suppose*_____ we saw on Buford Road?

8. What are we _____*supposed*_____ to do with these three-by-five-inch cards?

9. Mindy _____*supposed*_____ that the factory would reopen in the fall.

10. I _____*suppose*_____ Ron is willing to shovel the snow this time.

PRACTICE 2

On separate paper, write two sentences using *suppose* and two using *supposed to*.

Their/There/They're

Their is a possessive pronoun and shows ownership.

(1) They couldn't find *their* wigs.
(2) *Their* children are charming.

There indicates a location.

(3) I wouldn't go *there* again.
(4) Put the lumber down *there*.

There is also a way of introducing a thought.

(5) *There* is a fly in my soup.
(6) *There* are two ways to approach this problem.

They're is a contraction: *they + are = they're*. If you cannot substitute *they are* in the sentence, you cannot use *they're*.

(7) *They're* the best poems I have read in a long time.
(8) If *they're* coming, count me in.

PRACTICE 1

Fill in *their*, *there*, or *they're*.

1. If you move over _____*there*_____, I can get everyone into the picture.

2. _____*There*_____ are three ways to mix paint, all of which are messy.

3. If _____*they're*_____ here, we can set out the food.

4. Please hang your coats over _____there_____.

5. My uncle and aunt always helped _____their_____ children with _____their_____ homework.

6. _____They're_____ preparing for a hot, sticky summer.

7. Is _____there_____ a faster route to Topeka?

8. _____They're_____ never on time when it comes to paying _____their_____ phone bills.

9. _____Their_____ products contain no sugar and no preservatives.

10. Is _____there_____ a wrench in the toolbox?

11. If _____they're_____ the winners, that is the kind of encouragement they need.

12. Is _____there_____ a small tear in this scarf?

PRACTICE 2

On separate paper, write two sentences using *their,* two using *there,* and two using *they're.*

Then/Than

Then means "next" or "at that time."

> (1) First, we went to the theater, and *then* we went for pizza.
> (2) I was a heavyweight boxer *then.*

Than is used in a comparison.

> (3) She is a better student *than* I.

PRACTICE 1

Fill in *then* or *than.*

1. Carlos works harder _____than_____ anyone else in this office.

2. San Francisco has colder winters _____than_____ San Diego.

3. Get your first paycheck; _____then_____ think about moving into your own apartment.

4. Thinking you are better _____than_____ everyone else can get you into trouble.

5. If you receive straight A's this semester, will you _____then_____ apply for a scholarship?

6. You asked me a question and _____then_____ interrupted me before I could answer.

7. This red convertible gets more miles to the gallon _____*than*_____ any other car on the lot.

8. Now I'm ready for marriage; _____*then*_____, I was confused.

PRACTICE 2

On separate paper, write two sentences using *then* and two using *than*.

Thought/Taught

Thought is the past tense of the verb *to think.* It can also mean "an idea."

> (1) She *thought* it was an interesting idea.
> (2) Now that's a strange *thought!*

Taught is the past tense of the verb *to teach.*

> (3) Last summer, César *taught* his daughters how to swim.
> (4) She once *taught* mathematics at Stanford Community College.

PRACTICE 1

Fill in *thought* or *taught.*

1. Nora _____*taught*_____ me how to decipher my boss's handwriting.

2. I _____*thought*_____ about the company's offer but decided to refuse it and wait for a better one.

3. Perry _____*thought*_____ that he could make extra money driving a cab.

4. Charlie _____*thought*_____ he could always borrow anything he needed.

5. Every great deed begins with a _____*thought*_____.

6. Who _____*taught*_____ you how to balance your checkbook?

7. When she_____*thought*_____ about next summer, Louisa promised herself that she would learn to relax.

8. Mr. Gold _____*taught*_____ carpentry for three years before he opened his own shop.

PRACTICE 2

On separate paper, write two sentences using *thought* and two using *taught.*

Threw/Through

Threw is the past tense of the verb *to throw.*

> (1) Charleen *threw* the ball into the bleachers.

Through means "in one side and out the other" or "finished."

> (2) He burst *through* the front door laughing.
> (3) If you are *through* eating, we can leave.

PRACTICE 1

Fill in *threw* or *through.*

1. I went _____through_____ my notes, but I couldn't find any reference to Guatemala.

2. He _____threw_____ the pillow on the floor and plopped down in front of the TV.

3. Gail _____threw_____ her raincoat over her head and ran out into the storm.

4. You go _____through_____ that door to get to the editor's office.

5. If you are _____through_____ with that reference material, I would like to take a look at it.

6. I am not sure why he _____threw_____ the towel over the mirror.

7. I can see _____through_____ the window if I stand on a step stool.

8. It took Beverly over an hour to go _____through_____ airport security.

PRACTICE 2

On separate paper, write two sentences using *threw* and two using *through.*

To/Too/Two

To means "toward."

> (1) We are going *to* the stadium.

To can also be combined with a verb to form an infinitive.

> (2) Where do you want *to* go for lunch?

Too means "also" or "very."

> (3) Roberto is going to the theater *too*.
> (4) They were *too* bored to stay awake.

Two is the number 2.

> (5) Ms. Palmer will teach *two* new accounting courses this term.

PRACTICE 1

Fill in *to*, *too*, or *two*.

1. If you want ____*to*____ enroll in college this fall, you will need ____*two*____ letters of recommendation.

2. It will be ____*too*____ awkward ____*to*____ leave the dinner before the dessert is served.

3. She ____*too*____ has a birthday in June.

4. It's ____*too*____ early ____*to*____ leave for the football game.

5. That dance step may be ____*too*____ advanced for me right now.

6. No one is ____*too*____ old to learn.

7. The ____*two*____ students worked all night preparing for the debate.

8. On the express bus, there were ____*too*____ many people in the front and ____*too*____ few in the back.

9. Even the students admitted that the test was ____*too*____ easy.

10. Jimmy and I have ____*to*____ build the drawers by Friday if we want ____*to*____ stain the chest on Monday.

11. Albert expects ____*to*____ get the next promotion.

12. Tracey hates ____*to*____ complain, even when she is clearly right.

13. It's ____*too*____ much trouble to make my own salad dressing.

14. She ____*too*____ likes ____*to*____ watch professional wrestling.

15. We saw ____*two*____ undercover agents talking quietly ____*to*____ the bartender.

PRACTICE 2

On separate paper, write two sentences using *to*, two using *too*, and two using *two*.

Use/Used

Use means "to make use of." The past tense of *use* is *used*. The past participle of *use* is *used*.

> (1) Why do you *use* green ink?
> (2) He *used* the wrong paint in the bathroom.
> (3) I have *used* that brand of toothpaste myself.

Used means "in the habit of" or "accustomed"; it is followed by *to*.

> (4) I am not *used to* getting up at 4 a.m.
> (5) They got *used to* the good life.

REMEMBER: When you mean *in the habit of* or *accustomed*, always use the *-ed* ending—*used*.

Fill in *use* or *used*.

1. Terry is _____*used*_____ to long bus rides.

2. It may take a few days to get _____*used*_____ to this high altitude.

3. Do you know how to _____*use*_____ a buzz saw?

4. Vera hopes to get _____*used*_____ to her grumpy father-in-law.

5. Please _____*use*_____ the main entrance on Globe Avenue.

6. Carlotta and Roland still _____*use*_____ the laundromat on the corner.

7. We _____*used*_____ the self-service pump; it was cheaper.

8. Marguerite _____*uses*_____ my telephone every time she visits.

9. _____*Use*_____ your head!

10. Never _____*use*_____ big words to try to impress people.

11. He _____*uses*_____ an electronic typewriter because he cannot get _____*used*_____ to a computer.

12. Never get _____*used*_____ to failure; always expect success.

On separate paper, write two sentences using *use* and two using *used to*.

Weather/Whether

Weather refers to atmospheric conditions.

(1) In June, the *weather* in Spain is lovely.

Whether implies a question.

(2) *Whether* you pass is up to you.

PRACTICE 1

Fill in *weather* or *whether*.

1. Rainy _____weather_____ makes me lazy.

2. Be sure to tell the employment agency _____whether_____ you plan to take the job.

3. You never know _____whether_____ Celia will be happy or sad.

4. Good _____weather_____ always brings joggers to the park.

5. Norman wasn't sure _____whether_____ his boss would let him use the copier after 5 p.m.

6. I don't know _____whether_____ to go to the bank or to Ruby's house first.

7. The real estate agent must know by 10 a.m. _____whether_____ you intend to rent the house.

8. _____Whether_____ the _____weather_____ cooperates or not, we're going to the beach.

PRACTICE 2

On separate paper, write two sentences using *weather* and two using *whether*.

Where/Were/We're

Where implies place or location.

(1) *Where* have you been all day?
(2) Home is *where* you hang your hat.

Were is the past tense of *are*.

(3) We *were* on our way when the hurricane hit.

We're is a contraction: *we* + *are* = *we're*. If you cannot substitute *we are* in the sentence, you cannot use *we're*.

(4) *We're* going to leave now.
(5) Because *we're* in the city, let's go to the zoo.

Fill in *where, were,* or *we're.*

1. The desk was scratched, but ____*we're*____ not sure who did it.

2. ____*Where*____ did you put the tape measure?

3. Ted and Gloria ____*were*____ childhood sweethearts.

4. When you ____*were*____ at your aunt's house, ____*where*____ did your cat stay?

5. My convertible is not ____*where*____ I left it.

6. The librarians ____*were*____ very helpful in showing us ____*where*____ things ____*were*____.

7. ____*Were*____ you surprised that ____*we're*____ as good a team as we are?

8. The clouds ____*were*____ blocking the sun in exactly the spot ____*where*____ we ____*were*____ sitting.

9. Our children want a story every night, but sometimes ____*we're*____ too tired to read them one.

10. Do you know ____*where*____ the empty packing boxes are?

11. Everyone needs a little hideaway, a place ____*where*____ he or she can be absolutely alone.

12. ____*We're*____ not sure ____*where*____ the motel is.

PRACTICE 2

On separate paper, write two sentences using *where,* two using *were,* and two using *we're.*

Whose/Who's

Whose implies ownership and possession.

(1) *Whose* term paper is that?

Who's is a contraction of *who is* or *who has.* If you cannot substitute *who is* or *who has,* you cannot use *who's.*

(2) *Who's* knocking at the window?
(3) *Who's* seen my new felt hat with the green bows?

PRACTICE 1

Fill in *whose* or *who's*.

1. _____Who's_____ bored with these old reruns?

2. _____Whose_____ CDs are scattered all over the floor?

3. We found a puppy in the vacant lot, but we don't know _____whose_____ it is.

4. _____Who's_____ tapping on the window?

5. He's a physician _____whose_____ diagnosis can be trusted.

6. Grace admires the late Marian Anderson, _____whose_____ singing always moved her.

7. I'm not sure _____who's_____ coming and _____who's_____ not.

8. _____Who's_____ going to try the mambo with me?

PRACTICE 2

On separate paper, write two sentences using *whose* and two using *who's*.

Your/You're

Your is a possessive and shows ownership.

> (1) *Your* knowledge is astonishing!

You're is a contraction: *you + are = you're*. If you cannot substitute *you are* in the sentence, you cannot use *you're*.

> (2) *You're* the nicest person I know.

PRACTICE 1

Fill in *your* or *you're*.

1. Where is _____your_____ bottle opener?

2. If _____you're_____ tired, take a nap.

3. Does _____your_____ daughter like her new school?

4. I hope _____your_____ children haven't forgotten Father's Day.

5. If _____you're_____ in a rush, we can mail _____your_____ scarves to you.

6. _____Your_____ foreman was just transferred.

7. Please keep _____your_____ Saint Bernard out of my rose garden.

8. Is that _____your_____ rain hat or Shelley's?

9. When _____*you're*_____ optimistic about life, everything seems to go right.

10. Let me have _____*your*_____ order by Thursday; if it's late, _____*you're*_____ not likely to receive the merchandise in time for the holidays.

PRACTICE 2

On separate paper, write two sentences using *your* and two using *you're*.

PRACTICE: WRITING ASSIGNMENT

While away from home—perhaps at school, in the service, or at an out of town job—you have met the person you wish to marry. Write a letter to introduce him or her to your parents. Since you want your parents to like your fiancé or fiancée, your letter should explain his or her most appealing qualities: career success, education, kindness, generosity, poise, friendliness, dependability, good looks, and so on. However, since you want to be realistic, show that you and this person have some differences that will have to be accepted or resolved.

Proofread your letter for accurate spelling.

✔ Chapter Highlights

Some words look and sound alike. Below are a few of them:

■ **it's/its**

> *It's* the neatest room I ever saw.
>
> Everything is in *its* place.

■ **their/they're/there**

> They found *their* work easy.
>
> *They're* the best actors I have ever seen.
>
> Put the lumber down *there*.

■ **then/than**

> I was a heavyweight boxer *then*.
>
> He is a better cook *than* I.

■ **to/too/two**

> We are going *to* the stadium.
>
> No one is *too* old to learn.
>
> I bought *two* hats yesterday.

■ **whose/who's**

> *Whose* Italian dictionary is this?
>
> I'm not sure *who's* leaving early.

■ **your/you're**

> Is *your* aunt the famous mystery writer?
>
> *You're* due for a promotion and a big raise.

Proofread this essay for look-alike/sound-alike errors. Make your corrections above the lines.

The Olympic Games

(1) Although the Olympic games are almost three thousand years old, schol-

know ~~ ~~ *an*

ars ~~now~~ of an athlete who was ~~and~~ Olympic champion in 776 B.C. (2) Coroebus

was his name. (3) He won the two-hundred-yard footrace, the only event in the

By *new*

Olympics at that time. (4) ~~Buy~~ the fourteenth Olympic games, in 720 B.C., ~~knew~~

events, including boxing and discus throwing, had been added. (5) At these

sit

early games, women weren't allowed to ~~set~~ in the stadium as spectators. (6) A

lose

woman who broke this law could ~~loose~~ her life. (7) Eventually, women were

accepted

~~excepted~~ as spectators and even as participants. (8) After the decline of ancient

Greece, the games were abolished. (9) Although the last games were held in the

fourth century A.D., the idea of the Olympic games was not dead.

were

(10) In 1896, the first modern Olympic games ~~where~~ held in Athens, Greece.

(11) Of all the events, the marathon attracted the most attention. (12) The

supposed

marathon was ~~suppose~~ to represent the ancient games. (13) Actually, it commem-

orates a real event. (14) In 490 B.C., the Greeks defeated the Persians at the Battle

of Marathon. (15) Legend says that Pheidippides, a professional runner, ran to

and *Whether*

Athens, told of the victory, ~~an~~ fell to the ground dead. (16) ~~Weather~~ or not the

been

legend is true, the marathon has ~~being~~ the major attraction of the modern

Olympic games.

(17) At the first modern games, the Greek spectators were unhappy. (18) By

their *There*

the last day of the games, none of ~~there~~ athletes had won an event. (19) ~~Their~~

were twenty-five runners in the final event, the marathon. (20) One of the runners

a *whose* *used*

was ~~an~~ Greek shepherd ~~who's~~ name was Spiridon Louis. (21) He was ~~use~~ to

thought

running great distances, and he ~~taught~~ about winning the marathon and bringing

Then

glory to Greece. (22) For the first part of the race, a Frenchman led. (23) ~~Than~~

passed

runners began dropping out from exhaustion, and Louis ~~past~~ many of them.

(24) About seven kilometers from the Olympic stadium, Louis took the lead.

(25) When word reached the stadium, the Greek crowd went wild. (26) Louis
entered the stadium to ~~they're~~ *their* cheers. (27) The second- and third-place winners
were Greeks ~~to.~~ *too* (28) Spiridon Louis ~~excepted~~ *accepted* his honors ~~quitely~~ *quietly* and modestly.

(29) He returned to his life as a shepherd, but he left his mark on the Greek language. (30) The expression *egine Louis,* which means "became Louis," also means "ran quickly."

UNIT 8 WRITING ASSIGNMENTS

As you complete each writing assignment, remember to perform these steps:

- Write a clear, complete topic sentence.
- Use freewriting, brainstorming, or clustering to generate ideas.
- Arrange your best ideas in a plan.
- Revise for support, unity, coherence, and exact language.
- Proofread for grammar, punctuation, and spelling errors.

Writing Assignment 1: *Post a notice.* You are a member of a community action committee. For this year's project, the committee will collect clothing for the homeless, hold a sale to raise money to beautify a local park, or assist some other worthwhile cause. Write a bulletin-board notice that describes the project and invites people to participate. Be sure to name specific materials that might be needed or tasks that have to be completed. As you write, remember that your goal is to persuade your neighbors to volunteer their goods and services—and time— for this cause. Your notice will be posted on bulletin boards throughout the neighborhood. Proofread for accurate spelling.

Writing Assignment 2: *Discuss giving and getting advice.* We all give advice to and get advice from others. Sometimes that advice can have a great impact. Have you received advice that changed your life? Were you advised to return to school, marry, or change careers? Did you give advice to others that changed their lives? In your first sentence, explain who advised whom to do what. What happened? What were the consequences of the advice? End with advice to others about giving or receiving advice. Proofread for accurate spelling.

Writing Assignment 3: *Review a movie.* Your college newspaper has asked you to review a movie. Pick a popular film that you especially liked or disliked. In your first sentence, name the film, and state whether or not you recommend it. Explain your evaluation by discussing two or three specific reasons for your reactions to the picture. Describe as much of the film as you need to, to make your point, but do not retell the plot. Proofread for accurate spelling.

Writing Assignment 4: *Describe a family custom.* Most families have customs that they perform together. These customs often help strengthen the bond that the members of the family feel toward each other. A custom might be eating Sunday dinner together, going to religious services, celebrating holidays in a special way, or even holding a family council to discuss difficulties and concerns. Write about a custom in your family that was especially meaningful. Of what value was this custom to you or other members of the family? Proofread for accurate spelling.

UNIT 8 REVIEW

Proofreading

We have changed the following composition so that it contains a number of spelling and look-alike/sound-alike errors. First, underline any misspelled words. Then write each correctly spelled word above the line.

Grow <u>Youre</u> Own Houseplants
Your

(1) Every February, I begin turning seeds and pits into <u>lovly</u> houseplants.
lovely

(2) <u>Buy</u> Easter, I have small citrus, mango, and avocado trees, which I give away
By

<u>too</u> my <u>nieghbors</u> and friends. (3) You <u>two</u> can start plants that will grow
to   neighbors   too

<u>beautyfully</u> from seeds, pits, and parts of fruits or vegetables that you <u>normaly</u>
beautifully   normally

throw in the garbage.

(4) To grow a mango tree, for example, first scrub the mango pit. (5) Once

the pit is washed and <u>dryed</u>, trim the long hair on it. (6) <u>Than</u> use a small knife to
dried   Then

open the pit and remove the seed, which looks like a large bean. (7) Put this seed

into <u>to inchs</u> of <u>poting</u> soil, put another half-inch of soil over it, and add water.
two inches   potting

(8) Let the container drain, put it inside a clear plastic bag, <u>an</u> then close the bag
and

with a twist tie. (9) <u>Finaly, sit</u> the bag in a warm place, but not in direct sunlight.
Finally, set

(10) Wait <u>untill</u> the first leaves begin to show. (11) Then remove the plastic
until

bag, and place the young plant in bright shade or sunlight. (12) When <u>its'</u> about
it's

three inches tall, you can start <u>pincheing</u> back the newest leaves. (13) Pinching
pinching

every branch like this will produce extra <u>branchs, makeing</u> your tree bushy.
branches, making

(14) You will not <u>acheive sucess</u> with garbage seeds and pits 100 percent of the
achieve success

time. (15) Some store-bought fruits and vegetables have been exposed <u>too</u>
to

chemicals to keep them from sprouting, and some are just too old for <u>they're</u>
their

seeds to sprout. (16) If the process <u>dosen't</u> work the first time, just keep <u>tring</u>
doesn't   trying

until it does. (17) You will not be <u>dissappointed</u> as long as you don't <u>quite.</u>
disappointed   quit.

Iris Protinick, student

Examine Positive (or Negative) Values

One good way to develop a paragraph or essay is by supporting the topic sentence or the thesis statement with three points. A student uses this approach in the following essay. In your group or class, read her work, aloud if possible.

Villa Avenue

(1) The values I learned growing up on Villa Avenue in the Bronx have guided me through thirty-five years and three children. Villa Avenue taught me the importance of helping people, playing together, and having a friendly environment.

(2) Villa Avenue was a three-block, friendly environment. I grew up on the middle block. The other ones were called "up the block" and "down the block." Mary's Candy Store was up the block. It had a candy counter and soda fountain on the left and on the right a jukebox that played three songs for twenty-five cents. My friends and I would buy candy, hang out, and listen to the Beatles and other music of the sixties. A little down from Mary's on the corner was Joey's Deli. When you walked into Joey's, different aromas would welcome you to a world of Italian delicacies. Fresh mozarella in water always sat on the counter, with salami, pepperoni, and imported provolone cheese hanging above. On Sundays at Joey's, my father would buy us a black-and-white cookie for a weekly treat. No matter where you stood on Villa Avenue, if you looked up, someone's laundry was always hanging on a line.

(3) On Villa Avenue, everyone helped everyone else. Everybody's doors were open, so if I had to go to the bathroom or needed a drink of water, I could go to a dozen different apartments. If my parents had to go somewhere, they would leave me with a friend. When people on the block got sick, others went to the store for them, cleaned for them, watched their kids, and made sure they had food to eat. If someone died, everyone mourned and pitched in to help with arrangements. When I reflect on those days, I realize that the way the mothers looked out for each other's children is like your modern-day play group. The difference is that our play area was "the block."

(4) The whole street was our playground. We would play curb ball at the intersection. One corner was home plate, and the other ones were the bases. Down the block where the street was wide, we would play Johnny on the Pony with ten to fifteen kids. On summer nights, it was kick the can or hide and seek. Summer days we spent under an open fire hydrant. Everyone would be in the water, including moms and dads. Sometimes the teenagers would go to my Uncle Angelo's house and get a wine barrel to put over the hydrant. With the top and bottom of the barrel off, the water would shoot twenty to thirty feet in the air and come down on us like a waterfall.

Loretta M. Carney, student

1. How effective is Ms. Carney's essay?

   __*Y*__ Clear main idea?   __*Y*__ Good supporting details?

   (see #3 below)
   __*Y/N*__ Logical organization?   __*N*__ Effective conclusion?

2. What is the main idea of the essay? Can you find the thesis statement, one sentence that states this main idea? *Sentence 2*

3. The writer states that Villa Avenue taught her three values. What are they? Are these clearly explained in paragraphs 2, 3, and 4? Are they discussed in the same order in which the thesis statement presents them? If not, what change would you suggest? *No, change thesis to match body or vice versa: friendliness, helpfulness, playfulness.*

4. Does this essay *conclude,* or just stop? What suggestions would you make to the writer for a more effective conclusion? *Add a conclusion*

5. Proofread Ms. Carney's essay. Do you see any error patterns that she should watch out for? *No*

Writing and Revising Ideas

1. Describe a place or person that taught you positive (or negative) values.

2. Do places like Villa Avenue exist anymore? Explain why you do or do not think so.

See Chapter 5 for help with planning and writing. You might wish to present your topic with three supporting points, the way Ms. Carney does. As you revise, pay close attention to writing a good thesis sentence and supporting paragraphs that contain clear, detailed explanations.

Parts of Speech Review

A knowledge of basic grammar terms will make your study of English easier. Throughout this book, these key terms are explained as needed and are accompanied by ample practice. For your convenience and reference, below is a short review of the eight parts of speech.

Nouns

Nouns are the names of persons, places, things, animals, activities, and ideas.*

Persons:	Ms. Caulfield, Mike, secretaries
Places:	Puerto Rico, Vermont, gas station
Things:	sandwich, Sears, eyelash
Animals:	whale, ants, Lassie
Activities:	running, discussion, tennis
Ideas:	freedom, intelligence, humor

Pronouns

Pronouns replace or refer to nouns or other pronouns. The word that a pronoun replaces is called its *antecedent*.**

My partner succeeded; *she* built a better mousetrap!

These computers are amazing; *they* alphabetize and index.

Everyone should do *his* or *her* best.

All students should do *their* best.

---

*For more work on nouns, see Chapter 20.
**For more work on pronouns, see Chapter 21.

Pronouns take different forms, depending on how they are used in a sentence. They can be the subjects of sentences (*I, you, he, she, it, we, they*) or the objects of verbs and prepositions (*me, you, him, her, it, us, them*). They also can show possession (*my, mine, your, yours, his, her, hers, its, our, ours, their, theirs*).

Subject:	*You* had better finish on time.
	Did *someone* leave a red jacket?
Object of verb:	Robert saw *her* on Thursday.
Object of preposition:	That VCR is for *her.*
Possessive:	Did Tom leave *his* sweater on the dresser?

Verbs

Verbs can be either action verbs or linking verbs. Verbs can be single words or groups of words.*

Action verbs show what action the subject of the sentence performs.

Sonia *bought* a French dictionary.

Jack *has opened* the letter.

Linking verbs link the subject of a sentence with a descriptive word or words. Common linking verbs are *be, act, appear, become, feel, get, look, remain, seem, smell, sound,* and *taste.*

This report *seems* well organized and complete.

You *have been* quiet this morning.

The *present participle* of a verb is its *-ing* form. The present participle can be combined with some form of the verb *to be* to create the progressive tenses, or it can be used as an adjective or a noun.

Pat *was waiting* for the report.	(*past progressive tense*)
The *waiting* taxis lined up at the curb.	(*adjective*)
Waiting for trains bores me.	(*noun*)

The *past participle* of a verb can be combined with helping verbs to create different tenses, it can be combined with forms of *to be* to create the passive voice, or it can be used as an adjective. Past participles regularly end in *-d* or *-ed,* but irregular verbs take other forms (*seen, known, taken*).

He *has edited* many articles for us.	(*present perfect tense*)
This report *was edited* by the committee.	(*passive voice*)
The *edited* report reads well.	(*adjective*)

*For more work on verbs, see Unit 3.

Every verb can be written as an *infinitive: to* plus the *simple form* of the verb.

> She was surprised *to meet* him at the bus stop.

Adjectives

Adjectives describe or modify nouns or pronouns. Adjectives can precede or follow the words they describe.*

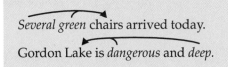

Several green chairs arrived today.

Gordon Lake is *dangerous* and *deep*.

Adverbs

Adverbs describe or modify verbs, adjectives, or other adverbs.**

Anita reads *carefully*.   *(adverb describes verb)*

She is *extemely* tired.   *(adverb describes adjective)*

He wants a promotion *very* badly.   *(adverb describes adverb)*

Prepositions

A preposition begins a *prepositional phrase*. A prepositional phrase contains a preposition (a word such as *at, in, of,* or *with*), its object (a noun or pronoun), and any adjectives modifying the object.†

Preposition	Object
after	*work*
on	the blue *table*
under	the broken *stairs*

Conjunctions

Conjunctions are connector words.

   Coordinating conjunctions (and, but, for, nor, or, so, yet) join two equal words or groups of words.††

---

*For more work on adjectives, see Chapter 22.

**For more work on adverbs, see Chapter 22.

†For more work on prepositions, see Chapter 23.

††For more work on conjunctions, see Chapters 13 and 14.

James is quiet *but* sharp.

Ms. Chin *and* Mr. Warburton attended the Ice Capades.

He printed out the report, *and* Ms. Helfman faxed it immediately.

She will go to Norfolk Community College, *but* she will also continue working at the shoe store.

Subordinating conjunctions (after, because, if, since, unless, and so on) join an independent idea with a dependent idea.

Whenever Ken comes to visit, he takes the family out to dinner.

I haven't been sleeping well *because* I've been drinking too much coffee.

Interjections

Interjections are words such as *ouch* and *hooray* that express strong feeling. They are rarely used in formal writing.

If the interjection is the entire sentence, it is followed by an exclamation point. If the interjection is attached to a sentence, it is followed by a comma.

Hey! You left your wallet in the phone booth.

Oh, she forgot to send in her tax return.

REMEMBER: The same word may be used as a different part of speech.

Harry *thought* about the problem. *(verb)*

Your *thought* is a good one. *(noun)*

Reading Selections and Quotation Bank

Unit 9 contains three parts:

✔ *Effective Reading: Strategies for the Writer*
This introduction to the readings section gives tips on how to get the most out of your reading.

✔ *The Readings*
Here you will find eighteen readings on a range of interesting subjects. Discussion questions and writing assignments follow each reading.

✔ *Quotation Bank*
This section contains seventy-four brief quotations for you to read and enjoy, be inspired by, and use in your writing.

Reading Selections

Effective Reading: Strategies for the Writer

We hope that the reading selections that follow will interest you and make you think. Many deal with issues you face at college, at work, or at home. Your instructor may ask you to read a selection and be prepared to discuss it in class or to write a composition or journal entry about it. The more carefully you read these selections, the better you will be able to think, talk, and write about them. Below are seven strategies that can help you become a more careful and effective reader.

1. **Underline important ideas.** It is easy to forget what you have read, even though you have recently read it. Underlining or highlighting what you consider the main ideas will help you later—when you review the essay—to remember what you have read. Some students number the main points in order to understand the development of the author's ideas.

2. **Write your reactions in the margins.** If you strongly agree or disagree with an idea, write *yes* or *no* next to it. Record other questions and comments also, as if you were having a conversation with the author. Writing assignments will often ask you to respond to a particular idea or situation in a selection. Having already noted your reactions in the margins will help you focus your thinking and your writing.

3. **Prepare questions.** You will occasionally come across material that you cannot follow. Reread the passage. If rereading and further thinking do not help, place a question mark in the margin to remind you to ask a classmate or the instructor for an explanation.

4. **Circle unfamiliar words.** If you come across an unfamiliar word that makes it difficult to follow the sense of what the author is saying, look up the word immediately, write the definition in the margin, and continue reading. If, however, you are able to get a general sense of what the word means from the context—how it fits into the meaning of the sentence—do not break your reading "stride" to consult a dictionary. Circle it, and look it up when you have finished reading the entire selection.

5. **Note effective or powerful writing.** If a particular line strikes you as especially important or moving, underline or highlight it. You may wish later to quote it in your written assignment. Be selective, however, in what you mark. *Too much* annotation can turn a selection into a mass—or mess—of underlinings, circles, and highlighting. An overly annotated essay can make it hard to focus on what is important when the selection is discussed in class or when you write about it.

6. **Vary your pace.** Some selections can be read quickly because you already know a great deal about the subject or because you find the material simple and direct. Other selections may require you to read slowly, pausing between sentences. Guard against the tendency to skim when the going gets tough: more difficult material will usually reward your extra time and attention.

7. **Reread.** If you expect to discuss or write about a particular selection, one reading is usually not enough. Budget your time so you will be able to give the selection a second or third reading. You will be amazed at how much more

you can get from the selection as you reread. You may understand ideas that were unclear the first time around. In addition, you may notice significant new points and details: perhaps you will change your mind concerning ideas you originally agreed or disagreed with. These benefits of rereading will help you to discuss and write about the selection more intelligently. They will also increase your reading enjoyment.

The following essay has been marked by a student. Your own responses to this essay would, of course, be different. Examining how this essay was annotated may help you annotate other selections in this book and read more effectively in your other courses.

Women Are Missing from Newspaper Pages

Ellen Goodman

bylines = a line identifying author of an article
Why "boys" and "girls"?

Take last week's papers out of the pile in the corner of the kitchen. Check the bylines. Check the photos. How many boys, how many girls? 1

kindling = used to light fires
tabulation = list

Now put the papers back in the recycle bin, or in the bird cage, or in the kindling box. Wherever. Compare your tabulation with the fourth annual report just released by the Women, Men and Media Project at the University of Southern California. 2

In the press women almost invisible!

1. Women underrepresented in newspapers

The folks there surveyed the front page and the local front page of 20 newspapers for the month of February. They came to the unsurprising and unhappy conclusion that women—52 percent of the population—show up just 13 percent of the time in the prime news spots. Lest you think that this is just a reflection of reality, even the stories about breast implants quoted men more often than women. 3

The names in the stories

Women's names appear *on* the stories more often than *in* the stories. Even so, two-thirds of the bylines on front pages were male and three-quarters of the opinions on op-ed pages were by men. To complete this, uh, picture, less than a third of the photographs on front pages feature women. 4

This small statistical reminder comes just in time for the American Society of Newspaper Editors' [ASNE] annual convention. In Washington this week, editors will be talking about America and the World, economics and politics, readers and nonreaders. Which brings them back to gender. 5

emergence = coming into existence
gender gap = difference in attitudes between women and men
2. Women read papers less.

One of the less heralded facts of declining newspaper readership in the 1990s is the emergence of a gender gap among people under 35 years old. Young women are seven to nine points less likely to be daily newspaper readers than men. 6

It would be nice to blame this on the infamous time crunch in young women's lives. Nice to find yet another reason for men to lift the double burden: Share housework, save a newspaper. But full-time working women are more loyal newspaper readers than women who are part-time workers or homemakers. 7

No wonder! ⟶

It turns out that women across the board are more likely than men to feel that the paper doesn't speak to them. Or about them. As Nancy Woodhull, a founding editor of *USA Today* who now runs her own consulting firm, says, "Women around the country really notice when the press doesn't report their existence. It's like walking into a room where nobody knows you're there. If you have choices, you don't go into that room anymore." 8

Too strong

The search for a welcome sign to hang on the newspaper door has brought ⁹ up the question of "women's pages." Back in the 1960s, these pages were the ghetto to which women, children, food, home, and family were restricted. In the crest of the women's movement, many of us in the business embarked on a movement to integrate the whole paper.

What happened was a kind of premature equality. The old women's pages ¹⁰ became more or less "unisex." Lifestyle sections wrote about and to women and men. But the rest of the paper remained nearly as lopsided as ever (see Page One [of your newspaper]). The result has been a net loss in the news about women.

Going backward or back to the future

Now there is a lively debate about whether to bring back women's pages. Is that ¹¹ going backward or back to the future? Is that admitting defeat in the struggle to get women's concerns into the rest of the paper or is it some unabashed recognition that women retain separate interests?

Experiments abound and so do opinions. Some women worry that a mar- ¹² keting move to target female readers will inevitably "dumb down" and talk down to them. Others believe that these pages can create a strong forum for a woman's different voice. And still others wonder if you can win the women who are drifting away without offending the loyal female readers who write in to ask, Why is the story about Hillary Clinton in the Lifestyle section?

As someone who has been around this argument for a couple of decades, ¹³ I have no problem with experiments in re-creating a woman's "place" in the paper *IF*—here comes the big if—the place doesn't become a ghetto again. And *IF* it doesn't take the pressure off changing the rest of the paper.

Men and women are more alike in their news interests than they are dif- ¹⁴ ferent. Moreover, the surveys on "difference" that I have seen suggest that what women really want are stories that go deep, that focus on matters close to their lives, that are less about institutional politics than about how institutions affect people. They want to read about families, relationships, health, safety, jobs, learning, the environment. That's a pretty good guide for any gender and any editor's story list.

News decisions rest with the editors and the number of women editors is ¹⁵ even smaller than the number of women on the front pages (see masthead). The female membership of ASNE is at an all-time high: 9.7 percent.

So, if newspapers want to make women feel welcome, begin the way a ¹⁶ reader begins. Start with Page One. And keep counting.

A Homemade Education

Malcolm X

Sometimes a book can change a person's life. In this selection, Malcolm X, the influential and controversial black leader who was assassinated in 1965, describes how, while he was in prison, a dictionary set him free.

It was because of my letters that I happened to stumble upon starting to acquire ¹ some kind of homemade education.

I became increasingly frustrated at not being able to express what I ² wanted to convey in letters that I wrote, especially those to Mr. Elijah Muhammad.¹ In the street, I had been the most articulate hustler out there—I

---

1. Elijah Muhammad: founder of the Muslim sect Nation of Islam

---

Margin notes:

some history of trends in journalism

3. "Women's pages" have become unisex.

4. People disagree over the value of "women's pages."

unabashed = not embarrassed

abound = are common

I'll ask some women class-mates of various ages what they think about this issue.

establishes she's an expert →

5. Author's opinion: OK for papers to have a high-quality women's section, but keep adding stories by and about women to rest of paper too.

Yes!

masthead = place in a newspaper or magazine where staff is listed

Malcolm X giving one of his many speeches (Corbis-Bettman)

had commanded attention when I said something. But now, trying to write simple English, I not only wasn't articulate, I wasn't even functional. How would I sound writing in slang, the way I would *say* it, something such as, "Look, daddy, let me pull your coat about a cat. Elijah Muhammad—"

Many who today hear me somewhere in person, or on television, or those who read something I've said, will think I went to school far beyond the eighth grade. This impression is due entirely to my prison studies.

It had really begun back in the Charlestown Prison, when Bimbi first made me feel envy of his stock of knowledge. Bimbi had always taken charge of any conversation he was in, and I had tried to emulate[2] him. But every book I picked up had few sentences which didn't contain anywhere from one to nearly all of the words that might as well have been in Chinese. When I just skipped those words, of course, I really ended up with little idea of what the book said. So I had come to the Norfolk Prison Colony still going through only book-reading motions. Pretty soon, I would have quit even these motions, unless I had received the motivation that I did.

I saw that the best thing I could do was get hold of a dictionary—to study, to learn some words. I was lucky enough to reason also that I should try to improve my penmanship. It was sad. I couldn't even write in a straight line. It was both ideas together that moved me to request a dictionary along with some tablets and pencils from the Norfolk Prison Colony school.

> "I saw that the best thing I could do was get hold of a dictionary—to study, to learn some words."

3

4

5

_____

2. emulate: copy

I spent two days just riffling[3] uncertainly through the dictionary's pages. **6** I'd never realized so many words existed! I didn't know *which* words I needed to learn. Finally, just to start some kind of action, I began copying.

In my slow, painstaking, ragged handwriting, I copied into my tablet **7** everything printed on that first page, down to the punctuation marks.

I believe it took me a day. Then, aloud, I read back, to myself, everything **8** I'd written on the tablet. Over and over, aloud, to myself, I read my own handwriting.

I woke up the next morning, thinking about those words—immensely **9** proud to realize that not only had I written so much at one time, but I'd written words that I never knew were in the world. Moreover, with a little effort, I also could remember what many of these words meant. I reviewed the words whose meanings I didn't remember. Funny thing, from the dictionary first page right now, that "aardvark" springs to my mind. The dictionary had a picture of it, a long-tailed, long-eared burrowing African mammal, which lives off termites caught by sticking out its tongue as an anteater does for ants.

I was so fascinated that I went on—I copied the dictionary's next page. **10** And the same experience came when I studied that. With every succeeding page, I also learned of people and places and events from history. Actually the dictionary is like a miniature encyclopedia. Finally, the dictionary's A section had filled a whole tablet—and I went on into the B's. That was the way I started copying what eventually became the entire dictionary. It went a lot faster after so much practice helped me pick up handwriting speed. Between what I wrote in my tablet, and writing letters, during the rest of my time in prison I would guess I wrote a million words.

I suppose it was inevitable that as my word-base broadened, I could for **11** the first time pick up a book and read and now begin to understand what the book was saying. Anyone who has read a great deal can imagine the new world that opened. Let me tell you something: from then until I left that prison, in every free moment I had, if I was not reading in the library, I was reading on my bunk. You couldn't have gotten me out of books with a wedge. Between Mr. Muhammad's teachings, my correspondence, my visitors—usually Ella and Reginald—and my reading of books, months passed without my even thinking about being imprisoned. In fact, up to then, I never had been so truly free in my life.

Discussion and Writing Questions

1. Malcolm X says that in the streets he had been the "most articulate hustler" of all, but that in writing English he "not only wasn't articulate, [he] wasn't even functional" (paragraph 2). What does he mean?

2. What motivated Malcolm X to start copying the dictionary? What benefits did he gain from doing this?

3. What does Malcolm X mean when he says that until he went to prison, he "never had been so truly free in [his] life" (paragraph 11)?

4. Have you seen the 1992 film *Malcolm X*? Do you think the film's prison scenes show how strongly Malcolm X was changed by improving his writing skills?

———
3. riffling: thumbing through

Writing Assignments

1. Did you ever notice a difference between your speaking skills and your writing skills? Write about a time when you needed or wanted to write something important but felt that your writing skills were not up to the task. What happened?

2. Malcolm X's inner life changed completely because of the dictionary he copied. Write about a time when a book, a story, a person, or an experience changed your life.

3. Choose three entries on a dictionary page and copy them. Then describe your experience. What did you learn? Can you imagine copying the entire dictionary? How do you feel about what Malcolm X accomplished? Where do you think he got the motivation to finish the task?

Mrs. Flowers

Maya Angelou

Maya Angelou (born Marguerite Johnson) is widely known today as the poet who read her work at President Clinton's inauguration and as the author of *I Know Why the Caged Bird Sings*. In this book, her life story, she tells of being raped when she was eight years old. Her response to the traumatic experience was to stop speaking. In this selection, Angelou describes the woman who eventually threw her a "life line."

For nearly a year, I sopped around the house, the Store, the school and the 1 church, like an old biscuit, dirty and inedible. Then I met, or rather got to know, the lady who threw me my first life line.

Mrs. Bertha Flowers was the aristocrat of Black Stamps. She had the grace 2 of control to appear warm in the coldest weather, and on the Arkansas summer days it seemed she had a private breeze which swirled around, cooling her. She was thin without the taut[1] look of wiry people, and her printed voile[2] dresses and flowered hats were as right for her as denim overalls for a farmer. She was our side's answer to the richest white woman in town.

Her skin was a rich black that would have peeled like a plum if snagged, 3 but then no one would have thought of getting close enough to Mrs. Flowers to ruffle her dress, let along snag her skin. She didn't encourage familiarity. She wore gloves too.

I don't think I ever saw Mrs. Flowers laugh, but she smiled often. A slow 4 widening of her thin black lips to show even, small white teeth, then the slow effortless closing. When she chose to smile on me, I always wanted to thank her. The action was so graceful and inclusively benign.[3]

She was one of the few gentlewomen I have ever known, and has re- 5 mained throughout my life the measure of what a human being can be. . . .

One summer afternoon, sweet-milk fresh in my memory, she stopped at 6 the Store to buy provisions. Another Negro woman of her health and age would have been expected to carry the paper sacks home in one hand but Momma said, "Sister Flowers, I'll send Bailey up to your house with these things."

She smiled that slow dragging smile, "Thank you, Mrs. Henderson. I'd 7 prefer Marguerite though." My name was beautiful when she said it. "I've been meaning to talk to her, anyway." They gave each other age-group looks.

---

1. taut: tight, tense
2. voile: a light, semi-sheer fabric
3. benign: kind, gentle

Momma said, "Well, that's all right then. Sister, go and change your dress. 8 You going to Sister Flowers's." . . .

There was a little path beside the rocky road, and Mrs. Flowers walked in 9 front swinging her arms and picking her way over the stones.

She said, without turning her head, to me, "I hear you're doing very good 10 school work, Marguerite, but that it's all written. The teachers report that they have trouble getting you to talk in class." We passed the triangular farm on our left and the path widened to allow us to walk together. I hung back in the separate unasked and unanswerable questions.

"Come and walk along with me, Marguerite." I couldn't have refused 11 even if I wanted to. She pronounced my name so nicely. Or more correctly, she spoke each word with such clarity that I was certain a foreigner who didn't understand English could have understood her.

"Now no one is going to make you talk—possibly no one can. But bear in 12 mind, language is man's way of communicating with his fellow man and it is language alone which separates him from the lower animals." That was a totally new idea to me, and I would need time to think about it.

"Your grandmother says you read a lot. Every chance you get. That's 13 good, but not good enough. Words mean more than what is set down on paper. It takes the human voice to infuse⁴ them with the shades of deeper meaning."

I memorized the part about the human voice infusing words. It seemed so 14 valid and poetic.

She said she was going to give me some books and that I not only must 15 read them. I must read them aloud. She suggested that I try to make a sentence sound in as many different ways as possible.

"I'll accept no excuse if you return a book to me that has been badly han- 16 dled." My imagination boggled at the punishment I would deserve if in fact I did abuse a book of Mrs. Flowers's. Death would be too kind and brief.

The odors in the house surprised me. Somehow I had never connected 17 Mrs. Flowers with food or eating or any other common experience of common people. There must have been an outhouse, too, but my mind never recorded it.

The sweet scent of vanilla had met us as she opened the door. 18

"I made tea cookies this morning. You see, I had planned to invite you for 19 cookies and lemonade so we could have this little chat. The lemonade is in the icebox."

It followed that Mrs. Flowers would have ice on an ordinary day, when 20 most families in our town bought ice late on Saturdays only a few times during the summer to be used in the wooden ice-cream freezers.

She took the bags from me and disappeared through the kitchen door. I 21 looked around the room that I had never in my wildest fantasies imagined I would see. Browned photographs leered or threatened from the walls and the white, freshly done curtains pushed against themselves and against the wind. I wanted to gobble up the room entire and take it to Bailey, who would help me analyze and enjoy it.

"Have a seat, Marguerite. Over there by the table." She carried a platter 22 covered with a tea towel. Although she warned that she hadn't tried her hand at baking sweets for some time, I was certain that like everything else about her the cookies would be perfect.

They were flat round wafers, slightly browned on the edges and butter- 23 yellow in the center. With the cold lemonade they were sufficient for childhood's lifelong diet. Remembering my manners, I took nice little lady-like bites off the edges. She said she had made them expressly for me and that she had a

> "I was liked, and what a difference it made. I was respected not as Mrs. Henderson's grandchild or Bailey's sister but for just being Marguerite Johnson."

---

4. infuse: to fill or penetrate

few in the kitchen that I could take home to my brother. So I jammed one whole cake in my mouth and the rough crumbs scratched the insides of my jaws, and if I hadn't had to swallow, it would have been a dream come true.

As I ate she began the first of what we later called "my lessons in living." 24 She said that I must always be intolerant of ignorance but understanding of illiteracy. That some people, unable to go to school, were more educated and even more intelligent than college professors. She encouraged me to listen carefully to what country people called mother wit. That in those homely sayings was couched the collective[5] wisdom of generations.

When I finished the cookies she brushed off the table and brought a thick, 25 small book from the bookcase. I had read *A Tale of Two Cities* and found it up to my standards as a romantic novel. She opened the first page and I heard poetry for the first time in my life.

"It was the best of times and the worst of times . . ." Her voice slid in and 26 curved down through and over the words. She was nearly singing. I wanted to look at the pages. Were they the same that I had read? Or were there notes, music, lined on the pages, as in a hymn book? Her sounds began cascading[6] gently. I knew from listening to a thousand preachers that she was nearing the end of her reading, and I hadn't really heard, heard to understand, a single word.

"How do you like that?" 27

It occurred to me that she expected a response. The sweet vanilla flavor 28 was still on my tongue and her reading was a wonder in my ears. I had to speak.

I said, "Yes ma'am." It was the least I could do, but it was the most also. 29

"There's one more thing. Take this book of poems and memorize one for 30 me. Next time you pay me a visit, I want you to recite."

I have tried often to search behind the sophistication of years for the en- 31 chantment I so easily found in those gifts. The essence escapes but its aura[7] remains. To be allowed, no, invited, into the private lives of strangers, and to share their joys and fears, was a chance to exchange the Southern bitter wormwood[8] for . . . a hot cup of tea and milk with Oliver Twist.[9]

I was liked, and what a difference it made. I was respected not as Mrs. 32 Henderson's grandchild or Bailey's sister but for just being Marguerite Johnson.

Childhood's logic never asks to be proved (all conclusions are absolute). I 33 didn't question why Mrs. Flowers had singled me out for attention, nor did it occur to me that Momma might have asked her to give me a little talking to. All I cared about was that she had made tea cookies for *me* and read to *me* from her favorite book. It was enough to prove that she liked me.

Discussion and Writing Questions

1. Angelou vividly describes Mrs. Flowers's appearance and style (paragraphs 2–5). What kind of woman is Mrs. Flowers? What words and details convey this impression?

2. What strategies does Mrs. Flowers use to reach out to Marguerite?

3. What does Marguerite's first "lesson in living" include (paragraph 24)? Do you think such a lesson could really help a young person live better or differently?

---

5. collective: gathered from a group
6. cascading: falling like a waterfall
7. aura: a special quality or air around something or someone
8. wormwood: something harsh or embittering
9. Oliver Twist: a character from a novel by Charles Dickens

4. In paragraph 31, the author speaks of her enchantment at receiving gifts from Mrs. Flowers. Just what gifts did Mrs. Flowers give her? Which do you consider the most important gift?

Writing Assignments

1. Has anyone ever thrown you a life line when you were in trouble? Describe the problem or hurt facing you and just what this person did to reach out. What "gifts" did he or she offer you (attention, advice, and so forth)? Were you able to receive them?

   If you prefer, write about a time when you helped someone else. What seemed to be weighing this person down? How were you able to help?

2. Mrs. Flowers read aloud so musically that Marguerite "heard poetry for the first time in [her] life." Has someone ever shared a love—of music, gardening, or history, for example—so strongly that you were changed? What happened and how were you changed?

3. Many people have trouble speaking up—in class, at social gatherings, even to one other person. Can you express your thoughts and feelings as freely as you would like in most situations? What opens you up, and what shuts you up?

The First Read

David Goddy

In this article, David Goddy explains the almost magical process by which his daughter Sonya learned to read. However, an ironic twist concludes this story: Each member of the family, it seems, has a different explanation of how this miracle occurred.

> "Her voice swells with confidence as I turn the pages. And when I don't keep pace, she shoots me a glance."

Among the images that make up my memories of parenthood, I have a favorite 1
I like to replay in my mind. It's my daughter Sonya learning to read.

The way I remember it, Sonya is about six years old. I am sitting on her 2
bed holding the book so she can follow along as I read. Sonya leans forward from the bedcovers until her face is perhaps a foot from the open pages and silently mouths the words as I say them aloud.

I pause for a brief moment to take a breath. 3

Suddenly, a different voice reads the next sentence . . . and the next. And 4
then, within seconds, she completely takes over my role of narrator.

Her voice swells with confidence as I turn the pages. And when I don't 5
keep pace, she shoots me a glance.

As the scene fades in my mind, I am beaming with the shameless pride of 6
parenthood and the realization that this magic moment was a precursor[1] of greater and deeper transitions[2]—graduations, proms, and perhaps even borrowing the car keys.

Sonya's version of the event is much different. Like a screenwriter 7
adapting my novel, she diplomatically[3] demotes me from my starring role. "That's not it, Daddy," she corrects me gently when I share my memory. "Of course, you and Mommy were very helpful, but I started to read before that."

---

1. precursor: forerunner
2. transitions: changes
3. diplomatically: politely, without being offensive

As she recalls, the moment happened in school. The director of her early 8
childhood program sat her down in the reading corner, put a familiar book in
her hands, and said, "Read this to me."

Sonya told the director that she couldn't read. The director reassured her 9
she could and said, "Go ahead." So she did. She read *The Carrot Seed* from start
to finish, with all the poise and dignity of someone who had "watered it and
pulled the weeds" many times before.

If my wife's version of the story is correct, however, Sonya and I are both 10
a little off the mark. The way she reconstructs what happened, learning to read
began with a toddler who barely sat still in our laps. In her mind, the crucial[4]
moments were when we started to read to our daughter, when we sat with her
and turned the pages of the board books again and again. Our voices filled her
eager mind with the words of simple stories. And she, in turn, began to associate the reassurance and stimulation of our attention with those flat, colorful
things of paper and cardboard that we found so fascinating.

Whose point of view is closest to the truth? I suppose it lies somewhere in 11
between. As my wife suggests, Sonya's reading was, of course, part of a continuing process. And if Sonya remembers first reading in her early childhood program, I am sure she did. But it's my prerogative[5]—and I choose to exercise it—
to stick to my own version.

So when I daydream of yesteryear, Sonya begins to read in her bedroom at 12
age six. And I am right there turning the pages—a little bit too slowly.

Discussion and Writing Questions

1. What is meant by Goddy's comment in paragraph 5 that whenever he
   doesn't keep pace, "she shoots [him] a glance"?

2. In paragraph 6, Goddy claims that "this magic moment was a precursor of
   greater and deeper transitions." What does he mean?

3. How does Sonya's understanding of the event differ from her father's?

4. Why might a child insist that she had learned to read even before her parents taught her?

Writing Assignments

1. Have you ever "compared notes" with someone about an incident you both
   experienced or witnessed—only to find that you each had a different version of what took place? Describe the incident, explain the two viewpoints,
   and tell why your stories did not match.

2. Can you recall a skill that your parents or someone else taught you—like
   riding a bike, swimming, playing an instrument, or driving a car? Was the
   learning experience enjoyable, difficult, painful, or satisfying? Your audience is a friend who wishes to teach his or her child a similar skill. Using
   examples from your experience, advise your friend what to avoid and how
   to make the experience as rewarding as possible.

3. Write about an incident in which you became aware that children have a
   special way of seeing and understanding the world around them.

4. crucial: important
5. prerogative: right

Papa, the Teacher

Leo Buscaglia

Leo Buscaglia was the youngest of four children of Italian immigrants. In this selection, he describes how a father with only a fifth-grade education taught his children to respect—and even love—learning.

Papa had natural wisdom. He wasn't educated in the formal sense. When he was growing up at the turn of the century in a very small village in rural northern Italy, education was for the rich. Papa was the son of a dirt-poor farmer. He used to tell us that he never remembered a single day of his life when he wasn't working. The concept of doing nothing was never a part of his life. In fact, he couldn't fathom[1] it. How could one do nothing? 1

He was taken from school when he was in the fifth grade, over the protestations[2] of his teacher and the village priest, both of whom saw him as a young person with great potential for formal learning. Papa went to work in a factory in a nearby village, the very same village where, years later, he met Mama. 2

For Papa, the world became his school. He was interested in everything. He read all the books, magazines, and newspapers he could lay his hands on. He loved to gather with people and listen to the town elders and learn about "the world beyond" this tiny, insular[3] region that was home to generations of Buscaglias before him. Papa's great respect for learning and his sense of wonder about the outside world were carried across the sea with him and later passed on to his family. He was determined that none of his children would be denied an education if he could help it. 3

"The greatest sin . . . was to go to bed at night as ignorant as we had been when we awakened that day."

Papa believed that the greatest sin of which we were capable was to go to bed at night as ignorant as we had been when we awakened that day. The credo[4] was repeated so often that none of us could fail to be affected by it. "There is so much to learn," he'd remind us. "Though we're born stupid, only the stupid remain that way." To ensure that none of his children ever fell into the trap of complacency,[5] he insisted that we learn at least one new thing each day. He felt that there could be no fact too insignificant, that each bit of learning made us more of a person and insured us against boredom and stagnation. 4

So Papa devised a ritual. Since dinnertime was family time and everyone came to dinner unless they were dying of malaria, it seemed the perfect forum for sharing what new things we had learned that day. Of course, as children we thought this was perfectly crazy. There was no doubt, when we compared such paternal[6] concerns with other children's fathers, Papa was weird. 5

It would never have occurred to us to deny Papa a request. So when my brother and sisters and I congregated in the bathroom to clean up for dinner, the inevitable question was, "What did *you* learn today?" If the answer was "Nothing," we didn't dare sit at the table without first finding a fact in our much-used encyclopedia. "The population of Nepal is . . . .," etc. 6

Now, thoroughly clean and armed with our fact for the day, we were ready for dinner. I can still see the table piled high with mountains of food. So large were the mounds of pasta that as a boy I was often unable to see my sister sitting across from me. (The pungent[7] aromas were such that, over a half century later, even in memory they cause me to salivate.) 7

---

1. fathom: understand; get to the bottom of
2. protestations: objections
3. insular: like an island; isolated
4. credo: a statement of belief
5. complacency: a feeling of satisfaction or smugness
6. paternal: having to do with fathers
7. pungent: sharp, spicy

Dinner was a noisy time of clattering dishes and endless activity. It was 8 also a time to review the activities of the day. Our animated conversations were always conducted in Piedmontese dialect[8] since Mama didn't speak English. The events we recounted, no matter how insignificant, were never taken lightly. Mama and Papa always listened carefully and were ready with some comment, often profound and analytical, always right to the point.

"That was the smart thing to do." "*Stupido,* how could you be so dumb?" 9 "*Cosi sia,*[9] you deserved it." "*E allora,*[10] no one is perfect." "*Testa dura* ('hard-head'), you should have known better. Didn't we teach you anything?" "Oh, that's nice." One dialogue ended and immediately another began. Silent moments were rare at our table.

Then came the grand finale to every meal, the moment we dreaded 10 most—the time to share the day's new learning. The mental imprint of those sessions still runs before me like a familiar film clip, vital and vivid.

Papa, at the head of the table, would push his chair back slightly, a gesture 11 that signified the end of the eating and suggested that there would be a new activity. He would pour a small glass of red wine, light up a thin, potent Italian cigar, inhale deeply, exhale, then take stock of his family.

For some reason this always had a slightly unsettling effect on us as we 12 stared back at Papa, waiting for him to say something. Every so often he would explain why he did this. He told us that if he didn't take time to look at us, we would soon be grown and he would have missed us. So he'd stare at us, one after the other.

Finally, his attention would settle upon one of us. "*Felice,*"[11] he would say 13 to me, "tell me what you learned today."

"I learned that the population of Nepal is . . ." 14

Silence. 15

It always amazed me, and reinforced my belief that Papa was a little crazy, 16 that nothing I ever said was considered too trivial for him. First, he'd think about what was said as if the salvation of the world depended upon it.

"The population of Nepal. Hmmm. Well." 17

He would then look down the table at Mama, who would be ritualistically 18 fixing her favorite fruit in a bit of leftover wine. "Mama, did you know that?"

Mama's responses were always astonishing and seemed to lighten the 19 otherwise reverential atmosphere. "Nepal," she'd say. "Nepal? Not only don't I know the population of Nepal, I don't know where in God's world it is!" Of course, this was only playing into Papa's hands.

"*Felice,*" he'd say. "Get the atlas so we can show Mama where Nepal is." 20 And the search began. The whole family went on a search for Nepal. This same experience was repeated until each family member had a turn. No dinner at our house ever ended without our having been enlightened by at least a half dozen such facts.

As children, we thought very little about these educational wonders and 21 even less about how we were being enriched. We couldn't have cared less. We were too impatient to have dinner end so we could join our less-educated friends in a rip-roaring game of kick the can.

In retrospect, after years of studying how people learn, I realize what a 22 dynamic educational technique Papa was offering us, reinforcing the value of

8. Piedmontese dialect: the language spoken in the Piedmont region of north-western Italy

9. *Cosi sia:* Italian for "so be it"

10. *E allora:* Italian for "oh, well"

11. *Felice: Felice* is Buscaglia's real first name. The name *Leo* was taken from his middle name, *Leonardo.*

continual learning. Without being aware of it, our family was growing together, sharing experiences, and participating in one another's education. Papa was, without knowing it, giving us an education in the most real sense.

By looking at us, listening to us, hearing us, respecting our opinions, af- 23
firming our value, giving us a sense of dignity, he was unquestionably our most influential teacher.

Discussion and Writing Questions

1. What does Buscaglia mean when he says that his father "wasn't educated in the formal sense" (paragraph 1)? In what way *was* his father educated?

2. How did Buscaglia's father and mother react to information that the children reported at dinnertime? How did their reaction affect Buscaglia as a child? As an adult?

3. Years later, Buscaglia realized that his father had offered the family "a dynamic educational technique" (paragraph 22). What does he mean?

4. What point does the author make by using the population of Nepal as an example in paragraph 14? Is it useful to know the population of Nepal? Why or why not?

Writing Assignments

1. Describe a typical dinnertime in your family as you were growing up. Was dinnertime a time for sharing? Fighting? Eating alone? What effect did this have on you? If you now live away from your birth family, are dinnertimes different?

2. Discuss your attitude toward education. Who or what shaped your point of view? Has your attitude changed since childhood? Why is education important?

3. Did *you* learn anything new today? If so, describe what you learned. If not, what got in the way of your learning?

Forever

Francine Klagsbrun

Francine Klagsbrun has written extensively on relationships between women and men. In this selection, she characterizes healthy marriage as a dynamic, ever-changing process between two people, one that begins only when romance wears off.

Probably every couple that ever existed has looked at one another at some point 1
during or after the honeymoon and wondered, "Who are you?" and "What am I doing here?" For every couple there are expectations and dreams that go unfulfilled. Those who remain married and satisfied with their marriages are willing to discard the fantasies and build a richer and deeper life beyond the illusions.

All marriages, not only those that fail, begin with unreal expectations that 2
color much of what happens between partners. Maggie and Robbie are a good example. They have known one another for years. They are not carried away in transports[1] of romantic blindness about one another, nor does either deny the

---

1. transports: ecstasies

other's faults. But they are so pleased about getting married, so wanting to be adults now, that they happily gloss over[2] those faults. "We're as different as two people can be, and we'll never change," Robbie says, as though his acknowledgment makes the differences unimportant. "We fight all the time," Maggie laughs, shoving aside the anger that must lie behind the constant bickering. "Of course I'll take off from work when we have a baby," Robbie asserts, denying to himself the drive of ambition that makes him spend every evening working at his desk, leaving little time for the two to be together. And Maggie accepts his assertion, pretending to herself and to him that he will be able to put aside his ambitions when the time comes.

3 There are many kinds of expectations with which people begin their marriages. "I'll change him/her after we marry" is one of the most common of these—trite,[3] actually, because it is so widely known and often laughed at. The "I'll be happy once I'm married" illusion is also widely held, an anticipation that marriage will take care of all one's emotional needs. Then there is the illusion that "if she loved me, she'd know how I feel," which may begin before marriage and continue well into it. This is the expectation that in some fantasy land of love you never have to tell your partner how you feel or what you want.

4 Underlying all the other expectations is the expectation of perfection. All of us begin marriages with such high hopes, it is hard to believe that anything about our life could be less than perfect. When imperfections appear (as they must), most couples look around at other marriages and wonder what is wrong with them. They are sure that everybody else's sex life is wonderful, while they have had trouble adjusting to one another; everybody else knows how to communicate feelings, while they have had vicious battles; everybody else is adept at handling finances, while theirs are in constant chaos. Since their marriage isn't perfect, as everybody else's is, they conclude that it is probably no good at all.

5 Marital therapist Carl Whitaker, who has written and lectured a great deal, believes that a real marriage doesn't begin until that time when the illusions wear off, or wear thin. It takes a couple about ten years, says Whitaker, to realize that the expectations with which they began marriage and the assumptions they held about each other are not quite the way they seemed. At this point they see themselves as having "fallen out of love." He no longer thinks he can change her, and she no longer thinks he can understand her. The characteristics that had once seemed endearing—his fear of flying, her fear of failure—now drive them crazy. They have come to see each other as real people, neither saviors nor therapists, saints nor charming rogues.[4] Each knows the other's vulnerabilities, and knows well how to hurt the other. Now their marriage is at a crossroads. They can become locked onto a pattern of fighting and making each other miserable; they can become involved in outside affairs; they can decide that this is not what they bargained for and split; or they can create a true marriage. That is, they can come to accept the frailties and vulnerabilities each has, accept them and respect them, and in doing so, discover a much more profound love for the real person whom they married.

6 It may not take ten years for Whitaker's "ten-year-syndrome" to occur. It may take three weeks or five months or two decades for the exaggerated expectations and fantasies to fall away and for a couple to find themselves face to face with one another, confronting the realities of their marriage.

7 If they make the decision to stay together, they will begin the real process of marriage. Marriage is a process because it is always in flux;[5] it never stays the same and it never completes itself. It is a process of changing and accepting

> "A marriage is a process . . . it never stays the same and it never completes itself."

---

2. gloss over: not take seriously; treat superficially

3. trite: too often used

4. rogues: rascals

5. flux: change

change, of settling differences and living with differences that will never be settled, of drawing close and pulling apart and drawing close again. Because it is a process that demands discipline and responsibility, it can bring frustration and pain, but it also can plumb[6] the depths of love and provide an arena for self-actualization as nothing else can.

If Maggie and Robbie stay married, their marriage will have a special kind 8 of romance. It will not be only the romance of loving one another and it will not be the romance of sexual excitement—although those will be part of their marriage. The romance of a marriage that lasts beyond the illusions comes in its incompleteness, and in the adventure of exploring the unfolding process together.

Discussion and Writing Questions

1. The author says that all marriages begin with unreal expectations (paragraph 2). Give some examples of unreal expectations. What does the author believe must happen to these expectations for a marriage to succeed?

2. What does the author think of the communication between Maggie and Robbie? Why?

3. The author believes that marriage "is a process" (paragraph 7). What does she mean by this? What predictable stages occur in this process?

4. Once the romantic illusions are gone, does the relationship become boring? What, according to Klagsbrun, is exciting about a long-term relationship?

Writing Assignments

1. Write about a relationship you have had or a relationship you are familiar with in which the couple found themselves "at a crossroads." How did they handle this turning point? What happened?

2. Write about a situation that you approached with high hopes. Did those early hopes change over time? Try to give your reader a sense of the events you experienced and feelings you had. Did you come to a more realistic understanding of the situation? Why or why not?

3. Klagsbrun describes the "real process of marriage" as one that "demands discipline and responsibility" (paragraph 7). What else do you think marriage, or any healthy relationship, demands? Describe the characteristics of a successful relationship, as you see them.

In This Arranged Marriage, Love Came Later

Shoba Narayan

Although arranged marriages are common in many parts of the world, most Americans believe that the best marriages start with falling in love. In this essay, an American-educated journalist from India discusses her decision to let her family find her a husband.

We sat around the dining table, my family and I, replete[1] from yet another 1 home-cooked South Indian dinner. It was my younger brother, Shaam, who asked the question.

---

6. plumb: examine deeply
1. replete: filled to satisfaction

"Shoba, why don't you stay back here for a few months? So we can try to get you married." 2

Three pairs of eyes stared at me across the expanse of the table. I sighed. Here I was, at the tail end of my vacation after graduate school. I had an airplane ticket to New York from Madras, India, in 10 days. I had accepted a job at an artists' colony in Johnson, Vermont. My car, and most of my possessions, were with friends in Memphis. 3

"It's not that simple," I said. "What about my car . . . ?" 4

"We could find you someone in America," my dad replied. "You could go back to the States." 5

They had thought it all out. This was a plot. I glared at my parents accusingly. 6

Oh, another part of me rationalized, why not give this arranged-marriage thing a shot? It wasn't as if I had a lot to go back to in the States. Besides, I could always get a divorce. 7

Stupid and dangerous as it seems in retrospect,[2] I went into my marriage at 25 without being in love. Three years later, I find myself relishing my relationship with this brilliant, prickly man who talks about the yield curve and derivatives,[3] who prays when I drive, and who tries valiantly to remember names like Giacometti, Munch, Kandinsky.[4] 8

My enthusiasm for arranged marriages is that of a recent convert. True, I grew up in India, where arranged marriages are common. My parents' marriage was arranged, as were those of my aunts, cousins and friends. But I always thought I was different. I blossomed as a foreign fellow in Mount Holyoke College where individualism was expected and feminism encouraged. As I experimented with being an American, I bought into the American value system. 9

I was determined to fall in love and marry someone who was not Indian. Yet, somehow, I could never manage to. Oh, falling in love was easy. Sustaining it was the hard part. 10

Arranged marriages in India begin with matching the horoscopes of the man and the woman. Astrologers look for balance . . . so that the woman's strengths balance the man's weaknesses and vice versa. Once the horoscopes match, the two families meet and decide whether they are compatible. It is assumed that they are of the same religion, caste[5] and social stratum.[6] 11

While this eliminates risk and promotes homogeneity,[7] the rationale is that the personalities of the couple provide enough differences for a marriage to thrive. Whether or not this is true, the high statistical success rate of arranged marriages in different cultures—90 percent in Iran, 95 percent in India, and a similar high percentage among Hasidic Jews in Brooklyn, and among Turkish and Afghan Muslims—gives one pause. 12

Although our families met through a mutual friend, many Indian families meet through advertisements placed in national newspapers. 13

My parents made a formal visit to my future husband's house to see whether Ram's family would treat me well. My mother insists that "you can tell a lot about the family just from the way they serve coffee." The house had a lovely flower garden. The family liked gardening. Good. 14

> "Stupid and dangerous as it seems in retrospect, I went into my marriage at 25 without being in love."

_____

2. in retrospect: looking back

3. yield curve and derivatives: technical terms from finance

4. Giacometti, Munch, Kandinsky: great twentieth-century artists

5. caste: one of four social classes in India

6. stratum: level

7. homogeneity: sameness, similarity

Ram's mother had worked for the United Nations on women's-rights is- 15
sues. She also wrote humorous columns for Indian magazines. She would be
supportive. She served strong South Indian coffee in the traditional stainless
steel tumblers instead of china; she would be a balancing influence on my
youthful radicalism.

Ram's father had supported his wife's career even though he belonged to 16
a generation of Indian men who expected their wives to stay home. Ram had a
good role model. His sister was a pediatrician in Fort Myers. Perhaps that
meant he was used to strong, achieving women.

November 20, 1992. Someone shouted, "They're here!" My cousin Sheela 17
gently nudged me out of the bedroom into the living room.

"Why don't you sit down?" a voice said. 18

I looked up and saw a square face and smiling eyes anxious to put me at 19
ease. He pointed me to a chair. Somehow I liked that. The guy was sensitive and
self-confident.

He looked all right. Could stand to lose a few pounds. I liked the way his 20
lips curved to meet his eyes. Curly hair, commanding voice, unrestrained laugh.
To my surprise, the conversation flowed easily. We had a great deal in common,
but his profession was very different from mine. He had an MBA from the University of Michigan and had worked on Wall Street before joining a financial
consulting firm.

Two hours later, Ram said, "I'd like to get to know you better. Unfortu- 21
nately, I have to be back at my job in Connecticut, but I could call you every
other day. No strings attached, and both of us can decide where this goes, if anywhere."

I didn't dislike him. 22

He called 10 days later. We talked about our goals, dreams and anxieties. 23

"What do you want out of life?" he asked me one day. "Come up with five
words, maybe, of what you want to do with your life." His question intrigued
me. "Courage, wisdom, change," I said, flippantly.[8] "What about you?"

"Curiosity, contribution, balance, family and fun," he said. In spite of my- 24
self, I was impressed.

One month later, he proposed and I accepted. Our extended honeymoon 25
in Connecticut was wonderful. On weekends, we took trips to Mount Holyoke,
where I showed him my old art studio, and to Franconia Notch in New Hampshire, where we hiked and camped.

It was in Taos, New Mexico, that we had our first fight. Ram had arranged 26
for a surprise visit to the children's summer camp where I used to work as a
counselor. We visited my old colleagues with their Greenpeace T-shirts and
New Age commune mentality. Ram, with his clipped accent, neatly pressed
clothes and pleasant manners, was so different. What was I doing with this
guy? On the car trip to the airport, I was silent. "I think, perhaps, we might have
made a mistake," I said slowly. The air changed.

"Your friends may be idealistic, but they are escaping their lives, as are 27
you," he said. "We are married. Accept it. Grow up!"

He had never spoken to me this harshly before, and it hurt. I didn't talk to 28
him during the entire trip back to New York.

That fight set the pattern of our lives for the next several months. In the 29
evening, when Ram came home, I would ignore him or blame him for bringing
me to Connecticut.

Two years into our marriage, something happened. I was ashamed to re- 30
alize that while I had treated Ram with veiled dislike, he had always tried to improve our relationship. I was admitted to the journalism program at Columbia,
where, at Ram's insistence, I had applied.

---

8. flippantly: lightly, thoughtlessly

Falling in love, for me, began with small changes. I found myself relishing 31
a South Indian dish that I disliked, mostly because I knew how much he loved
it. I realized that the first thing I wanted to do when I heard some good news
was to share it with him. Somewhere along the way, the "I love you, too" that I
had politely parroted[9] in response to his endearments had become sincere.

My friends are appalled[10] that I let my parents decide my life partner; yet, 32
the older they get the more intrigued they are. I am convinced that our successful relationship has to do with two words: tolerance and trust. In a country
that emphasizes individual choice, arranged marriages require a familial web
for them to work. For many Americans, that web doesn't exist.

As my friend Karen said, "How can I get my parents to pick out my 33
spouse when they don't even talk to each other?"

Discussion and Writing Questions

1. Why did the author agree to an arranged marriage?

2. What factors did her family consider as they matched her with a husband?
   Which of these factors do you think are important predictors of success in
   marriage? Which, if any, seem unimportant?

3. How did Shoba Narayan know, after two years, that she was falling in
   love? If you have ever fallen in love, how was your experience similar or
   different?

4. What might be the disadvantages, or even risks, of an arranged marriage?

Writing Assignments

1. Soon after they met, Ram asked Shoba what words she would choose to
   express what she wanted in life. She said, "Courage, wisdom, change."
   Ram chose "curiosity, contribution, balance, family and fun." What three to
   five words would you select in answer to Ram's question? Choose your
   words carefully; then explain why each one is important to you.

2. Would you consider letting your relatives pick your marriage partner? Take
   a stand, presenting the two or three most important reasons why you
   would or would not consider such a move.

3. How important is romantic love in a marriage or other intimate relationship? To help you answer this question, review or read Francine
   Klagsbrun's article "Forever," in this section. Klagsbrun states that the "real
   work of marriage" begins only when romantic illusions wear off. *Is* love
   just a romantic illusion?

Homeless

Anna Quindlen

When she was a columnist for *The New York Times*, Anna Quindlen often wrote
about such issues as the changing family, men's and women's roles, the work-
place, and sexual harassment. Here she examines one of our society's most difficult problems: homelessness.

---

 9. parroted: repeated mindlessly, like a parrot
10. appalled: shocked

Her name was Ann, and we met in the Port Authority Bus Terminal several Januarys ago. I was doing a story on homeless people. She said I was wasting my time talking to her: she was just passing through, although she'd been passing through for more than two weeks. To prove to me that this was true, she rummaged through a tote bag and a manila envelope and finally unfolded a sheet of typing paper and brought out her photographs. **1**

They were not pictures of family, or friends, or even a dog or cat, its eyes brown-red in the flashbulb's light. They were pictures of a house. It was like a thousand houses in a hundred towns, not suburb, not city, but somewhere in between, with aluminum siding and a chain-link fence, a narrow driveway running up to a one-car garage and a patch of backyard. The house was yellow. I looked on the back for a date or a name, but neither was there. There was no need for discussion. I knew what she was trying to tell me, for it was something I had often felt. She was not adrift, alone, anonymous,[1] although her bags and her raincoat with the grime shadowing its creases had made me believe she was. She had a house, or at least once upon a time had had one. Inside were curtains, a couch, a stove, potholders. You are where you live. She was somebody. **2**

I've never been very good at looking at the big picture, taking the global view, and I've always been a person with an overactive sense of place, the legacy[2] of an Irish grandfather. So it is natural that the thing that seems most wrong with the world to me right now is that there are so many people with no homes. I'm not simply talking about shelter from the elements, or three square meals a day or a mailing address to which the welfare people can send the check—although I know that all these are important for survival. I'm talking about a home, about precisely those kinds of feelings that have wound up in cross-stitch and French knots[3] on samplers[4] over the years. **3**

Home is where the heart is. There's no place like it. I love my home with a ferocity[5] totally out of proportion to its appearance or location. I love dumb things about it: the hot-water heater, the plastic rack you drain dishes in, the roof over my head, which occasionally leaks. And yet it is precisely those dumb things that make it what it is—a place of certainty, stability, predictability, privacy, for me and for my family. It is where I live. What more can you say about a place than that? That is everything. **4**

Yet it is something that we have been edging away from gradually during my lifetime and the lifetimes of my parents and grandparents. There was a time when where you lived often was where you worked and where you grew the food you ate and even where you were buried. When that era passed, where you lived at least was where your parents had lived and where you would live with your children when you became enfeebled. Then, suddenly, where you lived was where you lived for three years, until you could move on to something else and something else again. **5**

And so we have come to something else again, to children who do not understand what it means to go to their rooms because they have never had a room, to men and women whose fantasy is a wall they can paint a color of their own choosing, to old people reduced to sitting on molded plastic chairs, their skin blue-white in the lights of a bus station, who pull pictures of houses out of their bags. Homes have stopped being homes. Now they are real estate. **6**

People find it curious that those without homes would rather sleep sitting up on benches or huddled in doorways than go to shelters. Certainly some **7**

> "They are not the homeless. They are people who have no homes."

---

1. anonymous: nameless, lacking identity
2. legacy: something from the past handed down or passed on
3. cross-stitch, French knots: types of stitching in needlepoint
4. samplers: pieces of embroidered cloth
5. ferocity: fierce energy

prefer to do so because they are emotionally ill, because they have been locked in before and they are damned if they will be locked in again. Others are afraid of the violence and trouble they may find there. But some seem to want something that is not available in shelters, and they will not compromise, not for a cot, or oatmeal, or a shower with special soap that kills the bugs. "One room," a woman with a baby who was sleeping on her sister's floor, once told me, "painted blue." That was the crux[6] of it; not size or location, but pride of ownership. Painted blue.

This is a difficult problem, and some wise and compassionate people are working hard at it. But in the main[7] I think we work around it, just as we walk around it when it is lying on the sidewalk or sitting in the bus terminal—the problem, that is. It has been customary to take people's pain and lessen our own participation in it by turning it into an issue, not a collection of human beings. We turn an adjective into a noun: the poor, not poor people; the homeless, not Ann or the man who lives in the box or the woman who sleeps on the subway grate. **8**

Sometimes I think we would be better off if we forgot about the broad strokes and concentrated on the details. Here is a woman without a bureau. There is a man with no mirror, no wall to hang it on. They are not the homeless. They are people who have no homes. No drawer that holds the spoons. No window to look out upon the world. My God. That is everything. **9**

Discussion and Writing Questions

1. What does the author mean when she says, "You are where you live" (paragraph 2)?

2. Why does she say, "Homes have stopped being homes. Now they are real estate" (paragraph 6)?

3. Why do some people refuse to live in public shelters?

4. The author states in paragraph 9 that she believes it is important to concentrate on details when we talk about homelessness. Why? What does she believe we gain by concentrating on details?

Writing Assignments

1. What is (or is not) being done in your community about homelessness? As you write, follow Quindlen's example and use vivid details and examples.

2. Describe what you mean by "home." What little details, comforts, colors do you love about your home? In paragraph 4, Quindlen says home is "dumb things." Do you agree?

3. It has been said that America is becoming further divided into two nations: those who "have" and those who "have not." Do you believe America is divided this way? Explain why you feel the way you do.

Say Yes to Yourself

Joseph T. Martorano and John P. Kildahl

Do you believe your thoughts can change your life? If you can change the way you think, say therapists Martorano and Kildahl, you will change the way you feel—and act.

---

6. crux: the most important part of an issue
7. in the main: mainly

It's the classic story with a twist: a traveling salesman gets a flat tire on a dark [1] lonely road and then discovers he has no jack. He sees a light in a farmhouse. As he walks toward it, his mind churns: "Suppose no one comes to the door." "Suppose they don't have a jack." "Suppose the guy won't lend me his jack even if he has one." The harder his mind works, the more agitated he becomes, and when the door opens, he punches the farmer and yells, "*Keep* your lousy jack!"

That story brings a smile, because it pokes fun at a common type of self- [2] defeatist thinking. How often have you heard yourself say: "Nothing *ever* goes the way I planned." "I'll *never* make that deadline." "I *always* screw up."

Such inner speech shapes your life more than any other single force. Like it [3] or not, you travel through life with your thoughts as navigator. If those thoughts spell gloom and doom, that's where you're headed, because put-down words sabotage confidence instead of offering support and encouragement.

Simply put, to *feel* better, you need to *think* better. Here's how: [4]

1. Tune in to your thoughts. The first thing Sue said to her new therapist [5] was, "I know you can't help me, Doctor. I'm a total mess. I keep lousing up at work, and I'm sure I'm going to be canned. Just yesterday my boss told me I was being transferred. He called it a promotion. But if I was doing a good job, why transfer me?"

Then, gradually, Sue's story moved past the put-downs. She had received [6] her M.B.A. two years before and was making an excellent salary. That didn't sound like failure.

At the end of their first meeting, Sue's therapist told her to jot down her [7] thoughts, particularly at night if she was having trouble falling asleep. At her next appointment Sue's list included: "I'm not really smart. I got ahead by a bunch of flukes."[1] "Tomorrow will be a disaster. I've never chaired a meeting before." "My boss looked furious this morning. What did I do?"

She admitted, "In one day alone, I listed 26 negative thoughts. No wonder [8] I'm always tired and depressed."

Hearing her fears and forebodings[2] read out loud made Sue realize how [9] much energy she was squandering[3] on imagined catastrophes. If you've been feeling down, it could be you're sending yourself negative messages too. Listen to the words churning inside your head. Repeat them aloud or write them down, if that will help capture them.

With practice, tuning in will become automatic. As you're walking or [10] driving down the street, you can hear your silent broadcast. Soon your thoughts will do your bidding, rather than the other way around. And when that happens, your feelings and actions will change too.

2. Isolate destructive words and phrases. Fran's inner voice kept telling [11] her she was "only a secretary." Mark's reminded him he was "just a salesman." With the word *only* or *just,* they were downgrading their jobs and, by extension, themselves. By isolating negative words and phrases, you can pinpoint the damage you're doing to yourself. . . .

3. Stop the thought. Short-circuit negative messages as soon as they start [12] by using the one-word command *stop!*

"What will I do if . . . ?" *Stop!* [13]

In theory, stopping is a simple technique. In practice, it's not as easy as it [14] sounds. To be effective at stopping, you have to be forceful and tenacious.[4] Raise your voice when you give the command. Picture yourself drowning out the inner voice of fear.

---

1. flukes: accidents
2. forebodings: feelings that something bad is going to happen
3. squandering: wasting
4. tenacious: holding on; stubborn

Vincent, a hard-working bachelor in his 20s, was an executive in a large **15** company. . . . Although attracted to a woman in his department, he never asked her for a date. His worries immobilized[5] him: "It's not a good idea to date a co-worker," or, "If she says no, it'll be embarrassing."

When Vincent stopped his inner voice and asked the woman out, she said, **16** "Vincent, what took you so long?"

4. Accentuate the positive. There's a story about a man who went to a **17** psychiatrist. "What's the trouble?" asked the doctor.

"Two months ago my grandfather died and left me $75,000. Last month, a **18** cousin passed away and left me $100,000."

"Then why are you depressed?" **19**

"This month, *nothing!*" **20**

When a person is in a depressed mood, everything can seem depressing. **21** So once you've exorcised[6] the demons by calling a stop, replace them with good thoughts. . . . Be ready with a thought you've prepared in advance. Think about the promotion you got or a pleasant hike in the woods. In the words of the Bible: " . . . whatever is honorable . . . whatever is lovely, whatever is gracious . . . think about these things."

5. Reorient yourself. Have you ever been feeling down late in the day, **22** when someone suddenly said, "Let's go out"? Remember how your spirits picked up? You changed the direction of your thinking, and your mood brightened. . . . Practice this technique of going from painful anxiety to an active, problem-solving framework. . . .

> "Listen to the words churning inside your head. . . . Short-circuit negative messages as soon as they start."

By reorienting, you can learn to see yourself and the world around you **23** differently. If you think you can do something, you increase your chances of doing it. Optimism gets you moving. Depressing thoughts bog you down, because you are thinking, "What's the use?"

Make it a habit to remember your best self, the you that you want to be. In **24** particular, remember things for which you have been complimented. That's the real you. Make this the frame of reference for your life—a picture of you at your best.

You'll find that reorienting works like a magnet. Imagine yourself **25** reaching your goals, and you will feel the tug of the magnet pulling you toward them.

Over the years we've discovered that when people *think* differently, they **26** *feel*—and *act*—differently. It's all in controlling your thoughts. As the poet John Milton wrote: "The mind . . . can make a heaven of hell, a hell of heaven."

The choice is yours. **27**

Discussion and Writing Questions

1. What is the point of the story of the traveling salesman and the jack (paragraph 1)?

2. Martorano and Kildahl say that negative inner speech "shapes your life more than any other single force" (paragraph 3). Do you think this statement is true? Why or why not?

3. The authors offer five suggestions for changing negative thinking to positive thinking. Which suggestion do you think would be most useful for you? Why?

4. What is the meaning of John Milton's line "the mind . . . can make a heaven of hell, a hell of heaven" (paragraph 26)? Give examples from experience.

---

5. immobilized: kept from moving
6. exorcised: gotten rid of evil spirits

Writing Assignments

1. Describe a person you know who always makes you feel good about yourself. What does he or she say or do that makes you feel this way? Describe a time when you acted in a positive way because of that person's influence.

2. Most of us have negative mental "tapes" that influence the way we feel or act. These might concern our physical appearance, our abilities as a student or worker, or our relationships with other people. In your first sentence, describe a negative thought you have had about yourself. How could you change it and think more positively? How might your feelings and actions change if you did?

3. For a day or two, try using one or more of Martorano and Kildahl's suggestions for changing negative thoughts. Then write about your experience. What negative thoughts did you notice? Were you able to stop those negative thoughts? If so, did you feel better? Did you act in a more positive way? If the experiment didn't work, do you think it might work if you had more time or practice?

Yolanda

Julia Alvarez

Living in a new country and learning a new language are challenges for anyone. For a young child, whose experience of the world is limited, the challenges may be even greater. This fictional selection by a writer from the Dominican Republic captures one child's fear and wonder in a new country.

Our first year in New York we rented a small apartment with a Catholic school 1
nearby, taught by the Sisters of Charity, hefty[1] women in long black gowns and bonnets that made them look peculiar, like dolls in mourning. I liked them a lot, especially my grandmotherly fourth grade teacher, Sister Zoe. I had a lovely name, she said, and she had me teach the whole class how to pronounce it. *Yo-lan-da.* As the only immigrant in my class, I was put in a special seat in the first row by the window, apart from the other children so that Sister Zoe could tutor me without disturbing them. Slowly, she enunciated the new words I was to repeat: *laundromat, corn flakes, subway, snow.*

Soon I picked up enough English to understand holocaust[2] was in the air. 2
Sister Zoe explained to a wide-eyed classroom what was happening in Cuba.[3] Russian missiles were being assembled, trained supposedly on New York City. President Kennedy, looking worried too, was on the television at home, explaining we might have to go to war against the Communists. At school, we had air-raid drills: an ominous[4] bell would go off and we'd file into the hall, fall to the floor, cover our heads with our coats, and imagine our hair falling out, the bones in our arms going soft. At home, Mami and my sisters and I said a rosary for world peace. I heard new vocabulary: *nuclear bomb, radioactive fallout, bomb*

> "Slowly, she enunciated the new words I was to repeat: *laundromat, corn flakes, subway, snow.*"

---

1. hefty: heavy

2. holocaust: total destruction

3. what was happening in Cuba: During the Cuban missile crisis of 1962, the United States discovered that the former Soviet Union was building nuclear missile launch sites on Cuba. After several weeks of great tension and the threat of nuclear war, the former Soviet Union withdrew. In return, President Kennedy agreed not to try again to overthrow the Castro government in Cuba.

4. ominous: threatening

shelter. Sister Zoe explained how it would happen. She drew a picture of a mushroom on the blackboard and dotted a flurry of chalkmarks for the dusty fallout that would kill us all.

The months grew cold, November, December. It was dark when I got up 3 in the morning, frosty when I followed my breath to school. One morning as I sat at my desk daydreaming out the window, I saw dots in the air like the ones Sister Zoe had drawn—random at first, then lots and lots. I shrieked, "Bomb! Bomb!" Sister Zoe jerked around, her full black skirt ballooning as she hurried to my side. A few girls began to cry.

But then Sister Zoe's shocked look faded. "Why, Yolanda dear, that's 4 snow!" She laughed. "Snow."

"Snow," I repeated. I looked out the window warily. All my life I had 5 heard about the white crystals that fell out of American skies in the winter. From my desk I watched the fine powder dust the sidewalk and parked cars below. Each flake was different, Sister Zoe had said, like a person, irreplaceable and beautiful.

Discussion and Writing Questions

1. Yolanda tells us that the word *snow* is among the words she is supposed to learn (paragraph 1). What other words does she learn that she does not yet have the experience to understand?

2. In paragraph 3, Yolanda describes the scene outside her school window: "I saw dots in the air like the ones Sister Zoe had drawn—random at first, then lots and lots." What did she think she was seeing, and what was she actually seeing? When did you realize what was really happening outside her window that day?

3. Does Yolanda's mistake indicate that she pays attention in school and is a very bright child, or just the opposite? Explain your answer.

4. Yolanda likes her teacher, Sister Zoe, from the start. Is Sister Zoe a good teacher? How can you tell?

Writing Assignments

1. Did you ever have a teacher who was especially important in your life? What was that teacher like? What influence did he or she have on you?

2. Children and people learning languages sometimes draw wrong conclusions based on limited experience. A child, for example, might think that he has to learn to fly like a bird in order "to fly to Grandma's next week." Did you ever draw a mistaken conclusion because you misunderstood a word or words? How did you find out the correct (or generally accepted) meaning?

3. Did you (or anyone you know) ever leave home to live in a new country? What was it like to adjust to a new culture? Choose one or two incidents to write about that capture one aspect of the experience—wonder or frustration, for example. Your audience is a friend or family member from another country who is considering a move to your area.

The Gift

Courtland Milloy

Help sometimes comes from unexpected places. This newspaper story describes the generosity of a friend whose gift saved someone's life—and baffled most people who knew him. As you read, ask yourself how you would have acted in his place.

When Jermaine Washington entered the barbershop, heads turned and clippers **1** fell silent. Customers waved and nodded, out of sheer respect. With his hands in the pockets of his knee-length, black leather coat, Washington acknowledged them with a faint smile and quietly took a seat.

"You know who that is?" barber Anthony Clyburn asked in a tone re- **2** served for the most awesome neighborhood characters, such as ball players and ex-cons.

A year and a half ago, Washington did something that still amazes those **3** who know him. He became a kidney donor, giving a vital organ to a woman he described as "just a friend."

"They had a platonic[1] relationship," said Clyburn, who works at Jake's **4** Barber Shop in Northeast Washington. "I could see maybe giving one to my mother, but just a girl I know? I don't think so."

Washington, who is 25, met Michelle Stevens six years ago when they **5** worked for the D.C. Department of Employment Services. They used to have lunch together in the department cafeteria and chitchat on the telephone during their breaks.

"It was nothing serious, romance-wise," said Stevens, who is 23. "He was **6** somebody I could talk to. I had been on the kidney donor waiting list for 12 months and I had lost all hope. One day, I just called to cry on his shoulder."

Stevens told Washington how depressing it was to spend three days a **7** week, three hours a day, on a kidney dialysis machine.[2] She said she suffered from chronic fatigue and blackouts and was losing her balance and her sight. He could already see that she had lost her smile.

"I saw my friend dying before my eyes," Washington recalled. "What was **8** I supposed to do? Sit back and watch her die?"

Stevens's mother was found to be suffering from hypertension[3] and was **9** ineligible to donate a kidney. Her 14-year-old sister offered to become a donor, but doctors concluded that she was too young.

Stevens's two brothers, 25 and 31, would most likely have made ideal **10** donors because of their relatively young ages and status as family members. But both of them said no.

So did Stevens's boyfriend, who gave her two diamond rings with his **11** apology.

"I understood," Stevens said. "They said they loved me very much, but **12** they were just too afraid."

Joyce Washington, Jermaine's mother, was not exactly in favor of the idea, **13** either. But after being convinced that her son was not being coerced,[4] she supported his decision.

The transplant operation took four hours. It occurred in April 1991, and **14** began with a painful X-ray procedure in which doctors inserted a metal rod into

> "'I had been on the kidney donor waiting list for 12 months and I had lost all hope. One day, I just called to cry on his shoulder.'"

---

1. platonic: nonromantic
2. kidney dialysis machine: a machine that filters waste material from the blood when the kidneys fail
3. hypertension: high blood pressure
4. coerced: pressured into doing something

Jermaine Washington and Michelle Stevens two years after the surgery
(© Beverly Rezneck)

Washington's kidney and shot it with red dye. An incision nearly 20 inches long was made from his groin to the back of his shoulder. After the surgery he remained hospitalized for five days.

Today, both Stevens and Washington are fully recovered. Stevens, a graduate of Eastern High School, is studying medicine at the National Educational Center. Washington still works for D.C. Employment Services as a job counselor. **15**

"I jog and work out with weights," Washington said. "Boxing and football are out, but I never played those anyway." **16**

A spokesman for Washington Hospital Center said the Washington-to-Stevens gift was the hospital's first "friend-to-friend" transplant. Usually, it's wife to husband, or parent to child. But there is a shortage of even those kinds of transplants. Today, more than 300 patients are in need of kidneys in the Washington area. **17**

"A woman came up to me in a movie line not long ago and hugged me," Washington said. "She thanked me for doing what I did because no one had come forth when her daughter needed a kidney, and the child died." **18**

About twice a month, Stevens and Washington get together for what they call a gratitude lunch. Since the operation, she has broken up with her boyfriend. Seven months ago, Washington got a girlfriend. Despite occasional pressure by friends, a romantic relationship is not what they want. **19**

"We are thankful for the beautiful relationship that we have," Stevens said. "We don't want to mess up a good thing." **20**

To this day, people wonder why Washington did it. To some of the men gathered at Jake's Barber Shop not long ago, Washington's heroics were cause for questions about his sanity. Surely he could not have been in his right mind, they said. **21**

One customer asked Washington where he had found the courage to give away a kidney. His answer quelled[5] most skeptics[6] and inspired even more awe. **22**

"I prayed for it," Washington replied. "I asked God for guidance and that's what I got." **23**

---

5. quelled: quieted
6. skeptics: people who doubt or question

Discussion and Writing Questions

1. A year and a half after Jermaine Washington donated a kidney to Michelle Stevens, his friends are still amazed by what he did. Why do they find his action so surprising?

2. Washington says, "What was I supposed to do? Sit back and watch her die?" (paragraph 8). Yet Stevens' brothers and her boyfriend did not offer to donate a kidney. Do you blame them? Do you understand them?

3. In what ways has Stevens' life changed because of Washington's gift? Consider her physical status, her social life, her choice of profession, her "gratitude lunches" with Washington, and so on.

4. According to Washington, where did he find the courage to donate a kidney? How did his action affect his standing in the community? How did it affect other aspects of his life?

Writing Assignments

1. Have you ever been unusually generous—or do you know someone who was? Describe that act of generosity. Why did you—or the other person—do it? How did your friends or family react?

2. Do you have or does anyone you know have a serious medical condition? Describe the situation. How do or how can friends help? Can strangers help in any way?

3. Stevens and Washington do not have or want a romantic relationship. "We don't want to mess up a good thing," Stevens says (paragraph 20). Does romance "mess things up"? Write about a time when a relationship changed—either for better or for worse—because romance entered the picture.

Salvation

Langston Hughes

Many people have experienced a crisis in their beliefs. Here Langston Hughes, a poet who first became famous in the 1920s, recalls the day his beliefs, and his life, changed.

I was saved from sin when I was going on thirteen. But not really saved. It happened like this. There was a big revival at my Auntie Reed's church. Every night for weeks there had been much preaching, singing, praying, and shouting, and some very hardened sinners had been brought to Christ, and the membership of the church had grown by leaps and bounds. Then just before the revival ended, they held a special meeting for children, "to bring the young lambs to the fold." My aunt spoke of it for days ahead. That night I was escorted to the front row and placed on the mourners' bench with all the other young sinners, who had not yet been brought to Jesus. 1

My aunt told me that when you were saved you saw a light, and something happened to you inside! And Jesus came into your life! And God was with you from then on! She said you could see and hear and feel Jesus in your soul. I believed her. I had heard a great many old people say the same thing and it seemed to me they ought to know. So I sat there calmly in the hot, crowded church, waiting for Jesus to come to me. 2

The preacher preached a wonderful rhythmical sermon, all moans and [3] shouts and lonely cries and dire[1] pictures of hell, and then he sang a song about the ninety and nine safe in the fold, but one little lamb was left out in the cold. Then he said: "Won't you come? Won't you come to Jesus? Young lambs, won't you come?" And he held out his arms to all of us young sinners there on the mourners' bench. And the little girls cried. And some of them jumped up and went to Jesus right away. But most of us just sat there.

A great many old people came and knelt around us and prayed, old [4] women with jet-black faces and braided hair, old men with work-gnarled hands. And the church sang a song about the lower lights are burning, some poor sinners to be saved. And the whole building rocked with prayer and song.

Still I kept waiting to *see* Jesus. [5]

Finally all the young people had gone to the altar and were saved, but one [6] boy and me. He was a rounder's[2] son named Westley. Westley and I were surrounded by sisters and deacons praying. It was very hot in the church, and getting late now. Finally Westley said to me in a whisper: "God damn! I'm tired o' sitting here. Let's get up and be saved." So he got up and was saved.

Then I was left all alone on the mourners' bench. My aunt came and knelt [7] at my knees and cried, while prayers and songs swirled all around me in the little church. The whole congregation prayed for me alone, in a mighty wail of moans and voices. And I kept waiting serenely for Jesus, waiting, waiting—but he didn't come. I wanted to see him, but nothing happened to me. Nothing! I wanted something to happen to me, but nothing happened.

I heard the songs and the minister saying: "Why don't you come? My dear [8] child, why don't you come to Jesus? Jesus is waiting for you. He wants you. Why don't you come? Sister Reed, what is this child's name?"

"Langston," my aunt sobbed. [9]

"Langston, why don't you come? Why don't you come and be saved? Oh, [10] Lamb of God! Why don't you come?"

Now it was really getting late. I began to be ashamed of myself, holding [11] everything up so long. I began to wonder what God thought about Westley, who certainly hadn't seen Jesus either, but who was now sitting proudly on the platform, swinging his knickerbockered[3] legs and grinning down at me, surrounded by deacons and old women on their knees praying. God had not struck Westley dead for taking his name in vain or for lying in the temple. So I decided that maybe to save further trouble, I'd better lie, too, and say that Jesus had come, and get up and be saved.

So I got up. [12]

Suddenly the whole room broke into a sea of shouting, as they saw me [13] rise. Waves of rejoicing swept the place. Women leaped in the air. My aunt threw her arms around me. The minister took me by the hand and led me to the platform.

When things quieted down, in a hushed silence, punctuated by a few ec- [14] static "Amens," all the new young lambs were blessed in the name of God. Then joyous singing filled the room.

That night, for the last time in my life but one—for I was a big boy twelve [15] years old—I cried. I cried, in bed alone, and couldn't stop. I buried my head under the quilts, but my aunt heard me. She woke up and told my uncle I was crying because the Holy Ghost had come into my life, and because I had seen Jesus. But I was really crying because I couldn't bear to tell her that I had lied, that I had deceived everybody in the church, that I hadn't seen Jesus, and that now I didn't believe there was a Jesus any more, since he didn't come to help me.

> "I wanted something to happen to me, but nothing happened."

---

1. dire: terrible, dreadful

2. rounder's: dishonest person's

3. knickerbockered: wearing knickerbockers (trousers that end just below the knee)

Discussion and Writing Questions

1. What did Hughes expect to happen to him during the church meeting?

2. Why did he finally stand up? How was he like or unlike Westley, who apparently didn't see Jesus either?

3. Compare paragraph 12 with the paragraphs above and below it. Notice the number of sentences in paragraph 12. Why does Hughes use a different writing style in this paragraph? Why is the sentence so important?

4. Why was Hughes so upset that night? Do you think he would have felt any better if he had not stood up but had endured everyone's discomfort and insisted on being true to himself?

Writing Assignments

1. Hughes describes the tremendous pressure put on him to "be saved." Write about a situation in which pressure was put on you to believe something or to behave in a certain way. How did you handle the pressure? Looking back, do you feel that your actions were courageous or cowardly?

2. What are your own ideas about religion? Are these ideas the same or different from the ideas that your family holds? Did you become less or more religious (or spiritual) as you grew older? Why?

3. Did you ever make a discovery about something that changed your view of the world in an important way—for example, the circumstances of your birth or adoption, new information about a loved one? Write about that experience. How did your view of the world change?

Emotional Intelligence

Daniel Goleman

How important to a person's success is I.Q.—that is, his or her score on an intelligence test? According to a widely read recent book, other personality traits and skills are even more important than I.Q. The author, Daniel Goleman, calls these traits and skills *emotional intelligence.* How would you rate your emotional I.Q.?

1 It was a steamy afternoon in New York City, the kind of day that makes people sullen[1] with discomfort. I was heading to my hotel, and as I stepped onto a bus, I was greeted by the driver, a middle-aged man with an enthusiastic smile.

2 "Hi! How're you doing?" he said. He greeted each rider in the same way.

3 As the bus crawled uptown through gridlocked traffic, the driver gave a lively commentary: there was a terrific sale at that store . . . a wonderful exhibit at this museum . . . had we heard about the movie that just opened down the block? By the time people got off, they had shaken off their sullen shells. When the driver called out, "So long, have a great day!" each of us gave a smiling response.

4 That memory has stayed with me for close to 20 years. I consider the bus driver a man who was truly successful at what he did.

5 Contrast him with Jason, a straight-A student at a Florida high school who was fixated[2] on getting into Harvard Medical School. When a physics teacher

---

1. sullen: gloomy
2. fixated: rigidly focused

gave Jason an 80 on a quiz, the boy believed his dream was in jeopardy.[3] He took a butcher knife to school, and in a struggle the teacher was stabbed in the collarbone.

How could someone of obvious intelligence do something so irrational? The answer is that high I.Q. does not necessarily predict who will succeed in life. Psychologists agree that I.Q. contributes only about 20 percent of the factors that determine success. A full 80 percent comes from other factors, including what I call *emotional intelligence.* 6

Following are some of the major qualities that make up emotional intelligence, and how they can be developed: 7

1. Self-awareness. The ability to recognize a feeling as it happens is the keystone of emotional intelligence. People with greater certainty about their emotions are better pilots of their lives. 8

Developing self-awareness requires tuning in to . . . gut feelings. Gut feelings can occur without a person being consciously aware of them. For example, when people who fear snakes are shown a picture of a snake, sensors on their skin will detect sweat, a sign of anxiety, even though the people say they do not feel fear. The sweat shows up even when a picture is presented so rapidly that the subject has no conscious awareness of seeing it. 9

Through deliberate effort we can become more aware of our gut feelings. Take someone who is annoyed by a rude encounter for hours after it occurred. He may be oblivious[4] to his irritability and surprised when someone calls attention to it. But if he evaluates his feelings, he can change them. 10

Emotional self-awareness is the building block of the next fundamental of emotional intelligence: being able to shake off a bad mood. 11

2. Mood Management. Bad as well as good moods spice life and build character. The key is balance. 12

We often have little control over *when* we are swept by emotion. But we can have some say in *how long* that emotion will last. Psychologist Dianne Tice of Case Western Reserve University asked more than 400 men and women about their strategies for escaping foul moods. Her research, along with that of other psychologists, provides valuable information on how to change a bad mood. 13

Of all the moods that people want to escape, rage seems to be the hardest to deal with. When someone in another car cuts you off on the highway, your reflexive[5] thought may be, *That jerk! He could have hit me! I can't let him get away with that!* The more you stew, the angrier you get. Such is the stuff of hypertension and reckless driving. 14

What should you do to relieve rage? One myth is that ventilating[6] will make you feel better. In fact, researchers have found that's one of the worst strategies. Outbursts of rage pump up the brain's arousal system, leaving you more angry, not less. 15

A more effective technique is "reframing," which means consciously reinterpreting a situation in a more positive light. In the case of the driver who cuts you off, you might tell yourself: *Maybe he had some emergency.* This is one of the most potent ways, Tice found, to put anger to rest. 16

Going off alone to cool down is also an effective way to defuse anger, especially if you can't think clearly. Tice found that a large proportion of men cool down by going for a drive—a finding that inspired her to drive more defensively. A safer alternative is exercise, such as taking a long walk. Whatever you do, don't waste the time pursuing your train of angry thoughts. Your aim should be to distract yourself. 17

---

3. jeopardy: danger
4. oblivious: totally unaware
5. reflexive: automatic
6. ventilating: "letting off steam," raving

The techniques of reframing and distraction can alleviate[7] depression and anxiety as well as anger. Add to them such realization techniques as deep breathing and meditation and you have an arsenal of weapons against bad moods. "Praying," Dianne Tice also says, "works for all moods." 18

3. Self-motivation. Positive motivation—the marshaling[8] of feelings of enthusiasm, zeal and confidence—is paramount for achievement. Studies of Olympic athletes, world-class musicians and chess grandmasters[9] show that their common trait is the ability to motivate themselves to pursue relentless training routines. 19

To motivate yourself for any achievement requires clear goals and an optimistic, can-do attitude. Psychologist Martin Seligman of the University of Pennsylvania advised the MetLife insurance company to hire a special group of job applicants who tested high on optimism, although they had failed the normal aptitude test. Compared with salesmen who passed the aptitude test but scored high in pessimism, this group made 21 percent more sales in their first year and 57 percent more in their second. 20

A pessimist is likely to interpret rejection as meaning *I'm a failure; I'll never make a sale.* Optmists tell themselves, *I'm using the wrong approach,* or *That customer was in a bad mood.* By blaming failure on the situation, not themselves, optimists are motivated to make that next call. 21

Your . . . positive or negative outlook may be inborn, but with effort and practice, pessimists can learn to think more hopefully. Psychologists have documented that if you can catch negative, self-defeating thoughts as they occur, you can reframe the situation in less catastrophic terms. 22

4. Impulse Control. The essence of emotional self-regulation is the ability to delay impulse in the service of a goal. The importance of this trait to success was shown in an experiment begun in the 1960s by psychologist Walter Mischel at a preschool on the Stanford University campus. 23

Children were told that they could have a single treat, such as a marshmallow, right now. However, if they would wait while the experimenter ran an errand, they could have two marshmallows. Some preschoolers grabbed the marshmallow immediately, but others were able to wait what, for them, must have seemed an endless 20 minutes. To sustain themselves in their struggle, they covered their eyes so they wouldn't see the temptation, rested their heads on their arms, talked to themselves, sang, even tried to sleep. These plucky kids got the two-marshmallow reward. 24

The interesting part of this experiment came in the follow-up. The children who as four-year-olds had been able to wait for the two marshmallows were, as adolescents, still able to delay gratification in pursuing their goals. They were more socially competent and self-assertive, and better able to cope with life's frustrations. In contrast, the kids who grabbed the one marshmallow were, as adolescents, more likely to be stubborn, indecisive and stressed. 25

The ability to resist impulse can be developed through practice. When you're faced with an immediate temptation, remind yourself of your long-term goals—whether they be losing weight or getting a medical degree. You'll find it easier, then, to keep from settling for the single marshmallow. 26

5. People Skills. The capacity to know how another feels is important on the job, in romance and friendships, and in the family. We transmit and catch moods from each other on a subtle, almost imperceptible level. The way someone says thank you, for instance, can leave us feeling dismissed, pa- 27

---

7. alleviate: reduce, make better
8. marshaling: gathering together, using
9. chess grandmasters: experts at the game of chess

tronized or genuinely appreciated. The more adroit[10] we are at discerning the feelings behind other people's signals, the better we control the signals we send.

The importance of good interpersonal skills was demonstrated by psy- 28 chologists Robert Kelley of Carnegie-Mellon University and Janet Caplan in a study at Bell Labs in Naperville, Ill. The labs are staffed by engineers and scientists who are all at the apex[11] of academic I.Q. tests. But some still emerged as stars while others languished.[12]

What accounted for the difference? The standout performers had a net- 29 work with a wide range of people. When a non-star encountered a technical problem, Kelley observed, "he called various technical gurus and then waited, wasting time while his calls went unreturned. Star performers rarely faced such situations because they built reliable networks *before* they needed them. So when the stars called someone, they almost always got a faster answer."

No matter what their I.Q., once again it was emotional intelligence that 30 separated the stars from the average performers.

Discussion and Writing Questions

1. Goleman names five qualities that contribute to emotional intelligence. What are they?

2. Describe someone you observed recently who showed a high level of emotional intelligence in a particular situation. Then describe someone who showed a low level of emotional intelligence in a particular situation. Which of the five qualities did each person display or lack?

3. Did it surprise you to read that "ventilating" is one of the worst ways to handle rage? Instead, experts suggest several techniques. Suppose you are in the following situation, and your first reaction is anger: *You ask a salesperson for help in choosing a CD player. As she walks right past you, she tells you that the boxes and labels will give you all the information you need.* What might you do to calm yourself down?

4. In paragraphs 24 and 25, Goleman discusses a now-famous study of children and marshmallows. What was the point of this study? Why does Goleman say that the most interesting part of the study came later, when the children reached adolescence?

Writing Assignments

1. Write a detailed portrait of a person you consider an "emotional genius." Develop your paper with specific examples of his or her skills.

2. Daniel Goleman claims that weak emotional qualities can be strengthened with practice. Choose one of the five qualities (self-awareness, people skills, and so forth), and recommend specific ways for a person to improve in that area. Your audience is people who wish to improve their emotional intelligence; your purpose is to help them do so.

3. Review or read "The Gift" on page 429, and evaluate the emotional intelligence of the young man in the story, Jermaine Washington. Mr. Washington saved a friend's life by giving her one of his kidneys after her two brothers and her boyfriend refused to be donors. Most people in their town still think Mr. Washington was "crazy" to make this decision. What do you think? Does he have a high level of emotional intelligence? A low level? Why?

---

10. adroit: skilled
11. apex: top, topmost point
12. languished: stayed in one place

Sports Nuts

Dave Barry

Dave Barry is a Pulitzer Prize–winning humorist who writes a column for _The Miami Herald_. This essay, on men who are fanatic about sports, is written in Barry's usual tongue-in-cheek style.

Today, in our continuing series on How Guys Think, we explore the question: 1
How come guys care so much about sports?

This is a tough one, because caring about sports is, let's face it, silly. I 2
mean, suppose you have a friend who, for no apparent reason, suddenly becomes obsessed with the Amtrak Corporation. He babbles about Amtrak constantly, citing[1] obscure railroad statistics from 1978; he puts Amtrak bumper stickers on his car; and when something bad happens to Amtrak, such as a train crashes and investigators find that the engineer was drinking and wearing a bunny suit, your friend becomes depressed for weeks. You'd think he was crazy, right? "Bob," you'd say to him, as a loving and caring friend, "you're a moron. The Amtrak Corporation has _nothing to do with you._"

But if Bob is behaving exactly the same deranged[2] way about, say, the 3
Pittsburgh Penguins, it's considered normal guy behavior. He could name his child "Pittsburgh Penguin Johnson" and be considered only mildly eccentric. There is something wrong with this. And before you accuse me of being some kind of sherry-sipping ascot[3]-wearing ballet-attending MacNeil-Lehrer Report–watching wussy, please note that I am a sports guy myself, having had a legendary athletic career consisting of nearly a third of the 1965 season on the track team at Pleasantville High School ("Where The Leaders Of Tomorrow Are Leaving Wads Of Gum On The Auditorium Seats Of Today"). I competed in the long jump, because it seemed to be the only event where afterward you didn't fall down and throw up. I probably would have become an Olympic-caliber long-jumper except that, through one of those "bad breaks" so common in sports, I turned out to have the raw leaping ability of a convenience store. I'd race down the runway and attempt to soar into the air, but instead of going up I'd be seized by powerful gravity rays and yanked _downward_ and wind up with just my head sticking out of the dirt, serving as a convenient marker for the other jumpers to take off from.

So, OK, I was not Jim Thorpe,[4] but I care as much about sports as the next 4
guy. If you were to put me in the middle of a room, and in one corner was Albert Einstein, in another corner was Abraham Lincoln, in another corner was Plato, in another corner was William Shakespeare, and in another corner (this room is a pentagon) was a TV set showing a football game between teams that have no connection whatsoever with my life, such as the Green Bay Packers and the Indianapolis Colts, I would ignore the greatest minds in Western thought, gravitate toward the TV, and become far more concerned about the game than I am about my child's education. And _so would the other guys._ I guarantee it. Within minutes Plato would be pounding Lincoln on the shoulder and shouting in ancient Greek that the receiver did _not_ have both feet in bounds.

Obviously, sports connect with something deeply rooted in the male 5
psyche,[5] dating back to prehistoric times, when guys survived by hunting and fighting, and they needed many of the skills exhibited by modern athletes—

> " . . . I turned out to have the raw leaping ability of a convenience store. . . . but I care as much about sports as the next guy."

---

1. citing: offering examples of
2. deranged: crazed, insane
3. ascot: an English necktie
4. Jim Thorpe: famous Native American athlete
5. psyche: the mind

running, throwing, spitting, renegotiating their contracts, adjusting their private parts on nationwide television, etc. So that would explain how come guys like to *participate* in sports. But how come they care so much about games played by *other* guys? Does this also date back to prehistoric times? When the hunters were out hurling spears into mastodons,[6] were there also prehistoric guys watching from the hills, drinking prehistoric beer, eating really bad prehistoric hot dogs, and shouting "We're No. 1!" but not understanding what it meant because this was before the development of mathematics?

There must have been, because there is no other explanation for such 6 bizarre phenomena as:

- Sports-talk radio, where guys who have never sent get-well cards to their 7 own mothers will express heartfelt, near-suicidal anguish over the hamstring problems of strangers.

- My editor, Gene, who can remember the complete starting lineups for the 8 New York Yankee teams from 1960 through 1964, but who routinely makes telephone calls wherein, after he dials the phone, he forgets who he's calling, so when somebody answers, Gene has to ask (a) who it is, and (b) does this person happen to know the purpose of the call.

- Another guy in my office, John, who appears to be a normal middle-aged 9 husband and father until you realize that he spends most of his waking hours managing a *pretend baseball team*. This is true. He and some other guys have formed a league where they pay actual money to "draft" major-league players, and then they have their pretend teams play a whole pretend season, complete with trades, legalistic memorandums, and heated disputes over the rules. This is crazy, right? If these guys said they were managing herds of pretend caribou,[7] the authorities would be squirting lithium[8] down their throats with turkey basters, right? And yet we all act like it's *perfectly normal*. In fact, eavesdropping from my office, I find myself getting involved in John's discussions. That's how pathetic I am: I'm capable of caring about a pretend sports team that's not even my own pretend sports team.

So I don't know about the rest of you guys, but I'm thinking it's time I got 10 some perspective in my life. First thing after the Super Bowl, I'm going to start paying more attention to the things that should matter to me, like my work, my friends, and above all my family, especially my little boy, Philadelphia Phillies Barry.

Discussion and Writing Questions

1. Barry often humorously exaggerates to make a point. Find several examples of exaggeration in his essay.

2. What details or points of the essay do you find particularly funny?

3. Why do you suppose Barry talks about Einstein, Lincoln, Plato, and Shakespeare in paragraph 4? Could he have chosen other famous men to make his point?

4. Do you think that "sports connect with something deeply rooted in the male psyche," as Barry states in paragraph 5? What is that "something"? What about the female psyche?

---

6. mastodons: prehistoric animals resembling elephants
7. caribou: a kind of Arctic deer
8. lithium: a drug used to treat mental illness

Writing Assignments

1. Fill in the blank in the following line. "Today, in our continuing series on How Gals Think, we explore the question:

   _____ ?"

   Then write a newspaper column exploring your topic. Be as humorous or as serious as you wish.

2. Reread Barry's description of his attempts at the long jump in paragraph 3. Then describe your own efforts in a sport you thought you might be good at but weren't.

3. Is there a sport you really like—either watching or playing? Describe your love of this sport, giving at least two reasons why the sport appeals to you. Your audience is a group of people who know little about this sport.

Desert Kin

Edward Abbey

Edward Abbey was a park ranger, environmentalist, and nature writer. Here he describes his encounters with animals in the desert that lead him to examine his own behavior and the connectedness of all living things.

I share the housetrailer with a number of mice. I don't know how many but apparently only a few, perhaps a single family. They don't disturb me and are welcome to my crumbs and leavings. Where they came from, how they got into the trailer, how they survived before my arrival (for the trailer had been locked up for six months), these are puzzling matters I am not prepared to resolve. My only reservation concerning the mice is that they do attract rattlesnakes. 1

I'm sitting on my doorstep early one morning, facing the sun as usual, drinking coffee, when I happen to look down and see almost between my bare feet, only a couple of inches to the rear of my heels, the very thing I had in mind. No mistaking that wedgelike head, that tip of horny segmented[1] tail peeping out of the coils. He's under the doorstep and in the shade where the ground and air remain very cold. In his sluggish condition he's not likely to strike unless I rouse him by some careless move of my own. 2

There's a revolver inside the trailer, a huge British Webley .45, loaded, but it's out of reach. Even if I had it in my hands I'd hesitate to blast a fellow creature at such close range, shooting between my own legs at a living target flat on solid rock thirty inches away. It would be like murder; and where would I set my coffee? My cherrywood walking stick leans against the trailerhouse wall only a few feet away, but I'm afraid that in leaning over for it I might stir up the rattler or spill some hot coffee on his scales. 3

Other considerations come to mind. Arches National Monument[2] is meant to be among other things a sanctuary[3] for wildlife—for all forms of wildlife. It is my duty as a park ranger to protect, preserve and defend all living things within the park boundaries, making no exceptions. Even if this were not the case I have personal convictions to uphold. Ideals, you might say. I prefer not to kill animals. . . . 4

_____

1. segmented: divided in sections
2. Arches National Monument: a park near Moab, Utah
3. sanctuary: an area where wildlife is protected

I finish my coffee, lean back and swing my feet up and inside the doorway 5 of the trailer. At once there is a buzzing sound from below and the rattler lifts his head from his coils, eyes brightening, and extends his narrow black tongue to test the air.

After thawing out my boots over the gas flame I pull them on and come 6 back to the doorway. My visitor is still waiting beneath the doorstep, basking in the sun, fully alert. The trailerhouse has two doors. I leave by the other and get a long-handled spade out of the bed of the government pickup. With this tool I scoop the snake into the open. He strikes. I can hear the click of the fangs against steel, see the stain of venom. He wants to stand and fight, but I am impatient; I insist on herding him well away from the trailer. On guard, head aloft—that evil slit-eyed weaving head shaped like the ace of spades—tail whirring, the rattler slithers sideways, retreating slowly before me until he reaches the shelter of a sandstone slab. He backs under it.

You better stay there, cousin, I warn him; if I catch you around the trailer 7 again I'll chop your head off.

A week later he comes back. If not him his twin brother. I spot him one 8 morning under the trailer near the kitchen drain, waiting for a mouse. I have to keep my promise.

This won't do. If there are midget rattlers in the area there may be dia- 9 mondbacks too—five, six or seven feet long, thick as a man's wrist, dangerous. I don't want them camping under my home. It looks as though I'll have to trap the mice.

However, before being forced to take that step I am lucky enough to cap- 10 ture a gopher snake. Burning garbage one morning at the park dump, I see a long slender yellow-brown snake emerge from a mound of old tin cans and plastic picnic plates and take off down the sandy bed of gulch. . . . The gopher snake, *Drymarchon corais couperi*, or bull snake, has a reputation as the enemy of rattlesnakes, destroying or driving them away whenever encountered.

Hoping to domesticate this sleek, handsome and docile[4] reptile, I release 11 him inside the trailerhouse and keep him there for several days. Should I attempt to feed him? I decide against it—let him eat mice. What little water he may need can also be extracted from the flesh of his prey.

The gopher snake and I get along nicely. During the day he curls up like a 12 cat in the warm corner behind the heater and at night he goes about his business. The mice, singularly quiet for a change, make themselves scarce. The snake is passive, apparently contented, and makes no resistance when I pick him up with my hands and drape him over an arm or around my neck. When I take him outside into the wind and sunshine his favorite place seems to be inside my shirt, where he wraps himself around my waist and rests on my belt. In this position he sometimes sticks his head out between shirt buttons for a survey of the weather, astonishing and delighting any tourists who may happen to be with me at the time. The scales of a snake are dry and smooth, quite pleasant to the touch. Being a cold blooded creature, of course, he takes his temperature from that of the immediate environment—in this case my body.

> "The two snakes come straight toward me, . . . the forked tongues flickering, their intense wild yellow eyes staring directly into my eyes."

We are compatible.[5] From my point of view, friends. After a week of close 13 association I turn him loose on the warm sandstone at my doorstep and leave for a patrol of the park. At noon when I return he is gone. I search everywhere beneath, nearby and inside the trailerhouse, but my companion has disappeared. Has he left the area entirely or is he hiding somewhere close by? At any rate I am troubled no more by rattlesnakes under the door.

The snake story is not yet ended. 14

---

4. docile: obedient
5. compatible: able to get along well together

In the middle of May, about a month after the gopher snake's disappear- 15
ance, in the evening of a very hot day, with all the rosy desert cooling like a
griddle with the fire turned off, he reappears. This time with a mate.

I'm in the stifling heat of the trailer opening a can of beer, barefooted, 16
about to go outside and relax after a hard day watching cloud formations. I
happen to glance out the little window near the refrigerator and see two gopher
snakes on my verandah[6] engaged in what seems to be a kind of ritual dance. . . .
A shameless *voyeur*,[7] I stare at the lovers, and then to get a closer view run outside and around the trailer to the back. There I get down on hands and knees
and creep toward the dancing snakes, not wanting to frighten or disturb them.
I crawl to within six feet of them and stop, flat on my belly, watching from the
snake's eye level. Obsessed with their ballet, the serpents seem unaware of my
presence. . . .

They intertwine and separate, glide side by side, . . . turn like mirror im- 17
ages of each other and glide back again, wind and unwind again. This is the
basic pattern but there is a variation: at regular intervals the snakes elevate their
heads, facing one another, as high as they can go, as if trying to outreach or
overawe the other. . . .

I crawl after them, determined to see the whole thing. Suddenly and si- 18
multaneously they discover me, prone[8] on my belly a few feet away. The dance
stops. After a moment's pause the two snakes come straight toward me, still in
flawless unison, straight toward my face, the forked tongues flickering, their intense wild yellow eyes staring directly into my eyes. For an instant I am para-
lyzed by wonder; then, stung by a fear too ancient and powerful to overcome I
scramble back, rising, to my knees. The snakes veer and turn away from me in
parallel motion, their lean elegant bodies making a soft hissing noise as they
slide over the sand and stone. I follow them for a short distance, still plagued by
curiosity, before remembering my place and the requirements of common courtesy. For godsake let them go in peace, I tell myself. Wish them luck and (if
lovers) innumerable offspring, a life of happily ever after. Not for their sake
alone but for your own.

In the long hot days and cool evenings to come I will not see the gopher 19
snakes again. Nevertheless I will feel their presence watching over me like . . .
deities,[9] keeping the rattlesnakes far back in the brush where I like them best,
cropping off the surplus mouse population, maintaining useful connections
with the primeval.[10] Sympathy, mutual aid, symbiosis,[11] continuity. . . .

We are obliged, therefore, to spread the news, painful and bitter though it 20
may be for some to hear, that all living things on hand are kindred.[12]

Discussion and Writing Questions

1. The first animals that the author mentions are mice. How does he feel about
   them (paragraph 1)?

2. Abbey has more than one reason for not killing the rattlesnake when he first
   sees it. What are they (paragraphs 3–4)? Does he later kill it (paragraphs
   7–8)? Why?

3. Abbey's relationship with the gopher snake is simple in the beginning and

---

6. verandah: porch
7. *voyeur*: someone who finds excitement in watching others
8. prone: lying down
9. deities: gods and goddesses
10. primeval: ancient
11. symbiosis: a relationship between participants who depend on each other
12. kindred: related to one another; relatives

then becomes more complicated. What are his feelings at first? What different emotions does he have as he watches the mating pair (paragraphs 16–18)? Did your feelings about snakes change as you read this essay?

4. What does Abbey mean when he says that "all living things on hand are kindred" (paragraph 20)? How does the whole selection lead up to this conclusion? Why does he say that this news may be "painful and bitter" for some to hear?

Writing Assignments

1. Have you ever felt especially connected to the natural world? Did a special place or experience make you feel that way? If so, describe the experience, including the setting.

2. Write to the owner of an apartment building that does not allow pets, and persuade him or her to change this policy. Support your argument by describing your own positive experience of owning a pet, or the experiences of others.

3. Observe an insect, a bird, or an animal very closely for a period of time. Take notes on its appearance, its activities, its relationships, if any. Is it a creature that many people dislike or want to kill—a roach, for instance? Describe this creature in detail, explaining whether your feelings changed as you watched it.

Perfume

Barbara Garson

Some people work year after year at dull, repetitive jobs. Why do they do it? How do they stand it? To find out, journalist Barbara Garson interviewed hundreds of workers for her book *All the Livelong Day*. Here, she visits a factory that makes beauty products.

Helena Rubenstein makes over two hundred products (if you count different colors). Here in F&F—filling and finishing—there are usually about two dozen lines working at once. Each line is tended by ten to twenty women in blue smocks who perform a single repeated operation on each powder compact, deodorant bottle or perfume spray as it goes past. . . .

There are about 250 blue-smocked women in filling and finishing. They are mostly white, mostly middle-aged, and mostly earning "second" incomes. But there's a peppering of black and Latin women in the room, one or two unmarried girls on each line, and an increasing number of young mothers who are the main support of their families. . . .

Herbescence is a relatively simple line. The lead lady takes the filled bottles of spray mist out of cartons and places one on each black dot marked on the moving belt. The next two women put little silver tags around the bottle necks. Each one tags every other bottle. The next nine women each fold a protective corrugated cardboard, unfold a silver box, pick up every ninth spray-mist bottle, slip it into the corrugation, insert a leaflet, put the whole thing into the box and close the top. The next seven ladies wrap the silver Herbescence boxes in colored tissue paper. The women don't actually have to count every seventh box because, as a rule, when you finish the twists and folds of your tissue paper, your next box is just coming along with perhaps a half second to relax before you reach for it. The tissue-papered boxes are put into cartons which in turn are lifted onto skids[1] which, when filled with several thousand spray colognes, will be wheeled out by general factory help or skid boys.

Since the line doesn't involve any filling machines, it was a bit quieter at Herbescence. The women didn't have to shout. They could just talk loudly to each other and to me. 4

"You writing a book about cosmetics?" . . . "About Helena's?" . . . And then with greater disbelief: "About these jobs?" . . . "About *us?*" 5

Then I got my instructions. 6

"Write down how hard we work." 7

"How boring." 8

"You ought to come back here on a nice hot summer day. They got air conditioning upstairs in lipsticks but it's not for the women. Don't let 'em hand you a line. It's just 'cause the lipsticks might melt." 9

"Write about how fast the lines are now. It used to be a pleasure to work here. Now you can't keep up. They keep getting faster." 10

"Write about the new supervisors. Why should they treat you like dirt just because you work in a factory?" 11

"Be sure to say how boring." 12

> "After four minutes, or about two hundred bottles, the effects of the break seemed to be wearing off."

Some twenty years ago, before all the talk about job enrichment, Local 8–149 fought for the right to rotate positions on the assembly line. Now the women change places every two hours. In addition the entire crew of certain particularly unpleasant lines is rotated every three days. 13

"Not that one job is so much different from another," said Dick McManus, local union president, "but at least the women get to move around. They sit next to different women. They get to have different conversations." 14

Maxine Claybourne, a fortyish, flourishing, light yellow black woman, was the new leading lady of the Herbescence line. Since the break she had been putting the bottles out one on each black line. After four minutes, or about two hundred bottles, the effects of the break seemed to be wearing off. Eyes were hypnotized, hands reached heavily for the boxes, bottles, wrapping paper and tags. 15

"Here's a gift, girls," Maxine announced. She took a comb out of her pocket and, between every self-confident stroke, set a bottle down on the belt. They came out neatly on every *other* black dot. 16

Gradually the gift was carried down the line. "This is beautiful," said the boxers as the farther-spaced bottles arrived. "Thanks, Max." Then after a minute it reached the wrappers. "This is how it should always be." And finally: "It used to be this way when I first started here," said the woman filling cartons at the end. 17

And then, without any noticeable shift, Maxine began putting the bottles on every dot again. 18

"I can do things like that," she told me, "when the supervisor moves away. When he comes back . . . [and she cast her eyes in the direction of the man I had not seen approaching] well, at least the girls get to enjoy a little break. One way or another, you got to get through the day." 19

The line settled down to its old pace again. I left Maxine and headed down to the other end. 20

"I started here," a woman said, answering my question, "to send my kids to college, but they're all grown up now." 21

---

1. skids: platforms for stacking and moving heavy items

"That's what I did, " said the woman next to her. "First you put your kids 22 through school, then you start to pay for a car, then it's new rugs, and before you know it—I'm here fifteen years."

The women nodded. That seemed to be the story for the second-income 23 workers.

A young black woman who hadn't said a word till then muttered sullenly, 24 "Some of us are here to pay for the rent, not buy rugs."

The older women went on. Perhaps they didn't hear her. 25

"And then you stay because of the other girls." 26

"Yeah, you stay to keep up with the gossip." 27

"And there's self-improvement here. You come to work every day, you get 28 more conscious of your clothes, your hair."

"Real self-improvement," a woman objected. "You should hear the lan- 29 guage I pick up. My husband says, 'The language you use, you sound like you work in a factory.' "

The most important benefit from the past struggles in this factory, and 30 from the impartial rotation systems, has no official recognition. There is no clause in the contract that says the workers shall have the right to laugh, talk and be helpful to one another. Nor is there a formal guarantee that the workers can shrug, sneer or otherwise indicate what they think of the supervisors.

But most of the women at Helena Rubenstein are helpful to each other and 31 they present a solid front to the supervisors.

The right to respond like a person, even while your hands are operating 32 like a machine, is something that has been fought for in this factory. And this is defended daily, formally through the grievance process and informally through militant kidding around.

I spent my last hour at Helena Rubenstein back at the Herbescence line, 33 watching hands reach for piece after piece until my own eyes grew glazed and my head throbbed with each bottle that jerked past. And yet, when I looked up it was only four minutes later. I forced myself to stay for a full twenty minutes; then I finally blurted out, "How do you do it seven hours a day?"

"You don't do it seven hours a day," was the answer. "You just do it one 34 piece at a time."

Discussion and Writing Questions

1. Describe the process by which a perfume bottle is packaged on the Herbescence perfume spray assembly line.

2. What reasons do the workers give for working on the line? Why do some of them stay so long if they do not enjoy their work?

3. What "gift" does Maxine Claybourne give her coworkers?

4. Which would you prefer: a boring, high-paying job or an interesting, low-paying job? Why?

Writing Assignments

1. Have you ever worked at a dull, repetitious job? Describe step by step what the job involved and your reaction to it, so that the reader can experience it as you did. Did you do anything to make the job more pleasant or interesting? What?

2. "Most of us, like the assembly line worker, have jobs that are too small for our spirit," says Nora Watson in Studs Terkel's book *Working.* What do you think she means by this? Do you agree? Describe a job that would be "big enough for your spirit."

3. Some people believe that a positive attitude can make even the most boring job interesting. Agree or disagree, using examples from your own or others' experience.

Discovery of a Father

Sherwood Anderson

Children sometimes find it hard to understand and accept a parent's behavior. In this selection, classic American author Sherwood Anderson recalls the night he stopped blaming his father and discovered the bond between them.

You hear it said that fathers want their sons to be what they feel they cannot themselves be, but I tell you it also works the other way. A boy wants something very special from his father. I know that as a small boy I wanted my father to be a certain thing he was not. I wanted him to be a proud, silent, dignified father. When I was with the other boys and he passed along the street, I wanted to feel a flow of pride. "There he is. That is my father." 1

But he wasn't such a one. He couldn't be. It seemed to me then that he was always showing off. Let's say someone in our town had got up a show. They were always doing it. The druggist would be in it, the shoe-store clerk, the horse doctor, and a lot of women and girls. My father would manage to get the chief comedy part. It was, let's say, a Civil War play and he was a comic Irish soldier. He had to do the most absurd things. They thought he was funny, but I didn't. 2

I thought he was terrible. I didn't see how mother could stand it. She even laughed with the others. Maybe I would have laughed if it hadn't been my father. 3

Or there was a parade, the Fourth of July or Decoration Day. He'd be in that, too, right at the front of it, as Grand Marshal or something, on a white horse hired from a livery stable. 4

He couldn't ride for shucks. He fell off the horse and everyone hooted with laughter, but he didn't care. He even seemed to like it. I remember once when he had done something ridiculous, and right out on Main Street, too. I was with some other boys and they were laughing and shouting at him and he was shouting back and having as good a time as they were. I ran down an alley back of some stores and there in the Presbyterian Church sheds I had a good long cry. 5

Or I would be in bed at night and father would come home a little lit up and bring some men with him. He was a man who was never alone. Before he went broke, running a harness shop, there were always a lot of men loafing in the shop. He went broke, of course, because he gave too much credit. He couldn't refuse it and I thought he was a fool. I had got to hating him. 6

There'd be men I didn't think would want to be fooling around with him. There might even be the superintendent of our schools and a quiet man who ran the hardware store. Once I remember there was a white-haired man who was a cashier of the bank. It was a wonder to me they'd want to be seen with such a windbag. That's what I thought he was. I know now what it was that attracted them. It was because life in our town, as in all small towns, was at times pretty dull and he livened it up. He made them laugh. He could tell stories. He'd even get them to singing. 7

If they didn't come to our house they'd go off, say at night, to where there was a grassy place by a creek. They'd cook food there and drink beer and sit about listening to his stories. 8

He was always telling stories about himself. He'd say this or that 9 wonderful thing had happened to him. It might be something that made him look like a fool. He didn't care.

If an Irishman came to our house, right away father would say he was 10
Irish. He'd tell what county in Ireland he was born in. He'd tell things that happened there when he was a boy. He'd make it seem so real that, if I hadn't known he was born in southern Ohio, I'd have believed him myself.

If it was a Scotchman the same thing happened. He'd get a burr[1] into his 11
speech. Or he was a German or a Swede. He'd be anything the other man was. I think they all knew he was lying, but they seemed to like him just the same. As a boy that was what I couldn't understand.

And there was mother. How could she stand it? I wanted to ask but never 12
did. She was not the kind you asked such questions.

I'd be upstairs in my bed, in my room above the porch, and father would 13
be telling some of his tales. A lot of father's stories were about the Civil War. To hear him tell it he'd been in about every battle. He'd known Grant, Sherman, Sheridan[2] and I don't know how many others. He'd been particularly intimate with General Grant so that when Grant went East to take charge of all the armies, he took father along.

"I was an orderly at headquarters and Sim Grant said to me, 'Irve,' he said, 14
'I'm going to take you along with me.'"

It seems he and Grant used to slip off sometimes and have a quiet drink to- 15
gether. That's what my father said. He'd tell about the day Lee surrendered and how, when the great moment came, they couldn't find Grant.

"You know," my father said, "about General Grant's book, his memoirs. 16
You've read of how he said he had a headache and how when he got word that Lee was ready to call it quits, he was suddenly and miraculously cured.

"Huh," said father. "He was in the woods with me. 17

"I was in there with my back against a tree. I was pretty well corned.[3] I had 18
got hold of a bottle of pretty good stuff.

"They were looking for Grant. He had got off his horse and come into the 19
woods. He found me. He was covered with mud.

"I had the bottle in my hand. What'd I care? The war was over. I knew we 20
had them licked."

My father said that he was the one who told Grant about Lee. An orderly 21
riding by had told him, because the orderly knew how thick he was with Grant. Grant was embarrassed.

"But, Irve, look at me. I'm all covered with mud," he said to father. 22

And then, my father said, he and Grant decided to have a drink together. 23
They took a couple of shots and then, because he didn't want Grant to show up potted before the immaculate Lee, he smashed the bottle against the tree.

"Sim Grant's dead now and I wouldn't want it to get out on him," my fa- 24
ther said.

That's just one of the kind of things he'd tell. Of course the men knew he 25
was lying, but they seemed to like it just the same.

When we got broke, down and out, do you think he ever brought anything 26
home? Not he. If there wasn't anything to eat in the house, he'd go off visiting around at farmhouses. They all wanted him. Sometimes he'd stay away for weeks, mother working to keep us fed; and then home he'd come bringing, let's say, a ham. He'd got it from some farmer friend. He'd slap it on the table in the kitchen. "You bet I'm going to see that my kids have something to eat," he'd say, and mother would just stand smiling at him. She'd never say a word about all the weeks and months he'd been away, not leaving us a cent for food. Once I

> "Life in our town . . . was at times pretty dull and he livened it up. He made them laugh. He could tell stories."

---

1. burr: sound of a Scottish accent
2. Grant, Sherman, Sheridan: great Civil War generals
3. corned: drunk on corn whiskey

© 1998 Houghton Mifflin Company

heard her speaking to a woman in our street. Maybe the woman had dared to sympathize with her. "Oh," she said, "it's all right. He isn't dull like most of the men in this street. Life is never dull when my man is about."

But often I was filled with bitterness, and sometimes I wished he wasn't **27** my father. I'd even invent another man as my father. To protect my mother I'd make up stories of a secret marriage that for some strange reason never got known. As though some man, say the president of a railroad company or maybe a Congressman, had married my mother, thinking his wife was dead and then it turned out she wasn't.

So they had to hush it up but I got born just the same. I wasn't really the **28** son of my father. Somewhere in the world there was a very dignified, quite wonderful man who was really my father. I even made myself half believe these fancies.

And then there came a certain night. He'd been off somewhere for two or **29** three weeks. He found me alone in the house, reading by the kitchen table.

It had been raining and he was very wet. He sat and looked at me for a **30** long time, not saying a word. I was startled, for there was on his face the saddest look I had ever seen. He sat for a time, his clothes dripping. Then he got up.

"Come on with me," he said. **31**

I got up and went with him out of the house. I was filled with wonder but **32** I wasn't afraid. We went along a dirt road that led down into a valley, about a mile out of town, where there was a pond. We walked in silence. The man who was always talking had stopped his talking.

I didn't know what was up and had the queer feeling that I was with a **33** stranger. I don't know whether my father intended it so. I don't think he did.

The pond was quite large. It was still raining hard and there were flashes **34** of lightning followed by thunder. We were on a grassy bank at the pond's edge when my father spoke, and in the darkness and rain his voice sounded strange.

"Take off your clothes," he said. Still filled with wonder, I began to un- **35** dress. There was a flash of lightning and I saw that he was already naked.

Naked, we went into the pond. Taking my hand he pulled me in. It may be **36** that I was too frightened, too full of a feeling of strangeness, to speak. Before that night my father had never seemed to pay any attention to me.

"And what is he up to now?" I kept asking myself. I did not swim very **37** well, but he put my hand on his shoulder and struck out into the darkness.

He was a man with big shoulders, a powerful swimmer. In the darkness I **38** could feel the movement of his muscles. We swam to the far edge of the pond and then back to where we had left our clothes. The rain continued and the wind blew. Sometimes my father swam on his back and when he did he took my hand in his large powerful one and moved it over so that it rested always on his shoulder. Sometimes there would be a flash of lightning and I could see his face quite clearly.

It was as it was earlier, in the kitchen, a face filled with sadness. There **39** would be the momentary glimpse of his face and then again the darkness, the wind and the rain. In me there was a feeling I had never known before.

It was a feeling of closeness. It was something strange. It was as though **40** there were only we two in the world. It was as though I had been jerked suddenly out of myself, out of my world of the schoolboy, out of a world in which I was ashamed of my father.

He had become blood of my blood; he the strong swimmer and I the boy **41** clinging to him in the darkness. We swam in silence and in silence we dressed in our wet clothes, and went home.

There was a lamp lighted in the kitchen and when we came in, the water **42** dripping from us, there was my mother. She smiled at us. I remember that she called us "boys."

"What have you boys been up to?" she asked, but my father did not an- **43** swer. As he had begun the evening's experience with me in silence, so he ended it. He turned and looked at me. Then he went, I thought, with a new and strange dignity out of the room.

I climbed the stairs to my own room, undressed in the darkness and got **44** into bed. I couldn't sleep and did not want to sleep. For the first time I knew that I was the son of my father. He was a story teller as I was to be. It may be that I even laughed a little softly there in the darkness. If I did, I laughed knowing that I would never again be wanting another father.

Discussion and Writing Questions

1. In what ways was Anderson's father a disappointing or even a bad father and husband? What role do you think his drinking played in his behavior?

2. Anderson says that one night he saw on his father's face "the saddest look I had ever seen" (paragraph 30). Why do you think Anderson's father looked—and felt—so sad?

3. Why did the swimming incident change the relationship between the author and his father? How did their relationship change?

4. At the end of this selection, Anderson recognizes his similarities to his father (paragraph 44). What are these similarities?

Writing Assignments

1. Anderson says that "a boy wants something very special from his father" (paragraph 1). Is this true? What did you, as a boy or as a girl, want from your father? Did you get it?

2. Have you ever been embarrassed by the behavior of your parent (or guardian)? How did that person act? Why did you feel embarrassed? Perhaps choose one incident that reveals his or her behavior and your response. Did you ever discuss the incident with the person involved?

3. Have you ever come to see a person differently? What changed your mind—or your heart? Describe your impressions of this person before and after the change. In what ways did your relationship with that person also change as a result?

Four Directions

Amy Tan

Have you ever possessed a certain skill or strength, and then, as you grew, lost it? Amy Tan, a Chinese-American novelist who lives in San Francisco, writes about a young chess player who seemed unbeatable—at age ten.

I was ten years old. Even though I was young, I knew my ability to play chess **1** was a gift. It was effortless, so easy. I could see things on the chessboard that other people could not. I could create barriers to protect myself that were invisible to my opponents. And this gift gave me supreme confidence. I knew at exactly what point their faces would fall when my seemingly simple and childlike strategy would reveal itself as a devastating and irrevocable[1] course. I loved to win.

_____

1. irrevocable: impossible to cancel or halt

© 1998 Houghton Mifflin Company

And my mother loved to show me off, like one of my many trophies she ² polished. She used to discuss my games as if she had devised the strategies.

"I told my daughter, Use your horses to run over the enemy," she in- ³ formed one shopkeeper. "She won very quickly this way." And of course, she had said this before the game—that and a hundred other useless things that had nothing to do with my winning.

To our family friends who visited she would confide, "You don't have to ⁴ be so smart to win chess. It is just tricks. You blow from the North, South, East, and West. The other person becomes confused. They don't know which way to run."

I hated the way she tried to take all the credit. And one day I told her so, ⁵ shouting at her on Stockton Street, in the middle of a crowd of people. I told her she didn't know anything, so she shouldn't show off. She should shut up. Words to that effect.

That evening and the next day she wouldn't speak to me. She would say ⁶ stiff words to my father and brothers, as if I had become invisible and she was talking about a rotten fish she had thrown away but which had left behind its bad smell.

I knew this strategy, the sneaky way to get someone to pounce back in ⁷ anger and fall into a trap. So I ignored her. I refused to speak and waited for her to come to me.

After many days had gone by in silence, I sat in my room, staring at the ⁸ sixty-four squares of my chessboard, trying to think of another way. And that's when I decided to quit playing chess.

> "I could no longer see the secret weapons of each piece, the magic within the intersection of each square."

Of course I didn't mean to quit forever. At most, just for a few days. And I ⁹ made a show of it. Instead of practicing in my room every night, as I always did, I marched into the living room and sat down in front of the television with my brothers, who stared at me, an unwelcome intruder. I used my brothers to further my plan; I cracked my knuckles to annoy them.

"Ma!" they shouted. "Make her stop. Make her go away." ¹⁰

But my mother did not say anything. ¹¹

Still I was not worried. But I could see I would have to make a stronger ¹² move. I decided to sacrifice a tournament that was coming up in one week. I would refuse to play in it. And my mother would certainly have to speak to me about this. Because the sponsors and the benevolent associations² would start calling her, asking, shouting, pleading to make me play again.

And then the tournament came and went. And she did not come to me, ¹³ crying, "Why are you not playing chess?" But I was crying inside, because I learned that a boy whom I had easily defeated on two other occasions had won.

I realized my mother knew more tricks than I had thought. But now I was ¹⁴ tired of her game. I wanted to start practicing for the next tournament. So I decided to pretend to let her win. I would be the one to speak first.

"I am ready to play chess again," I announced to her. I had imagined she ¹⁵ would smile and then ask me what special thing I wanted to eat.

But instead, she gathered her face into a frown and stared into my eyes, as ¹⁶ if she could force some kind of truth out of me.

"Why do you tell me this?" she finally said in sharp tones. "You think it is ¹⁷ so easy. One day quit, next day play. Everything for you is this way. So smart, so easy, so fast."

"I said I'll play," I whined. ¹⁸

"No!" she shouted, and I almost jumped out of my scalp. "It is not so easy ¹⁹ anymore."

I was quivering, stunned by what she said, in not knowing what she ²⁰ meant. And then I went back to my room. I stared at my chessboard, its

---

2. benevolent associations: charities

sixty-four squares, to figure out how to undo this terrible mess. And after staring like this for many hours, I actually believed that I had made the white squares black and the black squares white, and everything would be all right.

And sure enough, I won her back. That night I developed a high fever, and she sat next to my bed, scolding me for going to school without my sweater. In the morning she was there as well, feeding me rice porridge flavored with chicken broth she had strained herself. She said she was feeding me this because I had the chicken pox and one chicken knew how to fight another. And in the afternoon, she sat in a chair in my room, knitting me a pink sweater while telling me about a sweater that Auntie Suyuan had knit for her daughter June, and how it was most unattractive and of the worst yarn. I was so happy that she had become her usual self.

But after I got well, I discovered that, really, my mother had changed. She no longer hovered over[3] me as I practiced different chess games. She did not polish my trophies every day. She did not cut out the small newspaper item that mentioned my name. It was as if she had erected[4] an invisible wall and I was secretly groping each day to see how high and how wide it was.

At my next tournment, while I had done well overall, in the end the points were not enough. I lost. And what was worse, my mother said nothing. She seemed to walk around with this satisfied look, as if it had happened because she had devised this strategy.

I was horrified. I spent many hours every day going over in my mind what I had lost. I knew it was not just the last tournament. I examined every move, every piece, every square. And I could no longer see the secret weapons of each piece, the magic within the intersection of each square. I could see only my mistakes, my weaknesses. It was as though I had lost my magic armor. And everybody could see this, where it was easy to attack me.

Over the next few weeks and later months and years, I continued to play, but never with that same feeling of supreme confidence. I fought hard, with fear and desperation. When I won, I was grateful, relieved. And when I lost, I was filled with growing dread, and then terror that I was no longer a prodigy,[5] that I had lost the gift and had turned into someone quite ordinary.

When I lost twice to the boy whom I had defeated so easily a few years before, I stopped playing chess altogether. And nobody protested. I was fourteen.

Discussion and Writing Questions

1. Why did the child and her mother fight? Do you think the mother really wanted "all the credit" for herself (paragraph 5)? Why did she refuse to speak to the child after their argument?

2. The mother and daughter almost seem locked in a chess match of their own after their argument. What do you think is happening between them? Does the daughter's age—adolescence—have anything to do with it?

3. Why do you suppose the author says she had lost more than the last tournament, she had lost her "magic armor" (paragraph 24)?

4. The author says that "nobody protested" when she gave up chess permanently at age fourteen (paragraph 26). Do you think people might have protested if she were a boy? Why or why not?

---

3. hovered over: paid close attention to
4. erected: built
5. prodigy: a person with enormous talents in a particular area

Writing Assignments

1. Did you possess a talent or strength as a young person that you later lost? What happened? What caused you to change?

2. Adolescence is for most people a time of enormous change, and change often produces great anxiety. Was there an incident in your adolescence that caused you such anxiety—because you or your surroundings were somehow changing? Describe this incident.

3. Research suggests that once they reach adolescence, many girls give up asserting themselves—in sports, in class, and in student government, for example—because they feel pressure to be "feminine." Do you think this is true? Discuss why or why not, using yourself or a young woman you know as an example.

For a Parent, There's No Language Dilemma

Ana Veciana-Suarez

The issue of bilingual education—the teaching of two languages in the public schools—has become an increasingly sensitive one in recent years. Some argue for the practice; others oppose it. In a recent issue of *The Miami Herald*, a concerned parent argues that two languages are better than one.

My son Christopher cannot roll his R's.[1]   1

I realize that on the seismic[2] chart of development this does not rate as   2
high as a diagnosis of dyslexia,[3] but in my book of milestones it falls squarely between not being able to tie your shoelaces and repeated fighting with classmates.

In increasingly Latin Miami, rolling R's is a survival skill. In Christopher's   3
future world, it will mean more money and better opportunities. It will allow him to communicate with his many older relatives, to connect with the culture of his heritage.

Having lived most of his life in Palm Beach County, Christopher can   4
barely speak Spanish. He understands most everything especially if the conversation has to do with food or play. But ask him to complete a sentence or answer a question and his eyes grow wide and blank. He hesitates. His tongue proves to be as stubborn as a pack mule at the foot of a hill.

This causes him much stress, and it mortifies[4] me. I'm the one to blame.   5
From the beginning, when he babbled his first words, I should have insisted on Spanish because eventually he would have learned, and preferred, English.

As a daughter of Cuban exiles, I grew up speaking Spanish at home. I   6
learned to read and write it. At one time, the rules of where to place the accents were second nature when I put pen to paper. No more. I make my living in English, and English is the language that comes more easily. This saddens me. I am losing an important and valuable part of my personal history.

Not everyone feels this way. In fact, language is a volatile[5] issue in South   7
Florida. It is the red flag that separates the "us" from "them," the rallying cry for those who feel that immigrants must melt in, not stay apart.

---

1. roll his R's: pronounce the letter R like a native speaker of Spanish
2. seismic: like an earthquake
3. dyslexia: a reading disorder
4. mortifies: badly embarrasses
5. volatile: explosive

Spanish and English signs mingle on this American street (© Rob Tringali/SPORTSCHROME)

I know both sides of the language argument. I've heard those complaints 8 from strangers as well as from those close and dear to my heart. A childhood friend, who moved north when she felt she could not compete in a job market that often required Spanish as well as English, confided that she wasn't sure people like me, people not willing to give up that part of their identity, would ever be American enough. These were not words of hate; they were of love and concern.

As a kid, I knew a few children in the neighborhood who spoke broken 9 Spanish, accented and irregular. They were teased and labeled "cubanos arrepentidos," which loosely translates into regretful Cubans.

My children, I vowed, would not grow up to be like them. They would 10 speak both languages fluently and, because I'm such a stickler for grammar, they would also learn them correctly.

But I have failed, and now the urgency of making up for lost years has be- 11 come as important for cultural reasons as economic and emotional ones. I want them to be able to speak to their grandparents as freely as they do with their neighbors. I want them to have an edge in what is quickly becoming a global village.

The two older ones, exposed to Spanish for a longer period, speak it well 12 enough to be acceptable. Their trouble lies in pronunciation and verb tenses.

But until our return to Miami, Christopher had spent more than half of his 13 seven years in a place where no one spoke Spanish. His exposure was limited to

> "From the beginning, when he babbled his first words, I should have insisted on Spanish."

periodic visits with grandparents, when the communication between them was an odd amalgam[6] of sign language and Spanglish.[7]

Not so long ago in school a teacher read a story with a few words in Spanish. He was the only child able to translate those words for the rest of the class. He came home triumphant and demanding. He wanted to know more. **14**

So now almost every night before bed, we sit together to make our way through an ancient reader his father's grandmother mailed page by page from Cuba in the early 1960s. **15**

"Va, ve, vi, vo, vu," he repeats after me. "Una uva. Una uva en la mesa." **16**

After the first lessons, the oldest two asked to read, too. "But not from a baby book," insisted the 10-year-old. "A real book." We got a real book. **17**

Together we have begun a lifelong journey into a place whose doors open only when the R's are rolling. This is where history takes on a face and a name, where lilt[8] and inflection[9] suggest identity, culture, an unusual past that enriches and assures a hopeful future. **18**

We are learning to double our L's and squiggle the top of our N's. We are learning from where we have come and where we are going, and perhaps more importantly, why the two cannot be separated. **19**

I know that their lives, like mine, will sometimes appear fractured. "What do you dream in?" a boss once asked me. "Depends," I answered. **20**

Their lives, like mine, will grow into a duality[10] of more than language, and they will be better for it. Rest assured, it will not make them any less American. **21**

Discussion and Writing Questions

1. What reasons does Veciana-Suarez offer for wanting her boys to speak Spanish as well as English?

2. The author speaks of "us" and "them" (paragraph 7). What does she mean by these terms?

3. Why does the author discuss her own experiences with two languages (paragraphs 6 and 9)?

4. Why did Christopher suddenly want to learn more Spanish after he translated Spanish words for his class at school (paragraphs 14–15)? What changed his attitude?

Writing Assignments

1. Write about an aspect of your own cultural, racial, ethnic, or religious background that makes you proud, that you don't want to lose. Do you feel, like the author, that you can hold on to this identity and still be American?

2. Do you speak a language other than English at home? If so, describe where and how you learned, or are learning, English. If English is your first language, have you tried to learn a second? If you have, describe your experience.

3. Can the United States continue to be called the "melting pot" if people speak a language other than English at school or at work? Why or why not? Argue for one side of this issue or the other, or, if you prefer, discuss both sides.

---

6. amalgam: mixture
7. Spanglish: a mixture of Spanish and English
8. lilt: lightness in the voice
9. inflection: change in pitch or tone when speaking
10. duality: having two parts or sides

Quotation Bank

This collection of wise and humorous statements has been assembled for you to read, enjoy, and use in a variety of ways as you write. You might choose ones that you particularly agree or disagree with and use them as the basis of journal entries and writing assignments. Sometimes when writing a paragraph or essay, you may find it useful to include a quotation to support a point you are making. Or you may simply want to read through these quotations for ideas and for fun. As you come across other intriguing statements by writers, add them to the list—or write some of your own.

Writing

Writing, like life itself, is a voyage of discovery. 1
—*Henry Miller*

Writing is the hardest work in the world not involving heavy lifting. 2
—*Pete Hamill*

I think best with a pencil in my hand. 3
—*Anne Morrow Lindbergh*

I write to discover what I think. 4
—*Daniel J. Boorstin*

I see but one rule: to be clear. If I am not clear, all my world crumbles to 5
nothing.
—*Marie Henri Beyle Stendhal*

To me, the greatest pleasure of writing is not what it's about, but the inner 6
music that words make.
—*Truman Capote*

Writing is the only thing that when I do it, I don't feel I should be doing some- 7
thing else.
—*Gloria Steinem*

I never travel without my diary. One should always have something sensa- 8
tional to read on the train.
—*Oscar Wilde*

Nothing quite new is perfect. 9
—*Cicero*

A professional writer is an amateur who didn't quit. 10
—*Richard Bach*

Learning

I could walk twenty miles to listen to my worst enemy if I could learn some- 11
thing.
—*Gottfried Wilhelm von Leibnitz*

The mind is a mansion, but most of the time we are content to live in the lobby. 12
—*Dr. William Michaels*

Education is . . . hanging around until you've caught on. 13
—*Robert Frost*

Prejudices, it is well known, are most difficult to eradicate [remove] from the 14
heart whose soil has never been loosened or fertilized by education; they grow
there, firm as weeds among stones.
—*Charlotte Brontë*

Many receive advice; few profit from it. 15
—*Publius*

Pay attention to what they tell you to forget. 16
—*Muriel Rukeyser*

Education is what you have left over after you have forgotten everything you 17
have learned.
—*Anonymous*

Only the educated are free. 18
—*Epictetus*

The basic purpose of a liberal arts education is to liberate the human being to 19
exercise his or her potential to the fullest.
—*Barbara M. White*

All things are possible to him [or her] who believes. 20
—*Brother Lawrence*

Love

Love consists in this: that two solitudes protect and touch and greet each other. 21
—*Rainer Maria Rilke*

To love and to be loved is to feel the sun from both sides. 22
—*David Viscott*

So often when we say "I love you," we say it with a huge "I" and a small "you." 23
—*Archbishop Antony*

Choose your life's mate carefully. From this one decision will come ninety per- 24
cent of all your happiness or misery.
—*H. Jackson Browne, Jr.*

Marriage is our last, best chance to grow up. 25
—*Joseph Barth*

A divorce is like an amputation; you survive, but there's less of you. 26
—*Margaret Atwood*

No partner in a love relationship should feel that she [or he] has to give up an 27
essential part of herself [or himself] to make it viable [workable].
—*May Sarton*

I can't mate in captivity.
—*Gloria Steinem*

28

Gold and love affairs are difficult to hide.
—*Spanish proverb*

29

Love doesn't just sit there, like a stone; it has to be made, like bread, remade all the time, made new.
—*Ursala K. Le Guin*

30

To be loved, be lovable.
—*Ovid*

31

Work and Success

The best career advice to give the young is, find out what you like doing best and get someone to pay you for doing it.
—*Katherine Whilehaen*

32

Can anybody remember when times were not hard and money not scarce?
—*Ralph Waldo Emerson*

33

Nothing great was ever achieved without enthusiasm.
—*Ralph Waldo Emerson*

34

There are two things to aim at in life: first, to get what you want and, after that, to enjoy it. Only the wisest . . . achieve the second.
—*Logan Pearsall Smith*

35

Money is like manure. If you spread it around, it does a lot of good, but if you pile it up in one place, it stinks like hell.
—*Clint W. Murchison*

36

If you have built castles in the air, your work need not be lost; that is where they should be. Now put foundations under them.
— *Henry David Thoreau*

37

It is never too late to be what you might have been.
—*George Eliot*

38

A celebrity is a person who works hard all his [or her] life to become well known, then wears dark glasses to avoid being recognized.
—*Fred Allen*

39

I think most of us are looking for a calling, not a job. Most of us, like the assembly line worker, have had jobs that are too small for our spirit.
—*Nora Watson*

40

The secret of joy in work is contained in one word—excellence. To know how to do something well is to enjoy it.
—*Pearl Buck*

41

A good reputation is more valuable than money.
—*Publius*

42

Very little is needed to make a happy life. 43
—*Marcus Aurelius Antoninus*

When you reach for the stars, you may not quite get one, but you won't come 44
up with a handful of mud.
— *Leo Burnett*

Family and Friendship

Making the decision to have a child—it's momentous. It is to decide forever to 45
have your heart go walking around outside your body.
—*Elizabeth Stone*

Any mother could perform the jobs of several air-traffic controllers with ease. 46
—*Lisa Alther*

Familiarity breeds contempt.— *Aesop;* 47

—and children.—*Mark Twain* 48

It takes a village to raise a child. 49
—*African proverb*

Nobody who has not been in the interior of a family can say what the difficul- 50
ties of any individual of that family may be.
—*Jane Austen*

If there is anything that we wish to change in the child, we should first ex- 51
amine it and see whether it is not something that could better be changed in
ourselves.
—*Carl Jung*

Insanity is hereditary—you get it from your children. 52
—*Sam Levenson*

Govern a family as you would fry small fish—gently. 53
—*Chinese proverb*

Everything that irritates us about others can lead us to an understanding of 54
ourselves.
—*Morton Hunt*

The meeting of two personalities is like the contact of two chemical sub- 55
stances: if there is any reaction, both are transformed.
—*Carl Jung*

The only way to have a friend is to be one. 56
—*Ralph Waldo Emerson*

Wisdom for Living

It is not easy to find happiness in ourselves, and it is not possible to find it 57
elsewhere.
—*Agnes Repplier*

Seize the day; put no trust in the morrow.   58
—*Horace*

Don't be afraid your life will end; be afraid that it will never begin.   59
—*Grace Hansen*

My life, my *real* life, was in danger, and not from anything other people might   60
do but from the hatred I carried in my own heart.
—*James Baldwin*

No one can make you feel inferior without your consent.   61
—*Eleanor Roosevelt*

Life is under no obligation to give us what we expect.   62
—*Margaret Mitchell*

What we anticipate seldom occurs; what we least expect generally happens.   63
—*Benjamin Disraeli*

Take your life in your own hands and what happens? A terrible thing: no one   64
to blame.
— *Erica Jong*

Regret is an appalling waste of energy: you can't build on it; it is good only for   65
wallowing in.
—*Katherine Mansfield*

Grief dares us to love once more.   66
—*Terry Tempest Williams*

Flowers grow out of dark moments.   67
—*Corita Kent*

Lying is done with words and also with silence.   68
—*Adrienne Rich*

Pick battles big enough to matter, small enough to win.   69
—*Jonathan Kozol*

You can't hold a man [or a woman] down without staying down with him   70
[or her].
—*Booker T. Washington*

A fanatic is one who can't change his [or her] mind and won't change the   71
subject.
—*Winston Churchill*

To me, old age is always fifteen years older than I am.   72
—*Bernard Baruch*

Time wounds all heels.   73
—*Jane Ace*

When you come to a fork in the road, take it.   74
—*Yogi Berra*

Acknowledgments

Pages 406–407—"Women Are Missing from Newspaper Pages" by Ellen Goodman. Copyright © 1985, *Washington Post* Writer's Group. Reprinted with permission.

Pages 407–410—"A Homemade Education" from *The Autobiography of Malcolm X* by Malcolm X, with Alex Haley. Copyright © 1964 by Alex Haley and Malcolm X. Copyright © 1965 by Alex Haley and Betty Shabazz. Reprinted by permission of Random House, Inc.

Pages 410–413—"Mrs. Flowers" from *I Know Why the Caged Bird Sings* by Maya Angelou. Copyright © 1969 by Maya Angelou. Reprinted by permission of Random House, Inc.

Pages 413–414—"The First Read" from *Parent & Child*, Sept. Oct. 1994 issue by David Goddy. Copyright © 1994 by Scholastic Inc. Reprinted by permission of Scholastic Inc.

Pages 415–417—"Papa, the Teacher" from *Papa, My Father* by Leo F. Buscaglia, Ph.D. Copyright © 1989, by Leo F. Buscaglia, Inc. Published by Slack, Inc.

Pages 417–419—"Forever" from *Married People: Staying Together in the Age of Divorce* by Francine Klagsburn. Copyright © 1985 by Francine Klagsbrun. Reprinted by permission of the Charlotte Sheedy Literacy Agency, Inc., 65 Bleecher Street, New York, NY 10012.

Pages 419–422—Shoba Narayan, "In This Arranged Marriage, Love Came Later." Reprinted by permission of the Ellen Levine Literary Agency. Copyright © by Shoba Narayan.

Pages 422–424—"Homeless" from *Living Out Loud* by Anna Quindlen. Copyright © 1987 by Anna Quindlen. Reprinted by permission of Random House, Inc.

Pages 424–427—"Say Yes to Yourself" from Joseph T. Martorano and Joseph P. Kildahl, *Beyond Negative Thinking*. Copyright © 1989 by Plenum Publishing. Reprinted by permission of the publisher and the author.

Pages 427–428—"Yolanda" from *How the Garcia Girls Lost Their Accents* by Julia Alvarez. Copyright © 1991 by Julia Alvarez. Published by Plume, an imprint of Dutton Signet, a division of Penguin USA and originally in hardcover by Algonquin Books of Chapel Hill.

Pages 429–431—"The Gift" by Courtland Milloy. Copyright © 1992, *The Washington Post*. Reprinted with permission.

Pages 431–433—"Salvation" from *The Big Sea* by Langston Hughes. Copyright © 1940 by Langston Hughes. Copyright renewed 1968 by Arna Bontemps and George Houston Bass. Reprinted by permission of Hill and Wang, a division of Farrar, Straus & Giroux, Inc.

Pages 433–436—"What's Your Emotional IQ?" by Daniel Goleman, "What's Your Emotional IQ?" *Reader's Digest*, January 1996. Condensed from *Emotional Intelligence* (New York: Bantam Books 1995). © Daniel Goleman.

Pages 437–439—"Sports Nuts" from *Dave Barry Talks Back* by Dave Barry. Copyright © 1991 by Dave Barry. Reprinted by permission of Crown Publishers, Inc.

Pages 439–442—"Desert Kin" by Edward Abbey. Reprinted by permission of Don Congdon Associates, Inc. Copyright © 1968 by Edward Abbey, renewed 1996 by Clarke Abbey.

Pages 442–445—Barbara Garson, "Perfume" from *All the Livelong Day* by Barbara Garson. Copyright © 1972, 1973, 1974, 1975 by Barbara Garson. This book is available in an expanded paperback edition, 1994, Penguin Books, USA. Reprinted with permission of the author.

Pages 445–448—"Discovery of a Father" by Sherwood Anderson. Reprinted by permission of Harold Ober Associates Incorporated. Copyright © 1939 by *The Reader's Digest*. Copyright renewed 1966 by Eleanor Copenhaver Anderson.

Pages 448–451—"Four Directions" by Amy Tan. Reprinted by permission of G.P. Putnam's Sons from *The Joy Luck Club* by Amy Tan. Copyright © 1989 by Amy Tan.

Pages 451–453—"For a Parent, There's No Language Dilemma" by Ana Veciana-Suarez. Reprinted by permission of *The Miami Herald*. Copyright © 1992.

Index

© 1998 Houghton Mifflin Company

© 1998 Houghton Mifflin Company

Index of Rhetorical Modes

The following index classifies the paragraphs and essays in this book according to rhetorical mode. Although we do not teach the rhetorical modes in this text, these examples are included for instructors who wish to use them.

No writing containing errors for correction is listed, with the exception of four Writers' Workshops — marked *WW with errors* — where otherwise excellent writing warrants inclusion.

© 1998 Houghton Mifflin Company

Index to the Readings

Rhetorical Index to the Readings